Who are you indeed who would talk
or sing to America?
Have you studied out the land,
its idioms and men?

(Walt Whitman, from *Leaves of Grass*)

second edition

The Twisted Dream

Capitalist Development in the United States Since 1776

Douglas F. Dowd
San José State University

Winthrop Publishers, Inc.
Cambridge, Massachusetts

Library of Congress Cataloging in Publication Data

Dowd, Douglas Fitzgerald
  The twisted dream.

  Includes bibliographies and indexes.
  1.   United States—Economic conditions.   I.   Title.
HC103.D75   1977   330.9'73   76-58379
ISBN 0–87626–883–1

Cover design by Sandra Rigney

© 1977, 1974 by Winthrop Publishers, Inc.
  17 Dunster Street, Cambridge, Massachusetts 02138

10 9 8 7 6 5 4 3

To Muh for some beliefs;
to M. M. for some skepticism.

Contents

7. Imperialism, American-style / 207

8. The State / 267

Figures and Tables

Preface to the Second Edition

The Preface to the original edition still stands as a statement of what the books seeks to accomplish, and why it is seen as necessary. The crisis within which U.S. and global capitalist societies continue to writhe is barely acknowledged, let alone explained, by conventional social and economic analyses; but we must seek to overcome the crisis in ways beneficial rather than harmful to people, and that requires understanding—whatever else it requires in the way of political action.

The analysis that ties the book together is that capitalism depends upon continuous economic and geographic expansion *and* upon ever widening and deepening exploitation, both of people and of the rest of nature. The ongoing crisis is seen as resulting from the steadily increasing difficulties attached to meeting those needs. The data that support the foregoing argument have been brought up to date; more importantly, the analysis has been altered and, I trust, strengthened, by incorporating the recent work of radical scholars on the general nature of capitalism, on the process of capital accumulation, and on the State.

There is one more change of a major sort; namely, the substantial expansion of the final chapter. Many friendly critics of the book sought to convince me that attempts at radical analysis, such as this one, should be joined to a socialist strategy and vision. The most persistent and finally effective voices were those of Daniel and Patricia Ellsberg, and I thank them for their support in that regard, as I very much thank once more the critical assistance of Bruce Dancis in helping me to avoid errors both of omission and commission. I do no more than suggest bare outlines, and do that with the hope merely of putting forth one of what should be many agendas for such discussion. In my view, it is in the very nature of what an American socialist movement and society could and should be that they will emerge from processes involving large numbers of people and many years of effort. So, still with some reluctance, I offer in Chapter 9 one small part of that process.

I remain indebted to those who helped so much with the first edition, mostly and always to Kay Dowd.

D. F. D., 1977

Preface to the First Edition

The United States is in the midst of a developing social crisis, at once economic, political, and moral, simultaneously domestic and international. *The Twisted Dream* seeks to identify and explain the nature of and the reasons for this crisis.

The complexity of society and the rapidity of social change in the United States are kaleidoscopic in their appearance and bewildering in their effects. Underlying both the complexity and the change is a coherent pattern that establishes the limits and the possibilities of social change, a set of fundamental institutions that may and must be understood as a *system*. The United States is an advanced industrial *capitalist* system, and the leading nation of the world capitalist system.

The very notion of a social system implies that all facets of social existence—economic life, politics, social behavior and attitudes, education and culture—continually interact with each other through the system of which they are a part. Rapid change and intermittent conflict are inherent to the functioning of modern capitalist systems. When substantial conflicts persist or become irreconcilable, the system is losing its ability to absorb or resist efforts to share its benefits in new ways. It then moves toward crisis.

Today's emerging crisis, which is one of American and therefore also of world capitalism, is resulting from the renewal and strengthening of dynamically related conflicts within and between the United States and the other powerful capitalist nations, and between all of them and the rest of the world. This is by no means the first crisis of capitalist society and probably not its last, just yet.

Capitalism was born in what is now seen as the European crisis of 1560–1660. Two centuries or so later, the capitalist world was once more rocked by abortive revolutions and (in the U.S. and France) by civil war. The ensuing decades were marked by explosive industrialization and imperialist expansion. The major powers enjoyed relative social stability, for a while. The twentieth century's first pervasive crisis was a direct outcome of the earlier industrialization and imperialism. The resulting stresses and conflicts produced World War I, the first major anticapitalist revolution, and then a breakdown of the world capitalist system. Out of that breakdown came fascism, the world's most serious depression ever, and World War II.

The two world wars and the social upheavals connecting them in the interwar period pounded the major powers to their knees, exposing both internal and external weakness—for all but the United States. Our global economic and military strength grew as others' declined. From 1940 on, the rising power of the United States was inextricably interwoven with war and Cold War, enormous and continuing military expenditures, and the expansion of our overseas influence and power. But for our system, as for so many others in the past, the diet that gave us our strength was also the source of our growing troubles.

The hot center from which the troubles of the United States seemed to have emerged was our prolonged involvement and attenuated defeat in Indochina. The appearance is based on more than illusion, but confuses effects with causes. Indochina was a vortex pulling the United States in deeper year after year, from the Truman Administration on. That the United States for so long could find no way either to give up on the area or to overcome the Indochinese peoples was not a result of particular personalities, mistakes, or accidents. The United States, as the leader of the world capitalist system, explicably and inexorably played out its role, in Indochina as elsewhere. The burdens were heavy; but so were the gains. All empires meet their limits; ours were found in part in Indochina, and in larger part in the relationships within the Rich Man's Club of the capitalist world.

What made for the gains of empire began, by the mid-1960's, to make for serious strains, in the form of increasing international competition, domestic unrest and economic imbalance, and looming national and international instability. The Indochina war hastened these developments, but was itself part of a larger development: the onset of world capitalism's latest crisis.

These are heady assertions, neither to be accepted nor rejected without systematic inquiry and analysis. Most Americans have had little or no exposure to such analysis; even worse, the "best-educated" in social analysis have been trained much as the feet of Chinese women used to be: bound from childhood, resulting in a crippled elegance.

If we do face a social crisis, and if it is a crisis of capitalist society, the manner in which society moves through time, and why, must be comprehended. We must learn to think in analytical terms that are historical *and* that bridge the gulfs now separating the social sciences from each other, and all of them from history. And if the system that requires this study and this understanding is a capitalist system, then we must learn the imperatives and the modes of capitalist development.

Conventional, or mainstream, social science is utterly weak in the face of this challenge. Its typically narrow, segmented, and static (that is, non-historical) analyses are doubtless useful and necessary for a broad range of purposes; for today's purposes we need something more than that, more (in Stephen Spender's image) than "lectures on navigation while the ship is going down."

The public has every right to expect that those who have studied and taught in the areas of economics, political science, sociology, and history would be well-equipped to understand the system within which and because of which the present crisis stirs, every right to assume that courses at all levels of formal education and an accompanying literature would clarify the nature of our system and how it has come to this pass. Such expectations are vain, as so many students and teachers have discovered in recent years. One can go through high school, college, and graduate school in the social sciences and history without either the obligation or the opportunity to engage in serious discussion let alone systematic analysis of the nature and development of American capitalism, or its place in the larger world capitalist system.

In economics, the subject matter is the functioning of an effectually hypothetical "market economy," with the institutions and the life processes of capitalist economy and society ignored, assumed away as not requiring more than casual comment or, more usually, given a quick and approving glance and taken as permanent and beyond question. Economists must study theory and usually study facts, but the selection of *which* facts to study—concerning, say, product or labor markets, matters of employment, foreign trade and investment, and the like—is determined by the questions arising out of the theory. That theory is carried out on such a high and wrong-headed level of abstraction that the matters most crucial for contemporary understanding are blurred and flattened, much as the great heights of modern air travel make it virtually impossible to distinguish between a plateau and a valley, one city or even one nation from another. Chapter 1 seeks to show how and why this lamentable state of affairs came to be in economics (and, by extension, in the other areas of social inquiry). I have sought to make this failure understandable both to those who have and those who have not studied economics, a study that should be exciting and informative but which is typically boring and obfuscating.

The problems of abstraction in studying economics apply to the other social sciences as well: while students of economics fail to study the connections of "economic" with vital and interdependent "non-economic" relationships and processes of their capitalist society, political scientists and sociologists abstract from the economic setting of capitalist society; historians, meanwhile, generally pursuing what J. H. Hexter has called "tunnel history," burrow through one branch or another of a history (political, diplomatic, military, etc.), walled off from each other and in abstraction from the socioeconomic system that gives the historical process its particular dynamics. There are, of course, exceptions—some books, some teachers—but only rarely do they enter the curriculum of even the most serious students of our society.

In the past few years, efforts at change have mounted. Many teachers, especially the younger ones, now seek to remedy the grave defects of social study, for themselves and with their students. The task they face is formidable. This book is an attempt to make it somewhat less so. If this seems an arrogance on my part, it may be softened somewhat by adding that what I have written is cast as nothing more than a general perspective, a treatment of the main paths along which further inquiry might and should move. Numerous suggestions for further reading are scattered throughout the text and at the ends of chapters to aid the student.* This book can be read by any person of any age or prior education, assuming only a serious concern with society.

The theme that ties the book together is the perception of the United States as a capitalist society, and of capitalism as a system that requires, offers, and imposes two principal conditions on society: expansion and exploitation. It is a work of synthesis, combining what I believe to be valuable from Marx, Veblen, and Keynes with recent works in economics, history, and other social studies. It sees the achievements, the problems, and the tragedies of American history as stemming from the needs and the ability of American capitalism to expand and to exploit in ever changing ways.

This is a critical analysis based on my own system of values and perceptions, which I should make explicit at the outset. Although I have lived what I consider to be a privileged existence, since adolescence I have been horrified by the unnecessary cruelties and deprivations of American (and world) society. Very early I came to the conclusion that although human beings as such need not live badly or at each others' throats, they must continue to do so for as long as they live under capitalist institutions. Capitalism's claims to fame have rested on its presumed ability to enhance production and freedom. But the production it enhances has been achieved at the cost of terrible distortions to the human spirit and to nature, and its products are as unevenly and unjustly distributed as its freedoms. When the choice has arisen between maintaining capitalist power or reducing human freedoms—and the choice has arisen many times—freedom has given way to power; it is doing so today, as these words are written. Oppression did not begin with capitalist societies, nor is it confined to them now, but the entire world has moved within a system of capitalist power and standards for the past few centuries. The most powerful set the tune to which others dance.

The American people have both the need and the opportunity to throw off the incubus of capitalist relationships. For reasons which I hope will become apparent in this book, the time is long past when any reasonable calculus of advantages from American capitalism can be seen as exceeding its costs to ourselves and others. If the United States emerges from the oncoming crisis as still a capitalist society, it will be

---

* An asterisk following the title of the works cited indicates that the book is available in paperback.

necessary for it to become more centralized, more militarized, more oppressive, at home and abroad; already we have gone much too far in all these directions. The human spirit, like our air and water, has been heavily poisoned, and cannot last forever as things now go.

We can and must begin to find ways to free ourselves from the deadly weight of acquisitiveness and combativeness, begin to see our lives, our fellow human beings, and our environment as requiring and enabling cooperation and peace, equality, and genuine economic and political democracy. Whatever else may be necessary to move along such new lines toward what I believe must be a democratic socialist society, understanding and political participation based on understanding head the list of priorities.

If this book contributes to those possibilities, it is in no small measure due to the substantial help I have been given by many friends with whom I have been associated professionally and politically for a few or for many years. The opportunity for me to thank them here is most welcome.

Bruce Dancis, David Danning, and Michael Rotkin read all of the manuscript more than once, and their comments and the standards they sought to have me reach have been of great importance. The knowledge, commitment, and energy displayed by these critics, all students in their twenties, well-represent to me the substantial hope for a new and better society; in *my* twenties, if there were such people around I never had the pleasure of meeting them. Lennie and Marilyn Power Goldberg, John Judis, John Roehmer, Chip Marshall, David de Hart, Kathy and Len Gilbert, Lee Polony, and my son Jeff all made useful suggestions for one or more chapters. Richard Davison, whom I first knew as a graduate student some years ago, is a little-known but most astute scholar in history and economic thought, and his careful and lengthy comments were very valuable to me, as were those of Barbara Wiget Davison.

To my great gratification, I have found the faculty and students at California State University at San José to be the liveliest and most congenial in my teaching experience. Many of the teaching staff read parts of early drafts: Rob McBride, David Landes, Marty Davis, Gayle Southworth, and Marvin Lee. Their comments were very helpful. James O'Connor, also at San José, influenced my thoughts on the State, the subject of Chapter 8, through his critical comments and his own recent book, to which I shall refer frequently.

Honora Moore did what she could to render my language into clear English, as did Nancy Benjamin, my excellent editor at Winthrop. Both she and the others at Winthrop—Paul O'Connell, Michael Meehan, Muriel Harman, and William Sernett—showed that a capitalist enterprise can be efficient, congenial, and sensitive, but perhaps only if it is as small as theirs.

My old friend and colleague from Cornell University, Chandler Morse, who fully represents what is best about both the United States and the university, worked hard through more than one draft. I have incorporated many of his extensive comments almost verbatim, so much so that he is almost a co-author. I am most grateful to him. In a different sense, these remarks may also be applied to Paul Sweezy. I refer not to the time he spent in criticizing this work in draft form, which was substantial, but to his own writings, to those of his late co-workers, Leo Huberman and Paul Baran, and his co-editor at *Monthly Review*, Harry Magdoff. For several decades, Sweezy and his close associates helped to sustain and to create a critical and radical position in America. In my view, they have done more than any others in this country, throughout many years of difficulty and confusion; they are owed a great debt by the Left as well as by many who do not consider themselves so.

Finally, Kay Dowd put up with more and contributed more than any other. She listened to or read through all the variations, contributing wisdom, clarity, and cheerful endurance. And that's not all.

D. F. D., 1974

I

Economics and Economies,
Past and Present

O this is not spring but in me
there is a murmuring of new things.
This is the time of a dark winter in the heart
*but in me are green traitors. . . .**

The American dream has always been complex, never single-minded. Both in its nature and in the struggles fought over its realization, the dream has encompassed a broad range of economic, political, and social aspirations. Still, what stands out most prominently in our history, what has most persistently and effectively absorbed the energies of Americans, is without question the individual and national aim of economic advancement. Sitting at the center of Americans' personal and national self-esteem has been the pride of material achievement; the frame of reference for national policy has had its limits and its directions set mostly by what is compatible with economic criteria. What has most frequently moved us to political excitement have been economic hopes and fears—until, perhaps, yesterday.

The United States has been the business society, par excellence. If, nowadays, support for business standards is on the wane, is it not because rising numbers of Americans have begun to believe that a business society at its best is none too good? Be that as it may, those now concerned to rid the U.S. of the ugly and threatening dynamics which are seen as transforming dream into nightmare are also reversing a long-standing assumption about the American process. An ingrained American

---

* Kay Boyle, *O This Is Not Spring.* From *Collected Poems;* copyright 1938 Kay Boyle.

1

belief has been that personal and national *economic* improvement would eliminate or facilitate the resolution of *noneconomic* problems. Today, by contrast, the suspicion grows that our very means of achieving economic success have created or exacerbated that long and tragic list of problems now dominating this society: racial and sex discrimination and oppression; poverty; the spread of coercion and militarization in our domestic and foreign policies, along with a growing dependence on military production; cities plagued by intractable fiscal, environmental, and social crises; widespread drug addiction, cutting through all segments of society and reaching down even into early adolescence; petty and large-scale crime and corruption in both private and public life that far outdistances what was thought scandalous only a decade ago; a failure of nerve, of imagination, and of morale in the entire educational system; the disaffection of large segments of the young; and a pattern of centralized and concentrated power, both private and governmental, which, taken together with the secrecy and manipulation that such a pattern requires, presides over all.

Hidden within that melancholic dirge are of course some cheerier notes; not least of them is that millions of Americans seek to set aright what has gone so badly askew. But nothing will be set aright without understanding why it is wrong. The question *why*, when asked of social problems, is always *historical;* whatever else is also necessary, understanding of a social present requires understanding of how it came to be.

The American dream that now seems so twisted became so over time, beginning with the conception of the dream itself. For our purposes, the conception of the dream can be related to two events of the year 1776. The first was a set of ideas—Adam Smith's *Wealth of Nations;* the second was a set of actions—the American Declaration of Independence. These two events had considerably more in common, in origin, intent, and consequences, than is usually supposed. In the intervening centuries the spirit that motivated both events has been transfigured. What became economics and what became the United States have moved in directions neither expected nor intended by their originators.

To understand why is to understand the dynamics of capitalist development, which in turn requires understanding how very much a capitalist economy requires of its associated social and political framework. The defining characteristics of a capitalist economy are that the means of production—mines, mills, factories, land, and so on—are privately-owned, and operated for the profit of the owners. Such an economy has existed for only a brief fraction of human history, the past few centuries. Special circumstances, in a process of violent change, were required to bring capitalism into existence; its continuation has depended upon a precariously balanced set of social institutions and economic processes: power must be held by the relatively few who own productive property, or by others who move in harmony with the needs of capitalism, in order to allow the *exploitation* intrinsic to capitalist development; and the economy must continually *expand*, both in its production and in its geographic sway. The interaction of these imperatives over time weaves together the economic, political, and social relationships that give capitalism its life, its strength, its dynamics, its virtues, and its defects.

Adam Smith (1723–1790) and the Founding Fathers were sophisticated thinkers, discerning of the complex web of relationships and processes required and enhanced by capitalist development. But, we may say, they viewed these matters through the rose-colored lenses of the upper crust. Their optimism, and their social values, led them to emphasize the gains possible from capitalist development and to minimize the social costs—or to assume that the material successes of capitalism would render such costs negligible. From the beginning there were some who thought otherwise; now there are many who sense, who believe, who understand that the social costs of capitalism are far too high and that much of its material achievement is not achievement at all: that too many are exploited and oppressed in too many ways for too little and too few, that capitalist economic expansion is heedless, too costly to human beings and to the rest of nature.

The historical and analytical support for these assertions constitute the heart of this book. Suppose for a moment the assertions are valid. To understand their whys and wherefores is it necessary to understand what is now called *economics?* No, but it is necessary to develop an analytical perspective on the American *economy*. It is both fortunate and unfortunate that mastery of economics is not equivalent to gaining the needed perspective, or necessary in order to do so. Quite apart from an ideological basis that accepts the status quo, conventional economics (as distinct from critical or radical economics) is neither broad enough in its reach nor deep enough in its penetration to suit today's analytical needs. This is not to deny the existence of valuable elements within conventional economics which, happily, can and must be incorporated into a more appropriate framework. But thinking and working solely within the framework of conventional economics does more to obstruct than to provide the possibilities of understanding the American economy.

Much the same can be said of the analytical state of affairs in the other social sciences and in history. What is needed badly is not further refinements of existing conventional economics and of the other social sciences, but the development of a dynamic social science that starts with our world, our needs, our possibilities. Central in that development must be a dynamic new *political economy:* one that allows us to integrate current with historical developments.

This book is an attempt to take a small but important step along that long and difficult path, a step which, if successful, will provide a general perspective that will assist in the development of more specific and more theoretical inquiries. Now some clarification of terms is necessary, in order both to clarify and to demystify "economics."

Classical and Neoclassical Economics

When the term *economics* is used here or, generally, by contemporary economists, the reference is to conventional ("mainstream") *economic theory* and its applications. Today's economics is an outgrowth and modification of classical economics; as such, it is called *neo*classical economics. The usage of these classifications is by no means standardized. Marx, for example, saw classical economics ending in the early nineteenth century and Keynes viewed all economists up to himself as classicists. Here, classical economics will be seen as having its first great thinker in Adam Smith, and its last in John Stuart Mill (1806–1873). Neoclassical economics will be viewed as having begun to take hold in the 1870's, with its most influential thinkers being Alfred Marshall (1842–1924) and John Maynard Keynes (1883–1946). Karl Marx (1818–1883) and Thorstein Veblen (1857–1929), unlike the classical and neoclassical economists, were profound critics of capitalism and of the economists of their own time; their ideas and their social values provide the critical guiding framework for this book's analysis.

All these thinkers were unusually sensitive to the nature, the needs, and the possibilities of their times; all were theorists; all were critics, reformers, or revolutionaries. Most decisive of all, and what made them great, was that the values, analyses, and purposes they expressed coincided with significant social interests in their day, and were thus reflected in practice. They not only studied society; in some measure they changed it. All were concerned with capitalism—lovingly, worriedly, or angrily.

Adam Smith (a Scot) was the first to be so concerned in a fully systematic manner, and the first theoretician of capitalism as a *system*. He laid the groundwork of what became the methodology of classical economics, altered but basically retained by neoclassical economists, thoroughly criticized, transformed, and transcended by Marx and Veblen.

All theory, social or physical, works from and within a *methodological* framework, which guides the theorist in what is examined, what ignored, what emphasized, what relegated to secondary consideration, what taken as "given" and what taken as the "variables" to be analyzed. For social theorists, methodology is developed in accord with basic social values, with their conception of human nature and of society, with their initial conception of what problems most require analysis and resolution.

The classical economists, who are also called political economists, had much the same set of social values as their successors, the neoclassicists. But the needs of early capitalism were different from those of Britain after, say, 1870. The classical economists were concerned with establishing the conditions within which capitalism and industrialism could successfully emerge from the confines still lingering from a precapitalist tradition; the neoclassicists were working with an already well-established industrial capitalist society. As will be seen, Smith and David Ricardo (1772–1823) theorized in order that political constraints holding back development could be understood as doing just that; J. S. Mill, writing some decades later, synthesized classical thought while at the same time seeking to puzzle through some of the consequences of the successes facilitated by the contributions of Smith and Ricardo. These classical economists all constructed analyses that encompassed developments over time, and all related economic to political and social relationships; it was this that made their economics *political economy*. The absence of these characteristics is the most relevant factor in identifying neoclassical economics up through Keynes. The narrowness of neoclassical economics gave it what strength it has possessed; its present grave inadequacies are owed to that analytical narrowness also. Neoclassical economics retains some uses for contemporary purposes, but these uses do not include adding to the possibility of comprehending the dynamics of modern capitalism—which must be understood by both the supporters and the critics of capitalism. Let us now proceed to examine what Adam Smith and the American revolutionaries had in common.

Mercantilism, Capitalism, and Political Economy

Both Smith and the revolutionaries were fighting against British mercantilism, Smith to get it off the back of British capitalism, the Americans to get it off their own backs. Smith correctly saw that mercantilistic restrictions were holding back the dynamic potential of the British economy; the Americans correctly perceived that the same system as applied to the colonies not only held back but skimmed the cream from American economic development. Smith had to undertake a full analysis of how capitalism works; much to their surprise, the Americans had to set off a national revolution.

It was Smith who introduced the concept of "mercantilism," or what he called *the mercantile system*.[1] Its importance in his argument and his

[1] Adam Smith, *An Inquiry into the Nature and Causes of the Wealth of Nations*. McCulloch edition (London, 1869), Book IV.

day requires examination of the term; the fact that much of what capitalist economies practice today is called "neomercantilist" increases the importance of doing so. First, it will be fitting to examine the times in which mercantilism came into being, and seek to extract the essence of those times in order to understand not only the term but its continuation in practice today.

The "mercantilist period" is generally seen as extending from the sixteenth century through the eighteenth century. The societies involved directly were the new nation-states of Western Europe. Although each of these societies practiced mercantilism in different ways and over different stretches of time during the three centuries, all were faced with the same general set of conditions, and all held two aims in common: profit and power. As the new nation-states struggled for power, territory, and gain all over the globe, they created an epoch of constant warfare. In the seventeenth century, when the mercantilist period was at its peak, there were at most four years not marked by international war.

The mercantilist period opened with the expansion of Europe into the Americas, Africa, and the Far East. Maritime trade and navies were essential and dangerous, costly and profitable. Piracy and warfare were inseparable from trade; plunder and slavery were its handmaidens. National economic strength was inseparable from national military strength. Not to win was to lose; national autonomy required national aggressiveness. It was the birth of the modern world, whose defects are thus congenital. If we owe much to those earlier centuries, in our cultural, political, and technological advance, they also set us on the paths of modern nationalism, militarism, imperialism, and capitalism. Then as now, all these were tightly intertwined.

Trade and control over resources in the overseas areas were highly interdependent: spices, sugar, tea and coffee, gold and silver, and slaves obsessed the economic, political, and military figures of that era. Private fortunes and national strength waxed and waned as rivalry and wars for domination of the sea lanes and the lands they connected saw first the Spanish, then the Dutch and, by the eighteenth century, the French and British struggle for leadership. The seventeenth century was dominated by the Dutch; the nineteenth by the British. The Dutch had wrested control from the Spanish; the British from the French. The decisive element in both cases was the ability to devise an appropriate blend of private and public institutions to enhance the profit and power necessary to national strength.

The Dutch depended upon their ability to make the most of water resources, beginning with fishing, to shipbuilding and shipping, to a complex pattern of overseas trade, premodern industry, and finance. The British, slowly coming from behind, took advantage of their agricultural and mineral resources and location (fronting on both Europe and the Atlantic) to put all that together into the first modern industrial society. The energetic development of capitalist institutions and impulses was both cause and consequence of the successes of the Dutch and the British; their global political ambitions and their complicated failure to break the crust of medieval and dynastic molds largely explains the undoing of the Spanish and the French.

Adam Smith sought a laissez-faire State for Great Britain; that is, a State that would serve as a "night watchman" over economic life rather than as a fussing and intrusive parent. He saw the latter role as characterizing the mercantilist State.[2]

More specifically, there was virtually no area of economic life untouched by State controls, subsidies, or regulations. Overseas trade was carried on through numerous Crown-chartered trading monopolies, only the most famous of which was the East India Company. Industries deemed critical by the State were similarly vested with monopolies of production, although key industries such as arms found themselves on a list which also included whiskey. The supply of labor, the conditions under which labor worked, and its possibilities of geographic movement were subject to intricate regulations. The manner in which the land was farmed was unregulated, but the conditions of land tenure (affecting the control and the sale of land) were subject to nonmarket constraints. Finance was dominated by taxation and, at the end of the seventeenth century, the Bank of England was chartered so as to gain a virtual monopoly over banking. The French cry of *laissez-faire, laissez-passer!* symbolized Smith's position: freedom of enterprise and movement.

Smith was a good historian and knew that the mercantilist network of private-public privilege and power had served a vital role in earlier periods. He knew that the military and economic risks of the early modern period required the protection and subsidization by the State; that the State's security required a strong economy and access to overseas colonies which would give it the strength to preserve itself. But he saw that what was positive in one historical setting had become negative later, precisely because the success of mercantilist policies had made them unnecessary.[3]

---

[2] "State" is capitalized here, to distinguish it from the American usage that almost always refers to the separate "states." This narrow question and the much more complicated set of matters concerning the State are discussed in Chapter 8.

[3] A misleadingly calm but comprehensive survey of the mercantilist period at its height throughout Europe is given by G. N. Clark, *The Seventeenth Century* ° (London: Oxford University Press, 1950). A series of analyses emphasizing the change and conflict of the period is Trevor Aston, ed., *Crisis in Europe, 1560–1660* ° (London: Routledge, 1965). An excellent study of England for the period stretching from 1530 to 1780 is Christopher Hill, *Reformation to Industrial Revolution* (New York: Pantheon, 1968).

What was negative about mercantilism? In ways that very much suggest current conditions, the intimate cooperation between the State and its private economic favorites had created a locus of power that ultimately and inexorably mixed corruption with economic stultification. Access to the favors of the Crown was the key determinant of private economic activity. Although the activities thus encouraged strengthened some of the muscles of Britain's economy, others remained undeveloped. Trade, industry, and finance by Smith's time required freedom more than parental protection; the laws and customs surrounding labor and the land held back their "rational" utilization. For Smith, not the State but the "law of supply and demand," the free market, was the best determinant of what should be produced, who should produce it, how it should be produced, and how the production should be distributed. This meant the elimination of *all* Crown-granted monopolies, *all* restrictions on trade, and the transformation of land and labor into commodities. The only State activities deemed worthwhile by Smith were those that private business could not—or should not—undertake: defense, justice, and "certain public works."

World trade had expanded enormously in the eighteenth century. The sea lanes were for England and its powerful navy becoming safe enough to allow a sharp distinction between mercantile and naval voyages: this had been quite impossible in the seventeenth century. Trading opportunities multiplied, but trade monopolies continued in the ruts of the past. The industrial revolution was growling beneath the surface while Smith wrote; industrial monopolies granted by the Crown impeded the possibilities. Surplus labor was bottled up in parishes where work was unavailable; the new factories would need that labor in the growing cities. And so on. *Laissez-faire!*

Smith was unquestionably correct in arguing that the mercantilist policies of the State were hampering private enterprise. In seeking to bring about an unhampered capitalist economy, he was of course seeking also to bring about a society in which the possession and use of private property in the means of production would determine both the qualitative and the quantitative aspects of social existence. Smith believed that by replacing State power with *market competition* as the dominant force in the economy that power itself would be dispersed. He, and those who still follow his faith, failed to see how very strong and effective the impulses would become to replace what we may call "*state* mercantilism" (Smith's target) with "*private* mercantilism." In Britain and the U.S.—the closest approximations to the Smithian ideal of laissez-faire capitalism in the industrializing nineteenth century—private economic power in the form of the corporation grew even more rapidly than the economy; in the process it was able to use the relatively weak State to protect, aid, and abet it in the carving out of modern baronies.

Competition, Power, and Property

Smith relied upon market competition, what he called the "invisible hand," to transform individual self-seeking into social well-being. He was a wise, observant, and humane person, and in no way innocent concerning the proclivities of businessmen, "an order of men," he said, "whose interest is never exactly the same with that of the public, who have generally an interest to deceive and even to oppress the public, and who accordingly have, upon many occasions, both deceived and oppressed it."[4]

His analytical enemy was the State, the Crown, what we would call the government. That was appropriate enough in his era. Monopoly in Smith's day was not privately achieved, but publicly granted. The truly private enterpriser did not and could not gain pervasive market power, which technology did not then allow. Thus it was reasonable for Smith, distrustful though he was of businessmen, to believe that distortions of economic life *and* of public life had their origins at the top of the society —in the State. He knew that businesses would do what they could to avoid market competition in what they sold for the very reasons that competition is deemed socially valuable: it keeps down prices and profits. He also knew that those same businesses would value competition among those from whom they bought, for the same reasons. What he failed to take into account was how very effective businesses would be in combining their *political* activities with their *economic* activities. The combination was made all the more effective as the development of modern industrial technology rendered small-scale production and therefore competitive market structures less tenable, while access to political power by the larger business firms became both easier and more necessary. Smith's shortcomings on this account are more comprehensible than those of subsequent economists. It is one thing not to foresee the future, and quite another to ignore the facts of everyday life.

One important source of Smith's optimism concerning the consequences of laissez-faire capitalism was a certain myopia regarding the relationship between property and power, and the decisive relationship between that relationship and capitalist development. Smith was not blind on this matter; far from it:

Whenever there is great property, there is great inequality. For one very rich man, there must be at least five hundred poor, and the affluence of the few supposes the indigence of the many. The affluence of the rich excites the indignation of the poor, who are often both driven by want and prompted by envy to invade his possessions. It is only under the

[4] Smith, *The Wealth of Nations*, p. 215.

shelter of the civil magistrate that the owner of that valuable property, which is acquired by the labour of many years, or perhaps of many successive generations, can sleep a single night in security. . . . The acquisition of valuable and extensive property, therefore, necessarily requires the establishment of civil government.[5]

Thus, Smith was not blind at all; but myopic if, as was true, the aim of his analysis was to benefit the society as a whole rather than the few most privileged within it. The last sentence of the foregoing quotation, at least in substance, could have been written by Karl Marx, who saw "the executive of the modern state [as] but a committee for managing the common affairs of the ruling class." But Smith did not perceive the private owners of productive property as a "ruling class." There is a difference between Smith's belief that property must be protected from the propertyless, and Marx's belief that the existence of a small class of property owners and a large population of the propertyless would set the tone and direction of social development. Smith believed that property had to be protected by the State; he also believed that society would be protected from property by the forces of market competition. That was not to be.[6]

The guiding theme around which the analysis of this book revolves, and that will be emphasized and elaborated upon time and again, is that capitalism thrives not only by *expansion,* which Smith advocated and facilitated, but as well by *exploitation.* Smith did not advocate exploitation but through his argument for the systematic elimination of social constraints, he provided, although doubtless unintentionally, a basic rationale for it. The exploitation of labor was intense long before Smith wrote and he fully recognized it as it existed in his own day; the means he proposed for increasing "the wealth of the nation" had as their ultimate end the improvement of the lot of the common people.[7] But the implantation of the Smithian social framework meant that his own social hopes would be brutally swept aside, and that human exploitation would be intensified in ways and to a degree unimagined by Smith.

Writing a century and a half after *The Wealth of Nations,* and thus with the benefit of hindsight, R. H. Tawney (1881–1966) attacked

[5] Ibid., p. 561.

[6] Problems surrounding Smith's position in this and related areas will be explored again in Chapter 2, pp. 45–49. The data on property and income in the United States will be the subject of Chapter 5.

[7] A readable presentation of Smith's main argument, and one which also centers in upon Smith's humanitarian and communitarian purposes, is Eli Ginzberg, *The House of Adam Smith* (New York: Octagon Books, 1964). A masterful treatment of the basic ideas of Smith and of his times is Samuel Hollander, *The Economics of Adam Smith* (Toronto: University of Toronto Press, 1973).

laissez-faire economics by contrasting it with medieval social thought, in these scathing words:

> . . . to found a science of society upon the assumption that the appetite for economic gain is a constant and measurable force, to be accepted, like other natural forces, as an inevitable and self-evident *datum* would have appeared to the medieval thinker as hardly less irrational or less immoral than to make the premise of social philosophy the unrestrained operation of such necessary human attributes as pugnacity or the sexual instinct.[8]

Classical Economics and Industrial Revolution

The impact of Smith's *magnum opus* was triggered more by his times than by the ideas themselves. At a critical moment, he had put together existing ideas into a new and compelling whole. His basic argument was not universally accepted, either ideologically or economically; the tendencies energized by the industrial revolution accomplished in fact what his persuasiveness had failed to do. Smith was the broadest in vision and highest in optimism of the classicists. David Ricardo narrowed the scope of argument in his *Principles of Political Economy and Taxation* (1817). In his *Essay on Population* (1798) and his *Principles of Political Economy* (1820) the Reverend Thomas Malthus (1766–1834) substituted apprehension for optimism. Because Malthus' arguments, whether or not attributed to him, have once more gained a relatively wide audience, it will be worthwhile to pause a moment to examine them.

Malthus was a pessimist. Economics came to be called "the dismal science" in part because of the gloominess of his anticipations. His gloom centered on two probabilities, both of them imperfectly but vividly argued for: 1) the prospect of population growth outrunning resources, and 2) the likelihood of what we would call stagnation or chronic depression, which he called "gluts of production." As a parson whose attachments were to the rural virtues, Malthus did not share the enthusiasms of Smith or Ricardo regarding capitalist development. This enabled him to peer more critically at its prospects, albeit quite literally as a reactionary. Taken seriously in his own time, especially by his noted theoretical antagonist Ricardo, Malthus came to be scorned by economists over the next century. In more recent years, the laughter has subsided.

This is not to say that Malthus was correct for all times and condi-

---

[8] In *Religion and the Rise of Capitalism* * (New York: Mentor, 1950), p. 35. Published first in 1926.

tions, although for the functioning of *industrial capitalism* he may well have been. He is best known for his argument that the limits of development are set by the fact that population increases geometrically (1, 2, 4, 8, 16 . . .) but that subsistence (that is, production, especially of food) increases only arithmetically (1, 2, 3, 4, 5 . . .). He was subsequently derided because technological development appeared to have intervened to allow subsistence to increase more dynamically than he foresaw, at the same time that industrial development appeared to reduce the rate at which population increased. By the end of the nineteenth century, economists believed that optimism had a solid grounding in fact: mainstream economists didn't foresee what imperialist expansion would do to upset the presumably benign relationships then apparent, and Marxists analyzed the problems foreseen by Malthus as the problems of *capitalism*, not of economic development as such. When international capitalism moved into the processes of imperialism over the past century—processes considerably more powerful in their impact than the earlier waves of geographic expansion—one consequence was to *increase* population growth rates in the imperialized areas while simultaneously engendering in them a process of retrogressive development (or underdevelopment). The technological developments that relieved population pressures in the advanced countries exacerbated those pressures in the rest of the world—to say nothing of the depletion of resources and environmental problems created by the same processes. Industrialization proceeding under *capitalist* auspices could benefit a fraction of the world's population, but only at the expense of the rest; ultimately, it appears, only at the expense of all. (Chapters 6 and 7 explore these and related questions more fully.)

In his other major argument, Malthus anticipated both Marx and Keynes in their theories of capital accumulation and the determination of the causes of depression. Here we may point to the simple contours of the argument. Production takes place for profit in a capitalist economy. Profit depends upon sales in generally buoyant—that is, sellers'—markets. The level of "effective demand" (a concept also used by Marx and Keynes) is the measure of total sales. That level is determined by the combination of sales to businesses (for equipment, etc.) and consumers. The former sales depend upon the actual and expected state of business. The latter depend upon the purchasing power of consumers. Since the state of business is partially and importantly dependent upon consumers' purchasing power, and since the mass of consumers are poor, the economy will periodically or even persistently be faced with gluts—that is, with inadequate levels of effective demand. Malthus therefore saw the need for what he called "unproductive consumption," anticipating Marx and Keynes in their conviction that private prosperity would come to depend upon public spending. The conclusions of Malthusian analyses had some validity, but not in his own time. The decades after he wrote were marked by rapid technological improvement and worldwide economic expansion. He was wrong, but only for a while, only for the adolescence of industrial capitalism.

David Ricardo was the most illustrious successor to Smith, in his effective contributions both to political change and to political economy. Ricardo developed "the principle of diminishing returns," which says that increases in the use of one factor of production (such as, labor) in combination with another *fixed* factor (such as, land) will mean increasing *inefficiency* after some level of production has been reached. Ricardo used that principle to carry forward Smith's aim of freeing the economy from political restrictions; in this case the restrictions were in the form of protective tariffs on imported grain (called "corn" in England). The Corn Laws made the price of bread unnecessarily high in England; the price of bread was a key determinant of wages; and wages were the strategic factor in manufacturers' costs. Therefore, the Corn Laws provided an unearned income to the better-off landowners but reduced the profits of manufacturers. Industrial development was held back by protective tariffs on grain; Ricardo argued the necessity to abolish the Corn Laws. They were, in 1846.

Ricardo's analytical focus was considerably narrower than Smith's; he used history less and logic more. The analytical procedures of subsequent economists were considerably more affected by Ricardian than by Smithian modes of analysis, although perhaps Ricardo would be unsettled by what he helped to bring about. His great work, *The Principles of Political Economy and Taxation,* was written after he had retired from a successful career in the London stock exchange, and was seen at the time as the highest development of economic science. It was the work of a man who was in close touch with the world he analyzed, combining close reasoning with observable fact and a clear emphasis on policy. Later economists who adopted his logical reasoning all too often tended to neglect the observable facts of their own, different times in favor of seeking more elegant and abstract theorems.

The decade of the 1840's saw the full triumph of Free Trade for Great Britain, both at home and in its foreign economic relationships. In that same decade John Stuart Mill composed the great synthesis of classical economics, his *Principles of Political Economy* (1848). Meanwhile, efforts to reintroduce protections for labor in the market were underway, in the form of Factory Laws, which sought to limit the working hours and conditions of women and children. Eighteen forty-eight was also the year of *The Communist Manifesto.* We shall begin to touch on Marxian ideas shortly; here the continuity and change in the development of conventional economics remains our focus.

John Stuart Mill, writing seventy years or so after Smith, could look back on an economy and an economics that Smith had helped to create. Both the economy and economics were of course very different from what Smith himself had proposed or developed. Mill lived at a time when the human suffering as well as the economic achievements of capitalism were both evident. Furthermore, the problems facing the society were those not of a struggling new capitalism but rather of one beginning to generate the problems of age. Or so it seemed to Mill, for he did not foresee the renewed explosion of economic growth that lay ahead: industrialization spreading all over Europe, North America, and Japan; a new wave of technological advance giving vitality to capitalism, through the cheapness of its metals, its fuels, its transportation and communications, its foodstuffs and raw materials; or, making all that possible, the completion and deepening of the imperialist conquest of the entire world by the major powers.

In 1848, Mill believed that the period of major vitality and expansion was drawing to a close. He pondered the probability and the implications of a "stationary state" (that is, a nonexpanding economy), which he, like many today, saw as desirable. He believed that the long hours of work from dawn to dusk were unnecessary, and the conditions of work in mine and mill inhumane; he saw the need for at least mild forms of social intervention. The increase of production had occupied the thoughts of Smith and Ricardo; for Mill the main problem was one of income distribution. He was an urbane and humane believer in capitalism, believing still in 1848 that political liberty and human decency were compatible with capitalist institutions. He was anything but rigid in his attachments, however, as revealed by this passage from his *Principles:*

> If, therefore, the choice were to be made between Communism with all its chances, and the present state of society with all its sufferings and injustices; if the institution of private property necessarily carried with it as a consequence, that the produce of labour should be apportioned as we now see it, almost in an inverse ratio to the labour—the largest portions to those who have never worked at all, the next largest to those whose work is almost nominal, and so in a descending scale, the remuneration dwindling as the work grows harder and more disagreeable, until the most fatiguing and exhausting bodily labour cannot count with certainty on being able to earn even the necessaries of life; if this, or Communism, were the alternative, all the difficulties, great or small, of Communism would be but as dust in the balance.[9]

It is generally believed that by the time he died in 1873, Mill had become a socialist. The development of British socialism in the late

---

[9] (New York: People's Edition, 1872), p. 128. When he wrote, *Communism* and *Socialism* were words used interchangeably.

nineteenth and early twentieth centuries, it is worth noting, depended considerably more upon Mill than Marx, both in its analysis and its politics.

Industrial Capitalism and Neoclassical Economics

Classical political economy may be viewed as an attack on and critique of the dying remnants of the feudal and mercantilist epochs. It was an economics of *development*. Development is a process extending over time, taking on its pace, direction, and forms because of the connections *within* the economy and *between* the economy and larger society.

Neoclassical economics came into being at a time when industrial capitalism was established, most especially in Great Britain. In the hands of some, neoclassical economics served as an apologia for capitalism, as a sustained argument showing why Marx was wrong, or why even moderate social intervention in economic life would harm the society. Of equal or greater significance, however, was its function in meeting the positive needs of the business economy. Those needs were not for institutional change, for the abolition of political constraints, and the like. That had been accomplished in Great Britain in the century or more preceding the 1870's, when neoclassical economics began to take the form it carried into the twentieth century. Neoclassical economics took the political setting for granted, and made *political economy* into *economics;* economics became the science of economizing. It became, in the words of one of its modern spokesmen, "the science which studies human behavior as a relationship between ends and scarce means which have alternative uses." [10]

A "science" of scarcity, of economizing, of maximizing, is *quantitative* in its focus. *Qualitative* relationships can be taken as "given," that is, left unexamined. Not being concerned with development, but with making the most of a good thing, neoclassical economics could ignore historical (that is, real) time; its analysis was static, not dynamic. Social and political institutions, technological change, technology itself, the structures and functions of wealth and power—all this and more could quite logically be taken as given. Those who developed neoclassical economics decided upon these "givens" deliberately and in keeping with those analytical problems they chose to emphasize. Some of their less self-conscious descendants often seem not to know what is even on the list of what is being ignored; as one wag has put it, some students and their

[10] Lionel Robbins, *The Nature and Significance of Economic Science* (London: Macmillan, 1932), p. 16.

teachers may now believe that "society," far from being the subject matter of the social sciences, is merely a synonym for "parameters."

In short, neoclassical economics works from a methodology that places both the social process and social relationships outside its ken, except insofar as posited abstractly for purposes of the argument. This is so for the works of all neoclassical economists, including the two greatest, Marshall and Keynes, and despite the quite different questions they confronted.

Economic theory today divides into two major sectors, *microeconomics* and *macroeconomics*. The fundamentals of the former are found in Marshall's *Principles of Economics* (1890) and of the latter in Keynes's *General Theory of Employment, Interest, and Money* (1936). Marshall was the great synthesizer of neoclassical economics; Keynes, finding it necessary in the midst of the disastrous depression of the 1930's to alter a key assumption of that economics, may very well have opened a floodgate in his attempt to plug a hole in the dam.[11]

The classicists, to repeat, were concerned with bringing about change, and the changes were both controversial and substantial. The differences between their focus and that of the neoclassicists is aptly suggested by the epigram on Marshall's title page: *Natura non facit saltum* —nature makes no leaps. It was not the intent of neoclassical economists to provide an analysis that would rationalize leaps; maximum efficiency and maximum profits was their focus: an explicable response to the needs and interests of business in the latter part of the nineteenth century, especially and perhaps solely for Great Britain.

Marshall saw nature and society as ruled by the "principle of continuity." Change was at the edges of life, slow, incremental, "marginal." In a world characterized by scarcity—of resources, of skilled labor, of capital—because caught up in a pervasive process of industrialization, the problem became one of making the most of what was available: the problem was economizing, or, what is saying the same thing, maximizing. Increased efficiency, enabled and enhanced by economic rationality, was the means to that end. Economics thus focused on the units where efficiency presumably would be achieved. On the supply side that was the individual firm, using materials, equipment, and labor in the most efficient combinations. The economy would be getting the most for the least when all firms produced where their costs and outputs were in

---

[11] Neoclassical economics subdivides more numerously than into two parts: welfare theory, capital theory, wage theory, general equilibrium theory, trade theory, monetary theory; or, in some versions, distribution theory, the theory of markets, and the like. For present purposes micro and macro will suffice. For a penetrating critique of neoclassical welfare economics, see Herbert Gintis, "Neoclassical Welfare Economics and Individual Development," *Occasional Paper No. 3* of the Union for Radical Political Economics (July, 1970). (Hereafter, URPE.)

quantitative *balance* with prices and purchases, with consumers maximizing "utility"—a subjective and empirically unknowable state. Obviously, the laws of supply and demand are a more complicated matter than this. More important, however, is the conception of human nature and society that the classical economists handed down to the neoclassicists, and the latter's modifications of that conception. A digression on this matter is essential.

Human Nature and Conduct

All competent social theorists begin with a working conception of human nature and the ways in which that presumed nature contributes and responds to social relationships and processes. Most of us merely inherit these ideas which lead us unknowingly to accept or reject social ideas and proposals. But the meaning and the validity of any social theory rests upon its view of the raw materials of that theory: the nature of our species and of the process of social change. The most profound differences between those who have accepted capitalism and those who have not are thus to be found in this area of analysis; the other differences follow.

Smith was a philosopher of high esteem before he turned his talents to economic affairs. He believed in an inherent "natural order" superior to anything humans might create, and that the wisest form of social organization is that which allows people to act as nearly as possible in harmony with the dictates of that "natural order." Those dictates, if not interfered with by human and especially governmental meddling—such as those of mercantilism—would lead to an "obvious and simple system of natural liberty." According to Smith, human beings are actuated by six motives: self-love, sympathy, the desire to be free, a sense of propriety, a habit of labor, and "the propensity to truck, barter, and exchange." Let them be, said Smith, and the beneficence of Providence will provide that social order which, though not perfect, is the best to be had. There is little we can do that will be anything but harmful except to let the natural order realize itself. This in turn meant allowing the self-interest which characterizes us to assert itself. Practically, this meant ridding society of the State's meddling and allowing a laissez-faire society to emerge. "Each for himself," as someone has put it, "and God for all." The subsequent development of capitalism led to an added phrase: "As the elephant said, while he danced among the chickens."

If Smith's conception of human nature was narrow—by comparison with Marx, Veblen, and John Dewey, for example—it was narrowed even further by the neoclassical economists (although broadened somewhat by John Stuart Mill who thought education could play a role in allowing people to expand social possibilities). For Smith's six human attributes, the neoclassical economists substituted *homo economicus,* compressing human nature into a mold of rational economic maximization, ignoring "sympathy," and seeing labor as something humans seek to avoid. They worked with the now discredited conception of "man as hedonist"—that is, one who seeks to maximize pleasure (especially by consumption) and minimize pain (by minimizing work). Thorstein Veblen, the most penetrating American critic of neoclassical economics and of American society, disposed of their notions of human nature in a brilliantly sardonic passage:

> The hedonistic conception of man is that of a lightning calculator of pleasures and pains, who oscillates like a homogeneous globule of desire of happiness under the impulse of stimuli that shift him about the area, but leave him intact. He has neither antecedent nor consequent. He is an isolated, definitive human datum, in stable equilibrium except for the buffets of the impinging forces that displace him in one direction or another. Self-imposed in elemental space, he spins symmetrically about his own spiritual axis until the parallelogram of forces bears down upon him, whereupon he follows the line of the resultant. When the force of the impact is spent, he comes to rest, a self-contained globule of desire as before.[12]

Marx and Veblen viewed the classical and neoclassical conceptions of both human nature and society as culture-bound and ahistorical, although they might disagree about other fundamental questions. Both saw the human species as a part of nature, rather than a species set apart from or against nature; more important, they saw human beings as transforming nature and (most clearly in Marx) as thereby being transformed as part of nature. Both also perceived human nature as being distorted—Marx used the term *alienated*—by the social conditions of capitalism. As for society, given this conception of the relationship between humans and nature, it followed that *no* form of social organization was "natural": all societies are in a process of continuous change, all are transitory, all are historically dynamic, all give rise to processes and relationships which displace them. The difference between Marx and Veblen on this latter score was not on the question of permanence or change, but on the question of how the process of change works out, and the directions in which it moves. Marx was optimistic, Veblen gloomy.

---

[12] In *The Place of Science in Modern Civilization* (New York: B. W. Huebsch, 1919; and Russell & Russell, 1961), pp. 73–74. This book contains the bulk of Veblen's methodological essays, including a critically friendly analysis of Marxism.

In addition to these differences between the classical–neoclassical economists and Marx and Veblen, there is one striking difference regarding labor. For Marx, the main motive forces of history revolved around the production and reproduction of life. For Marx, an animal's life—and people are animals—is its *activity,* what it does; first and foremost what humans do is produce and reproduce the stuff of life. Work is not only natural, but fulfilling. Under capitalist conditions, however, people do not labor for themselves. They labor for others, for those who own and control the means of production, who decide what will be produced and why—for profit—it will be produced, and by whom the workers, because they are propertyless and thus powerless, are exploited. Under such conditions, Marx said, the worker is *alienated.*

> First, . . . the work is *external* to the worker, . . . it is not part of his nature; . . . consequently, he does not fulfil himself in his work but denies himself, has a feeling of misery rather than well-being, does not develop freely his mental and physical energies but is physically exhausted and mentally debased. The worker, therefore, feels himself at home only during his leisure time, whereas at work he feels homeless. His work is not voluntary but imposed, *forced labour.* It is not the satisfaction of a need, but only a *means* for satisfying other needs. Its alien character is clearly shown by the fact that as soon as there is no physical or other compulsion it is avoided like the plague.[13]

Because the productive life of people under capitalism is necessarily alienating, Marx saw workers as therefore alienated from nature, from themselves, from other human beings, and from their essential and distinctive nature (which Marx called *species-being*). For the conventional economists' mechanical view of humans, Marx substituted a dynamic view, where human beings, nature, and society moved in a process of continuous interaction. Fundamentally, Veblen agreed.

Veblen put forth his views in *The Instinct of Workmanship* (1914). Before examining those views, it is necessary to show how he uses the term *instinct,* for many of the criticisms leveled at Veblen have sought to dismiss him as being "unscientific" for merely using the word. After stating that "instinct" is a concept "of too lax and shifty a definition to meet the demands of exact biological science," Veblen goes on to say the following:

[13] *Karl Marx; Early Writings,** translated and edited by T. B. Bottomore (New York: McGraw-Hill, 1963), pp. 124–25. This book contains the so-called "Economic and Philosophic Manuscripts" of 1844, where Marx's theory of alienation, which lies at the base of much of his later thinking, was first expressed. These manuscripts were unpublished until 1932. Although Veblen, who died in 1929, could not have known of these ideas directly, his own views are strikingly similar.

A genetic inquiry into institutions will address itself to the growth of habits and conventions, as conditioned by the material environment and by the innate and persistent propensities of human nature; and for these propensities, as they take effect in the give and take of cultural growth, no better designation than the time-worn "instinct" is available. . . . "Instinct," as contradistinguished from tropismatic action, involves consciousness and adaptation to an end aimed . . . , at the conscious pursuit of an objective end which the instinct in question makes worth while. . . . The ends of life, then, the purposes to be achieved, are assigned by man's instinctive proclivities; but the ways and means of accomplishing those things which the instinctive proclivities so make worth while are a matter of intelligence. . . . Men take thought, but the human spirit . . . decides what they shall take thought of, and how and to what effect.[14]

Veblen's "instinct of workmanship" virtually equates with Marx's notion of work as the life activity of human beings, in the sense that workmanship and what Veblen calls "the parental bent" refer to the production and reproduction of life. The sense of workmanship has for Veblen a "sub-instinct," that of "idle curiosity." It is this that accounts for the growth of technology, science, and culture, and that makes human beings into transformers of nature and not merely a part of it. For Veblen, as for Marx, what he calls "the regime of private property" leads people to shirk labor and to become reduced as human beings. Another "instinct" of Veblen's is worth noting: "the instinct of sportsmanship" is his ironic way of referring to the combative, warlike, and ultimately self-destructive penchants recorded in history. If Veblen is gloomier than Marx, part of the reason is that he sees workmanship and sportsmanship as running a sort of race between life- and death-giving activities, with little reason to believe that a society controlled by "force and fraud" would allow the race to be won by life. We will have occasion to return to these questions later. Now we turn our attention back to the nature, evolution, and inapplicability of neoclassical economics.

Transformation and Failure of the Market Economy

The narrow and mechanical view of human nature and the view of the basic outlines of nineteenth century British society as the representation of an essentially unchanging "natural order" verge on the ludicrous today. Even as the basic analytical framework of neoclassical economics

[14] *The Instinct of Workmanship* ° (New York: Macmillan, 1914), pp. 2–6.

was being constructed, it was being consigned to irrelevance. The market economics of Marshall assumed a competitive and small-scale economic structure; otherwise it made no sense. But in the very period in which he wrote, monopolies were moving toward center stage; today all the major industrial capitalist powers are characterized by monopolistic (technically, "oligopolistic") structures of ownership and control. (See Chapter 3.) Marshall assumed and advocated an unobtrusive, though not an unimportant, State; all modern States are interventionist, and obviously so. The world of Marshall was seen as one of market scarcity; although a desperate scarcity of needed goods exists for most of the people of the world today, *market* scarcity is not a major problem for the people of the industrial powers. Their problems, instead, revolve around questions of distribution, direction, and quality; their political economies are indeed the major *cause* of scarcity for the rest of the world. In Marshall's world, one power was preeminent: Great Britain. Today, there are noncapitalist and anticapitalist powers of great and lesser strength, and capitalist rivals for the once unchallenged strength of Britain and, now, of the United States. An "economics of choice" in such a world becomes something worse than a bad joke; it is positively dangerous to the degree that it is taken as a basis for thinking about *economies.*

One might think that the extraordinary turbulence of the period that began in the 1890's, that encompassed World War I, the Soviet Revolution, a decade of economic stagnation in Great Britain (in the 1920's), and the emergence of fascism in Italy and Germany, would have caused mainstream economists to reevaluate their theories. But it took the Great Depression of the 1930's to even begin that process; then, as will be seen, the changes brought about were theoretically peripheral, if also of great practical importance.

Depression, Keynes, and War

The central importance of economic expansion for the maintenance of capitalism is so great that we shall devote much of two chapters (4 and 7) to explaining why that is so, and under what conditions the need has and has not been met. Here our attention will be confined to the alteration of economics induced by the *failure* of expansion after World War I. Great Britain was economically stagnant throughout the twenties, suffering from an average of 10 percent unemployment for the decade. The entire capitalist world collapsed in 1929, and the collapse was most devastating in the two most highly-industrialized nations: the United States and Germany.

The enormity of that depression is suggested by the fact that industrial production in the United States and Germany fell by 50 percent. Since World War II, by way of contrast, it has never dropped more than a few percentage points, and then for very brief periods. Neoclassical economics was caught off guard by the Depression. The facts were plain, but the theory could not handle such facts. Neoclassical theory, until it was revised in 1936, taught that when unemployment occurred it was "voluntary"; that is, it was because workers were demanding excessive wages. When unemployment rose to 25 percent of the labor force (1933) and long bread and soup lines were a daily sight in all cities, it became difficult to believe that unrealistic expectations concerning wages had placed the unemployed on those lines. There were no jobs to be had at *any* wages for them.

The theoretical sticking-point for the economists was "Say's Law." Jean-Baptiste Say (1767–1832), who sought to implant Smith's ideas in France, had shown the theoretical impossibility of depression in arguing that "supply creates its own demand." That is, everything produced would be sold, either to consumers or to businesses, because 1) the value of production created money incomes of an equivalent value, and 2) that portion of incomes not spent on consumer goods but saved would be offset by business purchases of investment goods. The key notion allowing this conclusion was that consumers would reduce their expenditures to save *only* because the rate of interest on savings would induce them to do so; the rate of interest was determined by the demand for funds created by those investors. In short, consumption and investment were reciprocally motivated; if consumption declined it was *because* investment rose to the same degree. Thus, supply creates its own demand. If all that were so, there could *be* no involuntary unemployment: the jobless are thus lazy, witless, useless, or seeking excessive wages.

Keynes's *General Theory of Employment, Interest, and Money* jiggled one assumption in that theory and came out with opposite conclusions. It showed that consumption and investment are *not* reciprocally motivated; that savings are related more to changes in money income than to the rate of interest. Not only could depression and high unemployment occur, but in the normal and rational functioning of industrial capitalism they were downright likely, and, without government intervention, the economy could get stuck in them with no tendency to escape. Up to the time of the *General Theory*, classical–neoclassical economics had served to show why governmental intervention was both unnecessary and undesirable. Keynes, though himself a neoclassical economist of the highest order, showed why intervention was necessary in order to save capitalism itself. Capitalism had matured; it had to take care.

Like all the great thinkers who had preceded him, Keynes was not so much a creator of new ideas as one who integrated others' ideas *and* at a time when events compelled attention. Swedish economists had for several years been developing the basic ideas presented by Keynes, and Keynes was directly and indirectly assisted by a small group of young and brilliant economists such as R. F. Kahn, Joan Robinson, and Michael Kalecki.[15]

Depression or no, resistance to the new ideas in the economics profession was strong and lasting, as Keynes had anticipated. "The difficulty," Keynes wrote in the Preface to *The General Theory*, "lies, not in the new ideas, but in escaping from the old ones, which ramify, for those brought up as most of us have been, into every corner of our minds." [16] If anything, the opposition to Keynesian ideas was even greater among practical "men of affairs" who did not relish being told that thrift was not necessarily a virtue, and that not only government spending but *deficit* spending (that is, an excess of government expenditures over taxes) and perhaps even socialized consumption and investment had become at least intermittently necessary. For American businessmen and politicians, the blocks to understanding were all the higher, given the British citizenship and aristocratic mien of the theorist, theorists being suspect enough in any case.

President Franklin Roosevelt and Congress responded noticeably but ineffectually to the prescriptions of the "New Economics," but widespread acceptance came only after the practical experience of World War II and the Cold War taught both economists and businessmen that the ideas worked and that the policies were profitable when applied. The first textbook to incorporate Keynesian ideas was Paul Samuelson's *Economics* (1947), banned in several states as being "communistic"; the first administration after World War II to absorb and apply the ideas seriously was that of John F. Kennedy; by 1970, even the arch conservative Richard Nixon had announced "I am a Keynesian." Keynes died in 1946. It is doubtful that he would have been pleased with the narrowing and the application of his ideas which allowed their acceptance even in the farther reaches of American conservatism.

Such an evolution requires explanation of what Keynesian theory accomplished and what it left undone. Only its bare bones have survived; not only policy-makers but most economists are unaware of the body surrounding those bones in Keynes's original presentation and in his subsequent arguments. He caused neoclassicists to examine a few of

---

[15] Joan Robinson, herself a noted neoclassical economist at the time, has subsequently sought to reintegrate Marxian theory into what is valuable in conventional theory. Kalecki was even then a brilliant Marxist; he anticipated the basic ideas of Keynes, and did much to enrich theory before his death in 1970. See *The Last Phase in the Transformation of Capitalism*° (New York: Monthly Review Press, 1972), a collection of his essays.

[16] *The General Theory,*° p. viii.

their premises; the main machinery of their economics survived and has gone on to spin even finer webs of counter-factual analysis.

Keynesian theory is often called "the theory of effective demand." It places the cause of depression in inadequate levels of aggregate demand for goods and services, the key component of which is the demand of businesses for investment goods (plant, equipment, and so on). Such expenditures take place both to maintain existing productive capacity, and to expand productive capacity. The latter is called *net investment,* and is the source of economic expansion. Net investment takes place only when investment is expected to yield a satisfactory profit. In a business society, this sounds like common sense. It is a way of saying that the key economic *decisions* are made by businessmen, even though the largest share of all *expenditures* is made by consumers. When profit expectations are inadequate, investment will be inadequate to maintain adequate levels of production, employment, and income. The critical problem then becomes one of understanding what determines the state of profit expectations, thus of the volume of investment, thus of the degree to which the economy will or will not expand. That is the analytical problem; the real-world problem is that increases in production, employment, and income, far from providing the basis for their maintenance—as Say's Law proposed—guarantee instead that at some point investment will fall, and bring everything else down with it. Consequently, for Keynes, a source of demand other than private consumption and private investment must stand in readiness to fill in the gap: government spending.[17]

What was wrong with Say's Law? It did not recognize that as the national income rises so do savings. Consumer expenditures of course rise with income; but they rise at a declining rate. That is, savings rise at an increasing rate. Therefore, the volume of investment must rise as income rises. But money income has risen because production and productive capacity have risen (setting aside inflation). Thus the need for investment *increases* just when the likelihood rises that *excess* productive capacity, profitless productive capacity, will emerge. Expansion is brought to an end by its very successes. (Marx and Veblen came close to the same kind of argument.) Why is *deficit* government spending necessary at that stage? Because the government must spend, and if it were to do so while also raising taxes it would take with one hand what it is giving with the other. It may be added that when the economy is facing unduly rising price levels, Keynesian analysis applies equally well, but turned around: monetary and fiscal policies should aim to curb private spending, raise interest rates to discourage such spending, and

---

[17] Also, in times of slack demand, monetary policy (exercised by the Federal Reserve System) should seek to reduce interest rates to lower the *obstacles* to investment.

also tax more than the government spends. All capitalist governments have put these notions into practice in one setting or another and to one degree or another in the recent past.[18]

Keynesian economics constituted a significant improvement over what preceded it, but at least three things have rendered its meaning inadequate for the present. First, as suggested above, its acceptance was only partial. Although Keynes both in and subsequent to the *General Theory* showed that he understood the need for *structural* changes in the economy—in production, consumption, income distribution—today's Keynesians continue to analyze and prescribe in terms of marginal adjustments and aggregative policies. Their effect is to maintain rather than to change structures, at best. Second, Keynes developed a theory for an economy whose dynamics were national, or domestic; the internationalization of the American economy requires a substantial theoretical alteration, not merely an "adjustment," to handle those dynamics. Third, the theory Keynes developed was meant to apply to a fundamentally private economy, with government activities brought in to alter troublesome developments. Today's economy is privately dominated, but the structure of the economy is heavily and permanently infused with government as spender, taxer, employer. In different words, Keynesian theory pounded cracks in the wall of neoclassical laissez-faire philosophy and capitalist practice; in doing so, it necessitated a different theory, one that would incorporate an imperialist State into its analysis. Mainstream economics shows no inclination—nor did Keynes—to move along those lines; its principal tendencies in recent years have been to mathematize and refine the micro and macro economics of the past. At the edges of the mainstream, however, some attempts are underway, in economics and in the other areas of social analysis.

Toward a New Political Economy

The attempts now underway to change the various aspects of social analysis are a response to a society that is changing rapidly and under great stress, whose major characteristics interact in such a way as to threaten what has not already been damaged or destroyed. All the economists we have looked at were responding to the needs of their times for changes, large or small; except for Marx and Veblen, the changes they sought were designed to strengthen or to preserve industrial capital-

---

[18] For useful discussions of American and European practices since World War II, see Andrew Shonfield, *Modern Capitalism* * (New York: Oxford University Press, 1965). The details of the American experience and a fuller analysis will be traced in Chapter 4, below.

ism. The search for a new society, not the shoring up of the status quo, underlies today's search for a new social analysis.[19]

This chapter opened with the observation that a long and tragic list of social problems, from racism to centralized power, is now seen as having a close or significant connection with the successful functioning of American capitalism. No single one of those "problems" owes its existence to economic relationships alone, if by economic we mean what conventional economists mean—namely, supply and demand relationships. Even with that narrow definition of economics, however, it may be asserted that none of these problems exists except that in some way or in some degree its origins and persistence connect with the economic relationships of American capitalism. What degree? What ways? Why? How? Since when? With what prospects for improvement or worsening?

Conventional economists cannot, as such, be expected to answer such broad and complicated questions adequately; as *economics* is refined into ever more specialized compartments and techniques, it is reasonable to expect that conventional economists' understanding of the *economy* will decline further. There are depths below depths.

A capitalist economy rests upon and promotes private ownership of the means of production, and production for profit, the main breeding grounds of power in our society. It moves through time, and changes as it moves; it is dynamic and it requires a compatible social and political framework, one that appears to be incompatible with the needs and potentials of a large portion of its population.

As citizens, some conventional economists have found ways to understand some or all of these matters. When they do so, it is as reasonably informed and wise individuals. As economists (that is, as people working within and applying a body of economic theory), almost all of what now concerns the American people and themselves as citizens has been deliberately and in principle excluded from the reach of their theory. Conventional economic theory does not raise the appropriate questions; when conventional economists do raise such questions they do so without the guidance of their theory. If untrained people knew more of this they might understand why economists seem as mystified as the person in the street by problems such as simultaneous inflation and recession and world monetary crisis. And they might conclude, as many younger economists have concluded, that still another New Economics is needed.

The strong criticisms of conventional economics running through this chapter should not be construed to suggest that economics—let alone

[19] Critiques of conventional theory in all the social sciences, as well as an identification of "key problems" for contemporary analysis and some alternative analyses are set forth well in Robin Blackburn, ed., *Ideology in Social Science** (New York: Vintage, 1973).

theory as such—is useless. Neoclassical economics, or "marginalism," is a theory of minor adjustments within a given social and economic framework. It makes no pretense of providing understanding of socio-economic structures and processes, or of when and why it might be necessary to seek structural changes in production, consumption, trade, income distribution, investment, or, say, in the structure of power. Minor adjustments to achieve improved efficiency are always called for, in *any* economy; marginalism of the micro or the macro variety will be useful so long as that is so.

But at a time when structural changes are badly needed and loudly called for, society has the right to expect something more than marginalist theory from its economists. Economists are not but should be servants of all the people, not just of those presently in power. "The people" is of course an over-general abstraction. There are conflicting groups of all sorts among "the people." Economics claims to serve everyone and no one, and to do so in the name of objectivity. But of course the profession contains within it economists who do in fact, well or badly, serve one or another of those groups, whether the economist is in a university, the government, a trade union, or a corporation. Mostly they serve those closest to the maintenance of the status quo.

Under these circumstances objectivity becomes a pretense; it is also a state of confusion. Objectivity means writing, thinking, and teaching with scrupulous and fearless regard for evidence, logic, and honesty. That is what it means. If, however, one means by *objectivity* what most social scientists seem to mean—namely, social *neutrality*—the matter is transformed. Nobody should be neutral, and probably nobody can be, except by self-delusion. Everybody should be objective and everybody can be. Those who know where their sympathies lie on the omnipresent range of human controversies can be objective *and* they can consciously distinguish between objectivity and neutrality. Those who make no such distinction and who confuse the two are neither objective nor neutral. They mislead themselves and cannot help but confuse and mislead those with whom they communicate. It may be said that the classical economists did not work under such confusion; the confusion became rampant with the presumed scientism of neoclassical economics, whose training has encouraged it. This is one of the reasons why so many conventional economists today are taken aback by the politically candid, self-styled "radical economists," whom they criticize for *being* political. But everyone is political, those who wish to preserve things as much as those who wish to change them. Everyone cares; save us, especially in the social sciences, from those who don't.

Caring is not enough, of course. We need an appropriate framework of analysis. Whatever else it must be, this framework must be informed by history. What is changing cannot be understood except as part of a process that leads to change. To study historically is to study in terms of *connections;* it is to take fewer matters as *given.* Conventional economics shies away from such modes of inquiry; political economy in the past did not. The political economy of the present and the future cannot. We need not start from scratch. Not only Marx and Veblen, but many others less well-known have studied so. The analyses they have constructed remain inadequate for our time and place, but they are still a place to begin an examination of political economy.

The range of Marx's inquiries was as broad as society itself, although he bore down most heavily on economic analysis, in *Capital.* Almost all conventional social scientists, and not least the economists among them, have rejected the possibility of Marx having said anything of use to those living in capitalist society—and most of those have done so with the confidence that comes from not having bothered to read Marx. Veblen is a name that is now virtually unknown in professional circles, except perhaps as that quaint man who coined the term "conspicuous consumption" so long ago.

The indifference and scorn meted out to these two intellectual giants is something made comprehensible by their own analyses; that is, their analyses explained the manner in which critical theories are deflected by an intellectual status quo, as well as by those in practical life. Both also help us to understand why basic impulses toward change in economics and in the society have taken this long to appear. It is a matter of staying power, and of the enormous difficulties attaching to both intellectual and social change. Those out of power have little to work with and much to oppose; those in power have much to work with and little to oppose. Until, that is, the society finds itself in a crisis.

It appears that American society, and economics as well, is now in the first stages of a profound crisis. As the crisis deepens, the social consciousness of all is stimulated and enhanced, and those with power find it more necessary and more difficult to tighten their hold on things.

Since the 1930's, conventional economics has been in a process of transformation as it has attempted to cope with a whole new range of pressing questions: depression, endemic inflation, business monopolies and trade unions, modern public finance, economic growth and development, poverty, ecology, and a series of complicated international developments. But when those efforts have been informed by theory, the theory has remained neoclassical theory. If theory may be thought of as a compass, it may be said that a bad compass is likely to be worse than none at all: errors become systematic and cumulative. This cannot be taken as an argument for substituting hunches and intuition for inadequate theory; we need to develop much better theory.

Whatever else might characterize that theory, it must come to terms with history. In a time of rapid and troubling change, the minimum basis for understanding is that we know how we got to where we are, and why; in a time when change cuts through all quarters of social existence, we must know how the various aspects of social existence connect and interact. The specialization of social inquiry that has given us "economics," "sociology," and "political science," and innumerable specializations within each of those, has led to analytical compartments hermetically-sealed off from each other. The social analysis our times require must take society for what it is, an organic and dynamic whole. Were such an analysis to develop, many of the specialized efforts of conventional social scientists could take on a new and positive meaning.

Attempts are being made to move in these directions in all the social sciences. In economics the most noteworthy development has been the emergence of the Union for Radical Political Economics (URPE). Begun in the late 1960's, amidst a certain hilarity from the better-established members of the profession, URPE is now a growing and increasingly respected organization. Its journal, the *Review of Radical Political Economics (RRPE)*, has provided an outlet for numerous searching inquiries and critiques of conventional economics and of the American economy. We shall have reference to many of these contributions in this book.

Neither the tasks set by URPE for itself, nor those set by their counterparts in the other social sciences, will be easily or quickly fulfilled, anymore than a decent and safe society will be easily or quickly created. Among the matters on the agenda, one that compels immediate attention is the attempt to comprehend the whys and wherefores of capitalism as a social system, and the manner in which that system has worked itself out in the United States.

Reading Suggestions

In this and succeeding chapters we shall list books that will facilitate the serious reader's ability to push beyond the very general perspective offered here. Countless references could be listed; the criterion guiding these is some combination of accessibility, readability, breadth, and depth.

Robert L. Heilbroner, *The Worldly Philosophers** (New York: Simon and Schuster, 1953) is a lively introduction to the lives and works of the major figures in the development of economic thought. If it is occasionally too breezy, that quality is perhaps an inevitable accompaniment of the author's most readable style. Eric Roll, *A History of Economic Thought** (Englewood Cliffs, N.J.: Prentice-Hall, 1946—subsequent editions should be avoided) is by no means lively, but it does penetrate more deeply than Heilbroner, and is especially useful in relating the classical and neoclassical economists to each other and in placing Marx with respect to them. Leo Rogin, *The Meaning and Validity of Economic Theory: A Historical Approach* (New York: Harper's, 1956) is the most incisive and insightful analysis of how and why economic theory developed, up through Keynes. Unfortunately, the author died before he completed this work, and parts of the text reflect this. Nonetheless, it is a superb analysis.

The shortcomings of conventional analysis can be studied from various standpoints. Joan Robinson, *Economic Philosophy* * (Chicago: Aldine, 1962) is a cheerful but slashing critique of conventional theory by one who has made substantial contributions both to it and to Marxian theory. An excellent, mostly but not entirely Marxian collection of essays is E. K. Hunt and Jesse G. Schwartz, eds., *A Critique of Economic Theory* * (Harmondsworth, England: Penguin Books, 1972). Benjamin Ward, in his *What's Wrong with Economics?* (New York: Basic Books, 1972), laments the methodological inconsistencies and inadequacies of conventional economic theory in a detached but devastating analysis. Sidney Schoeffler, *The Failures of Economics: A Diagnostic Study* (Cambridge, Mass.: Harvard University Press, 1955) is an earlier technical critique of economic theory from a coolly logical standpoint, an attempt to reform from within that has been studiously ignored by the profession since its publication. A book concerned with the development of theory in the natural sciences, Thomas Kuhn, *The Structure of Scientific Revolutions* (Chicago: University of Chicago Press, 1962), which sought to show how and why the hard core of scientific theory—what Kuhn calls their "paradigms"—undergoes development and displacement, has stimulated controversy on the degree to which his analysis applies to *social* thought. URPE, in its *RRPE*, vol. 3, no. 2 (July, 1971), devoted an issue to that controversy: "Special Issue on Radical Paradigms in Economics." Responding to the Nixon policies of late 1971 and to the current state of macroeconomics, the *RRPE* devoted another issue to "On the New Economic Policy: The New Economics and the Contradictions of Keynesianism," Special Issue, vol. 4, no. 4 (August, 1972), perhaps best read after Chapter 4 below. James Weaver, ed., *Modern Political Economy: Radical and Orthodox Views on Crucial Issues* * (Boston: Allyn & Bacon, 1973), provides a useful series of contrasting views. A fine elementary text that places modern and conventional views against each other is E. K. Hunt and Howard Sherman, *Economics* * (New York: Harper & Row, 1975). Many of the criticisms of economics made here have their counterpart for sociology in C. Wright Mills, *The Sociological Imagination* * (New York: Oxford University Press, 1967).

The best introduction to Marxian *economic* theory is Paul M. Sweezy, *The Theory of Capitalist Development* * (New York: Monthly Review

Press, 1968; originally published in 1942), although it is somewhat dated in some of its contemporary judgments. I have sought to do something of the same thing in my *Thorstein Veblen* * (New York: Washington Square Press, 1964) for Veblen's entire range of social analysis. Dudley Dillard, *The Economics of John Maynard Keynes* * (Englewood Cliffs, N.J.: Prentice-Hall, 1948) does for Keynes what Sweezy did for Marx, for those who wish to "do" Keynesian theory.

I have stressed the importance of history and in the following chapters will take this advice, at the same time incorporating the ideas of Marx and Veblen, both historical in their approaches. William Appleman Williams, one of the very best American historians, in his *The Great Evasion** (New York: Quadrangle, 1964), argues that American scholars and citizens have been badly crippled in their ability to understand their country by their assumption that Marxism is irrelevant to American development. Others of Williams' books will be cited later.

A Marxian view of American and of world history may be found in two books of Leo Huberman: *We, the People* * and *Man's Worldly Goods*,* both available in paperback from Monthly Review Press. Both these books were written in the 1930's by a humane and brilliant man who was a lifelong socialist. Both can now be seen as having serious errors of omission and commission—regarding racism, sexism, and what now appears as an uncritical view of the Soviet Union. That so fine and learned a man as Huberman could make such "mistakes" is instructive. Thus, although we might hope that no decent white person would write of Native Americans today as Huberman did in his *We, the People,* we may be quite sure that virtually all whites did then. Regarding the Soviet Union, a different point must be made: in the 1930's to join in the general attacks on the Soviet Union was to join a reactionary crusade, setting aside entirely the difficulty of having access to reliable information. Young and old are still making "mistakes," and doing so honorably. Louis M. Hacker, *The Triumph of American Capitalism* (New York: Columbia University Press, 1940), puts forth a somewhat crude Marxian analysis through the nineteenth century, and departs entirely from that view for the twentieth century. Dudley Dillard, *Economic Development of the North Atlantic Community* (Englewood Cliffs, N.J.: Prentice-Hall, 1967), is a useful overall view of the development of European–U.S. capitalism.

Three other books, quite different from each other, are worth noting here. One shows that realism in economics has not always required radicalism in viewpoint. J. M. Clark, *Studies in the Economics of Overhead Costs* (Chicago: University of Chicago Press, 1923), sought to integrate "micro" and "macro" materials into a dynamic whole, connected to the facts of modern industrial life in the United States. Clark's father was perhaps the most eminent of American neoclassical economists; J. M. Clark himself was much influenced by Veblen's down-to-earth approach, although not by his social outlook. In any case, the economics profession has taken little or no advantage of Clark's major contribution. We have said a bit about alienation in this chapter, and will have reason to bring the matter to the fore again. A convenient and broad collection of fictional and nonfictional essays in the general area is Eric and Mary Josephson, eds., *Man Alone: Alienation in Modern Society* * (New York: Dell, 1962). A powerful and comprehensive treatment of alienation as seen by Marx is Istvan Meszaros, *Marx's Theory of Alienation* * (New York: Harper Torchbooks, 1970). Studs Terkel, *Working* * (New York: Pantheon, 1972), whose subtitle is "People Talk About What They Do All Day and How They Feel About What They Do," is an illuminating glimpse of what alienation on all kinds of jobs is like. It is compiled from interviews; the author is a Chicago-based journalist and TV-radio commentator.

Note: Many of the works cited throughout this book are available in relatively inexpensive paperback editions. Such editions are identified here by an asterisk following the title of the work (whether the reference pertains to the original work or to the paperback reprint).

2

Capitalism

Unhappy, eagle wings and beak, chicken brain
Weep (it is frequent in human affairs) weep for the terrible
magnificence of the means
The ridiculous incompetence of the reasons, the bloody and shabby
*Pathos of the result.**

Capitalism is a world-economic system with a global division of labor. Its emergence and development over the past several centuries has been the dominant force of world history. Capitalist nations have certain basic characteristics in common; each capitalist nation also has defining characteristics that set it apart from and often in conflict with the others. For certain analytical purposes, the defining national adjective—American, British, German—is critical; for other purposes the noun capitalism is decisive. For our purposes it is essential to grasp and integrate the meaning of both. As Maurice Dobb has put it:

> Capitalism is not a system that is cut to a certain pattern and remains the same for all time. Product of a complex process of historical development, capitalism is itself continually subject to historical development. It changes from one decade to the next, it is different in many respects in one country from what it is in another country, according to the specific features of that country and according to the peculiarities of that country's history. . . . But that does not mean that it is not valuable to pick out and to study certain *general features* of capitalism—to isolate and analyze certain relationships that are typical of capitalism in all its varied forms and manifestations. In fact it is essential to do this as a *preliminary* to a more detailed study, if we are to see the wood for the trees—if we

---

* Robinson Jeffers, *Eagle Valor, Chicken Brain.* Reprinted by permission of Jeffers Literary Properties.

are to grasp the general lie of the land as well as be acquainted with each separate bit of it.[1]

The focus of this book is on the nature and the development of capitalism in the United States. The latter part of this chapter will examine capitalism's beginnings and some of its features that are specifically American; the rest of the book will analyze its development up to the present. But first we must discuss in general the origins, the meaning, and the imperatives of capitalism.

Capitalism emerged historically in Western Europe, taking firm hold in the seventeenth century. It was and remains a unique historical development: although many capitalist societies have come into existence outside of Western Europe since then (such as the U.S. and Japan), they have not done so spontaneously, but as an extension or a result of European capitalism. That capitalism emerged at all, and when and where it did, resulted from the specific, distinctive features of *Western European feudalism*; in turn, these were owed to the combination of German tribalism with the legacy of classical antiquity.[2]

Thus, when capitalism as such emerged, it was in a specific historical context; the same is true, even more specifically, of capitalism in different countries. The ways in which, say, British capitalism evolved are due to the particular temporal, spatial, historical, and cultural characteristics of Great Britain. But all these were in turn strengthened, weakened, shaped, and distorted over time by the driving general forces of a developing world-economic system, a global division of labor under capitalist auspices—developing, it is important to note, in a *political* context of competing nation-states. As Wallerstein puts it,

> . . . [Three] things were essential to the establishment of such a capitalist world-economy: an expansion of the geographical size of the world in question [by comparison with medieval Europe], the development of variegated methods of labor control for different products and different zones of the world-economy, and the creation of relatively strong state machineries in what would become the core-states of this capitalist world-economy.[3]

[1] Maurice Dobb, *Economics of Private Enterprise* * (Sydney: Current Book Distributors, 1944), p. 3.

[2] This important argument cannot be pursued here; it is, however, especially vital for understanding the political "side" of capitalism, so frequently neglected by both supporters and critics of the capitalist system. For a comprehensive and powerful statement of this position, see the two volumes by Perry Anderson, *Passages from Antiquity to Feudalism* and *Lineages of the Absolute State* (London: NLB, 1974), esp. pp. 397–431 of *Lineages*.

[3] Immanuel Wallerstein, *The Modern World System: Capitalist Agriculture and the Origins of the European World-Economy in the Sixteenth Century* (New York: Academic Press, 1974), p. 38. By the "sixteenth century," he means 1450–1640.

As a given society moves through time it never totally loses all traces of its cultural characteristics, whether under the impact of feudalism, capitalism, or socialism. However, the special power of capitalism as a system of production has been due to its ability—indeed, its need—to subordinate all social relationships to its dynamism. Marx and Engels put it vividly in the *Communist Manifesto:*

> The bourgeoisie [i.e., capitalists] cannot exist without constantly revolutionizing the instruments of production, and thereby the relations of production, and with them the whole relations of society. Conservation of the old modes of production in unaltered form was, on the contrary, the first condition of existence for all earlier industrial classes. Constant revolutionizing of production, uninterrupted disturbance of all social conditions, ever-lasting uncertainty and agitation distinguish the bourgeois epoch from all earlier ones. All fixed, fast-frozen relations, with their train of ancient and venerable prejudices and opinions, are swept away, all new-formed ones become antiquated before they can ossify. All that is solid melts into air, all that is holy is profaned, and man is at last compelled to face with sober senses his real conditions of life and his relations with his kind.

What is it about capitalism that gives it such power? What needs does such a system have, what imperatives must it satisfy, that drive it so forcefully through time and space and tradition?

The answers to these questions cannot be supplied fully here, but a serious attempt to make headway on them can be. That attempt will revolve around examining the three prime needs of capitalism: for expansion, for exploitation, and for rule by what amounts to an oligarchy. More questions are raised: What makes expansion necessary, even compulsive? What makes it happen? What gives the process its push, its direction, its rate, its quality, its consequences? To answer those questions requires careful inspection of the socioeconomic relations within a given capitalist society and of those between it and other societies. Whatever else such relationships entail—and they entail very much indeed—their unwavering requirement is labor exploitation. And, feeding and being fed by the interaction of expansion and exploitation is a dynamic system of economic, political, and social power that buttresses, feeds upon, and guides the process of development.

"Variegated labor" refers to three distinct forms of labor control: wage labor, sharecropper/tenancy, and serf/slave labor, which work in core, semiperipheral, and peripheral economies respectively. The core economy stands as technologically advanced in relation to the others.

The Heart of the Matter: Expansion and Exploitation

Throughout its history, capitalist profitability has required, and capitalist rule has provided, ever-changing means and areas of exploitation and oppression. This may be seen as the essence of capitalist *social relations*—the necessary but not sufficient condition for capitalist development. *Given* these social relations, the strength of each capitalist enterprise and of national and global capitalist economies varies in accordance with the volume, scope, and rate of capital accumulation, what we term here *economic expansion*. In turn, the economic expansion relates closely to the processes of extensive and intensive *geographic expansion*. Expansion may be seen as the essence of the capitalist *process*, as the heartbeat of capitalism. The full meaning, the widespread recognition, and the political consequences of capitalist social relations have been obscured or blocked in the leading industrial capitalist nations most effectively by the recurring ability of global capitalism to meet its needs for expansion—the primary explanation for the containment of class conflict in those societies, and most notably in the U.S.[4]

Because expansion and exploitation are fundamental to the strength and the survival of capitalism, an inquiry into their causes and consequences necessarily carries deep into the nature and the dynamics of capitalism. Here we make only a brief and abstract foray into that territory; subsequent chapters will examine the American specifics.[5]

To repeat: *expansion* is a process; *exploitation* is a set of relationships. Both are necessary for capitalist development, and neither functions effectively without the other. Their interaction is decisive: the process moving within the relationships, changing them and being changed by them, sustained by and helping to sustain them. The means and ends of business behavior require and lead to expansion; these means and ends in a society in which people are economically powerless and socially and politically oppressed (because of their race or sex) produce and sustain exploitation.

The direct aim of the capitalist business is to make a profit; when it fails to do so, it goes under. Except for brief and exceptional circumstances, profit cannot be made unless businesses function within a process of economic expansion, as manifested in the growth of commodity markets—that is, expansion of the markets in which commodities are

---

[4] Those who call for a cessation or slowing of economic growth, on grounds of ecological damage, must—but seldom, if ever, do—contend with the fact that they are thereby calling for a new socioeconomic system, not just the ecological de-fanging of the present one.

[5] Arthur MacEwan, "Capitalist Expansion, Ideology, and Intervention," *RRPE* (Winter, 1972), is a useful general introduction that relates the abstract discussion to contemporary developments.

sold. This is so whether or not business is able successfully to exploit its labor force, the prime condition surrounding the *production* of commodities. Conversely, even in expanding markets, profits cannot be made unless production is carried on in an exploitive context. This was especially so in the relatively competitive conditions of the nineteenth century, when profits depended squarely upon direct labor exploitation, given expanding market conditions. A full understanding of contemporary U.S. capitalism will show that the combination of monopolistic structures, modern advertising, our overseas relationships, and the taxing and spending activities of the modern capitalist State makes for additional avenues of profitability. The dependence on expansion and exploitation does not decrease as capitalism moves from competitive to monopolistic structures; what changes is the nature and determinants of the expansion process and the burden and the forms of exploitation and oppression. Let us look more closely now at the importance of expansion.

Bigger is Better; More is Not Enough: The Political Economy of Expansion

The need for continuous expansion rises out of the motivations and the key institutions of capitalism: private ownership and control of the means of production in the hands of the very few and their use to make profit, depending upon and perpetuating a starkly unequal distribution of income, wealth, and power. More specifically:

1. Production is for profit, not use; it is production for sale, for the market. Although profits may be made *possible* by labor exploitation in the production process, they may be *realized* only in the market. The full realization of profits thus depends on market buoyancy, on the relative *scarcity* of commodities compared to the demand for them, which gives sellers relative power over buyers. In turn, the most generally beneficial and acceptable basis for scarcity (as compared with natural disasters or monopolistic restrictions of supply) is the expansion of the overall economy, brought about by and further contributing to expansion in productive capacity (that is, net real investment).

2. Capitalism rests upon individualistic ownership, control, and direction of production, and upon capitalist competition within and between industries and national economies, even in the era of monopoly capital. But there is a major difference between competitive and monopoly capitalism: competition in the earlier era led to *falling* prices and perhaps *to* expanding markets, whereas in our era competition (or, better,

rivalry) leads through "non-price" tactics to *higher* prices, thus increasing the need *for* expanding markets. If the disproportionalities and gluts that unavoidably arise from unplanned production are to be kept within bounds, and if the sharp edges of domestic and international competition are to be blunted, expanding markets are required.

3. Technological innovation (in both products and productive techniques), a natural and accelerating process under conditions of industrial capitalism, requires market expansion if the increased production and productivity that make technological change profitable are to occur. In addition, the largest part of such innovation takes place in and most affects the capital goods industries, the heart of an industrial economy (machinery, electricity, metallurgy, chemicals, heavy transportation). These industries depend upon expansion in the rest of the economy (and in their own sectors) if they are not to suffer losses through excess productive capacity.

4. Capitalist exploitation and accumulation depend upon and perpetuate a highly unequal distribution of income and wealth. As the mass of the population lives at levels of socially defined subsistence, a small minority is able to consume *and* save at relatively high levels. If capitalist savings are to be positive in their economic effects, they must be matched by the continuous expansion of real investment, by increases in productive capacity. That only takes place in the expectation of profit, which is to say in the context of actual and expected market scarcities—in turn dependent upon expansion.

5. Capitalism has always depended upon debt financing to some degree for its production and investment activities. Such dependence has increased over time (and spectacularly so since World War II), and extends throughout all spending activities—of consumers and governments, of working and investment capital. Debt financing is now based increasingly on short-term (under one year) borrowing, which requires even more rapid expansion of sales and jobs to provide the corporate and personal incomes and rising real tax base necessary to support markets and to refinance (or further expand) debt. The legend of the sorcerer's apprentice comes to mind.

6. From its beginnings, capitalist economic expansion has depended upon intermittent and deepening waves of *geographic* expansion. Increasing access to exploitable cheap labor, nonhuman resources, and more markets has lifted the volumes of trade, investment, and production for the core (that is, the center or imperialist) economies. This has allowed the maintenance or increase of profits and, in raising the level of socially defined subsistence, has helped to blunt social conflict in the core countries at the expense of external populations. There have undoubtedly been sociopsychological consequences of imperialism (taking the form, for example, of attitudes of superiority and vicarious power)

which, in association with the cultivation of patriotism in the nation-states of capitalism, have also contributed to political stability. Anything that might do so is welcome to capitalism, given the potentially explosive nature of its distributions of income, wealth, and power.

The interaction of *all* these "needs"—rather than any one of them—defines capitalism's dependence upon continuous expansion. The recurring inability of global capitalism throughout much of its history to fulfill all of them in adequate combination provides the major explanation for its tendency toward intermittent economic crisis and toward internal and international conflict. The experience since World War II, in contrast, has been spectacularly successful in all these respects for North America, Western Europe, and Japan, and it provides the major explanation for the reduction of conflict within and between the core capitalist nations—until the 1970's and the emergence once more of troubles, when the rate of capitalist economic expansion subsided. Of that, more in later chapters.

For the compulsive quality of expansion under capitalism to be understood more fully, let us examine further the historical meaning of business competition and rivalry, and the impulses of and relationships between capitalists. We must take a closer look at the class structure of society, the relationships between the powerful and the powerless, which underlies the profitability accompanying expansion. Engels caught part of this very well, when he wrote:

> Competition is the most complete expression of the battle of all against all which rules in modern civil society. This battle, a battle for life, for existence . . . , is fought not between the different classes of society only, but also between the individual members of these classes. Each is in the way of the other, and each seeks to crowd out all who are in his way, and to put himself in their place. The workers are in constant competition among themselves as the members of the bourgeoisie among themselves.[6]

It is fairly easy to see how and why workers would compete among themselves for jobs; nor is it difficult to imagine business competition. But why does the competition require and lead to expansion?

Capitalism emerged full-blown only when the traditions and restrictions of earlier times had been swept away. It was also a time of rapid geographic expansion and the ever-swifter growth of technology and science. The expanding production sought by Smith took place in a context of increasing productivity, brought about by technological improvement. Once set loose, the rate of technological change became in-

[6] Frederick Engels, *The Condition of the Working-Class in England in 1844* (London: Allen & Unwin, 1950), p. 75. Published originally in 1845.

creasingly rapid and pervasive in its impact. A competitive capitalist economy is one in which the only protection a given firm has is its own strength. That strength finally depends upon its profitability. In the modern world this means that each firm must adopt the latest in technology, for both defensive and offensive reasons. With all or most firms in a given industry doing so, both production and productivity increase. The market must expand to absorb the increased production. In the normal course of such processes, some firms succeed and others fall by the wayside. The surviving firms continue to expand, in themselves and by gobbling up others. The result is large-scale production, large-scale ownership, and large-scale control: a tendency toward monopoly. Along with economic expansion, both facilitating it and required by it, is geographic expansion—expansion of foreign markets, access to increasingly-needed foodstuffs and raw materials, and profitable foreign investments. Again, the *Communist Manifesto:*

> The need of a constantly expanding market for its products chases the bourgeoisie over the whole surface of the globe. It must nestle everywhere, settle everywhere, establish connections everywhere.

But there is more involved. The aim of profit under capitalist conditions, as earlier in the mercantilist period, sets up a corollary aim: *power.* Control over productive property is the *sine qua non* of profits; property and profits *are* private power, and private power has access to State power; such access allows protection and enhancement of an already privileged position. Smith, it will be recalled, knew that State power was essential to protect the unequal division of property in society, the division that has capitalists on one side and propertyless workers on the other. Power inheres in property ownership, and power begets power both at home and abroad, as powerlessness begets powerlessness.

The emergence of laissez-faire capitalism depended upon the abolition of State mercantilism. What Smith had correctly viewed as obstacles to the full increase of productive powers was also a system of protections and privileges. Labor was obliged to work, but it had also had the right to work and in principle the right not to starve. Capital, to the degree that it had the favor of the State, was likewise insulated from the market. Laissez-faire capitalism left individuals' and enterprises' fates in the hands of impersonal market forces, forces which changed swiftly and at times violently. In the absence of built-in social constraints on the free operations of the markets for labor power and goods, protection and privilege had to be gained through private efforts.

Ownership of the means of production, that is, property ownership, in such a society was the prime source of advantage. The means of enhancing that advantage for both offensive and defensive purposes was to move toward monopoly—the control over supply. For those whose incomes come from their work rather than from property, means of controlling *their* supply were even more indispensable. This is what trade unions, professional associations, licensing, and the like, achieve. Both for business and for labor, the seeking and the achievement of such ends require access to or the protection of State power. In nineteenth century American and British capitalism, property, business, and power were simply and clearly linked; in the more complicated world leading to the present, the basic relationships continue, but in a more intricate pattern. The nature of those relationships is suggested when economists refer to monopoly as "control over supply." They appear more clearly when we view control over supply in its monopolistic forms as being the monopolization of property and of skills. Property retains the advantage, for labor power must combine with property to become productive.

Businessmen agree that production is for profit, and that expansion is good and necessary. Neither they nor most social scientists, however, agree that exploitation is an actual, let alone a necessary, accompaniment of business success. Conventional social analysis leads few to think in terms such as these; it fails even to raise questions that might lead us to check a concept such as exploitation against social reality. Yet how is one to comprehend a situation in which incomes are distributed "almost in an inverse ratio to the labour," as J. S. Mill said, unless one recognizes that some are being exploited by others and that that relationship can persist, as Smith said, "only under the shelter of the civil magistrate"?

Such assertions and such questions require explanation, all the more essential because the existence of systematic and persistent exploitation is rejected or treated aloofly in conventional social analysis. The requisite analysis is necessarily historical: how did a small number of people gain the power to exploit the majority of the population?

Exploitation and Capitalism

Workers as such are propertyless. To produce they must work with materials and equipment owned by capitalists; to survive, they must produce. As Marx put it, ". . . the labourer purchases the right to work for his own livelihood only by paying for it in surplus-labour. . . ." [7] By "surplus-labour" Marx meant unpaid labor—that is, exploited labor. Exploitation as a concept leads directly to power as a reality.

The power of the employer derives from his position in the scale of income and wealth, his control over the means of production, and his

[7] Karl Marx, *Capital* * (New York: International Publishers, 1967), vol. I, p. 515. Originally published in 1867.

related political and social prestige and power. All these are inextricably linked. Conventional economics starts and ends with the capitalist producing for profit; it ignores the fact that what makes the process possible is the control over property exercised by the capitalist and the power preceding and accompanying the achievement of that control. Having ignored the relationship, conventional analysis is therefore under no obligation to explain its existence.

How did modern property and labor relationships come to be? Has it always been thus? Why and how does it persist? We need not posit some golden idyll of a dim past to answer that as capitalism came into being it did so on the wreckage of medieval property relationships. In the medieval world, private property as we understand the term did not exist. Neither land nor labor were commodities; neither could be bought or sold. The fundamental form of wealth was land. Let us examine what Marx called "the classic case," that of England.

Land was *held*, not "owned," within a set of concomitant obligations. The rights to the land, for lord or serf, were the rights of "usufruct": rights to the produce of the land. The holding of land was consequent upon a feudal "contract," in which those granted land were obliged to provide "aid and counsel" to their lord. Aid and counsel took the form of military, political, and religious service. The serf and his family were required to work the lands and to provide other forms of necessary labor for their lord. The serfs were attached to the land hereditarily, generation after generation on the same estate. The various strata of lords—knights at the lowest level, emperors at the highest—found their status within each generation. They were "free" to form their contracts. Free meant "honorable." They were the gentlemen and ladies of the medieval world. The serfs worked three to four days a week for their lord, farming his land, repairing paths and bridges, and the like; the rest of the week they worked for themselves. The work they did for their lord was surplus labor; it was the degree of their exploitation. It was, in its day, their taxes, paid in labor power. Custom and force in varying measure held the serfs to their tasks and the land on which they performed them. That simplicity gave way as the medieval world gave way to the modern, altering economic, political, and social structures and processes.

The medieval structure began to give way around the twelfth and thirteenth centuries in an irregular pattern, depending very much upon specific location and circumstances.[8] The more or less constant warfare of

[8] The diversity of the pattern in various parts of Europe, and the forces at work, are analyzed at their best in *The Cambridge Economic History of Europe, Vol. I: The Agrarian Life of the Middle Ages* (Cambridge: Cambridge University Press, 1942), edited by J. H. Clapham and Eileen Power. In the *Encyclopaedia of the Social Sciences*—an invaluable fifteen-volume work—under the entry "Feudalism," Marc

early medieval Europe had moderated by then, because of the success of feudalism in bringing relative peace—while also undermining the reasons for its own continuance as a social system. Peace allowed improvements in agricultural production, trade, and commerce. Serfs began to commute their labor services into money payments called "quitrents," an early version of what we call rent. In England, serfs became "copyholders." They were free in themselves and also free to use and sell the entire produce of their lands. Farming practices remained unchanged, but the holding of land was no longer medieval—nor was it yet a commodity. The copyholders are the "sturdy yeomanry" of renaissance literature. Their conditions were transformed and displaced as full commercialization took over.

The improvement in the conditions of life that began as serfdom and feudalism declined led to increased population as well as to increased trade and production; towns and cities grew; new and powerful nation-states emerged; technology improved; global expansion became the hallmark of the sixteenth and seventeenth centuries.

Alongside that set of changes, becoming disturbing in England in the sixteenth century, substantial in the seventeenth, and a landslide in the eighteenth, was the so-called *enclosure movement*—a movement that enclosed with a hedge or fence a whole estate, with its many "open" fields, into one "enclosed," unified farm, displacing many holders by one owner. That process, impelled by the gains to be made by a larger-scale and increasingly commercial agriculture producing wool and grains, entailed the transformation of a once populous and free peasantry, farming its own lands, into a propertyless and "free" working class. They, together with the increasing population that was already landless, became the modern working class, with nothing to sell but their labor power and with no way to stay alive without doing so.

The enclosure movement was a many-sided process. Its early beginnings were in thirteenth-century England, a time of prosperity and rising commercialism connected with the expanding wool trade and the rise of towns. The key period in terms of establishing precedents was in the sixteenth century, the century of the Reformation, of the disposition of Church lands on the market, and the creation of English mercantilist policies. The precedents established then led to rising enclosures in the seventeenth century; the statistical tidal wave took place in the latter part of the eighteenth century. By 1820 or so, almost all the agricultural land of England had been enclosed; by the close of the nineteenth century a few thousand families owned almost all of it. The means utilized to

---

Bloch provides a succinct and illuminating analysis of European feudalism and its decline. His own *Feudal Society* * (Chicago: University of Chicago Press, Phoenix Books, 1964), 2 vols., is the classic study, rich in wisdom and detail.

enclose lands—that is, to ease or force the peasantry or yeomanry from their lands—included force as well as law. The legalities were accomplished through the "Justices of the Peace" and through Parliament—by men who were generally of the enclosing class.[9]

The changes of the sixteenth through the eighteenth centuries in England were the social equivalent of an earthquake. The power of the Roman Catholic Church was broken in the sixteenth century, to give way to the "divine right of kings," which in the seventeenth century gave way to what later became the "divine right of capital." Land tenure and land utilization ceased to be determined by tradition, as commercialism and finally the making of land into a commodity transformed all of rural life. In the opening years of the nineteenth century, labor itself became a commodity, no less and no more than any other article of commerce, free from obligations and free of protection. All this seems natural to us today, but it was a process fought over every step along the way by those to whom it seemed unnatural and immoral. Neither land nor labor had been viewed as means to solely commercial ends in the earlier centuries; now they were. Only today is the view spreading in the U.S. that commercial considerations should not be dominant for either land or labor. Engels observed the connections between the two in 1843: "To make earth an object of huckstering—the earth which is our one and all, the first condition of our existence—was the last step toward making oneself an object of huckstering. It was and is to this very day an immorality surpassed only by the immorality of self-alienation." [10]

The enclosure movement in England, and its role in creating a wage-earning, propertyless and powerless, and therefore exploitable class of workers, was not unique to England in each of its respects, though it was when taken as a whole. The exploitation of labor had more diverse roots and took on forms other than wage labor in global and national capitalist developments. We need only mention the critical role imported black slaves played in the agricultural production of the New World—and not least in the United States—to see that exploitation is an outcome of powerlessness, and powerlessness is the outcome of many sociohistorical combinations and permutations.

[9] See R. H. Tawney, *The Agrarian Problem in 16th Century England* ° (New York: Burt Franklin Publishers, 1959), for a profound analysis of the critical breakdown of agricultural traditions. (Originally published in 1912.) For the nature and consequences of the later period see the definitive work on the period in all its respects, Paul Mantoux, *The Industrial Revolution in the Eighteenth Century*° (London: Cape, 1928), esp. Ch. 3. (Originally published in 1906.) William Lazonick, "Karl Marx and Enclosures in England," RRPE, Vol. 6, no. 2 (Summer, 1974) is a superb discussion both of that history and of the historiography of enclosures.

[10] From his *Outlines of a Critique of Political Economy,*° quoted in Meszaros, *Marx's Theory of Alienation*, pp. 314–15.

Earlier, we referred to Marx's conception of human nature and society. Marx saw alienation as intense under capitalist conditions, and ever-more intense with the development of industrial capitalism. The propertylessness of the worker, displaced from the land and without the tools of work, meant the loss of control over what is produced, or how, or why, or when. The natural relationship of people to production for use is mediated by the necessity to work for a wage, producing commodities for the market—for someone else's profit, and under harsh working conditions. The development of modern industry and the increased specialization accompanying it increases alienation but does not cause it; the cause lies in the separation of the workers from control over their work. Workers are alienated from each other, as they compete for jobs; from nature, from which they become separated; from their work; and from their own basic nature. The problem is not work, which is natural and fulfilling to humans; nor is it property, which is necessary for the work to be done. The problem is the conditions within which work takes place, and who controls the property. "Wages," Marx said, "are like the oil which is applied to a wheel to keep it running." [11] Like the commodities they produce, workers in industrial capitalism become things.

Faith, Hope, and Competition

Something else, perhaps most momentous of all, happened as the medieval gave way to the modern world. One of England's most searching political philosophers put it this way:

> The movement from feudalism to capitalism is a movement from a world in which individual well-being is regarded as the outcome of action socially controlled to one in which social well-being is regarded as the outcome of action individually controlled.[12]

[11] Bottomore, *Karl Marx: Early Writings,* p. 138. Stephen A. Marglin, "What Do Bosses Do? The Origins and Functions of Hierarchy in Capitalist Production," *RRPE,* Vol. 6, No. 2 (Summer, 1974), is an important analysis showing how the organization of work under capitalist conditions itself contributes to exploitation, whatever else it might mean. His emphasis is the long period into the nineteenth century; Harry Braverman, *Labor and Monopoly Capital* ° (New York: Monthly Review Press, 1974) shows this and much more for this century, with its "scientific management" of labor.

[12] Harold J. Laski, *The Rise of European Liberalism* (London: Allen & Unwin, 1936), p. 28.

That was the change given its fullest rationale by Adam Smith: the fate of society, and of the individuals in it, was entrusted to the outcome of a no-holds-barred economic contest. The only rules were those protecting property; all else was in the laps of the gods. No doubt, in the setting of the eighteenth and nineteenth centuries, such an economy would grow and change at rates that were, by previous standards, extraordinarily high, as dramatically portrayed in the *Communist Manifesto*:

> The bourgeoisie, during its rule of scarce one hundred years, has created more massive and more colossal productive forces than all preceding generations together. Subjection of nature's forces to man, machinery, application of chemistry to industry and agriculture, steam-navigation, railways, electric telegraphs, clearing of whole continents for cultivation, canalization of rivers, whole populations conjured out of the ground— what earlier century had even a presentiment that such productive forces slumbered in the lap of social labor?

Smith had been correct in anticipating that the abolition of social constraints upon the economy would enhance the "wealth of the nation." What he did not foresee was that the very competitive economy he posited, and the market competition that would transform individual self-seeking into social well-being, would be pushed aside. Nor did he see that the concentrated State power against which he railed successfully would be surpassed by an even more powerful private-State pattern of power. The latter was all the more substantial because, unlike explicit State power, it was difficult to identify and harder to control. Those who had to be controlled were in fact in control.

What emerged in the century after Smith wrote belied his intentions. Where had he gone wrong? We have noted some points earlier, but there are others. Smith did not anticipate that technology would develop in such a way that the forms of business organization that became both possible and necessary would be incompatible with small-scale industry, which was the basis of a competitive economy. Smith was not naïve. He assumed that businessmen would be unable to resist the temptation to monopolize when he noted, in a famous observation, that "people of the same trade seldom meet together, even for merriment and diversion, but the conversation ends in a conspiracy against the public, or in some contrivance to raise prices." [13] However, his fears on that score were neutralized by his key assumption that a highly decentralized market structure would block such natural inclinations. With the technology of his day, his view made sense. But the very success of the economy in subsequent decades also meant the failure of the "invisible hand."

[13] *The Wealth of Nations*, p. 130.

Smith tripped over another matter of greater weight: the distribution of income and wealth, and the ways in which those patterns affect both the process of expansion and the possibilities of exploitation. For this shortcoming, Smith had less excuse than for his failure to anticipate technological development adequately. The distribution of income and wealth when Smith lived was already highly unequal, and becoming more so. They were the days of high turmoil associated with the enclosure movement, a process which impoverished many while placing more wealth in fewer hands. It was a contemporary of Smith's, after all, whose epic poem "The Deserted Village" has done so much to tell us—if romantically and sentimentally—what was lost when efficient agriculture was gained:

Ill fares the land, to hastening ills a prey,
Where wealth accumulates, and men decay:
Princes and lords may flourish, or may fade;
A breath can make them, as a breath has made;
But a bold peasantry, their country's pride,
When once destroyed, can never be supplied.[14]

England had ceased to need "a bold peasantry" while Goldsmith wrote; to further its economic growth it needed a docile and powerless labor force that would work under wretched conditions in mine, mill, and factory. England got what it needed largely through the enclosure movement; other capitalist nations found both similar and different ways to create or to import a powerless working force. The conditions of Irish workers brought into England were even worse than those of the English; the great British historian Macaulay found those of German workers worse still, leading to his characterization of them as "degenerate dwarfs." That he was not entirely off the mark, setting aside his ugly language, is suggested by this observation concerning Germany: "In 1828 General von Horn warned the Prussian Government that these [Prussian] districts could not supply their quota of army recruits since the health of young factory workers was being undermined." [15]

[14] Oliver Goldsmith (1728–1774) was Irish, but the setting of the poem was England. This is but a fragment of a very long poem. The sixteenth century enclosures prompted Sir Thomas More to observe that "shepe are eating men," as those enclosures converted arable into pasture lands.

[15] W. O. Henderson, *The Industrial Revolution in Europe, 1815–1914*° (Chicago: Quadrangle, 1968), p. 23. This book is a useful source on developments in Europe, to balance our emphasis on England and the United States. It is dry, but informative. See Thorstein Veblen, *Imperial Germany and the Industrial Revolution* ° (New York: Viking, 1946) for a searching and witty comparison and analysis of British and German developments, accompanied by many general insights. Originally published in 1915.

What Smith failed to anticipate regarding technology, private economic power, and intensive human exploitation is less egregious as a defect for a moral philosopher than his failure to grasp what would become of a society loosed of all social constraints but those of the market. Recall Tawney's analogy concerning giving sex and pugnacity free reign and the central role in social organization. Then imagine how degraded and empty sexual relationships would become in a society knowing or caring little of ethics or love; how violent a society would be in which sheer physical strength dominated the relationships between people. Tawney knew that such a society would not be wished by anyone; the point is simply that allowing economic self-interest to function without constraint is equally destructive of human needs and possibilities.

Smith was right in believing that the abolition of social constraints would allow the capitalist economy to grow apace; indeed, the prime reason for the economic power of capitalism is that it is unconstrained. But the results were not benign, as Smith had hoped they would be.

Rapid economic growth taken alone is neither desirable nor undesirable. It must be judged in terms of its larger meanings to human beings and to natural resources; in what it elicits and what it deflects or suppresses in human beings; in what it does to the nature of human relationships; how it serves human needs; how it encourages human possibilities. In establishing competition as the ruling principle of social existence, a capitalist society makes combative relationships necessary for all. If there are quantitative rewards for those who are victorious, there are human losses for all. This is so even after the reintroduction of social constraints, for the basic processes remain competitive and combative. Human inclinations other than naked self-interest narrowly defined are pushed into the realm of the impractical, the "idealistic." As Tawney says,

> It is obvious, indeed, that no change of system or machinery can avert those causes of social *malaise* which consist in the egotism, greed, or quarrelsomeness of human nature. What it can do is to create an environment in which those are not the qualities which are encouraged. It cannot secure that men live up to their principles. What it can do is establish their social order upon principles to which, if they please, they can live up and not live down.[16]

To which may be contrasted, as Tawney points out, "the compound of economic optimism and moral bankruptcy which led a nineteenth-

[16] R. H. Tawney, *The Acquisitive Society* (New York: Harcourt Brace Jovanovich, 1920), p. 180.

century economist to say: 'Greed is held in check by greed, and the desire for gain sets limits to itself.' "[17]

Smith, Ricardo, and Marx all analyzed *competitive* capitalism. Neither Smith nor Ricardo foresaw the harshness of competition let loose; neither foresaw its leading to monopoly. But these were starting points for Marx. Marx saw competitive capitalism as an inhumane and dehumanizing social system, dependent upon greed for its energy and exploitation for its fuel. He took for granted that it would increase production and productivity over time; given its dynamics he also took for granted that monopoly would replace competition. Even after a century or more of evidence confirming Marx's judgment, conventional analysis continues without substantial recognition or analysis of these two major characteristics of capitalist development. What Marx took for granted is seen analytically as aberrant, or not seen at all.

The transition from competitive to monopoly capitalism was facilitated by but not *due* to technological change. It was the increasing scale and complexity of production *combined with* the major business impulses of those who controlled the means of production that led to monopoly. The concentration and centralization of capital that is characteristic of all industrial capitalist societies today arises out of, not despite, competitive capitalism. It is the way the system moves through time.

Those who survive capitalist rivalry do so by absorbing or by destroying the lesser firms. Capitalism is a predatory form of economic organization. For Smith's optimism to have been well-founded, limits would have had to have been set on the size of the bigger fish. Set by whom, the bigger fish? In the absence of any explicit institutions designed to control such a process—and Smith's laissez-faire capitalism excluded any such—the bigger fish become more and more immune to any constraints on their behavior or further growth. They are best able to respond effectively to changing technology, and are best able to survive intermittent blasts of depression. The history of the United States, most capitalistic of all capitalist nations, reveals these processes most clearly.

The American Setting: Capitalist Paradise

A generalization that will be agreed upon by both the critics and the supporters of our system is that both capitalism and industrialism have pushed further ahead in the United States than elsewhere. How and

[17] Ibid., p. 27.

why this came to be can be explained by all those matters that contribute to industrialism and to capitalist development, by the manner in which they interacted in our past. Let us note first the most obvious of these contributing factors—our geographic advantages—and place them in the American social context.

Everything and anything that might facilitate the emergence of capitalist institutions and the progress of industry was available to America. All that was lacking was control over our own destiny; that was achieved in our War for Independence. Most obvious and striking of American advantages has been our physical setting.

No nation has matched the quantitative or qualitative abundance of natural resources of this country, whether the reference is to climate, terrain, soils, coasts, bays, rivers, lakes, forests, and minerals or to the convenient locations of each of these with respect to each other. Nor can the vast oceans that give us almost total security from invasion be ignored as a developmental advantage. All these are obvious. But there were other and less obvious advantages, institutional and historical, which were of great importance in our evolution as a capitalist society.

The temporal and social conditions under which colonial America and the United States came into being were most auspicious. America as such had no medieval past, and thus no tradition of social controls to deny or to destroy. On this continent, all that had to be destroyed were the Native American and Mexican communities standing in the way. The settlement and development of America, as a colony of the British, represented the leading edge of British development, rather than the British past. In the seventeenth century, and even more in the eighteenth century, that meant a Britain moving rapidly toward capitalism.

Attempts to implant traditional agricultural forms (such as manorialism in upstate New York) or stringent social codes (theocratic attempts in Massachusetts) were made; the strong winds of commercialism and the extraordinary opportunities of the period combined to blow away such social structures. There were few people in America in comparison with the rich resources of the land. Labor was short in supply; workers were wanted in shipping, trade, fishing, petty industry, and agriculture. This was an especially severe problem for those who wished to exploit the valuable agricultural possibilities of the southern colonies. Serfdom was impossible; slavery was not.

Commercial slavery began well before significant settlement of the North American colonies. The African slave trade was well-established by the sixteenth century; slaves were widely-used in South America and in the Caribbean, especially for sugar cultivation. As the American South began to grow tobacco for the market, but even more so when rice, indigo and especially cotton plantations grew in number and importance, North America became the prime user of African slaves. Estimates of the numbers of Africans enslaved and carried to the Americas range from fifteen to twenty millions; it is estimated that from 50 to 85 percent of these died in route.[18]

The nonslave labor force of the colonies was made up of immigrants, many coming as indentured servants, which meant working three to seven years to pay for passage. Arriving largely as adults, immigrants were a boon to the young economy, for their childhood, their unproductive years, had been "paid for" in their home countries. This remained an advantageous characteristic of the expanding American labor force up to World War I. Apart from slaves, by that time well over thirty million had emigrated here.

In addition to the "social cheapness" of the American labor force over time, another feature should be noted: those who came voluntarily to this country, whether propelled or drawn by religious, political, or economic considerations, were clearly desirous of or suited to the non-traditional shape of American society. Their characteristics facilitated the growth of such a society.

From its first days, and setting aside those enslaved, the U.S. was a land of enterprisers—small or large farmers, artisans or petty manufacturers, domestic or foreign traders, low or high financiers. It was a capitalist society from birth; or, if not quite then, as soon as it could crawl. By the mid-eighteenth century, America had the ability to walk, but was increasingly held back by British capital and British power. What mercantilism had been to British capitalism in Great Britain, both in its positive and its negative aspects, British regulations were to the Americans, as Smith had noted.

Few indeed were the Americans who foresaw either the need or the possibility of revolution against Britain, until the mid-1770's. Once war broke out, the ability of the Americans to fight successfully was enhanced not only by the ocean between but also by the diverse interests and rivalries distracting the British from a sole preoccupation with the North American colonies; for instance, the Caribbean sugar colonies were seen as more important economically at the time. And, of course, Britain had to contend with its European rivals, particularly the French, who aided the Americans directly and indirectly.

Of great importance to the Americans before and after the Revolution were the expansive trends beginning to take hold in the world with the coming of the nineteenth century. The old structures of power were

---

[18] W. Schulte Nordholt, *The People That Walk in Darkness* * (New York: Ballantine, 1970) is an excellent and comprehensive treatment of the slave trade from its beginnings. It has a useful bibliography for further study.

cracking up in Europe, and new waves of economic and geographic expansion were transforming the world. In that setting, the United States found new and growing sources of trade, of technological innovation, of capital, and of immigrants. Added to our already substantial advantages in resources, attitudes, and labor supply, this dynamic new world context propelled American economic development along its path toward industrialism with an unmatchable set of advantages; the relative ease of our economic development did much to obscure and to suppress the social conflicts associated with capitalist development.

Next we should characterize the role of the State in our history. In rebelling against the British, Americans were also rebelling against the role of centralized State power. Consequently, even though the War brought Americans to a pitch of patriotism and nationalism which would still be considered intense by world standards, an affection for a strong *central* government did not result. But this did not mean a distaste for governmental assistance when it was necessary and useful. Thus, our first decades as a nation saw a minimal role of the *federal* government and a vital role for the separate *state* governments. The federal government presided over a unified foreign trade policy, a uniform currency, and a national policy for absorbing and conquering the lands to the west. The state governments played the decisive role in developing transportation (roads, canals, and railways), banking, and, among other economic matters, business and labor laws.

The upshot, for the first half-century of our existence as a nation, was far from the laissez-faire society proposed by Smith. That came later, in its American form. We may note very briefly three different periods regarding the role of the State in American economic life. The first period was American mercantilism, described above. The second period, replacing mercantilism after Jackson's presidency, occurred as American laissez-faire capitalism began to flourish. It came to its roaring climax in the decades after the Civil War, called by Mark Twain the "Gilded Age," and by Vernon Parrington the "Great Barbecue." The third phase leads up to the present, and was a response to the instabilities and beckoning possibilities of maturing industrial capitalism. This phase began to develop and to find coherence somewhat before but especially during Wilson's presidency and involved increased centralization of State power in Washington. This was both consequence and cause of the increasing concentration and centralization of economic power in the corporate world of industry and finance, and was accompanied by the first waves of overseas imperialism by the United States. Gabriel Kolko has called this the phase of "political capitalism." In Chapter 8 the background and functioning of this process will be examined intensively.

Mirror, Mirror, on the Wall . . .

Americans tend to view our national history as having made astounding economic achievements with a minimum of the coercive and violent practices associated with other nations' histories, and as having taken place within a political and social context at once humanitarian, egalitarian, and democratic. Such a view requires blindness to certain basic features of our development. The blindness is systematic and pervasive. It neglects the origins and the meaning of slavery as a central determinant of our early economic development, as it neglects in a connected way the other forms of labor exploitation hastening and shaping our economic achievements. It pays only the slightest attention to the connections between our rapid growth and the spoliation of our natural environment that cheapened the direct costs of that growth. In turn, our inability as a people to comprehend our history of human and resource exploitation has made it terribly difficult for us to comprehend or control the consequences of our past. And there is one further blind spot in the ways we view our history, one that has come to haunt us as it finally penetrates our consciousness: it concerns geographic expansion.

Economic expansion was noted earlier as being essential to capitalist health; geographic expansion must now be noted as playing a key role in our process of economic expansion. Capitalism began that way; the settling of the American colonies was itself an instance of geographic expansion for the British. Capitalism seeks to continue that way. Americans are generally critically conscious of the incessant attempts of *other* nations to enlarge their geographic influence and control; we are familiar with notions of British, or French, or German, or Japanese "imperialism." Our own processes of geographic expansion have been the most continuous and successful of all nations. Only rarely, however, do our histories speak of American imperialism; instead, we read of "westward expansion," or of "manifest destiny." We do not view our process of geographic expansion on this continent as imperialism, but as simply a filling of the space up to "our" natural boundaries. We do not see our history as one of exterminating or penning in the Native American population, or of holding back and pushing away the other contenders (French, British, Spanish, Mexican, Russian) for geographic control, but rather as merely securing "our" lands, lands that were in some unexamined sense "ours" to begin with, or "ours" when we could get around to settling and exploiting them.

Given that view of expansion on this continent, it was natural and easy to see our extra-continental expansion—into the Caribbean and Pacific, first, and directly and indirectly over the face of the entire globe, later—as having much the same qualities. If the rest of the globe was not "ours" in the same sense as actual settlement, it was ours to protect, to assist, to shape, to lead, to make "free." As finally became the case with Indochina, it was ours to destroy if necessary, in order to make "free."

A line from Jamestown to Indochina runs through our history. Its importance must be measured first in terms of what it has meant to those we have killed, caged, or shoved aside. But only at our peril can we overlook the importance to our past and our future that the studied innocence of that line has meant in shaping American policy and American consciousness, and how it connects with our treatment of human beings and nature here at home.[19]

Ensuing chapters will elaborate upon all the foregoing generalizations about American capitalist development. Here a few summary points may be of use. The United States had the easiest, swiftest, and most successful process of economic achievement of any society in history, whether we measure by the level or composition of production, by productivity, or by per capita real income. Most capitalist of all nations, the United States has had less open and sustained class conflict than other capitalist nations. Americans have seen more hope for themselves *within* the system than do their counterparts elsewhere; when they have moved to struggle—whether as workers seeking unions, or as those racially or sexually oppressed—they have almost always adopted both the means and the ends of those who rule and profit in the system.

Perhaps the best way of explaining the economic and the social strength and stability of U.S. capitalism is to see that it has possessed *within its own boundaries* and capacities as much of all that is essential for capitalist development, which other nations have possessed in much lesser part. Keep the United States in mind, in its early as well as its subsequent development, while reading this long quote from Wallerstein:

> The ability to expand successfully is a function both of the ability to maintain relative social solidarity at home (in turn a function of the mechanisms of the distribution of reward) and the arrangements that can be made to use cheap labor *far away*. . . . Expansion also involves unequal development and therefore differential rewards, and unequal development in a multilayered format of layers within layers, each one polarized in terms of a bimodal distribution of rewards. . . . [M]ulti-

[19] Historians did not even begin to pull this history together until very recently. See Richard W. Van Alstyne, *The Rising American Empire*° (New York: Oxford University Press, 1960; Chicago: Quadrangle, 1965) and William Appleman Williams, *The Contours of American History* ° (Chicago: Quadrangle, 1966) for two books that trace our expansionism to its early beginnings. Studies influenced by these initial breakthroughs will be noted and relied upon in Chapter 7, where our geographic expansion is a central topic.

layered complexity provide[s] the possibility of multilayered identification and the constant realignment of political forces, which provide[s] at one and the same time the underlying turbulence that permit[s] technological development and political transformations, and also . . . ideological confusion. . . .[20]

The U.S. got its "cheap labor" from "far away" in the form of slaves, indentured servants, and free laborers, in varying quantities and proportions at any time, but in important quantities in the critical eighteenth and nineteenth centuries. No other capitalist nation had such diversity in its *domestic* labor supply, nor did any other find it possible to use racism (against not only blacks, but others) at home in ways that combined economic and political advantage. In addition, the structure and traditions of government in the U.S.—symbolized best, perhaps, by "states' rights"—encouraged and allowed a "multilayered" political complexity which, in combination with other matters suggested above, enhanced the possibilities of "ideological confusion," in the context of the most successful and prolonged process of economic expansion of any of the capitalist nations.

Having come to be as a nation created in the name of minimal State power, the United States now functions as a highly centralized State at home. As the first society to fight a successful revolution for national independence, the United States now sits in the midst of a complicated web of neocolonial relationships constructed in this century in the name of what Williams calls "anti-colonial imperialism."

Nor can we fail to note that the land whose Declaration of Independence speaks in inspiring ways of human dignity and freedom has as its most fundamental and unresolved question an intensive form of racism practiced from our first years, and increasingly so after our independence. We continue despite repeated warnings from all quarters that if racism has not already been our undoing, it will one day be so. Much the same is said about our destruction of the environment, the deadly qualities of our air, the poisoning of our water supply.

In short, in creating the world's most powerful economy, the United States has also produced a society teeming with troubles. The troubles are connected in such a way that we must speak not of "social issues" but of a developing social crisis. Racism and imperialism were not invented by Americans. But the development of American capitalism has nourished them in ways and degrees going beyond that of the Europeans. The power of these monsters to create fear, tension, and violence cannot be viewed as separable from the power of the economy that has allowed or required them to grow.

[20] Wallerstein, *The Modern World System*, pp. 85–86, his emphasis.

American capitalism is the acme and the epitome of capitalism. As such, it departs further and further in time from inherited noncommercial values; in the process, institutions supportive of noncommercial values are vitiated, weaken, and disappear. At the same time, many people become increasingly aware of the essential inhumanity and amorality of a society dominated by profit-making and wealth-garnering, and the subjection of the human spirit and human activities to machine-like conditions. The tension between these two developments, between the natural course of capitalist development and the increasing resistance of the human spirit, lies at the root of our developing social crisis.

Human beings are inherently moral, possessed of feelings of sympathy, empathy, solidarity with our kind, and the need and ability to live creative and loving lives. These attributes continue to emerge, and manifest themselves, now as in the past, despite the presence of our baser capabilities. One need not be a Marx or a Veblen to see people as something more than creatures of material self-interest; all the major religions, psychiatry, and the landmarks of our literature, art, and music remind us of what we have been and what we can be, as do the numerous struggles fought by so many peoples for dignity throughout history. The crisis awaiting us shows itself first as a crisis of economic and political life; its root is a moral crisis, whose resolution will determine the realization or the destruction of our species' needs and possibilities.

Reading Suggestions

There are many books of selected readings; among the best as an accompaniment to the approach taken in this and subsequent chapters is Richard C. Edwards, Michael Reich, and Thomas E. Weisskopf, eds., *The Capitalist System** (Englewood Cliffs, N.J.: Prentice-Hall, 1972). For a closely-reasoned historical analysis of capitalism by a leading Marxist, see Maurice Dobb, *Studies in the Development of Capitalism* * (London: Routledge, 1946). Christopher Hill's excellent study of the early modern period of England's development was cited in Chapter 1; the succeeding period is excellently treated in E. J. Hobsbawm, *Industry and Empire* (New York: Pantheon, 1968).

Passages from the *Communist Manifesto* have been quoted several times. The *Manifesto* is available in many forms; a valuable selection of Marxian writings which includes the *Manifesto* is *Karl Marx and Friedrich Engels, Selected Works** (Moscow: Progress Publishers, 1968), also available in other editions. C. Wright Mills was much influenced by as well as honestly critical of Marxism. His views are put forth in *The Marxists** (New York: Dell, 1962). Shlomo Avineri, *The Social and*

*Political Thought of Karl Marx** (Cambridge: Cambridge University Press, 1971) is an excellent and thorough analysis, readable, critical, and sympathetic in treatment.

The difficulties and violence associated with economic development have been studied carefully by Barrington Moore, Jr., *Social Origins of Dictatorship and Democracy** (Boston: Beacon Press, 1966). Chapters on the English Civil War of the seventeenth century, the French Revolution, and the American Civil War are especially useful. The processes by which land and labor became commodities in England in the eighteenth and nineteenth centuries are studied exhaustively—and, for the reader, sometimes exhaustingly—by Karl Polanyi, *The Great Transformation** (New York: Holt, Rinehart ahd Winston, 1944). The effort to work through Polanyi's strangled prose is repaid. The nature of the medieval world and the manner in which commercialism grew in England are treated brilliantly and in human terms by Eileen Power in her *Medieval People** (New York: Anchor Books, 1956); her *Wool Trade in English Medieval History* (New York: Oxford University Press, 1941) is a superb analysis of the relationships between political and economic developments.

R. H. Tawney is one of the deservedly most influential historians of the rise of capitalism. In addition to works of his previously cited, his subtle and profound analysis of the manner in which religious thought changed in meaning, if not always in words, from the sixteenth to the eighteenth centuries is well worth study. It is found in his 175-page introduction to Thomas Wilson, *A Discourse Upon Usury* (London: Bell, 1925), itself the work of a sixteenth-century divine. E. P. Thompson, *The Making of the English Working Class** (New York: Vintage, 1966) has written that history "from the bottom up," and has very much influenced a new generation of historians. It is an excellent history, as well as an excellent model of historical writing.

Two comprehensive views of capitalist development, both affected by Marx and both differing in important ways from Marx, are Thorstein Veblen, *The Theory of the Leisure Class** (New York: Macmillan, 1899), and Joseph A. Schumpeter, *Capitalism, Socialism, and Democracy** (New York: Harper & Row, 1942).

A systematic and comprehensive introduction to Marxian social analysis, consisting entirely of thoughtfully selected quotations from Marx, Engels, and Lenin, is Howard Selsam, David Goldman, and Harry Martel, eds., *Dynamics of Social Change** (New York: International Publishers, 1970).

The succeeding chapters will be much concerned with aspects of the economic history of the United States. Frequent reference will be had to one or another of the books in a series published over the years by Holt, Rinehart and Winston (New York), entitled *The Economic His-*

tory of the United States. The separate volumes are generally valuable in themselves and each has a most useful bibliography. It seems appropriate to list all these books here for handy reference. Curtis P. Nettels, *The Emergence of a National Economy, 1775–1815;* Paul W. Gates, *The Farmer's Age: Agriculture, 1815–1860;* George R. Taylor, *The Transportation Revolution, 1815–1860;* Fred Shannon, *The Farmer's Last Frontier: Agriculture, 1860–1897;* Edward C. Kirkland, *Industry Comes of Age, 1860–1897;* Harold U. Faulkner, *The Decline of Laissez-Faire, 1897–1917;* George Soule, *Prosperity Decade: From War to Depression, 1917–1929;* Broadus Mitchell, *Depression Decade: From New Era Through New Deal, 1929–1941;* Donald L. Kemmerer, *The U.S. Economy, 1940–1960.*

A useful survey and critique of radical writings on U.S. history may be found in the journal *Radical America,* "Special Issue on Radical Historiography," Vol. 4, No. 8–9 (November, 1970.)

3

Business as

a System of Power

They pass through the great iron gates—
Men with eyes gravely discerning,
Skilled to appraise the tonnage of cranes
Or split an inch into thousandths—
Men tempered by fire as the ore is
And planned to resistance
Like steel that has cooled in the trough;
Silent of purpose, inflexible, set to fulfillment—
To conquer, withstand, overthrow. . . .
Men mannered to large undertakings,
Knowing force as a brother
And power as something to play with,
Seeing blood as a slip of the iron,
To be wiped from the tools
*Lest they rust.**

"The business of America," President Coolidge once remarked, "is business." More pointed, while also reflecting the subsequent progress of *big* business, was the famous statement thirty years later of Charles Wilson (of General Motors, and Secretary of Defense under Eisenhower); "What's good for General Motors is good for America." These pithy assertations, and others of the genre—"The public? The public be damned!"—have been much maligned by those with a loftier vision for America. But as matters now stand—that is, in the absence of fundamental institutional change—it is unquestionably true that when business is bad, Americans are badly off; when GM and the other giant corpora-

* Lola Ridge, *The Legion of Iron.* From *The Ghetto and Other Poems,* published by B. W. Huebsch. Reprinted by permission of David Lawson.

tions are in trouble, so is not only the entire economy, but the entire society.

In short, America is a business society, for better or for worse. It is, indeed, *the* business society, even in comparison with other capitalist societies. Unlike the others, we started that way; we have become even more so with the passage of time. If, in our own day, deep questioning of the performance of American society has become pervasive, is it not because business calculations rather than human needs and possibilities so much dominate the entirety of our lives—not only in industry, but in our foreign policies, our domestic politics, our schools, our health care systems, our environment, and even our culture?

That ours is so fully a business-like society and the most fully-developed of capitalist societies allows two major inferences about the historical development of the United States. First, *all* social activities— the production of all goods and all services from carrots to computers and from mechanics to ministers—have flourished or languished dependent upon the degree to which they have satisfied the finally financial criterion of *marketability*. Indeed, most Americans are unaware that other, essentially qualitative, criteria exist to be taken seriously. From the necessary evaluation of a business firm in terms of its income statement and balance sheet, American society has moved insensibly to evaluating virtually all activities in similarly quantitative and pecuniary terms: What does it cost? How much does he make? Will it sell? Is it profitable? So it is with our ways of speech, with paintings and movie stars, with professors and journalists, even with religious personages. The society has left or created no comfortable resting-place for means of evaluation, other than "the bottom line."

Second, if business criteria have made their way into all walks of life, the prime reason is that capitalist development has been so successful in its own terms in the United States. No other country has had so long and so impressive a history of expansion, production, and productivity, with over time our levels of per capita real incomes. Capitalism stresses material achievement as its promise. American capitalism has fulfilled that promise. If, in the process, large sections of the population have been shunted aside, exploited, and oppressed, left outside the charmed circle of material well-being drawn by the American Dream, then that is by no means unique to the United States where, in fact or in illusion, the majority has seen itself as blessed to reside in the most blessed of all nations.

To say that American capitalist development has been successful for so long is to point to two other major aspects of our development: the persistent and remarkable profitability, and the easy and comprehensive access to power, prestige, and authority by American businessmen and those who live by their criteria. These two processes have sustained and reinforced each other, and they bear closer examination, which must continue to focus most heavily on the questions of *expansion* and *exploitation*, the alpha and omega of capitalist development.

Onward and Upward with King Cotton

Expansion may be thought of as having two directions: upward, the growth of the economy in its productive capacity and its structure of production, and outward, the expansion of the land surface under the control or influence of the national economy.

The temporal and social advantages for capitalism in the United States were noted at the close of Chapter 2; those advantages were facilitated mostly by our *geographic* realities and possibilities. The meaning of the North American colonies to the British was slight by comparison with what could be made of the continent stretching westward from the lands the British had settled on the Eastern Seaboard. Given the limited maritime and military technology of the time, the new United States had virtually a free hand in moving into the wide open and very rich spaces to the west of the original thirteen colonies, and much more was made of the original land space because of that expansion into the West.

Consider briefly what access to the West stimulated and allowed and, more subtly, what it required (most especially, canals and railroads). For the South, the western lands were both a life-saver and a boon—a life-saver because the South's techniques of cultivating tobacco and cotton had depleted the soils; a boon because the new and even richer lands fitted most profitably into rapidly expanding markets in the Old World (most importantly, cotton for England's burgeoning textile mills). The South's movement westward into Alabama, Mississippi, and Louisiana meant, of course, the wholesale destruction of Native Americans and of their remarkable and healthy societies, as well as a vast increase in the numbers of black slaves imported and bred for plantation cultivation.[1]

But the South's geographic and economic expansion was an essential part of the developing capitalist world-economy and, of course, profitable—to the plantation owners, to the merchants and shippers and fi-

[1] See Paul Jacobs, Saul Landau, and Eve Pell, *To Serve the Devil* * (New York: Vintage, 1971), in two volumes. Vol 1, *Natives and Slaves,* * traces the early history of our treatment of Native Americans, African slaves, and Chicanos; Vol. 2, *Colonials and Sojourners,* * examines the lesser-known histories of Hawaiians, Chinese, Japanese, and Puerto Ricans in the American context. Besides a brief narrative history, the authors have collected valuable documents wherein these peoples speak for themselves; and there is a useful bibliography. An excellent anthology concerning Afro-Americans is Eric Foner, ed., *America's Black Past* * (New York: Harper & Row, 1970).

nanciers tied into plantation agriculture. Still more, the entire American economy depended very much upon the dynamism, the foreign exchange, and the internal trade generated by King Cotton in the first half of the nineteenth century. The importance of the South's economy in the United States was well-reflected in its power in the federal government. By any measure of population, land, or capital, the South's power was disproportionate, whether referring to the legislative, judicial, or executive branch of government. The South's power, not the moral issue of slavery, was the central issue leading to the Civil War; when the South lost, it was because the economic power of northern industry, agriculture, and finance had surpassed it. If we may judge the intentions of warriors by what they do after victory, the organization and functioning of the American federal government during and after the Civil War tells us that northern intentions were to adapt federal power to the needs of industrial, not planter, capitalism.

The North's economic strength rested on the commercial, industrial, and financial activities that had their small beginnings in colonial New England, New York, Pennsylvania, and New Jersey. The beginnings were small because of the less bountiful agricultural possibilities in the North as compared with the South. However, forced to diversify and to improvise, by the 1830's the small beginnings had become a torrent of economic life, with still greater dynamism lying squarely ahead.

Much of the North's early development had depended on the South, for the merchants of the North were heavily involved in the slave trade and in the associated rum and general mercantile trade in a series of "triangular" patterns linking North America with the Caribbean, Africa, and Europe. Veblen had a characteristically insightful and sardonic view of these northern activities:

> The slave trade never was a "nice" occupation or an altogether unexceptionable investment—"balanced on the edge of the permissible." But even though it may have been distasteful to one and another of its New-England men of affairs, and though there always was a suspicion of moral obliquity attached to the slave-trade, yet it had the fortune to be drawn into the service of the greater good. In conjunction with its running-mate, the rum-trade, it laid the foundations of some very reputable fortunes at the focus of commercial enterprise that presently became the center of American culture, and so gave rise to some of the country's Best People. At least so they say.
>
> Perhaps also it was, in some part, in this early pursuit of gain in this moral penumbra that American business enterprise learned how not to let its right hand know what its left hand is doing; and there is always something to be done that is best done with the left hand.[2]

[2] Thorstein Veblen, *Absentee Ownership and Business Enterprise* ° (New York: Huebsch, 1923; Viking, 1954), p. 171.

The North's process of economic development soon became the most dynamic industrialization process in the world up to that time; it was weaning itself from its heavy southern diet even at that time it was gaining the most from it. Of the several factors that loom large in northern economic development, one whole complex related to westward expansion. It was as vital as it was timely.[3]

The Dream Unfolds: Westward the Course of Empire

It is impossible to speculate beyond a certain point on what the United States would have been like had its geographic scope been confined to that of the original colonies. But we need not speculate. For the states north of the Mason-Dixon line, the trans-Appalachian West was not merely a beckoning frontier; it was a seemingly endless expanse of land teeming with excellent soils, waterways, minerals (including gold and silver), and forests. To exploit those lands, the United States had to import rising millions of people,[4] dig canals and build the largest rail network in the world—30,000 miles by 1860, 53,000 by 1870, twice that by 1882, and over 210,000 miles by 1904—import capital, and develop a technology that could master the great spaces and complex needs of such a land. But these needs had another side to them: they offered boundless possibilities to a society dominated and led by people with their eyes on financial gain.

The millions of immigrants contributed not just labor power, but imagination and enterprise and energy. The transportation network required new private and public financial institutions, and it constituted an enormous demand for a whole range of products—most importantly, metals and machinery and coal, the heart of nineteenth-century industrial development. A new technology was required to dig canals, to tame the

[3] The pre–Civil War history is rich in details that we are skirting over or ignoring. See the works of Nettels, Gates, and Taylor suggested at the close of Chapter 2; for the post–Civil War period, Shannon and Kirkland provide support for most of our generalizations. Harold Vatter, *The Drive to Industrial Maturity* * (Westport, Conn.: Greenwood Press, 1975) is an original analysis of the 1860–1914 era.

[4] The important surge that began in the 1840's was much facilitated by the revival of indentured labor during the Civil War, and became a headlong rush from 1861 on. Between 1861 and 1920, over twenty-eight million people came to the United States as immigrants. Movement to the West was principally by the "native-born" Americans, but their rush to take up western lands was reinforced and made possible by the filling up of eastern cities by the newcomers. Toward the close of the century immigration was induced largely to work the mines and the mills spreading over the whole country, and the immigrants were now coming from Eastern and Southeastern Europe, rather than the United Kingdom and Western Europe—with profound social and political results.

plains and the mountains with rails and powerful locomotives, and to exploit the surface and subsurface resources of America's varied lands. All this, taken together with a persisting labor shortage, meant that the United States became the first of all industrial nations to develop a comprehensive machine technology for all aspects of production—agricultural, mineral, manufacturing, and transportation.

The resulting high labor productivity, combined with the widespread ownership of land (relative to Europe) yielded a level and a distribution of income that provided the first *domestic* mass market for modern production. By the end of the nineteenth century, the structure of American production in both consumer and capital goods was broader and deeper than anywhere else in the world; and the process had just begun.

With unprecedented swiftness, the United States filled in its continental boundaries, and in doing so created an economy that dazzled the world. But the unprecedented swiftness was matched by unprecedented rapacity—a heedless exploitation of natural resources, and a pattern of human exploitation whose viciousness was obscured, on the one hand, by the widespread expectation that *everyone* would someday rise in the socioeconomic structure and, on the other, by the equally widespread indifference to the conditions of those (especially nonwhites) who in fact had no such prospects.[5]

From all this, a process of economic expansion whose buoyancy and profitability, despite intermittent business panics and crises, transformed the northeastern quadrant of the United States into a businessman's Eldorado. Meanwhile, cities grew like mushrooms over the face of the nation—New York, Philadelphia, and Boston, of course; but also Chicago, Cleveland, Cincinnati, St. Louis, New Orleans, Omaha, and San Francisco. The growth of the cities, like the growth of the economy, was a response to business needs and possibilities; as for anything more complicated, that could wait—or be forgotten.

Survival and success in the expansionist process required passing the test of the market, the test of a fully commercialized society. Those who

[5] The position and history of workers in its major aspects will be dealt with in Chapter 5. Meanwhile, serious students of American history will find it illuminating to read any one of several novels that explore the lives of ordinary people. See, for example, Upton Sinclair, *The Jungle* (slaughterhouse workers, turn of the century Chicago), O. E. Rolvaag, *Giants in the Earth* (Dakota farm life, nineteenth century), T. S. Stribling, *The Store* (southern tenants, post–Civil War), A. Cahan, *The Rise of David Levinsky* (Jewish immigrants, late nineteenth century), James Farrell, *Studs Lonigan* (slum life, Chicago, early twentieth century), and Agnes Smedley, *Daughter of Earth* (autobiographical novel, late nineteenth-early twentieth century). The list could be very long, and very rewarding. Films such as "The Emigrants" (Swedish)—which portray the harsh conditions pushing people toward the United States, and the harsh conditions endured in the process (around 1850)—are also good ways to improve one's sense of the past.

survived grew in strength, and they garnered the society's power, prestige, and authority. *Power* means the ability to decide, to influence, to control; *prestige*, both a source and a consequence of power, refers to the deference received by those who possess power in society; *authority* resides in those who have the weight of law, of custom, and of society's deepest values vested in them.

In the U.S., already by the close of the nineteenth century the strength of the business impulse had swept aside all noncommercial contenders for power, prestige, or authority—except those political figures who knew where the power lay. In practice, this meant a multitude of things; most especially it meant that what business needed, business got. When complications arose, it was almost always when one business group was in contention with another business group—small versus big business, farmers versus railroads, for instance. We now turn to the evolution of American business as "a system of power." [6]

Capitalism, American-style

Adam Smith's hopes for a benign capitalist order rested squarely on his prescription for a fully competitive economy. In such an economy, all firms would be small; that is, the percentage of a given industry's output produced by one firm (or by a few firms) would be insignificant as a percentage of the whole industry output. Without control over supply, each business would have to function in response to the free market; *with* control over supply, the powerful firm could control the market. Smith's policies were designed to eliminate the control provided by State-granted privileges and monopolies. He did not examine the future dynamics of the kind of private economy he sought. Marx and Veblen did.

The *general* development of capitalism was first analyzed and ex-

---

[6] This perspective is put forth most explicitly by Robert A. Brady. His *Business as a System of Power* (New York: Columbia University Press, 1943) analyzes the patterns of power and the directions of the major capitalist powers—Great Britain, France, Germany, Italy, Japan, and the United States. Though dated in detail, the basic analysis remains very valuable (and largely ignored by almost all economists). Brady was much influenced by Marx and Veblen, and he affected the development of this book's viewpoint because of my studies with him at the University of California (Berkeley). The approach to business power in the rest of this chapter will emphasize attempts to control the market directly. The use of power by business to affect the process of economic growth will be taken up in Chapter 4; the relationship of business power to the distribution of income and wealth and the organization of labor will be examined in Chapter 5; Chapter 6 will examine the functioning of business power in the cities and as affecting the environment; Chapter 7, business power in the world; and Chapter 8, The State, will seek to bring all this together.

plained by Marx, who sought to understand "the economic laws of motion of capitalist society." Marx barely touched upon the American experience. His empirical focus was Great Britain in the mid-nineteenth century. Britain was the leading industrial capitalist society of the time, and Marx was in Great Britain. As a contributing journalist to the *New York Tribune* in the 1850's and 1860's, Marx had occasion to observe and comment upon American developments; he never did more than that.[7]

It was left to Veblen to initiate the first systematic critique of American capitalism. Born in the U.S. almost a half-century after Marx's birth, Veblen was well-situated to study the more advanced and specifically American experience.[8] Veblen did not have to imagine or speculate on the course of capitalist development in America since the time of Marx, let alone that of Smith. He lived and wrote when the full sweep of American business and industrial practices was in evidence. His starting-point was to distinguish between "business" and "industry":

> The industrial arts are a matter of tangible performance directed to work that is designed to be of material use to man. . . . [The] arts of business are arts of bargaining, effrontery, salesmanship, make-believe, and are directed to the gain of the business man at the cost of the community, at large and in detail. Neither tangible performance nor the common good is a business proposition. Any material use which his traffic may serve is quite beside the business man's purpose, except indirectly, in so far as it may serve to influence his clientele to his advantage.[9]

In brief, business is a matter of making money; industry, of making goods.

Veblen was by no means unique in noting the aggressiveness and the "effrontery" of businessmen. But the way in which he combined this widespread view with a larger analysis doomed him to the role of a lonely and scorned prophet. In his *Theory of Business Enterprise* (1904) he foresaw the two leading developments of American capitalism as cen-

---

[7] And much of what he did say was without benefit of serious research, understandably. This is especially true regarding his observations on the developing Civil War, the most momentous process at the time in the United States. For astute criticisms of Marx by a Marxist in this respect, see Eugene Genovese, *In Red and Black* ° (New York: Vintage, 1972), especially Chapter 15.

[8] Lewis Corey, *The Decline of American Capitalism* (New York: Covici-Friede, 1934) is the first systematic Marxian attempt. Brady's book, published in 1943, combines Marx and Veblen. Paul Baran and Paul Sweezy, *Monopoly Capital* ° (New York: Monthly Review Press, 1966) brings together Marxian, Veblenian, and Keynesian theory with contemporary data in a comprehensive analysis of recent American capitalism. The authors describe their work as only "a brief sketch," but it is much more than that, in that it attempts to provide an up-dated Marxian *theoretical* framework.

[9] *Absentee Ownership*, p. 107.

tering on the drive for monopoly and the steady build-up of the forces of economic depression; in *Absentee Ownership* (1923) he was able to look around him and see his expectations confirmed. Another major probability as he saw it was an "increased unproductive consumption of goods," by which he meant the need to manipulate and persuade the population to buy unnecessary and trivial commodities, and the growth of arms production, accompanied by what he called "a strenuous national policy."

Precisely because the kind of competitive economy Smith desired would entail effective price competition, Veblen argued, businessmen would energetically move to eliminate the competitive structure that allowed and required it. Their view of price competition was effectively suggested when they described it as "cutthroat competition." Businesses, monopolistic or otherwise, continue to "compete." But the forms taken by modern business rivalry are not such as to reduce costs, prices, and profits to some optimal level, as predicated in the competitive model; quite the contrary. Price competition has been replaced by two major forms of business rivalry: 1) "nonprice competition," which takes the form of price-*increasing* advertising, packaging, and other forms of sales promotion; and 2) efforts to gain special privileges at all levels of government—to stabilize prices, to gain privileged contracts, to influence taxing and spending, labor and foreign policies, and the like. To recall an earlier observation, the *State* mercantilism that Smith fought against has been revived and joined by a *private* mercantilism. We can do no better than to refer to Veblen again:

> This decay of the old-fashioned competitive system has consisted in a substitution of competitive selling in the place of that competitive production of goods that is always presumed to be the chief and most serviceable feature of the competitive system. That is to say, it has been a substitution of salesmanship in the place of workmanship; as would be due to happen so soon as business came to take precedence of industry, salesmanship being a matter of business, not of industry; and business being a matter of salesmanship, not of workmanship. . . . Competition as it runs under the rule of this decayed competitive system is chiefly the competition between the business concerns that control production, on the one side, and the consuming public on the other side; the chief expedients in this business-like competition being salesmanship and sabotage. Salesmanship in this connection means little else than prevarication, and sabotage means a business-like curtailment of output.[10]

10 *Absentee Ownership*, p. 78. This was written in 1923; Veblen makes it clear elsewhere that the process of "decay" began decades earlier. For details, see Faulkner, *Decline of Laissez-Faire*, cited earlier, and Arthur Robert Burns, *The Decline of Competition* (New York: McGraw-Hill, 1936).

The hoped-for effects of a competitive economy need not depend upon the existence of textbook forms of "perfect" or "pure" competition. But they do depend upon the existence of pervasive and effective competition which, as data below will show, has little to do with the American reality. A competitive economy is one in which firms respond to the market, rather than setting the terms upon which the market responds to them. In such an economy there might be monopolies, but they would be under constant scrutiny and regulation, or they would be temporary. In the former case, which economists call "natural monopolies," the monopoly is justified by the technology of the industry; this is typical in utilities, where it is economically foolish to have duplicative large-scale water or gas-works, for example. The aim of the regulatory agency is to combine the advantages of large-scale production with the pricing results of a competitive industry where prices are set so as to attract the necessary amount of capital into the industry, but without the profits of monopoly. (In practice, those who sit on regulatory boards are predominantly from or in sympathy with those industries being "regulated.") Temporary monopolies, on the other hand, are presumed to disappear as soon as the new technology or unusual market circumstances giving rise to them are countered by long-run competitive forces.

What would *not* be, in an effectively competitive economy, is what exists in all the major capitalist countries today: patterns of concentrated power in all of modern industry and increasingly in trade, construction, finance, and in hitherto competitive sectors. To which must be added a State apparatus that, far from restraining private economic power, responds to it, represents it, and paves the way for it. Americans have become familiar with part of the pattern in recent years as they have become conscious of the so-called "military-industrial complex." The relationships exemplified in that pattern are not new; they are merely the latest development in the always close ties between business and government in the United States. These ties will be explored historically and in detail in Chapter 8.

Returning now to the question of business competition in the American economy, and assuming that the textbook model is neither necessary nor possible, did anything even approximating an effectively competitive economy ever exist in the United States? And if it did, how, why, and by what was it corrupted?

The Invisible Fist

Of the many points to be noted, perhaps the first is that the capitalist system posits the businessman as its dynamic center. He, the "entrepreneur," is expected to respond to stimuli and to overcome obstacles so as to produce what society needs and wants. But to do this, he must possess one form of power: ownership of productive assets. To the degree that he succeeds, he is likely to gain more economic power, and other forms of power as well.

In practice, the dice are loaded in favor of those who own and control society's productive assets; and they are a tiny percentage of the population. By design and by default, those who are *not* property owners are weak in influence and power. For the competitive system to work well economically and socially in Adam Smith's terms, in short, those who are powerful must be *frustrated* in what they seek—that is, profits and power. The social rationale for a competitive capitalist economy is thus a curious one: market competition will prevent those who have power in the society from realizing their aims. In reality, competition is eliminated and the benign principles are abandoned, except for their half-lives in textbooks and rhetoric.

The point may be made in another way. Social and economic policies are decided upon and implemented by those with power. The laissez-faire society is one in which all sources of public policy-making over the economy are eliminated on principle. What is left is economic power alone, private economic power, and that resides solely in the hands of those who own and control the means of production. Not, certainly, in the hands of the propertyless wage-earner (who in Smith's time didn't even have the vote); not, of course, in the hands of Church or State, by design. So in a society devoid of social controls other than the market, the capitalist will do what he can to mitigate the one threat to his strength and profitability: he will seek to eliminate competition. There is nothing to stop him, and much—including the political power he picks up along the way—to help him. In nineteenth and twentieth century America, the developing large-scale technology provided such assistance, for the small-scale structure implied by and required for a competitive economy is quite generally incompatible with modern technology, both on business and economic grounds. If a capitalist economy is made socially "safe" only by competition, what then remains of the social rationale for capitalism in the modern world?

Until the years just after the Civil War, the American economy may be said to have been effectively competitive. During that early period, businessmen's desires were no less profit-oriented than after the 1870's; what was different was technology and the extraordinary onrush of events associated with westward expansion. In the last quarter of the century, the westward movement began to stabilize while large-scale technology spread throughout the production process.

In the period before the Civil War (roughly speaking), there were, of course, large as well as small firms. The largest firms tended to be found in transportation, communications, finance, and trade; the occasional large *manufacturing* firm (in textile machinery, for example) had no substantial influence on the economy as a whole, which was changing its structure and growing so rapidly. Once more, however, the impact of the large-scale technology after the Civil War deserves emphasis.

The seller's impulse toward monopolization is a constant in history. (Thales, the ancient Greek philosopher, is known for his attempts to corner the market in olive oil.) That impulse becomes necessary and, when successful, much more profitable when it joins with the economics of modern—that is, large-scale—industry. The productive efficiency associated with modern industry is owed to the scale of production. This in turn entails not only widespread specialization in production, but also much in the way of expensive and long-lasting plant and equipment. The normal ups and downs of capitalist economic expansion and the intermittent glutting of markets combine with large-scale plants to yield destructive ("cutthroat") competition—price competition which entails selling below cost in bad times as a way to minimize losses. When that happens, or in order to prevent it from happening, the number of firms in a given industry shrinks, leaving the giants to endure and to prosper. For if eliminating competitors *diminishes* the prospects of price competition, it also *increases* the possibilities of enhancing profits in both bad and good times through controlling the market. ("Controlling the market" in this respect means controlling—that is, restricting—supply, something that cannot be accomplished in a competitive market.) Thus the key characteristic of modern business behavior becomes that of dominant firms restricting supply in order to dictate and sell at a desirable price, a process that distorts both the supply and demand sides of the market, and that gives the large firms access to broad power over society as well—in a society that systematically and in principle foregoes locating that power in *non*economic institutions.

From Mergers to Monopoly: The Giants Feed

Until about 1860, the corporate form of business was largely confined to transportation and finance. With few exceptions, the emergence of corporations in manufacturing awaited the new, large-scale technology that emerged and spread after the Civil War.

From 1873 until the mid-1890's the entire industrial capitalist world underwent what was then called "The Great Depression." Unlike the Great Depression of the 1930's, the most prominent feature of the earlier period was pressure on profits, rather than massive unemployment. That pressure was due to the steady and dramatic lowering of prices through the period, which was in turn the result of great increases in efficiency, combined with the inability to cut off domestic or foreign competition in the context of relatively free trade and relatively competitive market structures.

Consequently, that same period saw the first general attempts to control price competition through one form of business reorganization or another. "Gentlemen's agreements" not to cut prices, profit pools, and trusts (all of which maintained the separate identity of the member corporations) were all tried; but the form which won out was the merger. The process in which mergers occurred is called the *combination movement*. By the late 1890's, mergers or combinations (in which many firms were combined under one ownership and identity) became the rule; the years between 1897 and 1905 witnessed their first spectacular rush. During these years, over 5300 industrial firms came under the control, finally, of 318 corporations, the most advanced and powerful firms in the economy.

The turn-of-the-century wave of mergers was seen as spectacular, until subsequent waves surpassed it. As Figure 1 shows, a higher peak was reached in the 1920's; then, after what has been called a "ripple" in the 1940's, the largest wave of all began, in the 1960's. Economists have speculated as to what conditions are associated with increasing or decreasing merger activity. The evidence of the past seventy years or so suggests that the only period in which the *rate* of merger activity declines is that of depression; the impulse toward bigness and power is otherwise persistent.

The first waves of mergers were an outcome of the combination of expanding technology and businesses' aims of avoiding competition and of making profits. Technology then led to centralization of production facilities in a given location (for example, steel in Pittsburgh). Since World War II, however, technological development has led to *decentral*-ization of productive facilities geographically; at the same time the *control* over those facilities has become ever more centralized, spreading not simply over one industry but many different industries. Let us examine the process more closely.

Initially, mergers took place in each industry as it began to employ modern, large-scale technology. Sometimes the process was more like warfare than business in the late nineteenth century.[11] Mergers spread from transportation to manufacturing, to utilities and finance, to mining and construction and trade; by now mergers are the dynamic mode in all significant business, including entertainment, hotels and even agriculture, long considered the final preserve of effective competition.[12]

[11] Tactics ranging from outright gun battles (in the fight to control the Erie Railroad, for example) to the most relentless financial "terrorism" (in Rockefeller's successful steps toward monopoly in oil) are related and detailed in Matthew Josephson, *The Robber Barons* ° (New York: Harcourt Brace Jovanovich, 1934), for the period 1861–1901.

[12] Still most important in controlling the forces of the market in agriculture, however, is governmental policy, which was brought into being under the pressure of farmers beginning over half a century ago. More will be said of these matters in Chapter 6.

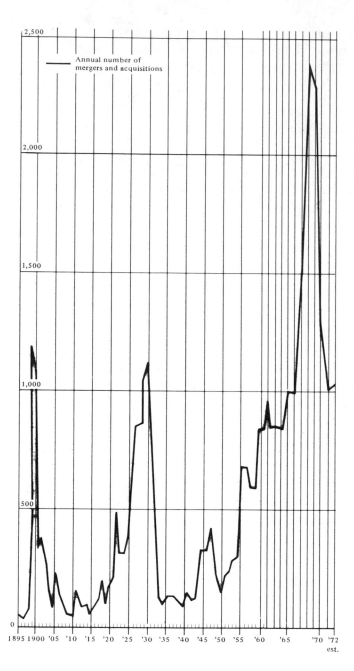

FIGURE 1 Acquisitions of Manufacturing and Mining Companies 1895–1972

SOURCE: Tom Cardamore Associates for *Fortune* Magazine.

The patterns of the merger movements are striking; most striking of all is the tidal wave that began during World War II and reached its historic peak in 1968–1969. Figures 1 and 2 reveal not only the recent upsurge in mergers but the domination of those mergers by the largest 200 corporations and the increasing size of the transactions. As *Fortune* points out, "from 1964 through 1966, there were 293 mergers in which the acquired companies had assets of more than $10 million; in the final three years of the decade there were 530. The average size of the transactions, $38 million in the first period, rose to $64 million during the second. In the peak year of 1968 the nation's top 200 industrial firms acquired a total of ninety-four large companies, with aggregate assets of more than $8 billion." [13]

Throughout all this merger activity there have been several subprocesses. At first, mergers were in one industry, where all the merging firms produced much the same product. These are called *horizontal* mergers, in which competitors in a given industry come under the ownership and control of one company (for example, one steel company buying out another). While those mergers continued, another form, *vertical* mergers, began to appear, especially in the 1920's, in which a company buys out its suppliers and/or its customers (for example, Ford gaining its own steel facilities; U.S. Steel buying out coal mines and a bridge-building company).

Horizontal mergers lead to concentration of power in a given industry, and to *oligopoly:* a few dominant sellers in an industry. Vertical mergers strengthen the hand of already large firms, while also creating higher barriers to entry by new firms. In the late twenties and early thirties another form of merger began to attract attention, as it does even more so today: the *conglomerate,* where the firms acquired by a corporation are only distantly related, if at all, to the industry of the acquiring firm. In the vast merger movement since 1950 all these forms—vertical, horizontal, and conglomerate—have been operating, with the conglomerate form taking the prizes for drama. The drama became especially vivid in the 1960's, with "the new conglomerates."

The expansion of the "new conglomerates" was dominated by eight companies: ITT, Gulf & Western, Ling-Temco-Vought, Tenneco, White Consolidated, Teledyne, Occidental Petroleum, and Litton Industries. "Each of these companies made acquisitions during the 1960's totaling more than a half-billion dollars; for six the asset value was over a billion

---

[13] *Fortune,* April, 1973, from which the charts are also derived. A useful and comprehensive analysis of mergers is Samuel Richardson Reid, *Mergers, Managers, and the Economy* ° (New York: McGraw-Hill, 1968).

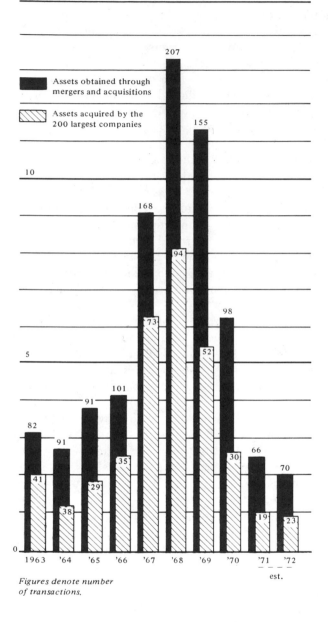

15 *Billions of dollars*

■ Assets obtained through mergers and acquisitions

▨ Assets acquired by the 200 largest companies

10

207

155

168

94

73

98

52

5

101

91

91

82

35

41

30

66

29

70

38

19

23

0

1963 '64 '65 '66 '67 '68 '69 '70 '71 '72

est.

Figures denote number of transactions.

FIGURE 2 Big Acquisitions 1963–1972

SOURCE: Tom Cardamore Associates for *Fortune* Magazine.

dollars." [14] Of the various important aspects of this movement, one worth noting is that it has sped up the process of bringing traditionally "small business" industries—for instance, food processing, nonelectrical machinery, and textiles—under the control of giant corporations.

The early merger movements, whether horizontal or vertical in origin, led to the *concentration* of economic power within the affected industries. When we add the conglomerate mergers to the earlier movement we come to an additional characteristic: *centralization*. Furthermore, combined with the concentration and centralization of *private* economic power is the associated concentration and centralization of *public* power. The concentration and centralization of State power shows itself in the enormously enhanced powers of the federal government today as compared with, say, 1900; it is revealed even more pointedly in the extraordinary powers increasingly arrogated by the presidency—and, conversely, the declining powers of Congress and the separate states.[15] The government at all levels represents the interests of many groups in American society, of course—doctors, organized labor, the aged, the poor—but it represents most and best the interests of the most powerful. The most powerful are unquestionably the most powerful business corporations. Let us examine some representative data suggesting their position in the American economy.

Facts are Stubborn Things

There is no mystery as to the size or the identity of America's giant corporations. *Fortune* annually publishes its "Fortune 500" and "Second 500," showing assets, sales, employees, income, and profits of the largest industrial corporations; their data in turn are derived from a multitude of governmental and private sources, all open to the public eye. Economists

[14] John M. Blair, *Economic Concentration: Structure, Behavior and Public Policy* (New York: Harcourt Brace Jovanovich, 1972), p. 285. This is probably the most comprehensive study of the whole question. The author has spent his life working on the problems of big business in the Federal Trade Commission. His data on conglomerates are drawn from Federal Trade Commission, *Economic Report on Corporate Mergers* * (Washington, D.C., 1969), the best factual study of the conglomerate movement.

[15] This development will be analyzed more fully in Chapter 8. In recent years, beginning in the Johnson Administration and accelerating under Nixon, the Supreme Court has become subject to crasser political considerations than earlier, as well, which has had the effect of placing more of the power of the judiciary in the White House. A careful and outraged analysis of the process may be found in Louis M. Kohlmeier, Jr., *God Save This Honorable Court* (New York: Scribner's, 1972), whose conclusion it is that "President Nixon's place in history is secure: Nixon politicized the Supreme Court more dramatically than any President in history" (p. 281).

are fully aware of these data, but they have yet to alter conventional economic *theory* to fit the data—quite possibly because to do so in any systematic manner would require abandoning the entire structure of the theory. One respected conventional economist, understanding this, has said (in the convoluted language used by economists when they address each other): "To argue that monopolistic deviations can be ignored because of their minor importance is to exhibit ideological bias. To argue that piecemeal antitrust leads to improvement is false. The only bias-free option is the option that leads to a centrally controlled economy. But how many believers in fact are prepared to accept this conclusion?" [16]

The information that follows concerns the concentration and centralization of control over productive assets, sales, profits, employment, and the like. The emphasis will first be on *industrial* (manufacturing and mining) *corporations,* of which there are about 215,000, and which do over 90 percent of all industrial business—the heartland of the economy. Unless otherwise specified, the data are for 1975:

1. The *sales* of the largest 500 industrials were $865 billion; their *profits* were $37.8 billion (after taxes); and they *employed* 14.4 million, amounting to about two-thirds of industrial sales, and about three-quarters of total industrial profits and employment.

2. The *sales* of the second largest 500 industrials were $83 billion; their *profits* after taxes $3.3 billion; and their *employment* 1.9 million; each figure was 10 percent or less of the top 500's. The top and second 500 together left very little indeed for the remaining 99 percent of industrial business. The *sales* of the largest 1000 industrial corporations totaled $948 billion; *gross national product* in 1975 (the total money value of all goods and services at their final stage) was less than twice that amount ($1,573 billion).

3. The top *ten* of the 500 (EXXON, GM, Texaco, Ford, Mobil Oil, Standard Oil of California, IBM, Gulf Oil, GE, and Chrysler) had *sales* of $214 billion in 1975, almost one-quarter of the sales of the top 500, more than two times the total sales of the second 500; the top 50 had over half the sales of the 500. Note that five of the top ten are oil companies, three are autos.

[16] Andreas G. Papandreou, *Paternalistic Capitalism* (Minneapolis: University of Minnesota Press, 1972), p. 26. Another "bias-free option" leads to a decentralized socialist society, in the minds of many. The author was Chairman of the Department of Economics at the University of California (Berkeley), until he became immersed in Greek politics as an important figure, and was expected to lead the government. The military junta that until recently ruled Greece jailed Papandreou when it seized power; he was freed and exiled after much pressure from outside. Papandreou saw the dictatorial government as the exact equivalent of the Thieu regime in South Vietnam, up to and including its installation and support by the United States. See pp. 121–34.

4. The *assets* of the top 500 industrials were $668 billion, of the second 500, $61 billion; the top ten had assets of $158 billion.

5. The industrial corporation with the greatest *assets* is EXXON: $33 *billion*. The company with the smallest assets of the top 500 in 1975 was Idle Wild Foods: $44 *million*—one seven-hundred-fiftieth of EXXON's. EXXON's sales were $45 *billion;* Idle Wild Foods' $323 *million*—less than one one hundredth of EXXON's, although both are in the top 500. EXXON's sales were almost half those of the second largest 500 combined.

6. The after-tax *profits* of the top ten industrials in 1975 were $9.2 billion, almost one-quarter of the profits of the first 1000 industrials. EXXON alone had profits of $2.5 billion, more than one-quarter of the top ten's.

7. In short, the concentration of the economy is continued within the top 500 and top 1000 corporations, where the bulk of industrial power is held by the very few.

8. What is true of industry is true in more and less degree of the rest of the economy. Thus, there were over 14,000 *commercial banks* in the U.S. in 1974, with assets of $927.5 billion. The assets of the fifty largest were $346 billion, and of the ten largest $196 billion. That is, fifty banks had well over a third of the assets of all commercial banks. Ten banks had well over half of that, and three banks—Bank of America, Citibank, and Chase Manhattan—own half or more of the assets of the top ten banks. The same pattern is true of deposits; the top ten banks hold just over 35 percent of all commercial banks' deposits.

9. The *five* largest *insurance* companies (Prudential, Metropolitan, Equitable, New York, and Hancock, in that order), with assets of $232 billion in 1975, account for nearly half of the total life insurance in force.

10. In the utilities group, AT&T is of course the giant among giants: $80 billion in assets, accounting for one-third of the top fifty's assets, revenues, net income, and stockholders' equity, and with 949,054 employees, more than any other company in any other business. In the world.

11. A final fact of a different sort: the top 500 do more and more business, but they do not necessarily hire more and more workers: they employed 14.6 million in 1970 and 14.4 million in 1975. In 1975, the top 500 laid off about one million employees, and four companies—GM, Ford, IT&T, and GE—accounted for one-fifth of that.[17]

---

[17] The data presented above are easily available. These are drawn primarily from Blair and Reid, both cited earlier, from Robert T. Averitt, *The Dual Economy* * (New York: Norton, 1968), from various issues of *Fortune,* but especially those of May and June, 1976, and from U. S. Bureau of the Census, *Statistical Abstract of the United States: 1975* (96th Edition), Washington, D.C., 1975.

These facts are striking in themselves. When they are seen as merely the latest stage of a continuing trend, they take on even more ominous overtones. In a similar examination of the top industrials, Ronald Müller points out that:

Between 1955 and 1970 the *Fortune* top 500 industrial corporations increased their share of total manufacturing and mining employment, profits, and assets from slightly more than 40 percent to over 70 percent. Whereas during the fifties the largest 200 were increasing their share of total industrial assets each year by an average of 1 percent, by the 1960's, this annual rate of increased concentration had doubled. . . .

He goes on to add, regarding banking, that:

From 1965 to 1970 the top fifty were increasing their share of total assets at more than double their expansion rate during the previous ten years. Federal Reserve Board studies show that almost all foreign deposits of U. S. banks are in the hands of the top twenty American global banks, with four holding 38 percent of these deposits, and twelve having 83 percent of all foreign banking assets. . . . Nine of the largest global banks account . . . for more than 26 percent of all total commercial and industrial lending by American banks . . . [and] these same nine hold 90 percent of the entire indebtedness in the U. S. petroleum and natural gas industry, 66 percent in machinery and metal products, and 75 percent in the chemical and rubber industries.[18]

Such are some of the facts of life of a concentrated economy. Economists seek to systematize these kinds of data with what are called concentration measures. Table 3–1 shows the percentages held by the largest four corporations in a given industry, using various measures.

Averitt's *Dual Economy* was used for some of the foregoing data. In his conclusion, he calls for a new microeconomic theory to build around the concentrated "center" and the weak "periphery." Having provided us with the data and an analysis showing that these describe a permanent feature of the American "dual economy," Averitt comes forth with the surprising conclusion that "we can attain perpetual prosperity while retaining a high level of what the business community calls 'economic freedom.' "[19] His optimism depends upon his hopes for governmental "moral suasion," which he takes to be "more effective in highly concentrated industries dominated by center firms than elsewhere."[20] To have

[18] Ronald Müller, "A Qualifying and Dissenting View of the Multinational Corporation," in George W. Ball, ed., *Global Companies: The Political Economy of World Business* * (Englewood Cliffs, N.J.: Prentice-Hall, 1975), pp. 24–25.

[19] Ibid., p. 200.

[20] Ibid.

TABLE 3-1 Concentration in Manufacturing Industries

Percentage of Sales, Total Assets, Net Capital Assets, and Profits after Taxes Accounted for by the 4 Largest Firms in Each Industry for 28 Selected Industry Groups, 4th Quarter, 1962

| | Percent of total | | | |
| | Sales | Total Assets | Net Capital Assets | Profits |
Industry				
Motor vehicles	80.8	79.7	83.1	89.1
Aircraft	47.3	41.9	32.6	46.6
Other transportation equipment	30.3	44.2	59.9	51.6
Electrical machinery	34.4	35.6	41.5	44.4
Metalworking machinery	14.5	16.3	18.5	19.1
Other machinery	20.6	24.3	31.5	39.6
Primary iron and steel	40.2	48.0	48.8	44.3
Primary nonferrous metals	27.3	41.1	47.7	37.1
Other fabricated metal products	14.7	19.9	30.3	17.7
Stone, clay, and glass products	18.1	19.9	19.8	23.4
Furniture and fixtures	5.2	8.4	9.6	5.3
Lumber and wood products	21.2	31.0	41.5	48.6
Instruments	37.9	41.2	50.2	56.6
Miscellaneous manufacturing	16.3	33.1	34.3	25.2
Dairy products	42.9	48.8	47.4	73.9
Bakery products	33.6	39.6	38.2	52.8
Other food	12.5	13.2	14.9	20.1
Textile mill products	22.0	26.1	25.7	30.5
Apparel	4.9	7.7	11.4	7.4
Paper	20.7	23.2	22.3	35.0
Basic industrial chemicals	42.0	45.5	44.6	64.6
Drugs and medicines	31.0	29.2	33.3	32.6
Other chemicals	28.5	30.0	33.6	35.8
Petroleum refining	50.3	50.1	47.7	54.3
Rubber	48.1	55.0	56.4	51.6
Leather	26.7	32.1	35.4	28.8
Alcoholic beverages	41.4	47.2	30.8	58.3
Tobacco	70.9	72.7	69.8	72.5

SOURCE: Bureau of Economics, Federal Trade Commission.

such hopes is to assume that private economic power is one thing and State power something else, something independent of private economic power.[21] In a capitalist society the shred of truth contained in those hopes

[21] Six case studies of how private and public power work together and separately to corrupt the presumed functions of both are collected in Robert L. Heilbroner et al., *In the Name of Profits* * (New York: Warner Paperback, 1973). The studies are illustrative of a much larger whole.

is completely out-weighed by the realities of power—a matter to be looked at more closely in Chapter 8.

The data above have been concerned with the functioning of the domestic economy. The figures show that the corporations involved constitute the hard core of power in the United States. When we look at the latest development of business power—the *multinational* corporation—we see the emergence of a powerful tendency for the same pattern of concentration and centralization in the capitalist world economy. Multinational corporations' main features are an integral part of the functioning of the American overseas empire; here it is appropriate to examine only the general shape of the development.

What's Good for America . . .

The multinational corporation, as its name suggests, has its origins and its headquarters in one nation, and it buys, invests, produces, and sells in many nations. As Stephen Hymer has pointed out,

> The multinational corporation is in the first instance an American phenomenon. Its precursor is the U.S. *national corporation* created at the end of the 19th century when American capitalism developed a multi-city continent-wide marketing and manufacturing strategy. . . . Though many U.S. corporations began to move to foreign countries almost as soon as they completed their continent-wide integration, the term *multinational* came to prominence only after 1960. . . . National firms think in terms of the national market; multinational firms see the whole world as their oyster and plan manufacturing and marketing on a global scale. . . . The shift in business horizons is closely connected to the aeronautical and electronic revolutions which made global planning possible.[22]

In 1972, about $500 billion of the world's production was attributable to multinational corporations. Of that amount, about half was produced by American multinationals, about one-quarter billion by foreign-based companies which also operate in the United States (for example, Royal-Dutch Shell), and the rest by interproduction in other countries. The proportion of world production contributed by multinational corporations

[22] Stephen Hymer, "The United States Multinational Corporations and Japanese Competition in the Pacific," an unpublished ms. which the late author kindly allowed me to use here. By the broadest definition, there are over 7,000 multinational companies in the world but fewer than 200 have about three-quarters of total assets, and comparable percentages of sales, income, employees, and so on. Since his tragic death, Hymer's doctoral dissertation has been published by the M.I.T. Press: *A Study of Direct Foreign Investments* (1976).

is now growing at the rate of about 10 percent per year. Were that rate to continue—and the turbulence and complexities of the world economy make it unlikely—the few hundred multinationals would generate about one-half of world production by the year 2000.

Naturally, almost all of the multinational corporations are among the very largest corporations in their own countries. Also, as might be expected, the emergence of this phenomenon for American corporations coincided with (was both cause and consequence of) our taking up primary status in the world economy from the 1920's on. Its most spectacular period of growth has been the past twenty-five years, the period in which the American economy has become internationalized, and the capitalist world-economy Americanized. The dynamic center of any future power struggle in the capitalist world-economy will surely find the multinationals taking leading roles.

The increasing proclivity of American corporations to locate their producing plants all over the world has vital consequences for the functioning of the American as well as other economies. Apart from what it means for the multinational corporations, it means a significant redistribution of productive jobs around the globe, and it affects resource flows, foreign policies, economic growth rates and patterns, and the international monetary system (as will be shown in Chapter 7). Whatever surprises and shocks the future holds, some of them will be due to the growing importance of these giants, as much of what has happened in the recent past has been clothed with their purposes and their needs.

Necessarily, the emergence of the American multinational corporation, like the emergence of the national corporation, has been facilitated by the State, which is much accustomed to responding to business needs and possibilities first, and asking and being asked questions about what it means to society, later—often too late. The internationalization of the American economy and the Americanization of the capitalist world-economy could not be accomplished without great changes in our global military posture, by comparison with any earlier period. Thus, there is an additional matter to be stressed in viewing the evolution of American business as a system of power: its relationship with the State and within that the relationships between business and the military. Here only the bare outlines will be suggested, anticipating fuller discussions later.

Among the justifications for capitalism as a system was one that, running contrary to the facts, is still frequently put forward. It claims that a "free enterprise" system minimizes the role of the State, and that it encourages everybody to pursue their rational material interests. One by-product of such a system would be efficiency; another would be material well-being; still another would be a government swayed by rational, meaning material, considerations.

But recently (that is, since about 1930), the United States has found itself confronted with developing needs and possibilities that cannot be resolved by a free market economy. There was the Great Depression of the 1930's, which only World War II resolved. There was the widespread unrest of that same period, taking the form of labor and socialist movements which, if they were never closely threatening, seemed so to the business class. There was the growth of fearsome Communist nations, assumed to be expansive and threatening to American interests, or even to "freedom" in the entire world. There was an already voracious and growing need for industrial raw materials, for markets, and for investment outlets, as well as a need for strategic sites to protect our expanding economic and political interests. Closely related to these developments was the growth of corporations that became usefully, vitally, or fully dependent upon military contracts—contracts typically constructed on a cost-plus (that is, guaranteed profit) basis.

These developments, taken together with the long-standing cultivation of patriotic attitudes among Americans, combined to produce a military-industrial complex most profitable to a hundred or so very large and thousands of smaller business firms, and a working force that was in fact or in its job fears dependent upon war production. Almost all Americans saw these developments, combining economic, military, political, and ideological needs, possibilities, and appeals, neither as malign nor as unreal; they saw them as responsibilities thrust upon America's economic and moral strength—thrust upon them by hostile, crafty, enigmatic and essentially peculiar foreigners. (Lyndon Baines Johnson once remarked, almost peevishly, "those foreigners weren't reared like us.") Later, we shall have occasion to cast doubt on whether the United States was forced by foreigners and/or hostile events to take up the role of Number One in the world. Here we may say merely that the processes of the past decades had the at least temporary effect, salubrious from the viewpoint of American capitalism, of bringing the majority of the American people closer to traditional conceptions of American virtues, a consequence anticipated by Veblen in 1904:

> The largest and most promising factor of cultural discipline—most promising as a corrective of iconoclastic vagaries—over which business principles rule is national politics. . . . Business interests urge an aggressive national policy and business men direct it. Such a policy is warlike as well as patriotic. The direct cultural value of a warlike business policy is unequivocal. It makes for a conservative animus on the part of the populace . . . [and] directs the popular interest to other, nobler, institutionally less hazardous matters than the unequal distribution of wealth or of creature comforts. . . . There can, indeed, be no serious question but that a consistent return to the ancient virtues of allegiance, piety, servility, graded dignity, class prerogative, and prescriptive authority would greatly

conduce to popular content and to the facile management of affairs. Such is the promise held out by a strenuous national policy.[23]

Reading Suggestions

Walter Adams, ed., *The Structure of the American Industry: Some Case Studies** (New York: Macmillan, 1961) is one of the best of several such books that examine many different industries in terms of their histories, their structures, and their performance. Leonard W. Weiss, *Case Studies in American Industry** (New York: Wiley, 1967) is similar and equally useful. Thurman Arnold, *The Folklore of Capitalism* (Garden City, N.Y.: Blue Ribbon Books, 1941), is a useful and critical study of the leading ideas and institutions of capitalist society. Arnold was at one time in charge of the Antitrust Division of the Justice Department, from which he was "booted upstairs" for being over-zealous. Joe S. Bain, Jr., *Industrial Organization,** rev. ed. (New York: Wiley, 1968) provides a thorough empirical and analytical study of the structure and functioning of American industry. A. A. Berle, *Power Without Property* (New York: Harcourt Brace Jovanovich, 1959) takes up an explosive issue and, characteristically, puts it down again as though it were not. See also his (with Gardiner Means) path-breaking *Modern Corporation and Private Property** (New York: Macmillan, 1932), a path that might have, but did not (either for him or his colleagues in economics), lead to disturbing conclusions and a new political economy.

John Kenneth Galbraith has the unusual virtue, for an economist, of writing bearable and even engaging English; this, certainly not any radical tinge to his ideas, is probably what has placed him near or beyond the pale for many in the economics profession. His *American Capitalism,** *The Affluent Society,** and *The New Industrial State** (Boston: Houghton

---

[23] *Theory of Business Enterprise*, pp. 391–93. In today's world, where so much of this has already been accomplished, it may be necessary to point out that Veblen's intent is sardonic, and that all his writings were devoted to preventing such developments from occurring. David Halberstam's *Best and the Brightest* * (New York: Random House, 1972) provides an extraordinarily detailed account of the personalities and policies of the 1960's, and abundant references back to the Truman and Eisenhower years. The treatment is journalistic rather than analytical, and the writing style is often indigestible, but those reading it will find that the Cold War in general and the Indochina War in particular were the outcome of some combination of private interest and capitalist ideology, rather than the interest of the American or any other nation's people, and that those making policy since (at least) 1945 did so in a continuous state of arrogance, ignorance, confusion, and systematic deception. Watergate's roots go deep.

Mifflin, 1956, 1958, and 1967, respectively) are worth reading—for information, for witty criticisms of the profession, and for examples of how a fine mind can stumble if it tethers itself in a pitted field. Andrew Hacker, ed., *The Corporation Take-Over** (Garden City, N.Y.: Doubleday, Anchor Books, 1965) is a useful collection of critical essays on various aspects of corporate power. Charles Perrow, ed., *The Radical Attack on Business** (New York: Harcourt Brace Jovanovich, 1972) covers much the same subject matter, from farther to the left. A radical treatment of the role of expansion in capitalist development is provided succinctly by Edwards in *The Capitalist System,* cited earlier, pp. 99 ff.

The basic history and central problems of combination and competition are treated conventionally and thoroughly in George W. Stocking and Myron W. Watkins, *Monopoly and Free Enterprise* (New York: Twentieth Century Fund, 1951). Watkins has written a fine and compressed analysis of the processes that lead to large-scale production, ownership, and control in the article entitled "Large-Scale Production," in *The Encyclopaedia of the Social Sciences.* The entry "Industrialism" by G. D. H. Cole is also praiseworthy in that encyclopaedia.

Those who wish to study one enterprise in depth can do so in many ways; one fine study of that sort is Keith Sward, *The Legend of Henry Ford** (New York: Holt, Rinehart and Winston, 1948). Ford, who once proclaimed "machinery is the new Messiah"—and "History is bunk"—comes out as something of a crank, and as a very lucky, quite ruthless, and not at all bright businessman, taking in profits at rates—$150,000 *a day* in the early 1920's—that economics textbooks neither describe, explain, nor imagine. Those wishing a good analytic account of the development of the giant corporation's organizational form should consult Alfred Chandler, Jr., *Strategy and Structure** (Cambridge: M.I.T. Press, 1962). Finally, the always close relationships between business and the State are examined from quite different perspectives by Bernard D. Nossiter, *The Mythmakers** (Boston: Beacon Press, 1964), and by Walter Adams and Horace M. Gray, *Monopoly in America: The Government as Promoter* (New York: Macmillan, 1955). Nossiter is a liberal journalist; Gray and Adams seek a reduction in the power and size of Big Business and Big Government. A revealing journalistic treatment of the crimes/shenanigans of one of the U.S. giant corporations at home and abroad is Anthony Sampson, *The Sovereign State of ITT* (New York: Stein and Day, 1973).

4

Growth and Development, Prosperity and Depression

As I sd to my
friend, because I am
always talking,—John I

sd, which was not his
name, the darkness sur-
rounds us, what

can we do against
it, or else, shall we &
why not, buy a goddamn big car,

drive, he sd, for
christ's sake, look
out where yr going.*

A capitalist economy cannot stand still. It must *grow* or shrink; it must continually change its patterns of production, consumption, and trade— that is, *develop*—or cease to grow; irrespective of growth and development, it must continually *fluctuate*. At any time and over time, the capitalist economy is marked by unevenness, uncertainty, and instability. Why is all this so? What are the characteristics of, and differences between, fluctuations, growth, and development? How do they relate, separately and in combination, to the defining traits of captalism—its need to expand and to exploit? Earlier we have touched on some of the relevant explanations; here we will explore them in greater depth.

* Robert Creeley, *I Know A Man.* From *For Love,* reprinted by permission of Charles Scribner's Sons. Copyright © 1962 by Robert Creeley.

However much they disagree on other matters, all economists who have studied capitalism—from Smith through Marx, Marshall, and Keynes—agree on the necessity of expansion. Disagreement centers upon what is required for expansion, what is associated with the process, the likelihood of expansion over time, and the consequences of either adequate or inadequate rates of expansion. How these matters are treated distinguishes classical from neoclassical economics and both of those from radical or dissenting economics.

The classical economists, and especially Smith and Ricardo, developed analyses whose aim was to enhance the possibilities of economic growth and development. J. S. Mill's examination of the likelihood and problems of a "stationary" economy ended the period of classical economics; as Mill's life was drawing to a close, neoclassical economics came to the fore. Until the astounding depression of the 1930's, that economics gave little sustained attention to the processes of growth and development. Neoclassical monetary theory, capital theory, and trade theory—all highly abstract—could be said to be *related* to such questions; since such theories generally took buoyant growth for granted, however, they did not systematically examine the life processes of growth. And, as we saw earlier, development—any sort of significant structural change—was neither sought nor discussed in neoclassical economics. Given the kinds of problems business faced in the late nineteenth century—centering mostly on market scarcities—and given the essential harmony between the viewpoints of business and economics, this was an understandable neglect. All that was rudely upset by the Depression and by the adjustments of neoclassical theory made by Keynes.

Alongside the aloof attitude of neoclassical economics, and developing in the same years (from the 1870's up to about 1930), there *was* a body of analysis that sought to approach questions of growth, fluctuations, and development directly. The significance of these ideas was not to become meaningful, however, until after the depression of the 1930's was well underway; nor did they divert the smooth flow of calm neoclassicism. In the United States, Veblen was unquestionably the most influential thinker in this area, although his influence was not always acknowledged by those he directly or indirectly influenced: J. M. Clark and Wesley Clair Mitchell, directly, and J. A. Schumpeter, indirectly. Economics in general went its merry way, unruffled by any serious concern with the prospect of untoward booms or slumps, while serious business cycle analysts managed to overlook the gloomy expectations of Veblen's analysis, which in turn was indebted to European, including Marxian, contributions.[1]

[1] A comprehensive and very useful study of this area of economics in its historical development and its contemporary state is Robert Aaron Gordon, *Business Fluctuations,** 2nd ed. (New York: Harper & Row, 1961). Gordon provides a thorough integration of Keynesian analysis with historical and current data. Chapters 12 and

In the decade or two preceding the Depression, the seriousness of the problems of expansion and contraction was only barely recognized, in short, as revealed by the credibility given to "theories" that explained aggregative movements in terms of sunspots, or, in one instance, by an inverse correlation with the length of women's skirts in Australia. It took a disaster to prompt either the economics profession or its audience to pay heed to the relationship between such disaster and the normal functionings of a capitalist economy.

Joseph A. Schumpeter, a conventional and very conservative economist, was one who—like Veblen, Clark, and Mitchell—stood as an exception to those who saw business downturns as temporary aberrations. Schumpeter was one of those rare people who can learn from those with whose purposes he disagrees; he learned much from Marx and perhaps from Veblen as well. Although he accepted much of the neoclassical mode of analysis, Schumpeter could not do so for the vital questions of growth and development. "Analyzing business cycles," he said, "means neither more nor less than analyzing the economic process of the capitalist era. . . . Cycles are not, like tonsils, separable things that might be treated by themselves, but are, like the beat of its heart, at the essence of the organism that displays them." [2] Schumpeter was an ardent supporter of capitalist society; his studies of capitalist development told him that the best one could hope for was the postponement of its disappearance. He developed this position most fully in his *Capitalism, Socialism, and Democracy.* The healthy dynamic of capitalism for Schumpeter was what he called "creative gales of destruction"—gales powered by technological innovation, leading to the elimination of *old* patterns of competition and monopoly by *new* patterns of competition and monopoly. In this view but not in others, he was close to Veblen and Marx, despite his quite different value system. They saw the life and death of capitalism more as undertakers than as doctors.

Writing in the heyday of neoclassical economics *and* of rampant American industrialization, Veblen combined a dour analysis of capitalist growth and development with a dim view of the associated economics:

---

13 examine "the variety of business-cycle theories." His more recent *Economic Instability and Growth: The American Record* * (New York: Harper & Row, 1974) examines the data from 1919 to 1970, and is the historical excerpt from and extension of the earlier book.

[2] Joseph A. Schumpeter, *Business Cycles: A Theoretical, Historical, and Statistical Analysis of the Capitalist Process,* two vols. (New York: McGraw-Hill, 1939), vol. I, p. v. This massive work ranges throughout the capitalist world in the terms of its title. Schumpeter was given the mantle of greatness by his contemporaries, but his approach and his ideas were given short shrift by them. (Gordon, cited above, is an exception.) Schumpeter was an Austrian, and taught at Harvard from 1932 until his death in 1950.

There are certain saving clauses in common use. . . . Among them are these: "Given the state of the industrial arts"; "Other things remaining the same"; "In the long run"; "In the absence of disturbing causes." Now, . . . the state of the industrial arts has at no time continued unchanged during the modern era; consequently other things have never remained the same; and in the long run the outcome has always been shaped by the disturbing causes. . . . The arguments [of the neoclassical economists] have been as good as the premises on which they proceed.[3]

For Veblen, the process of capitalist growth and development hurried through time under the domination of three major trends: a steady increase in monopolization, a continuing increase in technological strength, and a chronic tendency toward depression. Monopoly results from the native impulse of the business man to eliminate competition—"buy cheap and sell dear." Technological advance ". . . has in recent times been going forward at a constantly accelerated rate, and it is still in progress, with no promise of abatement or conclusion." [4] But why should depression be the outcome of monopoly and technological improvement? That takes us back to Veblen's distinction between business and industry. Business is a matter of making money; what business will produce, in what quantities, and when is determined by actual and prospective market conditions. The advance of technology means ever-increasing production and productivity; the combination of consumer and investment expenditures with the ability of monopolistic business to hold back production—Veblen called it "businesslike sabotage"—places steady downward pressure on the economy, relieved only by intermittent stimuli coming from outside the normal functioning of the economy. Thus,

> Since the seventies . . . , the course of affairs in business has apparently taken a permanent change as regards crises and depression. During this recent period, and with increasing persistency, chronic depression has been the rule rather than the exception in business. Seasons of easy times, "ordinary prosperity," during this period are pretty uniformly traceable to specific causes extraneous to the process of industrial business proper; [e.g., in] the one now drawing to a close, it was the Spanish–American War, coupled with the expenditures for stores, munitions, and services incident to placing the country on a war footing, that lifted the depression and brought prosperity to the business community.[5]

The remedy Veblen saw for this tendency toward chronic depression was for "the vested interests" to *create* these stimuli, for them to develop

[3] Thorstein Veblen, *The Vested Interests and the Common Man* * (New York: Huebsch, 1919; Viking, 1946), pp. 85–86.
[4] *Absentee Ownership*, p. 251.
[5] *Theory of Business Enterprise*, p. 250.

means of "unproductive consumption," through a "strenuous national policy," and a popular concern for "national integrity." Those who find this view out of keeping with what appears to be a different reality since 1904 may be reminded that the economy was saved from contraction by World War I and an ensuing prosperity, that it sank into deep depression in the 1930's from which it recovered only after our entrance into World War II, and that our prosperity since then has been accompanied by both Cold War and hot war involving the expenditure on military production of almost two *trillion* dollars since 1941—more than three-quarters of which was spent *after* World War II. These and other characteristics of our developmental process will be traced more fully later in this chapter. Let us look briefly now at Marx's approach to growth and development. There are implicit and explicit differences between his and Veblen's analysis, as well as many common features.

Marx spoke not of economic growth or development, but of the process of "capital accumulation." This was for Marx the rope on which capitalism climbed through time, aided by intermittent knots of expansion and threatened by periodic frayed stretches, which he called crises (and which are now called recessions or depressions). Marx believed also that this was the rope with which capitalism would ultimately hang itself—with the help of the working class, itself a product of capital accumulation. More exactly, both the expanding and the contracting phases of capitalist development are negative as well as positive in their meaning. Expansion means expanded production and profits, *but* only up to the point at which it also means overproduction and upward pressure on wages; contraction means decreased production and losses, *but* it also replenishes the "reserve army of the unemployed," ultimately reduces competition through the destruction of weaker firms, and lays the basis for renewed expansion and the tendency toward monopoly.

For Marx, the process of capital accumulation (that is, of expansion) is energized by what each individual capitalist *wishes* to do and what he and all capitalists *must* do: seeking to make profits in competition with others in the context of an ever-changing technology, the surviving capitalists and the economy are driven to "accumulate," or expand. The capitalist

> . . . shares with the miser the passion for wealth as wealth. But that which in the miser is a mere idiosyncrasy, is, in the capitalist, the effect of the social mechanism, of which he is but one of the wheels. Moreover, the development of capitalist production makes it constantly necessary to keep increasing the amount of capital laid out in a given industrial undertaking, and competition makes the immanent laws of capitalist production to be felt by each individual capitalist, as external coercive laws. It compels him to keep constantly extending his capital, in order to preserve it, but extend it he cannot, except by means of progressive accumulation.

Therefore,

> Accumulate, accumulate! That is Moses and the prophets! . . . Accumulation for accumulation's sake, production for production's sake. . . .[6]

A full treatment of Marxian and Veblenian theory along these lines would show that Marx had a more coherent and a more powerful *economic* theory of capitalist development than Veblen. On the other hand, the looseness and the breadth of Veblen's analysis, and the later period in which he wrote, allowed him to bring in the behavior and meaning of modern monopolistic business organization and of the State in ways that went beyond Marx.[7] What seems essential is to combine the strengths of Marx, Veblen, and Keynes with contemporary data and social analysis, an effort already begun by Baran and Sweezy in *Monopoly Capital*. Now let us explore what is meant by fluctuations, growth, and development, in general and in the American experience.

Fluctuations and Instability

In proceeding first to explain the pervasiveness and persistence of business fluctuations in a capitalist economy, it should be emphasized that fluctuations and instability are not *defects* in such an economy. The price of such instability may be high for particular businesses, industries, and workers at any time, but for a capitalist *economy's* health over time such fluctuations are essential. In what is no more than a suggestive analogy, we may think of the role of business fluctuations in a capitalist economy as comparable to the processes of inhaling and exhaling, of hunger and surfeit, of ingestion and digestion, in the human body. Extending the analogy a bit further, we can point out that it is not the processes as such that are harmful, but the quality of the air and the quantity and composition of the diet that make for health or sickness in the body.

Thus, business fluctuations are inherent to a capitalist economy. To rid

---

[6] The first passage is from *Capital*, vol. I, p. 592, and the second from p. 595.

[7] "Above all, Veblen was, and remains alone in assigning a decisive role in the development of capitalism to the reciprocating interaction of business principles and national politics. Others have described the economic impact of war, the psychological effects of militarism, the cultural incidence of nationalism; and none can deny that these forces have become increasingly important, if not actually dominant, in the world of the twentieth century. Yet only Veblen has built all these elements into a reasoned and coherent theory." Paul M. Sweezy, "Veblen on American Capitalism," in Douglas F. Dowd, ed., *Thorstein Veblen: A Critical Reappraisal* (Ithaca: Cornell University Press, 1958), p. 195.

the economy of them would require ridding it as well of its basic institutional characteristics: private ownership of the means of production, and the right and will to use those productive assets to make profits at the decision of the businessman. A capitalist *economy* is in its nature unplanned, however much each *enterprise* may plan. The economy is complex. It becomes more so as industrialization broadens and deepens specialization in all aspects of the economy—in agriculture, trade, industry, finance, and the broad variety of services. Time must pass between the initial decision to invest and produce; that is, decisions made on the basis of one set of market signals are realized either well or badly in markets that exist later. And all this is made infinitely more complex by virtue of the mediating role of money and finance, to say nothing of the impact of foreign trade.[8]

As noted in Chapter 3, competition, taken in its own terms, is essential to the economic and the social health of a capitalist economy; so is instability. However, just as businessmen have acted when they could to mitigate or eliminate competition (through driving out or buying up competitors, for example), they have also done what little they could to mitigate the harmful effects of instability on their own enterprises. But competition is an industry-wide phenomenon; instability is economy-wide. Consequently, no matter how effective steps may be to eliminate market competition when taken by an individual firm or corporation, the substantial amelioration of instability has depended upon economic intervention by the State. Such intervention became neither significant nor persistent until the onset of the Depression of the 1930's. This marked a major change both in the role of the State and in the structure of the economy. What these changes reflected was the necessity for a *developmental* change if adequate growth rates as well as the mitigation of instability were to be achieved.

If capitalism is *inherently* unstable, and if the United States was capitalist from its earliest beginnings, then our economic history should have been characterized by continuous ups and downs, as indeed it was. Table 4–1 indicates the basic economic fluctuations in the U.S. since 1800.

Growth and Development, Nineteenth Century

With such a dramatic pattern of seesawing throughout our history, why is it that nothing in the way of persistent and deliberate counteracting steps were made part of the State's functions until the past generation or so? It is not far-fetched to make an analogy with a young man

[8] See Gordon, *Business Fluctuations.* Chapters 1 and 8 provide a good explanation of instability and its causes.

TABLE 4–1

1800–1807	Prosperity	1894–1897	Mostly depressed
1808–1809	Depression		years
1810–1814	Gradual recovery	1898–1907	Prosperity
	and boom (in	1907	Panic
	1814)	1908	Depression
1815	Panic	1909–1914	Semi-stagnation
1816–1818	Depression	1914–1918	War prosperity
1819	Panic	1919	Mild postwar
1820–1821	Mild depression		recession
1822–1824	Prosperity	1919–1920	Prosperity
1825–1826	Recession	1921–1922	Sharp recession
1827–1836	Growing prosperity	1922–1923	Prosperity
1837	Panic	1924	Recession
1837–1843	Generally de-	1925–1926	Recovery
	pressed conditions	1927	Recession
1844–1848	Mild prosperity	1928–1929	Boom
1849–1856	Vigorous prosperity	1930's	Deep depression;
1857	Panic		short-lived
1858	Depression		"boom" in 1937
1859–1860	Revival and	1940's	War and postwar
	prosperity		prosperity; reces-
1861–1862	Generally de-		sion in 1946, and
	pressed conditions		in 1949
1862–1865	War prosperity	1950's	Recessions in
1866–1867	Depression		1953–54, and
1868–1872	Prosperity		1957–58
1873	Panic	1960's	Recession, 1960–61;
1874–1878	General depression		Expansion, 1961–69
1879	Recovery	1970's	Slowdown and
1880–1882	Prosperity		inflation,
1883–1885	Mild recession		1969–71
1886–1890	Vigorous prosperity		Inflation and
1891	Minor recession		rapid growth,
1892	Recovery		1972–73
1893	Stock market col-		Stagflation
	lapse		1974–?

SOURCE: Douglas F. Dowd, *Modern Economic Problems in Historical Perspective* (Boston: D.C. Heath, 1965), p. 143.

who gets periodic hangovers, or an occasional broken limb from skiing. Why does he not take more care, place himself under the advice of a doctor?

The nineteenth century was the American economy's reckless youth, a period of rapid expansion in every which way, as our geographic boundaries and structure of production were both filled in and expanded. It was a period of extraordinary buoyancy. Each panic or crisis was followed by successively higher peaks of economic activity. Optimism was the rule; for those at the top levels of business it was justified. They had neither inclination nor felt need for a "doctor's care."

In the early twentieth century, both the American and the European industrial economies reached maturity; business contractions, market instability, and insecurity became more dangerous. The consciousness of this grew in the United States, and especially among the most powerful of American corporate leaders. In turn, this consciousness led to a transformed view of the proper role of the State—away from laissez-faire. Although the State's role in the economy enlarged substantially after 1900, it did not take up any substantial monetary and fiscal functions; the creation of the Federal Reserve System in 1913, however, was a step in that direction. The postponement of the State's vital function may be explained by the deflecting impact of the expansion induced by World War I and the ensuing prosperity—until 1929. A closer examination of these patterns is now in order.[9]

In Chapter 3 we dwelt upon the dynamic interaction between economic and westward geographic expansion in the nineteenth century. Viewed from the perspective of this chapter, we may observe that process as almost chaotic; we may also understand how its individual and social costs were both softened and obscured by the generally rapid quantitative expansion and the developmental changes accompanying it. In addition, prior to the stage of advanced industrialism of the twentieth century, troubles in one part of the economy were felt less immediately *and* less seriously in the rest of the economy than became the case in this century.

The advance of productive efficiency is related to an ever more extensive specialization of function or division of labor, in turn implying increasing economic interdependence. Greater efficiency is thus paid for with greater precariousness. The chronological listing of expansions and contractions earlier shows many depressions and "panics." The very term "panic" suggests the spread of trouble over the economy; in some cases in the nineteenth century they spread like a prairie fire. What was noteworthy about such instances, however, was that their origins were almost always in the loose and speculation dominated *financial* system of the country, which in turn was usually responding to land and railroad speculation. But underneath the turbulent surface was a deepening and spread-

[9] Intensive examination of the growing and changing role of the State is postponed until Chapter 8. Those wishing to explore these matters now, however, may do so in Faulkner, *Decline of Laissez-Faire*, and in two major revisions of American history centering upon these developments: Gabriel Kolko, *The Triumph of Conservatism: A Reinterpretation of American History, 1900–1916* ° (New York: Quadrangle, 1967), and James Weinstein, *The Corporate Ideal in the Liberal State: 1900–1918* ° (Boston: Beacon Press, 1968).

ing industrial system, providing ongoing buoyancy to the economy and optimism to its businessmen. There was no felt need for an activist State to set limits to bad times, for the times were not seen as threatening to become or stay bad enough. "Depression," when it occurred in the nineteenth century does not signify deep—or, if deep, lasting—(recorded or known) unemployment until the massive depression of the 1930's. (However, that kind of unemployment, industrial unemployment, began to be noticed seriously in the 1890's for the first time.) The generally "depressed" years between 1873 and 1897 were years of steadily falling prices, due to the combination of rapid technological improvements and the tying together of world markets, resulting in foreign competition plus intense domestic competition. Both in Europe and in the United States the response to these conditions was a growth of monopolies, trusts, imperialism, cartels, and tariff protection—relatively simple matters by comparison with what developed in the twentieth century.

World War I and the New Era

There are two important matters requiring explanation for the period from 1914 to 1929: first, the sustained quality of its expansion, by comparison with earlier periods; second, the manner in which that long expansion connects with the great collapse after 1929. If the prosperity of the fifteen years preceding 1929 was unusual in our history, it is even more the case that the depression following 1929 was totally unprecedented in its severity, its duration, and its pervasiveness. Something new was going on; it probably began before World War I in the period we have called "semi-stagnation."

When we seek analytically to integrate the prosperity preceding 1929 with the depression following it, we place ourselves in the arena of growth and development analysis, rather than of short-term business cycle theory, let alone the abstract income and employment theory of Keynes's *General Theory*. That takes us into an exceptionally complex area of analysis; here we can only point to the major elements of what such an analysis has to put together.

First we should note that in the years preceding World War I, the United States had reached the limits of economic complexity then allowed by technology, real income, and business conditions. The limits reached were significantly beyond those attained elsewhere, whether the judgment is made in terms of productivity, the balance between consumer and capital goods production, the total of all production, or the scale of plant production. Second, although the years after 1909 are conventionally seen as a period of "recovery" from the panic and depression of 1907–1908, if there was a recovery it was quite uneven and very feeble. The uncertainty and rocky quality of the American economy had its counterpart in what was, if anything, a worse situation in Europe, where what was by then a "North Atlantic economy" was, by 1914, beginning to slip toward major economic troubles. Because each major segment of the capitalist world economy interacted critically with the rest, these developing weaknesses in the two strongpoints of the world system were ominous portents of the collapse that began in 1929.

Much of the talk about the causes of these difficulties in the United States in the decade before 1914 pointed to the inadequacies of our banking and monetary system. Because those inadequacies were quite real, and their consequences so vivid, they took attention away from deeper problems:

> An inefficient and inelastic credit system, however, was by no means the only cause for the unstable condition of American economic life between 1907 and 1914. High finance had overloaded railroads and other corporations with fantastic capital structures; industrial "trusts," as in the case of United States Steel after the panic of 1907, were reluctant to adjust prices to decreasing demand. Wages were barely keeping up with the increased cost of living, whereas unemployment in manufacturing and transportation amounted to 12 percent or over in 1908, 1914, and 1915. . . . [Despite] a vigorous speculative advance . . . in the early months of 1914 on both the London and New York stock exchanges . . . , the world saw no revival in trade and industry. In the United States the recession of 1913 sank into a depression in 1914 with an increase in gold exports, a decline in foreign trade, a weakening of commodity prices, and an increase in unemployment.[10]

What Faulkner portrays as a condition of substantial instability, in the preceding quote, Baran and Sweezy see as the onset of *stagnation*. Stagnation is another term for chronic depression where, in the absence of "external stimuli" such as war, the economy tends to limp along with unutilized productive capacity, depressed business, and high unemployment. Pointing to the increasing severity of the contraction phases of the business cycle from 1908 until the War, and to a sharp increase in unemployment in the same period (averaging 6.6 percent, from 1908 to 1915), Baran and Sweezy conclude that the years after 1907 displayed:

[10] Harold U. Faulkner, *The Decline of Laissez-Faire, 1897–1917*, pp. 31–32. This book is rich in information concerning all aspects of American economic (and associated political) developments for the period. What is striking, however, is that the author's devastating recital of facts—devastating to a relaxed view of American capitalism—is accompanied by an essentially complacent analysis. Kolko, in *The Triumph of Conservatism*, working from the same facts, takes them to quite different conclusions. Where Faulkner sees the upshot of what he has reported to be a revival of the "reform movement," (p. 382) Kolko concludes his book with a chapter entitled "The Lost Democracy."

. . . the kind of "creeping stagnation" with which we have become familiar in the later 1950's and the early 1960's. If there is any other interpretation of these facts, we are certainly ready to consider it on its merits. But until we know what it is, we shall feel justified in concluding that if the First World War had not come along, the decade 1910–1920 would have gone down in United States history as an extraordinarily depressed one.[11]

The outbreak of war in August of 1914 entirely altered the economic prospects of the American economy. Instead of having to struggle with what might well have been an intractable depression, both national and international, the United States found itself faced with rapidly growing demands from abroad for its production and its capital. Internally this meant that a likely downturn was replaced by a strong upswing in business and jobs, and an even further extension of our already advanced industrial system. It also meant a substantial boost toward the concentration and centralization of economic power, and explicit business–State coordination and planning, when the U.S. entered the war in 1917. A full panoply of new war agencies brought representatives of agriculture, business, and labor into the government, where they were schooled in new ways to gain and to use power.[12]

Out of these war needs the American economy was able to generate rising instead of falling incomes for the whole range of "ordinary people," and both sustained and high profits for the business world (including farmers). This, taken together with the technological developments facilitated by the war, laid the basis for the "New Era" for the United States economy in the twenties. Added to the advanced development of durable *capital* goods was the introduction on a mass basis of a broad range of durable *consumer* goods (such as automobiles and appliances) and a vast boom in residential, commercial, and public construction (of buildings and roads). Similar developments did not take hold in other industrial economies, if at all, until much later (and, on a mass basis, radios excepted, not until after 1950).[13]

Another outcome of World War I which must be noted is the manner in which the war speeded up and facilitated the emergence of the United

[11] The authors go on to make clear that they are not saying the depression of the 1930's would have taken place after 1910, for "by 1915, the automobile era was already well under way, and the great shake-up in living patterns and consumption habits which it brought with it would probably have created a boom. . . ." *Monopoly Capital*, p. 234. Their analysis concerning 1907–1915 begins on p. 228. The stagnation *theory* will be discussed in more detail below, pp. 111 ff.

[12] See George Soule, *Prosperity Decade*, Chapters 1, 2, and 3, for a complete story.

[13] The "mass basis" referred to, for the United States and other economies, is defined economically; that is, in terms not of the "masses" having access to the relevant goods, but of sufficient numbers of buyers existing to allow *mass production*. Thus, a fair estimate is that not more than about a third of the American people were able

States as the supreme power in the world economy—a position signified by the change from our *owing* over $3 billion before the War and being *owed* over $6 billion by other countries after the War. World War II strengthened us even more—much more, for a while. As will be discussed in Chapter 7, the domestic economic meaning of America's new world role after World War I was not vital to the prosperity of the twenties, both because the postwar upsurge in economic nationalism (protective tariffs and the like) placed stringent limits on American possibilities abroad, and because domestic prosperity reduced Americans' need to look far afield for profitable possibilities. Nevertheless, seen in a long-term perspective, World War I and its aftermath were critical in placing the United States in the forefront of world economic powers; after 1940, the United States was able to take conscious advantage of what had come within reach when the European powers entered upon the suicidal path of World War I.

With all the enormous stimuli provided during and by the War it is not difficult to understand the subsequent "prosperity decade." But what brought it to an end? And, more to the point (for under capitalism expansions always come to an end), why was the depression of the thirties so deep? Why did it last so long? Why, even more, did it require World War II to lift us out of that depression?

One way to begin to answer such questions is to dwell for a moment on the word "prosperity." Like so many other pleasing terms we find to describe our history, it has to be viewed with an eye to who uses it and what they mean by it. Up until very recently, almost all of those who have informed us about our society—as historians, economists, sociologists, journalists, politicians, et al.—have been in or from the upper ranks of society. They have spoken to us from the vantage point of the middle class, and are the comfortable beneficiaries of the society's achievements. As Veblen said, speaking of professors of social science, "their intellectual horizon is bounded by the same limits of commonplace insight and preconceptions as are the prevailing opinions of the conservative middle class." [14]

---

to buy throughout the range of consumer durables during the twenties, to say nothing of the depressed thirties. An automobile, for example, was something not even dreamed of by the bottom two-thirds of Americans in the twenties. See George Soule, Ibid.

[14] *The Higher Learning in America, A Memorandum on the Conduct of Universities by Businessmen* * (New York: B. W. Huebsch, 1918; Sagamore Press, 1957), pp. 135–36. This citation is from the Sagamore paperback, one of many editions. Originally written in 1908, but not published for a decade, Veblen's *Higher Learning* identified the basic elements of university "corruption" that were rebelled against by students (and some faculty) in the 1960's. However, Veblen was not as surprised as many are today that in a business society the universities (among other institutions) would live under business criteria. As a brilliant and confirmed scholar, this was among the most tragic of his conclusions by his own lights.

Thus, to say that the American economy was prosperous in the 1920's, as these words are commonly used (still to this day), is quite compatible with the existence of widespread misery in American society in the same period. It is also compatible with serious economic problems in a whole range of industries. The "system" was doing just fine in the twenties: it was expanding in its production and power, it was yielding all sorts of new and attractive products for a significant fraction of its population, and it was setting new records for returns to owners of productive assets and of securities and real estate. The period was not only one in which millions of Americans were realizing the life-long dream of "getting something for nothing" but it was also one in which much of what was being gotten hadn't even been thought of only a few years before. But railroads had already begun their long decline, and cotton textiles, staple agriculture (wheat, corn, cotton, tobacco) and coal mining were in serious trouble. Therefore those who depended for jobs on those industries were in even more serious trouble.

Unemployment statistics until the 1930's are notoriously unreliable [15] and there is no way now to establish the hard facts. Estimates for the years 1920–1929 range from an average of 5 percent to something over 13 percent unemployed. Even if we accept the conservative lower figure, we are faced with a jobless rate that would suggest something other than "prosperity" for those directly involved and the even larger number of those peripherally involved. What was true of the twenties has become even more pronounced and better understood in the past decade or so, a period in which extraordinary gains in production and profits have been associated with hard-core poverty for tens of millions of people, and unemployment rates of 10 to 40 percent for important segments of the population (blacks, Chicanos, and especially the young men and women among them). Thus, even with the exceptionally rapid expansion of 1973 (at an annual rate of 14 percent, 8 percent of which was seen as "real," the rest as inflation) officially recorded unemployment hovered around 5 percent. When the process of "stagflation" took hold in 1974, unemployment rose to a peak of 8.9 percent (in 1975) as consumer prices increased at 12.2 percent (in 1974); both rates fluctuated between 6 and 8 percent in 1976.

[15] Since the 1930's they have remained unreliable, but now scandalously, rather than notoriously, so. It was not until the Depression that systematic attempts to gather and analyze aggregative data (concerning income, jobs, investment, etc.) were institutionalized, so the economists for the twenties and earlier may be excused for the shortcomings of their data. That excuse no longer exists; but it is widespread knowledge that the number of jobless is vastly and systematically understated. Of which, more below.

The Dual Economy

At this point it seems appropriate to suggest an analysis that will connect the dubious prosperity of the twenties with the mixed prosperity–poverty conditions of our own times. The analysis will take the form of positing the development of a "dual economy." [16]

From its first years, the American economy has contained industries that were lively and growing, together with those that were stagnating and depressed; it has always had groups of people making high, medium, and low incomes—and, until the Civil War, millions of slaves without any money income. But, until the years just before World War I, such disparateness did not constitute a firm basis for *duality* in the economy. The term *duality* as used here suggests not only differences as between groups and sectors in the economy, but the evolution of two paths of change, one dynamic and profitable, the other marked by difficulties and stagnation. That bifurcation began to take hold as the American economy "settled in" to its industrial and organizational patterns before 1920.

Students of American development for the past half century will object to the notion of any "settling in" process for the American economy because, after all, that long period has seen an extraordinary amount of change in products, techniques, and patterns of distribution and finance, along with a great increase in real per capita income. All that is, of course, indisputable. The important aspect about that dynamism, however, is that it has been carried by what O'Connor calls the monopolistic sector and the State sector; meanwhile the competitive sector has drifted into something like a backwash—increasingly dependent upon the monopolistic sector and the State for viability or even livelihood, and increasingly resentful of both.

The prosperity of the twenties is attributable to the dynamism of the monopolistic sector: high rates of technological innovation in production, and a whole new spread of expensive durable consumer goods, combined with an associated and enormous expansion in the petroleum (and linked industries, such as oil pipe) and construction industries.[17] If one were to

---

[16] Economic duality as a concept solves some puzzles regarding the American economy, but complicates understanding of underdeveloped economies. (See Chapter 7.) In the forefront of developing these ideas are Professors Barry Bluestone and James O'Connor. Professor Bluestone put forth the concept at the *Hearings* of the Joint Economic Committee on the President's Economic Report of 1972, in Washington, D.C. (February, 1972), and O'Connor's argument, which moves along some of the same lines but with different terminology, will be found in his *Fiscal Crisis of the State* ° (New York: St. Martin's Press, 1973).

[17] Economists can rightly point out that the construction industries—building materials, contractors, and the building trades workers—are competitive in structure, with thousands upon thousands of separate firms. However, they might also know

locate the hot center of this dynamism in the twenties, it would be in the expansion of the automobile industry, which meant the expansion of industries directly (metals, machinery, paints, leather, rubber and glass) and indirectly (petroleum, highway, residential housing and service station construction, etc.) connected to the automobile. Today the automobile industry claims that one out of six jobs is tied into it, even if they also deny that it is the instance par excellence of a monopolistic and overweening industry, with GM as the virtual symbol of American economic power.[18]

In the twenties, Americans took great pride in their "New Era." Those who wrote about it, whether F. Scott Fitzgerald or the economist Irving Fisher, paid little or no attention to the seamy side; yet Veblen in 1923 had come down hard on the fact of monopoly and the probability of severe depression, and Sinclair Lewis (in *Main Street* and *Babbitt,* especially) had seen the emptiness of middle-class existence accompanying its "success." The seamy side was where most of the people lived, depending for their jobs on the competitive sector and its "sick" industries.[19]

"An economic system based on private investment decisions thus tends to produce a *dual economy* both in the structure of industries and in the structure of the labor force," said Bluestone in his statement to the Joint Economic Committee in 1972. This pattern was well underway already in

---

that the *organization* of construction in any given locality has been monopolistic through trade associations, building codes, and cooperating trade unions. More recently, giant corporations such as Bechtel have begun also to lessen the competitive *structural* characteristics of the industry.

[18] See, for example, Federal Trade Commission, *Report on the Automobile Industry* * (Washington, D.C., 1939), Keith Sward, *Legend of Henry Ford,* and the summary chapter on the industry in Walter Adams, *Structure of American Industry.* The incredible power and impact of automobiles and petroleum are discussed lucidly and factually by Barry Weisberg, *Beyond Repair: The Ecology of Capitalism* (Boston: Beacon Press, 1971), Chapter 5. This point will be discussed in Chapter 6 below, when environmental questions are examined.

[19] Thus, productivity rose between 1920 and 1929 such that a given volume of manufactured goods could be produced in 1929 with only 70 percent of the man years of labor required in 1920; employment in manufacturing rose only slightly in the period despite great increases in production, because of that increased productive efficiency. Meanwhile, employment in mining fell by 200,000. Overall employment rose by 16 percent, while the labor force (those working and seeking work) rose by 21 percent. As manufacturing, mining, and agriculture hired fewer people, jobs opened up in distribution, finance, and services—but not enough jobs, as indicated by the gap between them and the labor force. For data of this sort (and much else besides), consult U.S. Bureau of the Census, *Historical Statistics of the United States, Colonial Times to 1970* (U.S.G.P.O., 1975). The annual *Economic Report of the President* * is useful and convenient for a broad range of aggregative data, but its scope is narrower both in subject matter and time.

the twenties; this development also lies at the base of an explanation for the depression of the thirties.[20]

In the midst of the prosperity of the twenties, trouble had begun to develop even in the dynamic sector. The impulses of the corporate leaders of that sector, and their power to realize those impulses, disguised the trouble and postponed the collapse. It is quite likely that the collapse was therefore somewhat more severe than it otherwise might have been. The troubles appeared in the two leading industries: automobiles and housing construction.

Let us examine first the automobile industry.[21] There are three kinds of car buyers: new owners, those replacing an old with a new car, and used-car buyers. By 1924 new car buyers were no longer the focus of the auto industry's attention; their numbers had begun to shrink. What was needed was stepped-up replacement, and a large used-car market to support it. In turn, this led to what has since become the hallmark of consumer goods production and distribution: deliberate product obsolescence, extensive advertising, and consumer finance. General Motors took the lead in all three; advertising, yearly model changes, trade-ins, and living in constant debt were thereby elevated to what many take to be the American way of life. They also postponed the day when the industry would find itself with chronic excess capacity, as in the 1930's. However, as Soule points out:

> . . . installment buying could not obviate the eventual retardation of expansion. There was certain to come a time when all families who would utilize installment loans were loaded up with all the debt they could carry. In the long run the only possible means of keeping these new industries expanding would have been to augment the cash purchasing power of the consumers through sufficient increases in wages and salaries or through sufficient reduction in retail prices.[22]

[20] Because of the importance of the U.S. in the world economy, and vice versa, a complete explanation of the severity of the Depression must give high importance to the weakness of the world economy in the twenties, and its utter collapse in the thirties. But much of that explanation fits well within a "dual economy" framework for the world economy—with the industrial nations dynamic, and the raw materials-supplying (Third World) nations exploited and depressed. That will become part of the discussion in Chapter 7. For the twenties, and an explanation of the Depression that depends squarely on the weakening position of the Third World countries, see W. Arthur Lewis, *Economic Survey, 1919–1939*° (London: Allen & Unwin, 1949), especially Chapter 12. This small book provides a useful summary of developments in the major industrial nations in the interwar period.

[21] Paul M. Sweezy, "Cars and Cities," *Monthly Review* (April, 1973), provides a succinct historical analysis of the automobile industry in its broader meanings, as well as its impact on the environment, which will be taken up in Chapter 6.

[22] *Prosperity Decade*, p. 288. But, despite great increases in productivity, prices did not decline in the twenties (after 1922). As for wages, they rose 8 percent in manu-

The same kinds of problems affected the construction and sale of housing, with variations due to the different nature of the product. Again, Soule:

> Only a fraction of the population was able to buy or rent new houses or new apartments at the prices charged, and the number which could do so provided an upper limit to the market. After a few years of active building, this limit was being approached [by 1926]. There was still an actual need for better housing in large quantities, but this need could not be converted into a market demand unless either the number of those who could afford the housing was increased by sufficient enlargement of income, or the prices of the new housing could be materially decreased. Neither of these developments occurred.[23]

There is a vital difference between the prosperity of the period encompassing the 1920's and the ensuing depression, and the period since World War II. Although there were six or so recessions in the latter period, they were relatively minor with none showing signs of becoming a major depression; until, perhaps, 1974. What differentiates the two periods is the changed role of the State. The change is well-symbolized by the data on government expenditures, which do not, however, inform us on the full meaning of expanded State power.

In 1929, the combined expenditures of federal, state, and local governments, as a percent of gross national product (GNP),[24] were about 10 percent; in 1975 they were over 30 percent, and rising. In the earlier year, such expenditures were about *half* of total *private investment* expenditures, whereas by 1975 they were more than 50 percent *greater* than those expenditures. We have here one mark of how the structure of the economy has changed in the interim. If the structure has changed so much, the economic theory that presumes to tell us how the economy functions must change accordingly; but it has not. Keynesian theory still considers private investment as *the* key variable, and the role of government has

---

facturing and railroads, stayed the same for farm laborers, and declined 14 percent for miners. Meanwhile (1923–1929), corporate profits rose 62 percent, while the national income rose by 21 percent; and, tax policies were changed to lower the taxes paid as a percentage of income the higher the income (one percent reduction at $5000, 31 percent reduction for incomes above $1 million.)

[23] Ibid.

[24] GNP, as noted in Chapter 3, is defined as the dollar value of the total annual output of *final* goods and services (where "final" means that a good is counted only once—for instance, cotton cloth going into shirts is not counted until the shirt is sold at retail, except for what might be inventoried at the end of a year in intermediate stages). GNP only counts marketed goods and services; it takes no account of valuable activities that are not marketed (such as housework), or illegal activities of any sort. But the costs of both gasoline and smog control devices, for instance, are counted, as is napalm and the like.

not been incorporated into the theory—nor can it be, without a theory of the State that will allow such incorporation. Wherever such a theoretical advance might carry us, it would surely carry us toward a new "political economy."

Before resuming our analysis of the movement from prosperity into depression, a further comment on the concept of the dual economy is in order. As we have seen, in the 1920's a duality in the economy had become pronounced. The monopolistic sector, and those benefitting from it, moved dynamically through the 1920's; the competitive sector lagged behind, afflicting those dependent upon it. What was relatively insignificant then, as the discussion above makes clear, was the third sector emphasized by O'Connor: the State sector. Governmental expenditures were small as a percentage, and they were dominated by state and local expenditures (mostly for highways and education) rather than by federal expenditures. States and localities move *with* the direction taken by the economy; the desired role of governmental fiscal policy is to move in the opposite direction (to stimulate a weak economy, and restrain an inflating one). States and localities do not have the fiscal power (or, by their constitutions, the right) to operate in the desired way, and in the twenties no pressures were being placed on the federal government to do so.

Collapse and Depression

As seen by contemporaries, the twenties was a period not only of prosperity, but of endless prosperity. Irving Fisher (the Paul Samuelson of the economics profession at the time) proclaimed, only a few months before the Depression began, that the economy had solved the problem of the business cycle and that it was settled on a high plateau of endless prosperity. The well-off believed him, until, within the next year, many were desperate enough to commit suicide from the shock of their losses.

Individual losses for speculators were indeed great, but of more importance was what happened to the economy. The collapse was so substantial as to be virtually incomprehensible to those born since World War II. Between 1929 and 1933, GNP fell from $104 billion to $56 billion; per capita disposable income (after personal taxes) fell from $678 to $360; the income of farm proprietors from $5.7 billion to (in 1932) $1.7 billion; and unemployment rose from 1.5 million to 12.8 million—25 percent of the labor force! [25]

The quantitative disasters suggested by those numbers are impressive enough, and they were staggering at the time; but, quantitatively, there

[25] Data taken from *Historical Statistics of the United States* and *Economic Report of the President* (1976).

was more to the Depression than that and more still when its qualitative impact is taken into account. The Depression left no sector of the economy standing upright; the entire capitalist world underwent the same collapse (as did the dependent nonindustrial countries). Each nation had its own crisis, and each had a share of a worldwide crisis. Then as now, however, the United States was the leading economy, and, as W. Arthur Lewis says,

> It is clear that the center of the depression was the United States of America, in the sense that most of what happened elsewhere has to be explained in terms of the American contraction, while that contraction is hardly explicable in any but internal terms. The slump was also worse in the United States than anywhere else (with the possible exception of Germany, whose severe contraction was a direct result of American events).[26]

A recession or a depression is a process of contraction, which, whatever else it means, implies a serious underutilization of the society's productive resources. Unemployment is the most tragic measure of such underutilization, but as such it does not capture the imagination of business leaders unless it leads to social turbulence. What is of greater moment to those in business is the implication of shrinking markets for the profitable use of their productive assets. Just how far markets contracted in the 1930's is well-signified by figures for capacity utilization. Industrial producers usually find it desirable (depending upon the technology of their industry) to utilize capacity at rates lying between 85 and 95 percent. Already by 1928, the figures had begun to drop below 85 percent; but witness what happened in the thirties:[27]

1930	66 percent	1935	68 percent
1931	53 percent	1936	80 percent
1932	42 percent	1937	83 percent
1933	52 percent	1938	60 percent
1934	58 percent	1939	72 percent

[26] Lewis, *Economic Survey*, p. 52. Lewis notes that U.S. national income, a narrower figure than GNP, "contracted by 38 percent, and the unemployment figure increased to fifteen millions." The official American statistic for unemployment, used above, was 12.8 million; but that is quite probably an understatement. In 1929, U.S. industrial production was 46 percent of the total industrial production of the twenty-four most important producers in the world. (Lewis, p. 57.)

[27] Donald Streever, *Capacity Utilization and Business Investment*, University of Illinois *Bulletin*, vol. 57, no. 55 (March, 1960), p. 65; quoted in Baran and Sweezy, *Monopoly Capital*, p. 242. From 1969 through 1972, the rate vacillated around 73 percent; since 1974 it has stayed around 75 percent. The lowest rate in the twenties was 82 percent (1928).

When business is bad in a capitalist society, everyone is in economic trouble. Therefore, we may find a close correlation between the capacity utilization figures and unemployment rates for the corresponding years (remembering that the official rates are, if anything, understated):[28]

1930	8.7 percent	1935	20.1 percent
1931	15.9 percent	1936	16.9 percent
1932	23.6 percent	1937	14.3 percent
1933	24.9 percent	1938	19.0 percent
1934	21.7 percent	1939	17.2 percent

In 1941, the year the United States entered World War II, unemployment was 10 percent; it was still 4.7 percent in 1942.[29]

The decline in utilized capacity and the rise in unemployment after 1929, and the persistence of bad news on both scores until the U.S. entered the war in 1941, was matched by the performance of the economy as reflected in the following components of GNP listed in Table 4–2. Note that GNP did not regain its 1929 level until 1937, then fell back, and barely surpassed the 1929 level again in 1939.[30]

In studying Table 4–2, note first the comparative magnitudes of the several components—consumption, investment, net exports, and government; and note especially how their relationships have changed between 1929 and the present. The one stable relationship in that period is between GNP and personal consumption, with the latter running at about two-thirds of the former (except for the years of World War II). The most volatile component is gross private domestic investment. The one that rises most as a percentage of GNP is government *purchases*, from 1929 to the present. Today, government *expenditures* (including transfers) occupies about one-third of GNP in current dollars.

As might be expected, per capita consumption dropped seriously after 1929. Population increased by about nine million from then until 1938;

[28] *Historical Statistics of the U.S.*, Part 1, p. 135.

[29] The rate has gone close to 7 percent twice since then (in 1957 and 1961) and has been under 6 percent in all the other years, until 1975, when it rose to 8.5 percent. For three years (1943–1945) the rate was under 2 percent; for another three years (1951–1953) near 3 percent; for four years (1966–1969) under 4 percent; and all those "good" years were years of hot war, which added substantial military expenditures to already high and ongoing military expenditures. Note also the move from 2, to 3, to 4, to 5 percent, even in war years.

[30] The main components of expenditure are "personal consumption," "gross private domestic investment," "net exports of goods and services," and "government *purchases* of goods and services." "Government purchases" is a lower figure than "government expenditures," which includes "transfers"—social security benefits, welfare payments, and the like, at all levels of government. In 1975, federal "transfers" were $132 billion, greater than "purchases" by the federal government, which were $121 billion.

TABLE 4–2 Selected Categories of Gross National Product or Expenditure (In Billions of 1958 Dollars, for Selected Years)

	Total GNP	Personal Consumption Expenditures	Gross Private Domestic Investment	Net Exports	Government Purchases of Goods and Services		
					Total	Fed.	State and Local
1929	204	140	40	1.5	22	4	19
1930	184	130	27	1.4	24	4	20
1931	169	126	17	.9	25	4	21
1932	144	115	5	.6	24	5	20
1933	142	113	5	.0	23	6	17
1934	154	118	9	.3	27	8	19
1935	170	126	18	−1.0*	27	8	19
1936	193	138	24	−1.2	32	12	20
1937	203	143	30	− .7	31	12	19
1938	193	140	17	1.9	34	13	21
1939	209	148	25	1.3	35	13	23
1940	227	156	33	2.1	36	15	21
1941	264	165	42	.4	56	36	20
1942	298	161	21	−2.1	117	99	18
1943	337	166	13	−5.9	164	148	17
1944	361	171	14	−5.8	182	165	16
1945	355	183	20	−3.8	156	140	17
1946	313	204	52	8.4	48	30	18
1950	355	231	69	2.7	53	25	28
1955	438	274	75	3.2	85	51	34
1960	488	316	72	4.3	95	51	44
1965	618	398	99	6.2	115	58	57
1966	658	418	109	4.2	127	65	61
1967	675	430	101	3.6	140	75	66
1970	723	478	103	2.3	139	65	74
1974	821	540	127	9.0	146	57	89

* The minus sign for net exports signifies an excess of *imports* of goods and services, i.e., net imports.

SOURCE: Derived from U.S. Department of Labor, *Handbook of Labor Statistics 1975—Reference Edition*. (U.S. Government Printing Office, 1975) pp. 446–47. This edition of the *Handbook* has series generally going back to 1929 (and in a few cases earlier than that); beginning with the 1976 edition, data go back no further than 1967. Figures have been rounded off to the nearest whole number (except for net exports); consequently for government the total is occasionally greater or less than the sum of federal plus state and local. All figures are in "1958"—that is, "constant"— dollars, a procedure aimed at achieving comparable magnitudes by "deflating" for price changes over time. As an example of the difference when "current" dollars are used, GNP for 1929 would be $103 billion, and for 1970, $974 billion.

but personal consumption expenditures were the same for both years, and of course much lower in most of the intervening decade. Investment almost vanishes in 1932 and 1933; and, in fact, *net* investment did in 1933 (where "net" refers to increasing productive capacity, while "gross" also includes support and maintenance of existing capacity). During that year utilization rates in industry were at about the half mark, and expectations for the future were gloomy at best.[31] Gross private domestic investment does not begin to approach its 1929 proportion to GNP until 1946, after which time, in response to rapidly growing domestic, military, and foreign markets, it rises rapidly.

The government columns are especially notable, given the general understanding—or misunderstanding—most Americans have about the *spending* impact of the New Deal in the 1930's. Until 1940, federal purchases remained consistently lower than state and local purchases, which themselves remained stable through the decade. Between 1940 and 1941 —when President Roosevelt was said to have completed the transition from being "Dr. New Deal" to "Dr. Win-the-War"—federal purchases more than doubled, after which they rose to the point where in 1944 they (plus state and local purchases) amounted to *half* of GNP (with only a slight increase in consumption and a drop in private investment in the same years). A further comment on the alteration in federal spending rates is called for and will help to put the New Deal in perspective.

The New Deal and World War II

The period of the New Deal was intensely controversial and, not for the first or the last time in our history, one in which both supporters and opponents of New Deal policies took positions they would later alter. To understand the period, it is necessary to make several distinctions: one, between the sub-periods of the New Deal, and two, between the two main activities that gave it its name—deficit spending and institutional reform.

First, we should distinguish the "periods" of the New Deal or, more properly, of the Roosevelt Administration. FDR was first elected president in 1932, and died in 1945, at the beginning of his fourth term. The policies of the "first New Deal" extend from 1933 into 1935; the second —or "real" New Deal—goes into 1938. From 1938 on, Roosevelt is gen-

---

[31] The low rates of gross *private* domestic investment in the peak war years (of World War II) may be explained by looking at the high rates of federal purchases. The government built and paid for war plants, which were sold off at bargain basement prices to private corporations after the war.

erally seen as having become obsessed with the coming world war. Consistent with his electoral campaign, when he first took office Roosevelt stood for little in the way of institutional change; but he was of course a new president, faced with our most major depression, already in its fourth and most severe year. Essentially and initially, Roosevelt pursued the policies laid down by his predecessor, Herbert Hoover, but the unforgettable FDR spirit was different. His policies were emergency policies, but they were "conservative." In this respect, FDR was at one with the Democratic Party at the time: in the campaign of 1932, "National Democratic party leaders criticized Hoover not because he had done too little but because he had done too much. [Their] main criticism . . . was that [Hoover] was a profligate spender. In seeking to defeat progressive measures, Republicans in Congress could count on the votes of a majority of Democrats on almost every roll call." [32]

Roosevelt's statement that they "had nothing to fear but fear itself" was doubtless a good tonic to the fallen spirits of American workers, farmers, businessmen, and speculators. However, more than a tonic was necessary for a body as damaged as the American economy. In that respect, the first months of the New Deal were not encouraging: the federal government spent less in FDR's first five months than had been spent by Hoover in the same period of the preceding year.[33]

Like Hoover, Roosevelt was faced with massive unemployment, and an almost total collapse of agricultural, industrial, and financial markets:

Item: The Dow-Jones dollar average per share of sixty-five stocks (different from their index method of today) fell from $125 to $36 between 1929 and 1933. (Mitchell, p. 438)

Item: The average number of bank suspensions in 1928 and 1929 was 566; in 1930, 1931, and 1932 the average number was 1,700. (Ibid., p. 128)

Item: Merchandise exports fell from $5.2 billion to $1.7 billion in 1933. (Ibid., p. 444)

Item: The value of building construction of all sorts was $4 billion in 1925, $3 billion in 1929, and $500 million in 1933. (Ibid., p. 447)

[32] William E. Leuchtenburg, Franklin D. Roosevelt and the New Deal * (New York: Harper & Row, 1963), p. 3.

[33] See Broadus Mitchell, Depression Decade, cited earlier, p. 40. This is an unexciting but thorough treatment of the economic history of the period; and it has a full bibliography for further work. Taken together with Leuchtenburg's political history and bibliography, it will enable the reader to get a good grip on the depression years, especially if some of the general and fictional works noted in the Reading Suggestions at the end of this chapter are read.

Item: Farm prices (at wholesale) fell by more than half, 1929–1933. (Ibid., p. 448)

As we have noted earlier, at least one-quarter of the labor force was unemployed by 1933. In this early period of FDR's presidency he emphasized "relief" and "recovery"; the second New Deal (beginning in 1935) undertook the more controversial "reform." The distinction is somewhat too sharp, as will be seen; the point remains that the "liberal" reforms of the New Deal await 1935, for reasons to be discussed.

The major steps taken by Roosevelt in 1933 were taken in the name of emergency and in a context in which no opposition to the new president was feasible; Roosevelt had what was called a "honeymoon" for his first "Hundred Days." He closed all banks for four days, by proclamation, and embargoed the export of gold; with Congress he created the Agricultural Adjustment Administration, which followed the path laid down by Hoover in 1928 in supporting farm prices (at the 1909–1914 average), and went beyond Hoover by also limiting production. FDR legislated several "emergency relief acts" which provided simple relief (money payments) and work (usually make-work) relief, and which also continued and expanded the Reconstruction Finance Corporation (from Hoover's days), a forerunner of the sort of federal financial assistance given to Lockheed in 1971. To attempt to bring some order out of the shambles in the securities markets—a shambles in no small part due to the assorted malpractices and downright crookedness characterizing the stock and bond markets—the Securities Act of 1933 and the Securities and Exchange Act of 1934 were passed, providing for supervision and regulation of stock and bond markets. The powers of the Federal Reserve System were expanded, deposit insurance was enacted to prevent the recurrence of bank runs, in which panicky depositors lined up to retrieve money that wasn't there for all (nor can be in a fractional reserve system such as exists in all modern economies), and the Home Owners Loan Corporation was created to refinance home mortgages. And much more.

Probably most indicative of the conservative-mindedness of these first years was the National Recovery Administration (NRA); although "right-wing" is a better term than conservative to describe the NRA if right-wing is meant to suggest a design to disrupt and reverse the process of social change to place more power in the hands of the already powerful. The NRA (established by the National Industrial Recovery Act [NIRA] of 1933) deliberately replaced the "free market" as the approved and impersonal arbiter of production and price with hundreds of "code authorities." These usually consisted of the leading representatives of the business trade associations in each industry, associations in which policies were generally established by the most powerful firms. In the name of establishing codes of "fair competition," the code authorities could set prices below which members could not sell; that is, the NRA made price competition illegal and agreements to restrict production (or virtually *any* agreements) common. In effect, the NRA suspended the antitrust laws.

The NIRA also, in its Section 7A, gave labor the right to organize and to bargain collectively but provided no means of enforcement to make those "rights" meaningful. That would await 1935, and the Wagner (National Labor Relations) Act. The NRA was declared unconstitutional in May, 1935, its function in part to be performed thereafter by the "Fair Trade Laws."

Some slight economic recovery had taken place by 1935, but there were still 20 percent or more unemployed. Social unrest had spread over the country in all regions, evoking memories of the 1890's, only more so. After a long period of decline, socialist ideas took on a new life and received increasing attention, and for the first time explicitly fascist groups began to organize successfully. Neither those on the Right or Left had any national electoral significance, but their growing appeal on local and state levels and in workers' circles began to move to the front of the political stage.

The Communist Party of the United States probably had its greatest influence in this period, mostly through its successful organization activities in trade unions; they also constituted a bloc of only slightly critical support for the New Deal.[34] The Socialist Party revived, and also constituted a supporting bloc for the New Deal, pulling it slightly to the left. Father Coughlin's National Union for Social Justice was the leading fascist-type group, most effective in the Detroit region, serving up a stew combining racial, religious, and class hatred with economic appeals. Both the demogogically appealing and the poisonous sides of Populism ran through these movements of Right and Left, as they did in Huey Long's "Share the Wealth" movement in Louisiana and Upton Sinclair's "End Poverty in California" movement. The turbulence grew and spread.

Roosevelt was repeatedly and pointedly made aware of all this dissatisfaction. The Second New Deal was his response; his overwhelming reelection in 1936 was his reward for moving with the political winds of the day. The period from 1933 into 1935 was not entirely illiberal; nor was the period from 1935 to 1938 entirely liberal. But the change in emphasis was as obvious at the time as it is today. For the aged, especially, the Social Security Act of 1935 was a beginning, if a weak one. The legislation saw to it that the rich would continue *not* to pay for the alleviation of the poor, irrespective of age; but a crack in the wall of social unconcern had been made. By far the most controversial aspect of the New Deal was

[34] See James Weinstein, "The Left, Old and New," in *Socialist Revolution* 2, no. 4 (July-August 1972), pp. 29 ff.

the Wagner-Connelly Act, which not only reaffirmed the right of workers to organize and bargain collectively, but spelled out a list of unfair practices by employers and set up a National Labor Relations Board to adjudicate disputes. This "Magna Carta" of labor was a watershed in American history—a watershed whose affirmative meaning labor had to fight for continuously, however, until World War II. The major cause of labor disputes between 1935 and 1941 was union security, presumably *guaranteed* by the Wagner Act. All this, despite the fact that the Supreme Court upheld the constitutionality of the Wagner Act in 1938. As with the Depression itself, it took World War II to bring an at least temporary end to the perennial conflict between labor and business. The war not only enhanced production enormously and in doing so created a shortage of labor—with altogether sixteen millions entering the armed forces—but it also brought cost-plus contracts to assure profits for business, a free hand for labor to organize in war plants, and thus maximum production for the government.[35]

Secular Stagnation?

So the Great Depression came to an end, requiring the most massive war in history and its attendant demands upon production and manpower to turn the trick. Why had the depression been so stubborn? The only serious attempt to come to grips with that question during the depression years originated with Professor Alvin Hansen of Harvard, the "translator" of Keynes *General Theory* into the U. S. setting. Keynes's focus was static and short-run; Hansen applied the abstract theory to the historical conditions of the U. S., and in doing so he developed what was called a theory of "secular stagnation," or of "economic maturity." Hansen argued that three principal factors contributed to the long-run expansion of the United States through the nineteenth and into the early twentieth century: (1) rapid and sustained population growth, (2) geographic expansion over the continent, and (3) intermittent waves of technological change (especially the railroad in the nineteenth and the automobile in the twentieth century). These three processes in combination had re-

[35] The Taft-Hartley Act of 1947 was designed to limit and reduce the strength of unions. Although vetoed by President Truman, it was made into law by a Congress which, in overriding the presidential veto, revealed how very strong the voice of business was in Congress, and how temporary the peace between business and labor. As will be seen in Chapter 8, the State has been quite successful in more recent years in taming the chiefs of organized labor, mostly with the carrot of job-creating military expenditures.

sulted in an interacting and long-term expansion of both investment and consumer expenditures. Thus the normal cyclical contractions of capitalist accumulation were swiftly ended and followed by ever-higher levels of output, employment, and income. However, Hansen noted, population growth and geographic expansion diminished by the 1920's, and the burden of economic expansion thus fell heavily on technological change, which, though continuing, could not be expected to rise to the challenge alone.[36]

Nor could the economics profession rise to Hansen's analytical challenge; narrow though his argument was, for what it purported to explain, it was both too broad and too unsettling to be more than casually dismissed. The normal tendency of conventional economists to ignore the bearers of bad news was aided and abetted in this instance, of course, by the onset of World War II. In the long expansion that took hold during and after the war, Hansen's stagnation thesis became nothing more than a quaint memory; those few among the mainstream older economists who had once grappled with it saw the sustained expansion as a clear refutation of Hansen's dour analysis. They were wrong.

Hansen had not maintained that stagnation could not be overcome; rather he had proposed that to *offset* the inability of the "private" economy to create satisfactory levels of production and jobs the State would have to fill the gap. Since World War II the State has, of course, done so—in ways that go beyond (and, ethically, beneath) anything proposed by Hansen. As has been suggested earlier and will be pursued further below, massive military expenditures, facilitation of U. S. overseas in expansion, underwriting of "social consumption and investment" (such as welfare and highways) and of debt accumulation, and an active monetary and fiscal policy were all employed by the State to transform stagnation into expansion. The ensuing expansion did more than to rescue mature capitalism, however; we shall see that its ways and means, the ways and means of monopoly capitalism, also bred further structural imbalance—and stagflation.

Mainstream economists, having successfully ignored Hansen's theoretical challenge and having failed to integrate the role of the imperialist monopoly capitalist State into their analysis of economic behavior, now remind one of doctors who, having administered enormous doses of drugs to suppress the symptoms of disease, go on to diagnose and pre-

---

[36] See Alvin H. Hansen, *Full Recovery or Stagnation?* (New York: Norton, 1938). For a more radical "stagnation theory" that systematically relates monopoly structures to the accumulation process, see Josef Steindl, *Maturity and Stagnation in American Capitalism* (New York: Monthly Review Press, 1976. First published in 1952). Baran and Sweezy's *Monopoly Capital* relies heavily upon Steindl. A review of stagnation theory, and a useful criticism of its strengths and weaknesses, may be found in "The Status of Stagnation Theory," by H. R. Smith, *Southern Economic Journal* 15 (October, 1948 and January, 1949).

scribe for the patient as though unaffected by either disease *or* drugs. Thus, in a widely-used text by a Harvard economist, we read:

> As it turned out, the postwar economy of the United States was far more buoyant than the stagnationists had anticipated, and it is reasonable to say that these theorists had been unduly influenced by the Great Depression of the 1930's.[37]

Let us continue with a summary examination of the changes during and after World War II (with a fuller discussion in Chapter 8), changes that allowed such illusions to be sustained.

Warfare, Welfare, and Economic Growth

The Roosevelt years had been dubbed "New Deal," so it was probably inevitable that succeeding administrations would be given their own nicknames, as indeed they were. Truman's "Fair Deal" was followed by what Adlai Stevenson called Eisenhower's "Big Deal." Kennedy initiated the "New Frontier" (which in the Johnson Administration's "Great Society" was revealed to have more geographic than institutional meanings); the years since have been called the "Raw Deal" by some and the "Cruel Deal" by others. The labels tell very little, but the repetition of the term *deal* is not without a meaning of its own. Since the Depression, what Kolko calls "political capitalism" has meant an endless series of deals between various power blocs within the U.S., and also between American and foreign power groups.

The basic techniques of this modern political economy had been discovered, or rediscovered, in the Wilson administration, and especially during World War I. However, the euphoria and dynamism of the twenties caused relaxation for the powerful and helplessness for the rest. The Depression and the Roosevelt years implanted once more, and for the foreseeable future, that process of power-broking.

Neither the institutional reforms nor the deficit spending of the New Deal had substantial effect before World War II. Precedents were established, however, and habits and experience developed. The revelation of just how useful close relationships with the growing State could be for business, labor, and agriculture combined with the massive spending of World War II to place the impact of the New Deal on the years *after* World War II.[38] For purposes of this chapter, that impact can be under-

[37] Richard T. Gill, *Economics* (Pacific Palisades, Calif.: Goodyear, 1975).

[38] A suggestion of how minimal the New Deal years were in terms of federal spending is shown by the fact that in no year of the thirties, despite massive unemployment, did the federal deficit rise to $5 billion; and in only one year, 1936 (an election year), did it exceed $4 billion.

stood in its effects on the process of economic expansion. (Domestic policies that affected relationships between classes and groups at home, and foreign policies that promoted geographic expansion will be examined in succeeding chapters.)

In aggregative terms, the striking fact is that in the years since the end of World War II GNP has never dropped in current dollars, and until the 1970's dropped only infinitesimally (in 1947, 1954, and 1958) in constant dollars. After a tiny drop in 1970, GNP fell two consecutive years, 1974 and 1975, for the first time in the postwar period. Even more revealing is the record of disposable personal income (income of persons after federal income taxes and transfers): after 1946, real disposable personal income never fell, until 1974. The key to this process of sustained growth—that is, the absence of even a serious recession, let alone a depression—is to be found in the record of federal purchases, and in that category, the key factor is purchases geared to the military.[39] Although, as we shall discuss shortly, even that may not be working any more.

Between 1946 and 1975 federal purchases of goods and services totaled almost $2 *trillion*. Of that, 75 percent, or $1.5 *trillion* were for "defense" expenditures; over 10 percent of the remainder was for highway construction. This says nothing about state and local purchases, which rose steadily from about $10 billion in 1946 to 208 billion in 1975. By 1975, in addition, federal governmental transfers came to 132 billion. When all this is put together with exports of goods and services (which rose one-and-a-half times in the same period), a process also aided substantially by State policies, it becomes easy to understand why the American economy suffered no major relapse from buoyancy after 1946. Naturally, going along with this was a steady increase in private investment and in consumer expenditures with the explosion of suburban housing and commercial developments, and the rapid spread of automobile and consumer durables ownership.

The policies that underlay this expansion were initiated at the top levels of business, government, agriculture, and labor; but they were almost universally supported at all levels of society. Consciously and unconsciously, since the Depression Americans have allowed and encouraged the creation of a political economy that, whatever else it has meant, was designed never to allow a repetition of severe depression: it is the political economy of monopoly capitalism. Some of the feaures of monopoly capitalism have been discussed earlier, and others will be examined in later chapters; here it seems appropriate to summarize the main de-

[39] Our reference here has been to *federal* activities. Between 1940 and 1970, while personal income (incomes of persons before taxes) rose 926 percent, *all* taxes (federal, state, and local) rose by 1,840 percent—twice as fast. *Wall Street Journal*, November 13, 1972.

velopments that have shaped the accumulation process since World War II.

None of these developments was unique to the post–World War II era, but all have been more extensive, deeper and stronger, and their existence more consciously enhanced and coordinated than earlier; nor could any one development have persisted or had any effects except in combination with all the others. These developments include: (1) the vast increase in both the absolute and the relative power of supercorporations—within and between industries, sectors, and nations; (2) the equally striking increase in both the quantitative and the qualitative role of the State in all functional and geographic levels; (3) the strengthening and spread of "consumerism" in the United States and its replication in all of the leading capitalist economies and many of the lesser ones; (4) the re-creation and strengthening of a global capitalist empire, under American leadership; (5) the concomitant growth of a "military-industrial complex"; (6) and, required and facilitated by all these changes, the extension and refinement of mass communications techniques for commercial and political exhortation and manipulation: the lubricant of monopoly capitalism.

Taking hold in the early 1950's and running strongly by the early 1960's, sustained economic expansion became the rule and the continuing expectation in the capitalist world among businesses, consumers, and governments. Such expansion produced a state of economic euphoria and, not for the first time, an accompanying relaxation of customary prudence. Interestingly, *none* of the major institutional stimuli just referred to could find support in the traditional social philosophy of capitalist societies—neither monopoly nor its giant state, neither imperialism nor militarism, not even consumerism (with its emphasis upon borrowing instead of thrift, upon leisure rather than work). But the strength and the pervasiveness of the economic expansion deflected attention from and altered attitudes toward such ways and means, as it also obscured the negative possibilities that might flow from such a process. In the late 1960's, U. S. economists, echoing their predecessors of the late 1920's, came to believe that "the business cycle has been tamed," just as stagflation loomed up ahead.

Stagflation and More

In 1973, of the twenty-four capitalist nations that comprise the OECD (Organization for Economic Cooperation and Development, accounting for over 90 percent of world capitalist production), over half had double-digit inflation rates; in 1974, only two (West Germany and Switzerland) did not. In the capitalist dependencies, such as Brazil and Chile, rates were running anywhere from 35 to 350 percent per annum. In the same years, a worldwide recession began, bringing with it rising unemployment and shrinking markets within and between nations. Although inflation and unemployment rates have generally decreased, their levels are still serious and the combination is unprecedented: only a few years earlier the idea that the rates could be simultaneously high and persist would have been thought impossible.

By mainstream economists, it still is: whether in government or in the academic world, analyses of the developments of the early and mid-1970's explain the process as short run both in origin and in prospect: "normalcy" is just around the corner. But reality has also crept into their speculations, if by the side door: for many years, economists accepted the "Phillips Curve" as revealing a basic truth about the relationship between unemployment and inflation—to reduce either from about 3 percent requires increasing the other. The Phillips Curve was developed by a British economist; when translated for U. S. conditions by Paul Samuelson and Robert Solow (and called the "PSS Curve"), it asserted that price stability would require a 5.5 percent annual unemployment rate, and that full employment (defined as 3 percent unemployed) would require price inflation of 4.5 percent. However, as Dale Tussing has shown, their calculations included the years of both the Great Depression and World War II; when those years are omitted, "the 'cost' of price stability turns out to be an unemployment rate of around 6.5 percent, while the 'cost' of full employment may be an inflation rate as high as 9 percent!" [40] Later we shall argue that the presumed "inexorability" of the Phillips Curve is but an excuse for harming the relatively powerless to the gain of those who preside over the status quo.

It appears that global capitalism, including the U. S. economy, has begun a process quite different from anything in the past: one in which a 1930's-type of depression is unlikely, but one in which unemployment will remain serious (between 6 and 10 percent) and in which the means of keeping it from becoming as serious as the much higher rates of the 1930's will produce continuing inflation (also between 6 and 10 percent). But this is to point to something whose origins and implications go beyond the worrisome aggregative performance of the economy, which may thus be seen as the symptom of a deeper malady: the present system has lost its vitality, and we are probably in an era of transition. [41]

---

[40] A. Dale Tussing, *Poverty in a Dual Economy* * (New York: St. Martin's Press, 1975), p. 190. This is an excellent analysis of poverty in its many dimensions, and in its discussions of duality—in the economy, in labor markets, in welfare programs—it is valuable companion reading for many of the arguments put forth in this book.

[41] The general argument is developed in my "Stagflation and the Political Economy of Decadent Monopoly Capitalism," *Monthly Review,* October 1976. A comparison

In short, the social relations that were necessary and beneficial for the capitalist economies of the 1950's and 1960's, and whose continuation remains necessary in the 1970's—lest a worse fate befall—now yield growing troubles, only one of which is stagflation. In the language of sociology, what was *functional* for capitalism has now become, increasingly, *dysfunctional*. In other words, monopoly capitalism as a system is in decay— where the metaphor is meant to suggest a process that is protracted and confusing, rather than swift and obvious. The means that enabled capitalism to regain health and strength after World War II now work to eat away at its strength. Let us examine some of the ways in which the developments that constitute monopoly capitalism have turned back on themselves:

1. The era of big business and big government is perforce the era of vast and unavoidable private and public bureaucracy. The costs, wastes, and inefficiencies associated with their existence, functioning, and continuing growth have come to compete with the positive effects of the incomes generated in and by them—as, with the passage of time and changing circumstances, the essential functions of bureaucracy serve less for creating new bases of strength and more for holding on to what has been gained earlier.

2. The normal practices within and between businesses, and between businesses and politicians and governments—classified as "corruption"— have, with the exfoliation of giant corporate and governmental entities and of their functions, deepened and spread to new and spectacular levels, producing financial and political difficulties for businesses and governments.

3. The creation by North American, Western European, and Japanese capital of productive capacities for durable consumer and capital goods was, of course, a major stimulus in the long expansion. More recently, these facilities have become duplicative, producing intense competition for critical raw materials and for markets, with consequent whipsaw effects—the competition for raw materials yielding upward pressures on costs, the competition for markets causing downward pressures on sales and (in the absence of effective collusion) prices.

4. The stupefying increases in the levels of debt and the spread of dubious financial practices from the 1960's on—for individuals, businesses, and governments, nationally and internationally—were essential to finance and to sustain the unprecedented expansion; it is now known that this

---

between the present and the interwar period is developed extensively in my "Accumulation and Crisis in U. S. Capitalism," *Socialist Revolution*, Number 24 (Vol. 5, No. 2), June, 1975. In the preceding and subsequent issues, respectively, Samir Amin and André Gunder Frank explore the crisis in comparable ways.

process has brought about precarious debt/revenue ratios for all concerned, ratios whose threat to stability can be lessened, if at all, only through heightened economic expansion—in turn requiring a degree of further indebtedness which is, among other problems, realistically implausible.[42]

5. The replacement of traditional imperialism by neocolonialism (to be examined in Chapter 7) was vital in providing Third World economic stimuli and support to the expansion of the major powers. The military expenditures facilitated and required by that effort, and by the concomitant Cold War with the Soviet Union and China, also did much to sustain economic expansion. However, the great increase in military expenditures (most inflationary of all forms of effective demand, other things being equal) occasioned by the Indochina War, taken together with the most vigorous segment of the expansion (the mid-1960's), was a critical addition to already increasing inflationary pressures. Because these same years had relatively low unemployment, it was easier for those previously unorganized to organize and, along with already organized labor, to make and to achieve wage and nonwage demands, which intensified inflationary pressures and tax needs while simultaneously straining profits.

6. And then, of course, the war in Indochina was lost, which must be seen as one of several factors that contributed to the subsequent further shrinkage of the neocolonial area and of the power of the major capitalist nations vis-à-vis the Third World. We may add that the enormous amount of military expenditures, although they came to mean "more bang for a buck" as military technology became ever more complex and capital-using, also came to mean "fewer jobs for the buck." *If* government expenditures were now made on school construction or public housing instead of on arms, for example, it is reliably calculated by government agencies that 30 percent to 100 percent more jobs would be created per federal dollar of expenditure. (Space expenditures create fewer than one-third the jobs of straight military expenditures.)

7. The swift alteration of rural/urban and occupational patterns, and, within the cities, of the pre–World War II urban political economies, was an integral and profitable ingredient of the postwar accumulation process. Investment and incomes boomed with the expansion of industrial and residential suburbs and all that attends them; but recently attention has focused on the loss of city jobs and tax bases, together with rising expenditures. As will be seen in Chapter 6, virtually all major cities now

---

[42] For a comprehensive survey of the spectacular increase of debt since 1946 *and* the recommendation for facilitating more debt, see "The Debt Economy," *Business Week*, October 12, 1974. Further data and alarming analysis may be found in Hyman P. Minsky, "Financial Resources in a Fragile Financial Environment," *Challenge*, July/August, 1975.

face a seemingly intractable set of economic, political, and social problems, intensified greatly by the continuing demands of organized groups—demands that, whether granted or refused, worsen the urban condition. We can attribute much of the fiscal crisis of the cities to the high level of federal expenditures (over half) on the military.

8. Last but by no means least has been the increasingly "perverse" impact of consumerism. Unquestionably a major effect and cause of the long expansion and of the political stability associated with it, consumerism necessarily depends upon the mass media and its universal audience for purposes of persuasion. The entire population, not just those of middle and higher incomes, was led to accept, to want, and in an important sense to need, a level and composition of consumer expenditures that is quite simply beyond the present or potential income capacities of a good half of the population, as the data in Chapter 5 will show.

Consumerism, which means, creates, and depends upon rising expectations throughout the population, has thus raised the popular definition of what is economically necessary to keep the social peace. At the same time, related processes lowered the economy's ability to satisfy that definition for one-third to one-half of the population. This is a unique development in the history of capitalism. It comes now not because of some new inequality in the distribution of income and wealth (even though the degrees of inequality have probably become steeper in recent years); severe inequality is a constant in the history of capitalism, essential if capitalism is to exist and capital accumulation to occur. What is novel today is the social definition of an adequate level and composition of consumption which, as a necessary accompaniment of recent accumulation, has produced in the same process a new and higher level of socially necessary *waste:* in monopoly capitalism's advertising and sales promotion, in its vast bureaucracies, and among other areas and most draining of all, in its military expenditures—not only pure waste, but large-scale waste of scarce raw materials and advanced technology (setting aside what it means in terms of wasted human effort and damage).

Brother, Can You Spare a Tank?

The 1976 presidential campaign was characterized by one theme more than any other: antigovernment spending and antitaxation. Many of the existing ills were blamed squarely on Big Government. But it is not government as such, let alone taxation or spending as such, that is the problem: rather it is *who controls* the government, the *incidence* of taxation (who pays, in what proportions), and the direction or *composition* of government spending (who benefits). The U. S. economy requires much doctoring in its mature years. But it will not be lifted out of its chronic tendency to stagnate by following the same diet. A real war on poverty, a real war against ignorance, a real war against poor health and housing would stimulate the economy and end unemployment; continuing dependence on military expenditures and investment subsidization of the large corporations—on the principle enunciated (not for the first or last time) by President Nixon in 1971: "profits for business mean jobs for the people"—means continuing unemployment, poverty and inflation.[43]

As matters now stand, taxes and expenditures spiral in ways that do little to mitigate the "problems" they are designed to affect, and do much to perpetuate and contribute to social misery. An important case in point is dependence upon military production to maintain effective demand and jobs: it does create jobs (though decreasingly per dollar of expenditure); it is also the prime source of inflation for in adding to incomes it does not add to marketed commodities. Also, to develop the political support for high arms expenditures it is necessary to alter the universe of discourse in society, to push it to the political Right, thus making it harder for other needs to be financed and progressively easier for the military to enlarge its foothold. Thus, even after "Vietnam," members of Congress were so fearful of voting against military appropriations that they voted for more (in 1976) than either the Ford administration or the Pentagon had asked. But *is* the infiltration of the military into our economy so substantial?

"The general problem which confronts us and our statesmen," a business economist states,

> . . . is that a large section of the labor force turned surplus in the mid-1930's, and since then, year in and year out, there has been this 10 to 12 million excess of manpower to deal with. Administrations came and went over the years, but always the hard nut remained about the same. The particular programs of this or that party seems to have had little effect on the size of the surplus, more likely it would affect only how the surplus was split.[44]

The "split" the author refers to is between rising military employment or rising unemployment and underemployment.

The editors of the *Monthly Review* have conducted an intensive analysis of this question. Using figures for December, 1970, they argue that

[43] The "war on poverty" initiated under President Johnson reveals much concerning the weak impulses in that direction, as compared with military expenditures, for instance. For a thorough explanation and description of the whole matter, see Ben Seligman, *Permanent Poverty: An American Syndrome* (New York: Quadrangle, 1968), especially Chapters 9 and 10.

[44] *Jeremiad: Economic Intelligence,* no. 44 (July 24, 1972). Also see the important analysis of James Cypher, "Capitalist Planning and Military Expenditure," *RRPE,* Vol. 6, No. 3 (Fall 1974).

the then official rate of 6.2 percent should be 9.1 percent, and would be were it not that male labor force participation rates have declined sharply in the age group twenty-five to sixty-five. Unless we assume that those in that group are "members of a new leisure class (a high improbability considering that they are poor), the explanation must be that such people have given up hope of earning a living in the normal way in the economy today." [45]

In 1970 about one-quarter of manufacturing productive capacity was lying idle. Taking that as a starting point, the authors go on to calculate the role of military outlays in obscuring the stagnation of the American economy. In 1970 there were 2.9 million members of the armed forces, 1.2 million civilian employees of the Department of Defense, 3.0 million employees in defense industries, and 7.1 million employed because of the indirect effects of military spending. Adding in the unemployed— 7.9 million by their calculations—Magdoff and Sweezy come to a figure of 22.1 million dependent upon military activity, plus the unemployed, or 25.6 percent of the labor force, including armed forces. That figure is slightly above the official figure for unemployment in 1933, the worst year of the Depression. *Jeremiad's* calculations are much lower; still, he says, "Combining the military with the unemployed, when the total touches down at 10 million, as it did in 1965, that is prosperity. When it exceeds 12 million, as at the end of 1970, you have bad times." [46] And nowadays, whether it does or doesn't, we have inflation.

Permanent Inflation: Who Benefits? Who Pays?

The costs of business have risen as a result of rising prices for raw materials and labor and the inefficiencies of modern corporate (and other) organization. Monopoly power enables these costs to be passed on to consumers and small businesses as higher prices, with only token interference from the State. This is shown in the recent years of falling demand joined to rising prices for, say, autos and steel. Increased interest rates are also passed on by the giant corporation. Also, because the giants

[45] This comment and the argument surrounding it is found in two articles, "Economic Stagnation and the Stagnation of Economics" (April, 1971), and "On the Theory of Monopoly Capitalism" (April, 1972), *Monthly Review*. The authors are Harry Magdoff and Paul M. Sweezy.

[46] Ibid. Speaking of the official estimates of unemployment, *Jeremiad* says: "For true unemployment there is no solution except to open a path from the worker to a livelihood. Such unemployment should be distinguished from the statistical unemployment rate. That rate is sculpted politically, according to a man-made definition of what to count as unemployment. As it diverges from the facts, it verges on the propagandistic." June 26, 1972.

dominate the production and sales of the entire economy, a restrictive monetary policy may well promote *more* inflation (and increased hardship for small business) as will an easy money policy. A perverse question not yet pondered by conventional economists: which is more inflationary, an anti-inflationary monetary policy or no policy at all?

But inflation never means merely rising prices; it also means upward income redistribution, favoring the sellers of commodities. One notable consequence of the current inflation is thus increased demand for "luxury goods" combined with diminished demand and excess capacity for the general run of manufactures: while Chevrolet lays off workers, Cadillac produces on overtime.

In this latter way, among others, prolonged inflation under monopoly capitalism moves to worsen the processes producing stagnation; and the politics of inflation are institutionalized. Whether or not inflation begins is one matter, and may be seen as economic in its origins; how and whether it continues is a matter of politics, of power. Inflation can *always* be curtailed and eliminated; the question is finally at whose expense. The Phillips Curve tells us it must be at the expense of those ultimately unemployed—the weakest people in society. That is so, other things being equal. But those "other things" are essentially a way of referring to the balance of privilege and gain in the society. Tax policies *could* be designed that would curb inflation at the expense of the upper income groups; expenditure policies *could* be altered to achieve the same result, without damage to those who can bear that damage least. Monetary policies *could* be utilized that would reduce inflationary pressures with a minimum of adverse employment effects. Between the possibility and the reality falls the shadow of the structure of power that devises and implements policies. Not surprisingly, those who have power are at the top of the economic and political structure; obviously, their natural inclination is to shape policies that hurt themselves least and benefit themselves most.[47]

Thus, within and alongside the many structural, developmental changes of the period since World War II—internationalization, militarization, consumerism, and statism—one constant of fiscal and monetary policy orientation has persisted and strengthened: the continuing search for tax, expenditure, and monetary policies that will keep the wheels of business turning rapidly, smoothly, and, of course, profitably.[48] Most

[47] A clear explanation of how these relationships work out in economic terms and thus what the conventional political options are is Francis M. Bator, *The Question of Government Spending: Public Needs and Private Wants* * (New York: Harper & Row, 1960). We shall have more to say in this area in Chapter 8.

[48] See the important analysis of Raford Boddy and James Crotty, "Class Conflict and Macro-Policy: The Political Business Cycle," in *RRPE*, Vol. 7, no. 1 (Spring, 1975).

relevant in this connection are the policies designed explicitly to encourage business investment. Their results have been many; for present purposes their effects in *maintaining* the basic structure of production and control are most pertinent. They have guaranteed that the economy will remain locked in that condition of alternating or combined inflation and unemployment, mixing fever with sluggishness. These policies became obvious in the Eisenhower administration, and ever more pronounced under Kennedy and Johnson; since then they have become institutionalized. The latest development, in the face of persisting excess industrial capacity is to proclaim a "capital shortage," and the associated necessity for "tax reforms" that will allow a heightened rate of profit that in turn will encourage expanded productive capacity. And that adds up to reduced real incomes for those whose livelihood depends upon their work, not upon property ownership.[49]

The Bitter with the Better

The essence of monopoly capitalism is that it is a social not merely an economic system. The basic changes that have made the economy work "better" required a vast array of symmetrical changes in the rest of social existence: in the process we had become the "bureaucratic society of controlled consumers," in the phrase of Henri Lefebvre.[50]

As noted earlier, the institutional development of monopoly capitalism, whether separately or combined, could not have found support in the traditional social philosophy of nineteenth-century capitalism. That social philosophy had to be displaced; it was, but by what? Whatever the defects and the associated cruelties of what may be called the social philosophy of capitalism, it was at least the work of political, social, and economic theorists. By what social philosophy, devised by which Madison Avenue philosophers, do the rulers and the ruled of monopoly capitalist society live? It is simple, and can be summed up simply: "More!" "Why not?" It is the social philosophy of a decadent society; we'll discuss this further at a later point.

Now we may note merely that the United States, in seeking to forestall the evil of economic depression, has created a society whose achievements seem increasingly negative and whose problems link together in what steadily emerges as a   social crisis. That it is seldom seen as such is partly because of our altered standards: in seeking to master the art of

[49] For the appropriate data and analysis, see *Monthly Review*, April, 1976, by Harry Magdoff and Paul Sweezy.

[50] See his *Everyday Life in the Modern World* (New York: Harper & Row, 1971) for a radical sociological analysis of what is here called monopoly capitalism.

quantitative advance we have not only engendered qualititative deterioration but we have lost the ability to tell the difference between "good" and "bad" so long as there is *more*. One indication is the process by which, in the midst of the highest accumulation of commodities in history, the attitudes toward those who live on the bare edge of existence becomes increasingly hostile. And it is repaid in kind, with good reason. The other side of the nature, the direction, and the pace of economic growth and development is, on the one hand, by whom and for whom it is shaped, and, on the other, by whom its burdens are borne. To that we now turn.

Reading Suggestions

The more or less technical matters discussed in this chapter can be better understood and appreciated if also approached through lighter works, fictional and nonfictional. They allow us to regain the flavors, bitter and sweet, of the so-called interwar period. Here is a short list of such works.

A very high percentage of people today are still responding to the trauma of the years between the two world wars. They were years of middle class euphoria in the 1920's and of despair in the 1930's; of desperate unemployment for workers; surprisingly to young people today, they were bitter years for the militarists, for they were years of pervasive antimilitarism (different in roots and manifestations from that of the Indochina War). For an overview beginning well before World War I and going into the 1930's, see John Dos Passos's exciting and informative trilogy *USA** (*The 42nd Parallel, 1919,* and *The Big Money*). For the 1920's, anything of Sinclair Lewis, but especially *Babbitt.** Anything of F. Scott Fitzgerald, but especially *The Great Gatsby** and *Tender is the Night.** The noneuphoric side is brought out in Upton Sinclair, *Oil!* (union struggles in the Los Angeles area) and Pietro di Donato, *Christ in Concrete** (immigrant construction workers). The classic and most enjoyable social history of the decade of the twenties is F. L. Allen, *Only Yesterday.** J. K. Galbraith's *Great Crash** is a lively if bland analysis of the stock market debacle. Some idea of the period 1930–1960 can be gotten from Clancy Sigal's novel *Going Away** (Boston: Houghton Mifflin, 1962).

Comparable to Allen, for the thirties (and more solid), is Dixon Wecter, *The Age of the Great Depression, 1929–1941.* Steinbeck's *Grapes of Wrath** tells more than just about migrant farm workers, and is must reading for any who wish to understand an important part of the American mind; his *In Dubious Battle** is a penetrating fictional inquiry into a farm workers' struggle in Salinas, California (and provides some insights into the contemporary struggles of the United Farm Workers). There is a very special and valuable work recently made available: Studs Terkel, whose *Working* was noted earlier, has put together a broad range of human experience and responses from the 1930's, called *Hard Times,* in the recorded voices of people of all ages and from all walks of life who lived through the period—or, in some cases, the impressions they left with their children. It is a great way to learn about those years; it is also warm and enjoyable as moving reading. Representative fictional materials for the same period are collected in Harvey Swados, ed., *The American Writer and the Great Depression* (Indianapolis: Bobbs-Merrill, 1966).

Back to dryer stuff. To understand Keynesian theory, Dillard's book, cited earlier, is an apt summary. Useful controversies from right, middle, and left concerning Keynesian theory have been brought together in Robert Lekachman, ed., *Keynes and the Classics* (Boston: D. C. Heath, 1964). Lekachman's *National Income and the Public Welfare* (New York: Random House, 1972) is a clear and succinct statement of contemporary income and employment analysis. Lester V. Chandler, *America's Greatest Depression, 1929–1941* (New York: Harper & Row, 1972), is a readable and comprehensive survey of main processes and policies in the 1930's. A critical perspective on Roosevelt's New Deal may be found in articles by Ronald Radosh, "The Myth of the New Deal," in R. Radosh and Murray Rothbard, eds., *A New History of Leviathan* (New York: Dutton, 1972) and by Barton Bernstein, "The New Deal: The Conservative Achievements of Reform," in Barton J. Bernstein, ed., *Towards a New Past: Dissenting Essays in American History* (New York: Vintage, 1972) —a book of generally useful essays largely in accord with the interpretations of this work.

A critical Marxian analysis of the U.S. growth record since World War II is Victor Perlo, *The Unstable Economy: Booms and Recessions in the U.S. Since 1945* (New York: New World Paperbacks, 1973).

The Popular Economics Press (Box 221, Somerville, Mass. 02143) specializes in producing economic literature in a visual and conceptual format that combines easy readability with solid understanding of important economic issues, especially valuable for those trying to learn by themselves, or those involved in community work. Their publications run about fifty pages, cost a bit over one dollar, and are magazine-size. Two of them are *Why Do We Spend So Much Money?* and *Q. What's Happening to Our Jobs?*

5

Income,
Wealth,
and Power

Who can make a poem of the depths of weariness
bringing meaning to those never in the depths?
Those who order what they please
when they choose to have it—
can they understand the many down under
who come home to their wives and children at night
and night after night as yet too brave and unbroken
to say, "I ache all over"?
How can a poem deal with production cost
and leave out definite misery paying
a permanent price in shattered health and early old age?
When will the efficiency engineers and the poets
get together on a program?
Will that be a cold day? Will that be a special hour?
Will somebody be coocoo then?
And if so, who?*

Capitalism is a system whose vitality is given to it by everyone trying to make as much money as possible, and the devil take the hindmost. From its beginnings to the present, capitalist development has taken place within a pattern of income, wealth, and power characterized by great inequality. That history has been marked by constant changes in technology, in products, in markets, in institutions and in attitudes; among all

---

*Carl Sandburg, from *The People, Yes* by Carl Sandburg, copyright, 1936, by Harcourt Brace Jovanovich, Inc.; copyright, 1964, by Carl Sandburg. Reprinted by permission of the publishers.

these patterns, those comprising income, wealth, and power have been the most resistant to substantial change. Inequality is intrinsic to capitalism. It is another way of viewing the existence of exploitation; without inequality, economic expansion would be inexplicable.

Variations in the patterns of inequality have of course occurred. Given the complexity of capitalist development, and its dynamic changes in economic structure, such alterations have been unavoidable. In the nineteenth century, a simple division between property-owners and the propertyless wage-earner was both cause and consequence of the unequal distribution of wealth and income. In our day, a more complex cause and effect relationship exists: (1) there is a sharp line to be drawn between *Big Business* and all other owners of (some) productive assets; (2) substantial income and wealth distinctions must be drawn between those who "own" *professional* labor power and those who do not; (3) in the nonprofessional ranks of labor, there are significant differences in the incomes of those whose labor power is protected and sustained by strong trade unions and those who are not. Within these *class* divisions, further distinctions occur because of racial and sexual barriers.

Arising out of the growing complexity of functions and incomes of modern capitalist society has been growing speculation concerning the emergence of a "new working class," or an "extended working class." The intention of these inquiries has been to establish the degree to which the members of the last two categories (2) and (3) might be expected to develop attitudes antagonistic to the continuation of a society whose prime beneficiaries are mostly those in category (1), those who control the productive assets of the economy. For despite the complexity, American society continues to move in ways resulting from a highly unequal distribution of power, wealth, and income, the key determinant of which is wealth. So long as capitalist society *remains* capitalist in its basic institutions—private property in the means of production, and production for profit—it will function "healthily" only insofar as the pattern of income and wealth distribution is highly unequal and can be expected to remain that way by those at the top.

Let us look briefly at the historical variations within the basic pattern. What is noteworthy about them is the small number of lasting changes, the directions in which they have moved, and the extent of overall *social* change required to accomplish them. The period of *least* inequality in the United States—*if* black slaves and Native Americans are excluded from the calculations—was in the several decades preceding 1850. After that came a long period up to the 1930's of *increased* inequality of income and wealth. Overlapping that period and extending to the present, and accompanied by greatly expanded State activity in both taxing and spending, has been a process in which although it is possible to find some slight reduction of income inequality in the statistics, it is also necessary to show that both wealth and power have become more highly unequal.[1]

The lesser inequality of income and wealth for whites in the period 1800–1850, although it cannot be pinned down precisely, is suggested not only by impressionistic data, but by the economic structure and processes of the period: widespread and growing access to land, a shortage of nonslave, nonindentured labor, and light industrial production. The years after 1850 constituted a major turning-point in American capitalist development, when heavy as well as light industrialization caught hold. From then on, income and wealth came to be held in a steadily more unequal pattern, as the small farmer disappeared, business became bigger, and the power of business in government became increasingly strong. The economic transformation was accompanied by a geographical shift in power, leading to and flowing from the convulsion of the Civil War.

It should be noted that as the distributive *shares* of income and wealth became more unequal, the *levels* of real per capita income rose. This pertained to ex-slaves as well, though as a group they, like their descendants today, remained at the bottom of the scale. An important by-product of rising real incomes was a mitigation of internal conflict.

Rapid and widespread industrialization made for more inequality; it also made for more instability of business activity and increased insecurity in employment, as noted in Chapters 3 and 4. In turn, these changes marked the beginning of a new phase not only in private–State relationships, but, accompanying that, a new set of developments impinging upon the patterns of income, wealth, and power: a much enlarged role of federal, state, and local governments in taxation and expenditure. Setting aside careful analysis of this development for the moment, let it suffice here to say that although the distributional phenomena were of course much affected by the enormous increase of governmental fiscal activities, the resulting reduction of income inequality was at most marginal; nor have the changes benefited those at the very bottom. On the contrary, through the role of the State in strengthening capitalism, "political capitalism" has been of considerable advantage to those at the top and in the middle ranges.

Them That Has, Gits

Income is a flow of money and purchasing power over time; *wealth* is a stock of things owned that have market value. Money income includes wages and salaries, social security benefits, dividends, interest and rents received, welfare payments, pensions, alimony received, net income from

[1] An informative analysis of the nineteenth century changes may be found in Alfred Conrad's essay "Income Growth and Structural Change," in Alfred Conrad and John R. Meyer, *The Economics of Slavery* (Chicago: Aldine, 1964). For points under discussion here, see esp. pp. 168–77.

self-employment (for instance, from farming or by doctors), and other periodic income. Wealth includes automobiles and homes as well as trucks and mines and corporate stock; but for analytical purposes the ownership of productive—that is, income producing—assets is the vital factor. Let us look first at the facts of *income* distribution.

The data on these matters come primarily from the federal census conducted every ten years, and from income tax forms (though individuals' data are not made public). There is of course reason to doubt the detailed accuracy of such information, but the general outlines provided by the data over time are reliable. One major reservation, however, concerns understatement of high *incomes* (due to the 50 percent exclusion of capital gains, the hiding of income in expense accounts, and the like) and the understatement of the real *wealth* of the wealthy. Nevertheless, the extreme disparity between the rich and the poor stands out:

> Since World War II, the poorest fifth of families has received less than 6 percent of money income; the richest fifth has received over forty percent. Put another way, the average income of the 10.4 million families in the bottom fifth in 1970 was $3,054; the average income of the 10.4 million families in the top fifth was $23,100. If money income had been divided equally among families in 1970, the average income for each family would have been over $11,000.[2]

These figures are for "personal income distribution," and, as may be noted, they are generally couched in terms of "fifths" of the population, from the lowest 20 percent to the highest, as shown in Figure 5–1. (They are also available in terms of the highest 5 percent and the top 1 percent, as indicated in Table 5–1.)

These are before taxes on incomes; but as will be shown later, taxes make no substantial difference in the shares. What is remarkable is the constancy of the distribution in the past twenty-five years, despite massive socioeconomic changes, which Figure 5–2 shows.[3]

---

[2] Letitia Upton and Nancy Lyons, *Basic Facts: Distribution of Personal Income and Wealth in the United States* ° (Cambridge: Cambridge Institute, 1971), p. 1. This is a clear and succinct statement, objectively bringing together available data from all major official and private sources. It is available inexpensively from the Cambridge Institute, 1878 Massachusetts Avenue, Cambridge, Mass. "Family" as used in income data means two or more people residing together, related by blood, marriage or adoption. The statistical size of the average American family today is about 3.6 persons. See also, Herman P. Miller, *Rich Man, Poor Man* ° (New York: Crowell, 1971) for a handy compendium of facts and analysis on most of the matters discussed in this chapter—income, wealth, race, sex, education, and poverty—seen from a moderate viewpoint. Miller has been with the Bureau of the Census for over thirty years.

[3] *The Review of Radical Political Economics* (Summer, 1971), is devoted entirely to distributional questions, with seven essays examining "Capitalism, Inequality, and Poverty," from different vantage points. Most pertinent for our concerns here are pp. 20–43, "Income Distribution in the U.S.," by Ackerman et al.

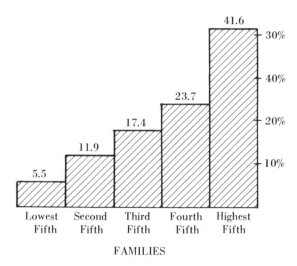

FAMILIES

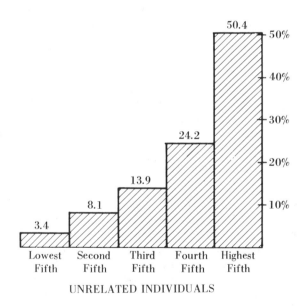

UNRELATED INDIVIDUALS

FIGURE 5–1 **Percentage Share of Aggregate U.S. Income in 1971 Received by Each Fifth of Families and Unrelated Individuals, Ranked by Income**

SOURCE: U.S. Department of Commerce, Bureau of the Census, *Current Population Reports, Consumer Income,* P–60, no. 85, December, 1972, p. 38, table 14. Reprinted from Pamela Roby, ed., *The Poverty Establishment,* by permission of Prentice-Hall, Inc.

TABLE 5–1

Families ranked from lowest to highest income	Income range (dollars)	Percent of income received
Lowest fifth	0–3,070	3.2
Second fifth	3,070–5,890	10.5
Middle fifth	5,890–8,620	17.0
Fourth fifth	8,620–12,260	23.9
Highest fifth	12,260 and over	45.8
Top 5 percent	19,920 and over	19.1
Top 1 percent	44,560 and over	6.8

SOURCE: Joseph A. Pechman, "Distribution of Federal and State Income Taxes by Income Classes," Presidential Address, American Finance Association Annual Meetings, New Orleans, La., December 28, 1971, p. 6. Quoted in Upton and Lyons, *Basic Facts,* p. 16. Some in the lowest fifth have "negative incomes"; i.e., they fall into debt.

Using a broader conception of income, Joseph Pechman (one of the most authoritative tax economists) has compiled figures from 1966 that show a somewhat higher degree of inequality, especially for the top 5 percent "after adjustment for nonreporting and underreporting of income." (See Table 5–1.)

What about constancy of income shares if we go further back than 1947? Partially because the data are unreliable, and partially because the question of constancy is itself so controversial in the present period—when we are frequently told that inequality is lessening and that the poor are taking money from the rich—any arguments about comparisons over the past half-century are sharply contested. On close examination, however, the sharpness is more that of needles than of swords. The main warrior arguing for constancy is Kolko, who asserts:

> A radically unequal distribution of income has been characteristic of the American social structure since at least 1910, and despite minor year-to-year fluctuations in the shares of the income-tenths, no significant trend toward income equality has appeared. . . . Throughout the 1950's the income of the top tenth was larger than the total for the bottom five income-tenths—about the same relationship as existed in 1910 and 1918. . . . While the income share of the richest tenth has remained large and virtually constant over the past half century, the two lowest income-tenths have experienced a sharp decline.[4]

[4] Gabriel Kolko, *Wealth and Power in America* * (New York: Praeger, 1962), pp. 13–15. Kolko's Table I, p. 14, shows the richest tenth receiving 33.9 percent in 1910 and 28.9 percent in 1959 (his latest year). This was something of a decline, but in relative terms not as much as the decline in the share of the poorest: the lowest tenth received 3.4 percent in 1910 and 1.1 percent in 1959. Note that Kolko is using *tenths*, not *fifths*.

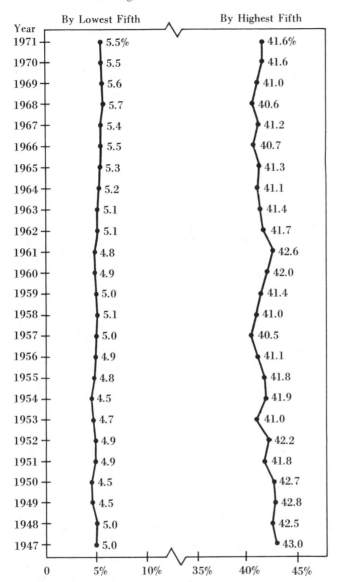

Percentage Share of Income Received

Year	By Lowest Fifth	By Highest Fifth
1971	5.5%	41.6%
1970	5.5	41.6
1969	5.6	41.0
1968	5.7	40.6
1967	5.4	41.2
1966	5.5	40.7
1965	5.3	41.3
1964	5.2	41.1
1963	5.1	41.4
1962	5.1	41.7
1961	4.8	42.6
1960	4.9	42.0
1959	5.0	41.4
1958	5.1	41.0
1957	5.0	40.5
1956	4.9	41.1
1955	4.8	41.8
1954	4.5	41.9
1953	4.7	41.0
1952	4.9	42.2
1951	4.9	41.8
1950	4.5	42.7
1949	4.5	42.8
1948	5.0	42.5
1947	5.0	43.0

0   5%   10%   35%   40%   45%

FIGURE 5–2 Percentage Share of Aggregate U.S. Income in 1947 to 1971 Received by Lowest and Highest Fifths of Families Ranked by Income

SOURCE: U.S. Department of Commerce, Bureau of the Census, *Current Population Reports, Consumer Income,* P–60, no. 85, December 1972, p. 38, table 14; and U.S. Bureau of the Census, *Trends in the Income of Families and Persons in the United States: 1947 to 1960,* Technical Paper No. 8 (Washington, D.C.: U.S. Government Printing Office, 1963), table 1, pp. 36–43. Reprinted from Roby, *The Poverty Establishment,* by permission of Prentice-Hall.

Herman Miller (p. 51) argues that Kolko's assertion is "very questionable," but the persistence of highly unequal income is unquestionable. There are occasional indications of departures from long-run stability. *Year-to-year* fluctuations in distributional shares take place, but shifting percentage shares in a given year have less meaning than is apparent, if the year in question is unusually prosperous *or* depressed, for example, or if a new short-run trend has been at work. Thus, the mid-1960's were years of lessening poverty and lower unemployment, in association with the economic height of the Indochina War. After 1969, poverty, unemployment, and inequality in income and wealth distribution all slowly and steadily increased.

Another important set of points requires emphasis. Those with the highest incomes and the greatest wealth benefit most from increases in the *national* income. They are in the best position to take advantage of the increased opportunities in expansion periods. In the early phases of an expansion out of a depressed period, although workers will find their incomes rising—not least because they are more fully employed—the *share* going to the lower income groups declines. In a sustained expansion that brings about full employment, the share of the lower income groups will later begin to rise, accompanied at the very peak of the expansion by falling profit rates (due both to rising wages and to softening markets for commodities). But a period of contraction means fewer jobs, and falling incomes for employed workers; although it also means falling incomes for those at the top, their *share* rises—and, of course, they are quite unlikely to suffer, as those in the lower income groups do. Over time, the gap between rich and poor widens obviously in absolute terms, if less so in relative terms. Thus (in *constant* 1970 dollars), between 1958 and 1968 the average income of the *poorest* fifth of families moved up from $1,956 to $3,085; of the *highest* fifth from $15,685 to $21,973. The difference in average incomes between the lowest and highest fifths increased from $13,720 to $18,888. The poor may or may not see their money incomes—and even, now and then, their income shares—rise; in in general they do well to hold on to their relative share. But even when they manage to do that, poverty increases when the absolute gap widens. Poverty is a *social* condition. An American family receiving many times the money income of a family in India can be poorer than the Indian family. *Absolute* poverty exists when starvation enters the picture; poverty then is physical as well as social. But poverty is always first and foremost social. Marx puts it well:

> Rapid growth of productive capital calls forth just as rapid a growth of wealth, of luxury, of social needs and social pleasures. Therefore, although the pleasures of the labourer have increased [through higher wages], the social gratification which they afford has fallen in comparison with the increased pleasures of the capitalist, which are inaccessible to the worker, in comparison with the stage of development of the society in

general. Our wants and pleasures have their origin in society; we therefore measure them in relation to society; we do not measure them in relation to the objects which serve for their gratification. Since they are of a social nature, they are of a relative nature.[5]

Marx's view helps to clarify why it is in periods of economic expansion that social protest tends to rise among those at the bottom of the heap. It is worth noting also that what is true of the distribution of income and wealth and the widening gap between rich and poor *within* this country is also true of the widening gap *between* rich and poor *nations*. When we look at the underdeveloped nations in a later chapter, we shall see it is a commonplace that the absolute and relative gap between the industrialized and nonindustrialized nations has widened substantially in the postwar years of sustained expansion. And, of course, turbulence has increased in that same period. Let us now turn to the distribution and accumulation of *wealth*.

The Accumulation of Wealth

The old saw, "the rich get richer and the poor get poorer," has more to it than spite and envy. The rich own most of society's wealth, and wealth yields incomes that in turn are invested in more wealth, to produce even more income. More importantly, great *wealth* yields great *power*. The simple relationship between income and wealth emerges clearly from Figure 5–3, a *Business Week* chart which is an application of recent data to the so-called "Lorenz Curve."[6]

Wealth measures the sale value of possessions and property. Almost everyone owns something of value; but only a small percentage of the population owns the society's income producing assets, the most vital part of which is its corporate stock. The considerably more unequal distribution of wealth than income is directly connected to economic power, and economic power is directly connected to political power. These connections mean that the wealthy are in a position to neutralize the apparent redistributive income and wealth effects of governmental income, estate, and inheritance taxes.[7]

[5] Karl Marx, *Wage-Labour and Capital* * (New York: International Publishers, 1933; originally published in 1849), p. 33. The data for the widening income gap in the preceding paragraph are from Upton and Lyons, op. cit., p. 4.

[6] The Lorenz Curve seeks to show degrees of inequality graphically: the straight line (45 degree angle) shows a relationship of exact equality between percent of persons and of income (or wealth); the greater the deviation from that straight line, the greater the degree of inequality.

[7] Philip M. Stern has written two books showing the facts, procedures, winners and losers, and bases of our tax system, which works very much the opposite of its presumed intent: *The Great Treasury Raid* * (New York: Signet, 1965), and *The Rape of the Taxpayer* (New York: Random House, 1973).

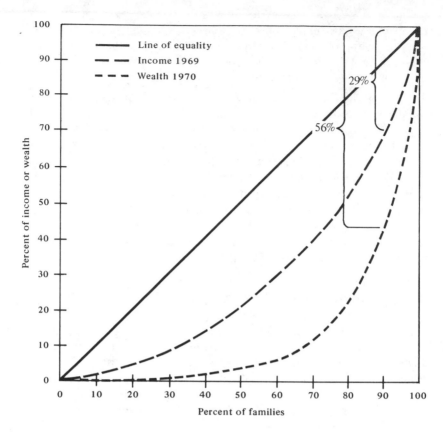

FIGURE 5–3 Relation Between Income and Wealth

SOURCE: *Business Week,* August 5, 1972.

U.S. income is shared unevenly, but wealth distribution is more unequal.

With equal distribution:
 •each 10 percent of the people would get 10 percent of all income.
 •each 10 percent would own 10 percent of total wealth.

But actually . . .

The top 10 percent of the people:
 •get 29 percent of income.
 •own 56 percent of wealth.

The bottom 10 percent of the people:
 •get 1 percent of income.
 •owe more than they own.

TABLE 5–2 Percentage Share of Wealth Held by Fifths, Top 5 Percent and Top 1 Percent, 1962.

Consumer units ranked from lowest to highest wealth	Total Wealth	Corporate Stock
Poorest fifth	(—)*	(—)
Second through fourth fifth	23%	3%
Richest fifth	77	97
Top 5 percent	53	86
Top 1 percent	33	62

SOURCE: Upton and Lyons, p. 22.

* (—) means less than 1/2 of 1 percent. These figures were derived by Upton/ Lyons from Edward C. Budd, ed., *Inequality and Poverty** (New York: Norton, 1967), p. xxii.

In 1962, as was noted earlier, the highest fifth of *income* receivers had over 40 percent of personal income; in that same year, the highest fifth ranked by *wealth* size owned 77 percent of personal wealth. When we examine the corporate stock component of total wealth, the concentration is considerably higher. (See Table 5–2.)

If the figures in Table 5–2 are startling standing alone, behind them matters are even more startling, showing how wealth feeds wealth. The top 1 percent of personal wealth holders own 30 percent or more of all wealth, although the top 1 percent of personal income recipients receive "only" something under 10 percent of income. But all the wealth could be translated into income. Why is it not? First, because wealth produces income, and the law of the rich is "never live off capital." Second, the higher incomes involved would, if allowed to go higher through converting wealth to income, be taxed away, at least in part. Third, wealth in the form of stock ownership (among other things) means increased wealth through undistributed corporate profits. Fourth, wealth means power. Last, in the case of the very rich, on what would they spend higher incomes? "Accumulate! Accumulate!" is what they have done.

It is a popular belief that stock ownership has become less unequal in recent decades, and in one sense that is so. The number of individual stock investors rose from nine million in 1956 to thirty-one million in 1970; but the wealthiest 1 percent of the population increased its percentage of stock ownership from 69.5 percent in 1953 to 71.6 percent in 1962.[8] *Business Week*, basing its analysis on the most recent scholarly studies of wealth concentration, concludes that "the degree of wealth

[8] Ibid., p. 31. In addition to books already cited for data on income and wealth, see Ferdinand Lundberg, *The Rich and the Super-Rich* * (New York: Lyle Stuart, 1968), a racy but thorough tome on the subject; and for basic work that is bone-dry, see Robert J. Lampman, *Changes in the Share of Wealth Held by Top Wealth-Holders, 1922–1956* * (New York: National Bureau of Economic Research, 1960).

concentration increased during the 1920's, decreased from 1929 to the late 1940's, and remained fairly stable in the 1960's." But they go on to cite the belief of Professor James D. Smith, a leading analyst of wealth distribution, that the figures since 1962 would certainly show no decrease in concentration of wealth; "if anything, it increased slightly."

Whether or not there is great inequality in the distribution of income and wealth is not debatable; as such, it is not debated. But what to do about it, whether it is either desirable or possible to move toward more equality—such questions are very much debated. Setting aside radical voices, however, the arguments that range around this question uncritically take property rights for granted, and rarely question the desirability of the basic institutions that have created and that require great inequality. Thus, *Business Week*, although it had three major essays during 1972 on the distribution of income and wealth, all of which show the same data used by us above, comes out bemused and puzzled: "Neither side can come up with hard answers as to how it [income redistribution] can—or should—work." And, "some inequality may serve as an incentive for growth in a profit-oriented economy." "Some" inequality is not what their own essays show, nor are their conclusions more or less helpful than those of mainstream economists. The worst-kept family secret about the relationship between capitalist development and *great* inequality in the distribution of income and wealth is that they need each other.[9]

Nobody, and certainly not the rich, needs to be told that property ownership is the key to high incomes. Nor could anyone seriously believe that being nonwhite or being a woman is a matter of indifference to one's income. What is less accepted or understood is the systematic and long-standing *class* pressures to maintain the relationships that allow the gains from property, and that perpetuate the low incomes of all workers—men and women, whites and nonwhites. Discussion of such matters is normally in the nature of asides, or with the unexamined assumption that some good will, some intelligence, and some time are likely (if anything can or should be) to rid American society of such patterns.

A critical analysis of capitalist development teaches otherwise. The causes of existing patterns of income and wealth distribution are far from accidental and, so far as basic patterns are concerned, are unchangeable. Capitalism requires expansion; expansion requires savings and investment; the required savings and investment depend upon past and expected profits; persistent profitability in the economy is the telltale sign of both expansion and exploitation; it requires people who must work for what they can get even when that means they work part of the time "for nothing," that is, for the benefit of the employer and of capitalism's health. If the alternative to being exploited for those with little or no property is harsh, it is harsher still for the man who is nonwhite, and still

[9] The *Business Week* articles are those of April 1, June 17, and August 5, 1972.

more for women as compared with men.[10] Let us examine what *average* incomes are and what they mean.

The Accumulation of Misery

Every year the Bureau of Labor Statistics (BLS) calculates the annual money income that a family of four (husband, wife, eight-year-old daughter, and thirteen-year old son) needs to enjoy a "moderate but adequate standard of living" in the "average American city." About two-thirds of Americans live in urban areas, and most of those who do not get and spend in roughly comparable ways. The BLS also calculates budgets for a "lower" or "austere" level of living, within a "minimum budget," and one for a "higher" level which "allows for some luxuries." The moderate budget may reasonably be viewed as the "American standard of living," if in a pinched version. It allows, for instance, for one suit every three to four years for the father, and three street dresses for the mother every two years; it assumes a new TV every ten years, a new refrigerator every seventeen years, a toaster every thirty-three years. The adults are entitled to nine movies a year, with none for the children (who presumably watch the aging TV set). It includes no allowance for savings to meet periods of unemployment, illness, or higher education for the children. A *used* car may be purchased every four years (the "higher budget" allows a new one every four years). And out of the budgeted amount social security, income, and other taxes must be paid. The lower or "austere" budget pares everything down to food, clothing, and shelter, leaving virtually nothing for other items.[11]

The BLS budgets for 1975 were designated as follows: "moderate" was $15,500; "lower" was $9,800; "higher" was $22,500. These figures constitute increases of 8 percent from 1974, which in turn had risen about 13 percent from 1973. Yet the average annual factory wage in durable goods production in 1975 was about $10,500 for fifty-two weeks' work. The average factory workers, therefore—those with the strongest unions— earned only a little over the urban "lower" level and were almost one-third shy of meeting the "moderate" budget, unless, of course, more than one person in the family worked.

In 1971, *median* money incomes for American families for the first time

[10] See the data in Table 5–3, below.

[11] Donald Light, "Income Distribution: The First Stage in the Consideration of Poverty," *RRPE* (Summer, 1971), conducts a useful and critical examination of these concepts, only touched upon here. It is worth noting that although those who live in rural areas have generally lower expenses than urban residents, the figures for the "average city" understate by $1,000 or more the cost-of-living in the big cities such as Boston, Greater New York, Milwaukee, San Francisco, Chicago, Philadelphia, Los Angeles, and several others. All figures have to be adjusted upward to reflect continuing inflation.

rose above $10,000 to $10,285. "Median" refers to the middle unit of an entire population, with half above and half below the median number. In 1971, the "moderate" budget was $10,971, as against the median family income, which was about $700 less; in 1975, the median family income was $12,840, as against a "moderate" budget of $15,500, producing a deficit of $2,660. The budget figure had risen by $4,529 between 1971 and 1975, while median family incomes rose only $2,555.

The explanation is, of course, that prices rose more rapidly than median (to say nothing of the lower) family incomes; another way of saying that those in the very *highest* income groups were increasing their incomes more rapidly than the rate of price increase. The costs of inflation, as noted in the last chapter, are borne asymmetrically: what is a loss for one segment is, necessarily, a gain for some other. In mid-1973, the Census Bureau reported that the 1972 percentage of all blacks' median incomes to all whites' median incomes was continuing the decline begun in 1970; since 1973 the percentage has fallen even more as the unemployment of blacks has risen in conjunction with worsened inflation and reduced governmental transfer payments. As Table 5–3 (below) shows, women workers were relatively worse off than "nonwhite" men (about 90 percent of whom are blacks); in 1975, the median income for all women for full-time work was $6,957, about 57 percent of the amount for all men, which was $12,152.[12]

In short, a good half of all American families in 1975 had money incomes below the "moderate but adequate budget" established by the BLS. The "poverty level" (whose definition will be questioned later) was redefined as $5,500 per year for a family of four for 1975: 25.9 million persons—10.7 percent more than in 1974—lived at or (most of them, of course) below that level.

These *quantitative* standards, even when embellished by the kinds of expenditures they allow on clothing, appliances, and the like, do not realistically describe what the money income levels of the majority of Americans mean in terms of the *quality* of life. To have too little money to have adequate possessions in a society that defines the good life by such standards is bad enough. It is even worse not to have enough money to maintain decent levels of health or minimal comfort. Those bureaucrats who set and define standards such as "moderate" and "lower," can hardly imagine what life is like for an urban family of four that pays excessive rents to a slumlord for an apartment which, and among other things, has faulty plumbing at best, peeling (and poisonous) paint, and numerous rats.

---

[12] The data in the foregoing paragraphs are taken from *Statistical Abstract, 1975*, and the *Handbook of Labor Statistics*, cited earlier, and from *Business Week*, December 8, 1975, "Egalitarianism: Mechanisms for Redistributing Income." See also, for, data in the preceding and following paragraphs, the annual report, *Characteristics of the Low-Income Population; Money Income, 1971 (et seq.)* USGPO, 1972 (*et seq.*)

Most people can not identify with those whose health is chronically poor because of rotten housing and poor diets and who must suffer the indignities of the inadequate health care meted out to the poor. In short, in this as in so many other instances of social measurement, quantitative standards, useful though they may be, often disguise more than they reveal; in doing so, they mislead more than they instruct.

Thus, in this, the richest of all societies, the majority of the population is not, by its own government's conservative measurements, living well; and inflation steadily increases that percentage.

But some few are living very well indeed. In 1971, fewer than one percent (.7) of American families received more than $50,000 a year; in 1973 the number had risen to 1.1 percent, and it has continued to rise as a result of both the income increasing and the upwardly redistributive effects of price inflation. (The percentages for incomes over $25,000 were for 1971, 7.8 percent, and for 1973, 10 percent.) These are the cream of the income crop, the owners and managers of the profitable companies, and the top professionals (doctors, lawyers, engineers, and the like). They are doubtless among those who in 1976 were awaiting delayed deliveries of the $13,000 plus Cadillac Seville, the "small luxury car." A survey of these buyers reported their median incomes as $67,150.

As far back as 1971 and 1972, executive salaries and fringe payments were staggering: the Board Chairman of Westinghouse in 1972 had a salary of $236,000, incentive compensation of $180,000, and profit on stock options of over $1 million. GM chairman Gerstenberg was paid $889,963, Henry Ford II $887,795, and Chrysler Chairman Townsend $649,850. In 1975, some representative incomes noted for the San Francisco Bay Area showed four executives of Kaiser Industries receiving between $260,000 and $450,000, two each from Levi Strauss getting $267,691, two each from Standard Oil of California $247,500; and so on. These are not entirely exceptional figures, as a reading of *Business Week's* annual survey of "Executive Compensation" would reveal.

The 1970's have been years of increased inflation and unemployment, of international monetary crisis, real or contrived food and energy shortages, record drops and increases in car sales, and rising military expenditures alongside presidentially impounded funds on health, education, job-training, and other socially needed programs. It should not stretch the imagination to discern close connections between the various elements of the pattern of production, of income, wealth, and power distribution, and the coexistence of very high and rising incomes for some with deep and increasing hardships for many millions more.[13]

[13] In a book that quintessentially manifests the socialized incapacity and the moral myopia of the mainstream economist, Stanley Lebergott, a life-long quantitative economist, analyzes each assertion that might allow one to believe there is socioeconomic misery in the U. S. with an electron microscope, and comes up with con-

Oligarchic Democracy

How are such patterns maintained, in what is not only the richest but, by its own standards, the most democratic country in the world? The answer must begin with the role of power, the power to defend and to enhance the prerogatives of property. The holders of such power in capitalist society have been seen as "the ruling class" by Marx, "the vested interests" by Veblen, "the power elite" by C. Wright Mills, "the establishment" by Papandreou, and "the governing class" by G. William Domhoff. Their terminological differences arise from analytical differences in the way each of these men has viewed our society. Whatever those differences are, all agree on one matter: the holders of power are few in number, and at their center sit those who control—by virtue of concentrated ownership—the wealth of the society.

Americans are a strange lot when it comes to questions of power and class. Although workers "hate the bosses"; although it is universally assumed that "you can't beat City Hall" (which means also state and federal equivalents) and that "City Hall" is a nest of corruption; although the media are alleged by figures as diverse as Abbie Hoffman and Spiro Agnew to be in the service of powerful financial interests; although there is widespread recognition that schools and churches and social occasions divide clearly in terms of the wealth and income of those participating; although those at the top act and frequently speak in ways explicable only in class terms (FDR, for instance, was said to be "a traitor to his class"—quite mistakenly, as it happens); although all this and much more of the same sort is taken for granted, *class analysis* of American society is rejected and scorned, not only by the conventional social scientist but quite generally by all the people whose attitudes are noted above. This contrast between popular attitudes and systematic understanding is not as apparent in other capitalist countries; it is very much an American trait. Why it should be so is of course a matter of our history, which thereby stands in contrast to the history of other capitalist societies.

Among all capitalist societies, the United States alone has no precapitalist history; for other societies, this was a history of clear-cut class relationships with power graded in terms of class. The United States was born in a *nationalist* struggle. Understandably, at the time that struggle could be seen as a social revolution as well. The distinction between a national and a social revolution requires clarification. Nationalist struggles

---

clusions that would make Voltaire's Dr. Pangloss—who saw this as "the best of all possible worlds"—weak with envy. See his *Wealth and Want* (Princeton: Princeton University Press, 1975), which earns Professor Lebergott the sobriquet of "the William F. Buckley of the economics profession."

unite people of different classes in pursuit of a common cause. They either succeed or fail. Social revolutions are struggles to alter the pre-existing internal class structure of power. Their success or failure is thus a matter of degree, depending on the extent to which the class structure is changed. (The Vietnamese struggle was a combination of these two forms, which helps to explain its vitality.)

By this criterion, the American Revolution does not qualify as much of a social revolution, for its internal structural effects were peripheral and ephemeral. Despite this, however, Americans have historically seen themselves living in a society characterized since the Declaration of Independence by widely diffused power and a fluid class structure, where movement from one level to another is a matter of pluck and luck and effort. Nor is it unimportant that a great measure of fluidity does exist. What is important about that fluidity, however, is not that it has existed, but that along with the social mobility has gone a *continuation* of the relative power of classes—indeed, as this book argues, an increase of power at the top. Why?

The upward mobility of American *individuals* has not altered the class structure because those who have moved up have been absorbed and co-opted by the stratum into which they have moved; only those who are willing to be thus co-opted get a chance to move up (except for a few "respectable" criminal and otherwise corrupt "deviant" exceptions, who get wealth by "out-system" means, and then buy in for themselves or their children). As will be noted again later, the education process and most especially the higher levels of education are the prime socializing agents in this process of co-optation; once a "lower-class" person makes his or her way on to the upper reaches of the social ladder—whether in a corporation, in government, in the military, or in the professions—the absorption process is intensified. Or the person falls off the ladder. Social fluidity is one matter; class structure and the concentration of power is another. They can exist side by side, and they have and do in America. If one consequence has been analytical confusion in the social sciences, the other and connected result has been a virtually unchallenged role for the class that has gained and held power by virtue of its wealth and control of the upward mobility ladders.

But has there not been class *struggle* in the United States, between capital and labor? There has been, but it has taken particular forms that require careful analysis if their meaning is to be understood. Kolko, relying upon Veblen, has pointed to a key characteristic of the process in the United States:

American society could also be understood as a class structure without *decisive* class conflict, a society that had conflict limited to smaller issues that were not crucial to the existing order, and on which the price of satisfying opposition was relatively modest from the viewpoint of the continuation of the social system. In brief, a static class structure serving class ends might be frozen into American society even if the interests and values served were those of a ruling class.[14]

The power of the ruling class in the United States has come principally from its ownership and control of the nation's productive wealth. That is a matter of class. But that power has also been enhanced by the depth and persistence of racial, ethnic, religious, and sexual discrimination, rivalry, and hatred. Whatever else in the United States may have held back the consciousness and strength of the working class, these divisions have surely been additional sources of weakness. Nor, of course, have such matters been confined to the United States. Discussing Ireland as a British colony, and the conditions of Irish workers in England (in a letter written in 1870), Marx said:

> And most important of all! Every industrial and commercial center in England now possesses a working class *divident* into two *hostile* camps, English proletarians and Irish proletarians. The ordinary English worker hates the Irish worker as a competitor who lowers his standard of life . . . [,] feels himself a member of the *ruling* nation, and so turns himself into a tool of the aristocrats and capitalists of his country *against Ireland*, thus strengthening their domination *over himself*. He cherishes religious, social and national prejudices against the Irish worker. His attitude toward him is much the same as that of the "poor whites" to the "niggers" in the former slave states of the U.S.A. The Irishman pays him back with interest in his own money. . . . This antagonism is artificially kept alive and intensified by the press, the pulpit, the comic papers, in short, by all the means at the disposal of the ruling classes. This *antagonism is the secret of the impotence of the English working class*, despite its organization. It is the secret by which the capitalist class maintains its power. And that class is fully aware of it.[15]

Before examining further how such *non*class relationships have operated, it is appropriate to explore very briefly the history of trade unionism in the United States, as trade unions were the main avenue taken by American workers to offset their weaknesses in the face of business power.

[14] Gabriel Kolko, "The Decline of American Radicalism in the Twentieth Century," in James Weinstein and David W. Eakins, eds., *For a New America* ° (New York: Vintage, 1970), p. 208. This book contains many exciting essays evaluating and re-evaluating American history. The point made by Kolko above suggests the analysis of ruling class "hegemony" made by the Italian Marxist Antonio Gramsci, which will be pursued more fully in our concluding chapter.

[15] Quoted in Selsam et al., *Dynamics of Social Change*, p. 136. Emphasis in original.

Nothing to Lose, But . . .

American trade unions, by comparison with similar groups in other capitalist countries, are conservative. Neither in principle nor in practice are they class conscious; they do not seek basic institutional changes. They work within the framework of existing society, seeking to improve the economic conditions of their members *within* that framework. To succeed, some institutional change is of course required; broad changes are not. American unionism is generally characterized by the term "business unionism," or, sometimes, as "pork-chops unionism." There have been exceptions to these generalizations, but mainly in early or very bad times.[16]

Right after the Civil War, groups such as the Knights of Labor formed which had as an important part of their aims a reconstitution of society, along lines which were then considered radical, although they might not seem so today. Even the very conservative American Federation of Labor (AFL) in the 1890's faced a moment when whether or not it would be explicitly socialist was debated (and rejected); before World War I about one-third of AFL members were also members of the Socialist Party. In the depression of the 1930's, the newly-formed Congress of Industrial Organizations (CIO) worked closely with New Dealers seeking broad social reform. And the most radical labor organization of all in America, the Industrial Workers of the World (IWW, called the "Wobblies"), was uncompromisingly anticapitalist. The IWW was ruthlessly and effectively crushed by the events surrounding World War I, the "Red Scare" of the 1920's, and the force of deeply hostile public opinion (including that expressed by the AFL), which more than once took the form of lynchings. Today a few so-called left-wing unions manage to hang on to life and members, but they survive because they are successful *business* unions.

How may the general conservatism of American trade unions be explained? It begins with the origins and the hopes of American workers, *and* with the socioeconomic context within which they worked. From its beginnings until the 1920's, ours was a land of labor shortage, when the labor supply is set against the amount of land open to cultivation and the rapid rate of economic growth—with one important proviso: the "labor shortage" was not as intense as it appears in retrospect if the several millions of unemployed and severely under-employed blacks and whites

---

[16] This characterization is of *trade unions*, and of their *leadership*. Like so much else in capitalist society, the trade union form is democratic, but the practice is more often than not oligarchic. *Workers* in general are not conservative, as Andrew Levinson makes solidly clear in his *The Working Class Majority* (New York: Coward, McCann, Geoghegan, 1974); Peck, in his *Rank-and-File Leader*, cited below, makes the same point about shop stewards (that is, low level union leadership).

in the South are taken into account and explained. From 1865 until the 1930's, migration from the underdeveloped South to the labor-hungry North was a mere trickle. Whites chose not to leave for an "enemy country," and blacks were generally restrained—by force of circumstance or by sheer force—from doing so. World War I and World War II, the agricultural depression of the 1930's and the mechanization and chemicalization of southern agriculture in the past generation gradually and then suddenly unlocked the substantial unused labor supply of the South substituting, in recent years, substantial urban for rural unemployment and under-employment.[17]

Given the foregoing institutional or artificially-created shortage of labor, the labor supply was persistently inadequate, despite a rapid rate of population growth. That rapid rate of increase was due in part to the high birth rate among residents, but the vital addition was due to heavy immigration, which was partly a result of the positive lure of the United States, partly due to the negative push of population pressure and political, social, and economic discontent in other countries. Acting as a link between the labor shortage and the influx of labor were American agents in Europe (and, later, in Asia)—sometimes of shipping companies seeking profits, sometimes of employers seeking workers, or of land companies seeking customers—who hawked the virtues of life in America much as soap is advertised today. The population rose from 31.5 million in 1860, to 63 million in 1890, to 106.4 million in 1920, about 29 million accounted for by immigration in that same period.[18]

In the period between the Civil War and 1920, the proportion of male immigrants to the total immigration never fell below half, more often than not was above 60 percent, and in many years was above 70 percent. The men were overwhelmingly between fifteen and fifty years old, ready to become members of the labor force. Our total population more than tripled in this period. Still, in 1920 a congressional committee was told "there is a labor shortage in practically every industrial activity. It amounts to not less than that of 5 million men." From then on, excepting the peak years of World War II, labor moved into surplus.

But in those earlier years, the United States was one of the few countries where people were more likely to be needed than needy, poor though many were throughout. Wages and working conditions were terrible, but except for the most highly skilled trades, unions did not form. Why not?

The heavy percentage of foreign-born in the labor force provides one

[17] I have analyzed this question more fully in the essay "A Comparative Analysis of Economic Development in the American West and South," included in Harry Scheiber, ed., U.S. Economic History: Selected Readings * (New York: Knopf, 1964), a generally useful collection of analytical studies.

[18] A useful analytical and factual study of the immigration process is Oscar Handlin, The Uprooted (Boston: Atlantic Monthly Press, 1951).

explanation. For immigrants America seemed a land of unparalleled opportunity and social mobility. Bad though conditions were, they were better than the harsh conditions of the home country, which usually meant the harsh conditions of the peasantry. Here there was hope, at least, hope for themselves and especially for their children; hopes not infrequently realized in the second generation. Why fight the bitter fight for unions if, perhaps, next year, or ten years from now, you would no longer *be* a worker?

Add to this the uncertainties and the hardships and the dangers of becoming involved in a union organizing drive and it may be understood why unions had difficulty in attracting converts. Employers' opposition to unions was unremitting and relentless, and they were greatly assisted by their friends in court and in the press—to say nothing of the pervasive view that *individual* hard work was the sure way to economic well-being. But the multiplicity of languages, religions, and national and cultural backgrounds of the labor force also rendered communication and solidarity among workers a most difficult thing. Employers did what they could to drive these wedges in deeper; "divide and rule" is as useful a stratagem for employers as it was for the British Empire.

Employers' determination to resist union organization took many forms: discrimination against union men on the job and in hiring, the use of labor spies within plants and unions, physical force or its threat, so-called "yellow-dog" contracts (where the condition of employment was to sign away the right to join a union), and moving plants to non-union areas in response to union activity. The press cooperated along the way in alerting the general public to anarchism, communism, and other schemes to destroy all that is good, in the name of unionism. Local police, state militias, and federal troops could be relied upon to maintain "law and order," when and if the occasion arose, and private police (for example, "the Pinkertons") could do the job when it became especially nasty. And then there were the laws of the land and their interpretation by a friendly judiciary.

The law did not forbid unionism; it merely made the rights of labor quite explicitly inferior to those of property. In 1842 it was decided that a trade union was *not* a conspiracy (in *Commonwealth* v. *Hunt*); workers had a right to organize. Local, state, and federal courts up until 1930 interpreted that decision as meaning the right was effective only when it did not interfere with employers' rights—and strikes were seen as such interferences. Unions without the right to strike are like armies without weapons. Antitrust legislation was used more frequently against unions ("combinations in restraint of trade") than against business until 1914, when the Clayton Act exempted unions from such laws, but in 1921 that too was reversed (*Duplex Printing* v. *Deering*).

By 1915, about 8 percent of the labor force was in unions (2.5 million workers). World War I and its accompanying upswing in production and the need for cooperation between business, labor, and government allowed the figure to double. Although the labor force increased between 1920 and 1933, union membership declined from five million to fewer than three million. The 1920's were a period of friendship between business and government, the years of Harding, Coolidge, and Hoover, of the "American Plan," of the "Red Scare," of "welfare capitalism." The American Plan was an open shop—*nonunion* shop—program. Its nature was epitomized by Mr. Dooley, the journalistic creation of Peter Finley Dunne, in a dialogue with his friend Hennessy: "But," says Hennessy, "these open shop min ye menshun say they are f'r unions if properly conducted." "Sure," says Mr. Dooley, "if properly conducted. An' there we are; an' how would they have thim conducted? No strikes, no rules, no contracts, no scales, hardly iny wages and damn few members."

In 1929 the Great Depression began. The prestige and power of the business community suffered. Businessmen had taken credit for all that was great in America; now business had somehow to explain how its genius had brought 25 percent unemployment, falling prices, bankruptcies, and the broad range of disasters of the Depression. Their explanation, which often placed the blame abroad, as did President Hoover, fell on deaf ears.

Enlightened corporate leaders had for decades seen the advantages of trade unionism, with effects both before and during World War I. But the largest number of businessmen were not so conscious of their own best interests over the long run, and in the euphoric 1920's even the "enlightened" leaders had changed their minds somewhat. In the Depression this view revived, and was given strength by the general unrest and by organizing drives of workers themselves. The government responded.

Inadequate legislation favoring unionism was made a part of the same law that created the National Recovery Administration in 1933. The inadequacy centered on the lack of provisions concerning business practices to fight against unionism, and of provisions that would enforce the legislation. These were substantially remedied by the Wagner (National Labor Relations) Act of 1935. After its passage the number of organized workers rose rapidly—from the low of 2.9 million in 1933, to 4 million in 1936, 7.3 million in 1938, 9.5 million in 1942, 13 million in 1946, and about 18 million by 1960, after which the rate of growth slowed down and stopped.

A casual reading of that numerical development might indicate that the labor legislation of the 1930's was the *cause* of this upsurge in trade union membership. It is perhaps more surprising that trade union growth was held back until the 1930's, than that it took place in and after that period. The development of mass production industries, the steady growth of the labor force, the virtual cessation of immigration in the 1920's, the loss of prestige by business after 1929, and the widespread social unrest of the Depression all must be given full weight in explaining the development of unions. So must the struggle of workers. The Wagner Act removed the legal obstacles to union organization and deprived employers of some of their traditional anti-union weapons. But the Act did not *establish* trade unions: the fight for union recognition was the major cause of industrial disputes between 1935 and World War II. Many of these disputes were extremely bitter and bloody; the waterfront strike in San Francisco of 1934 and the Republic Steel Strike of 1937 were the bloodiest of all.[19]

If the increase in the ranks of organized labor after 1935 resembled a flood, the Wagner Act was not the cause of the flood so much as the opener of the flood gates. Be that as it may, the legislation was important, and since then there has been an increasing reliance upon government by both business and labor to develop "anti" or "pro" labor legislation. Since World War II, the balance has tipped in favor of business—with the Taft-Hartley Act of 1947 (which reduced the benefits of the Wagner Act), and the Landrum-Griffin Act of 1959 standing out prominently. Of no little importance for the future of industrial relations was the process by which this more recent legislation was supported and framed: it occurred in an atmosphere of klieg lights, spectacular and unrepresentative revelations and headlines, and the whole gamut of techniques increasingly associated with congressional investigations. As one authority has put it:

> The method by which the provisions of the [Landrum-Griffin Act] were enacted justifies the most extreme cynicism toward the legislative process. Quite simply, the purposes of the various amendments were consistently and deliberately misrepresented to the general public, and for a good reason: Without the tremendous pressure exerted by public opinion, the Landrum-Griffin bill might never have passed the House. In a sense . . . it represents the failures of our democracy, for which all interested groups are in part to blame. Organized labor brought the new restrictions on its own head by insisting that amendments to the NLRA which it favored be included in any new legislation dealing with racketeering, corruption, and democratic union practices, and liberal legislators like Senator Kennedy yielded, presumably against their better judgment, to the union demands. Organized industry exploited the popular concern over dishonesty in labor-management relations and the lack of democracy in internal union affairs, and rallied support for NLRA amendments having little or no relevance to those issues. Finally, the average citizen continued to avoid acquainting himself with the basic problems involved, and fell back on the ingrained American habit of declaring, "There ought to be a law!" [20]

[19] Irving Bernstein, *The Lean Years: A History of the American Worker 1920–1933* and *The Turbulent Years: A History of the American Worker 1933–1941* (Boston: Houghton Mifflin Company, 1960 and 1969) are useful treatments of the years indicated.

[20] Benjamin Aaron, "The Labor-Management Reporting and Disclosure Act of 1959," *Harvard Law Review,* vol. 73, no. 6 (April, 1960), pp. 1126–27. Both the Taft-Hartley and Landrum-Griffin Acts are amendments to the Wagner Act, or NLRA.

I'm All Right, Jack

Up to this point in our discussion of organized labor we have been examining the development of a *trade union movement,* not a *labor movement.* The difference in terms is by no means a semantic one. Trade unions do and must fight for decent wages, working conditions, pensions, and, not least, their own continuity (which is called union security). Were they to cease to do so, general deterioration on all those matters would ensue. The union seeks to control the market in which labor power is sold; just as businesses seek to control the markets in which they sell their commodities. The goal in both cases is monopolistic control of the market; both cases are instances of what we have called *private mercantilism* earlier.

Without a trade union movement a labor movement could have no foundation of strength. But a labor movement goes beyond the terms of unionism; it is *political,* in the deepest sense of the term. A labor movement seeks State power, and seeks to gain it through being, or becoming affiliated with, a socialist movement.

As noted above, American trade unionism has had its political periods. One was from 1870 into the 1890's, before industrialism had taken a strong hold. The issues in that early period had to do with the money supply, with monopoly, with the manner of electing senators, and the like, issues affecting people in general, rather than workers in particular. Trade unions as such had little basis for national efforts, nor against nationally powerful corporations. Urban workers did cooperate with the angry farmers of the period to bring about, finally, the Populist Movement, which had a radical wing. In the 1930's, the CIO worked closely with what they hoped would be a continuing and ever-more liberal New Deal, and a social context favorable to the needs of working people. Since the 1940's, trade unions have stayed political, but in a narrow sense; at the leadership level (at least) this has more often than not meant working *with,* not against, the interests of corporate power and the military, and this has been more than symbolized by the hawkish and conservative positions of the leader of the AFL-CIO, George Meany. Labor leadership functions within the context of a rigid bureaucratic structure, which it is to the leadership's interests to exploit and maintain; the best means of doing that is for them to concentrate the efforts of the union on "wage-only" types of issues—quite apart from their own political attitudes.

But the political attitudes of labor leaders, however they may have begun, are not fixed in concrete. They are apt illustrations of the cooptation process noted earlier. The clear tendency of Big Business is to make it evident that they will only "do business" with business-minded unions— except when conditions warrant an attempt to destroy them, too. They do this by coming down with overwhelming power—their own and power that they can muster in the media and the courts—on socialist-minded labor leaders and movements.[21] Only those leaders and unions that find ways of working *within* the system find survival and success a feasible matter. Samuel Gompers, the first leader of the AFL, spread the slogan "reward our friends and punish our enemies." Business has found that to be a useful strategy in its dealings with organized labor, also.

It is more than understandable that trade unions would concentrate as much as they have on job control; the alternative is utter helplessness in the face of business power. In confining themselves largely to that aim and in doing so little to organize the overwhelming majority of *unorganized* workers, however, the unions have also found themselves adopting much the same aims and means as their business opponents. Thus, not only do unions attempt to control the supply of labor and use the strike as their principal weapon—both essential means—but they have also resorted to gangsters, racketeers, and physical violence for both defensive and offensive purposes, against both business and rival union organizers. The record in all these cases shows not only that the tactics of labor find their counterparts in the tactics of business, but also that business used each of these tactics first (and simultaneously). In the absence of a prolonged and deep commitment to fundamental social change on the part of labor—a labor movement—little else could be expected.[22]

None of this should be construed, it must be repeated, to mean that labor's efforts to organize or their uses of strength have been either unnecessary or damaging from the viewpoint of *all* workers. Unorganized workers have gained from the successes of the organized; the organized themselves have gained more, and have also learned organizational discipline which has been and can still be of fundamental importance for larger struggles. Nor would it be wise to overlook the difference between the functioning of the top bureaucracy of labor and the quite different functioning of *local* leaders, to say nothing of the growing militancy and enlarged focus of rank and file union members. Still, much more is needed if the ordinary people of this country are to have a decent existence in an

---

[21] A striking instance of this was in the attempt of the Waterfront Employers Association to have the leader of the longshore union, Harry Bridges, deported. Six trials occurred (beginning in the 1930's), in which the charge against Bridges (an Australian by birth) was that he was a member of the Communist Party and therefore deportable. The employers had the constant cooperation of the Immigration Service and what was proved to be their stable of paid informers. By the time of the sixth trial (after World War II), the *employers* moved to end the process, having found that the ILWU was a stabilizing influence on the waterfront.

[22] An analysis and history of these matters (up to the early 1930's) is provided by Louis Adamic, *Dynamite* ° (New York: Viking, 1934). C. Wright Mills, *New Men of Power* (New York: Harcourt Brace Jovanovich, 1948) provided an early study of the nature and probabilities of labor bureaucracy.

economic, political, and social sense.[23] Without the participation of trade unions in that larger struggle, the prospects for working people in this country are seriously, perhaps fatally, diminished. It is not only the success of trade unions in making some headway on "pork-chops" issues for themselves that holds them back from a broader view; it is also the degree to which organized workers participate in the patterns of racial and sexual discrimination and fear that so much characterize our history.[24] This is the Achilles heel of labor's strength in America; it is quite likely to be the terminal cancer of any viable American body politic. Further examination of this point is in order.

All Against All

We have to go back to the 1880's, at the very latest, to tie labor history in with the more general social history of America. Although immigration had been increasing since the 1850's, as we have seen, it was during the 1880's that the great waves of immigration from the poorer parts of Europe and from Asia began. By 1910 over one million immigrants a year were arriving, mostly from southern and southeastern Europe (over 200,000 southern Italians alone came in that year). These people came at a time when industrialization had taken strong hold and when the conditions of factory and city were becoming increasingly ugly. From the viewpoint of settled Americans (who were themselves immigrants from an earlier period, and from "better" areas of northern Europe such as England and Germany) these newcomers were also "increasingly ugly." Their language, their religion, their appearance—strange, "swarthy," Catholic, Jewish—set them against their predecessors, who, apart from the Irish, were mostly Protestant, and likely to be reasonably well-established.

America had been well-prepared for a translation of all this into divisions and hostility that were many-faceted. It had been prepared by our

[23] Sidney Peck, *The Rank-and-File Leader* * (New Haven: College & University Press, 1963) and Stanley Aronowitz, *False Promises* * (New York: McGraw-Hill, 1974) have similar hopes and fears concerning the workers of the U.S., and in their different ways they give reasons for both, regarding the possibilities for a genuine labor movement in the U.S. Both write from experience as workers.

[24] Which is not to overlook the many efforts made by unions throughout their history who fought for the breaking down of racial barriers—most notably in the Communist-led unions in the 1930's—and "equal pay for equal work" in the face of sex discrimination. Whether self-interested or not, such efforts are no less noteworthy, not least because unions were usually unique in pursuing them.

habituation to oppressing and even exterminating red, black, and brown peoples. The Populist Movement of the 1890's, which saw unprecedented political cooperation between poor whites and blacks, was the occasion for an intensification of racism. From the mid-1890's on, Jim Crow laws spread and deepened, and lynching became so common that it went unnoticed in the press (there were as many as a thousand a year officially recorded). The prior and continuing oppression of Native Americans joined with stepped-up oppression of black people and a rapid growth of American nationalism, religious bigotry and attitudes of cultural superiority. Savage developments in the eastern half of the country combined with savage developments in the western half, as Spanish-speaking and Asian immigrants were mistreated and killed (the lynching of Chinese was common in San Francisco at the turn of the century) while being exploited in the fields, mines, factories, and railroads.

Racial oppression and ethnic and religious hatreds did not begin in the United States, it should go without saying. But the competitive and combative atmosphere of the United States, taken together with the long-standing and well-entrenched acceptance of the Puritan work ethic and its corollary of economic individualism, made it easy for bigots and unscrupulous businessmen to exploit those pervasive inclinations. Given the enormous power and prestige of business in this country, workers would have had difficulty under the best of circumstances in forming unions or developing a labor movement. But workers accepted and developed internalized obstacles in their thinking and behavior, obstacles to thinking of themselves in terms of class solidarity.

The "Wobblies," never very influential in American labor or politics, lived by the slogan "an injury to one is an injury to all." The development of America has allowed most white men to see injuries to some as necessary to their own well-being—or even as desirable in and of themselves. Solidarity is a precious and delicate plant; it can scarcely grow or survive in a desert windstorm. It would be foolish to posit some inherent defect in the "American character" to explain the depth and pervasiveness of racism and sexism in our country, as foolish as it would be to ignore their existence in other countries. But it is not foolish to note how these characteristics have become accentuated and institutionalized in the United States to the point where it now appears that the very possibility of a decent future depends squarely on whether or not Americans can find ways to eliminate these practices and attitudes from our society.

Racism is one of the two leading social cancers that lead some human beings to view others as being less than human; the other is sexism. Historical and contemporary records point conclusively to one set of facts: nonwhite people and women of any color have been systematically deprived of basic human rights, have been systematically discriminated against in the kinds and levels of education normally available, have been systematically denied access to higher levels of work, and have been paid less for the same work when they could get it.[25]

TABLE 5–3 Median Incomes, 1964

FOR MEN	
Nonwhites' as a percentage of whites'	66 percent
FOR WOMEN	
Nonwhites' as a percentage of whites'	69 percent
FOR WHITES	
Women's as a percentage of men's	59 percent
FOR NONWHITES	
Women's as a percentage of men's	52 percent

SOURCE: Marilyn Power Goldberg, "The Economic Exploitation of Women," originally in *Liberation* (October, 1969). Reprinted in part in *RRPE* (Spring, 1970), in David M. Gordon, ed., *Problems in Political Economy: An Urban Perspective* (Boston: D. C. Heath, 1971), and in Edwards et al., *The Capitalist System,* cited earlier. These are U.S. Department of Labor data.

Summarizing the data, Goldberg points out that so far as money incomes are concerned, "this relative earning position, moreover, has not improved in the last twenty-five years, except for nonwhite women. White men have the highest median income, then nonwhite men, then white women, and finally nonwhite women." In December, 1972, the U.S. Department of Labor's Women's Bureau reported that the gap between men's and women's salaries and wages had widened substantially in the preceding years: full-time working women's wages as a percentage of men's had dropped from 64 percent in 1955 to 57 percent in 1970 (*New York Times,* December 28, 1972). As noted above, they were still at 57 percent in 1975: that is, women received five days' pay for nine days' work.

Incomes are of course an important measure of life in this society, but they are only a quantitative measure, and not an adequate measure even of that. It would of course be desirable if nobody's income were below the government's "poverty line" or, even better, if nobody lived below the level of "austerity." That so many people live below those lines in this very rich society should tell us that the elimination of poverty is not

[25] There is at least one important difference between racism and sexism that gives the former a different *economic* meaning than the latter. It is that women share the status and class of their fathers and husbands, quite generally. That is of course part of the meaning of sexism. But it does mean that there are fewer women as a percentage of all women who are *poor,* say, than blacks as a percentage of all blacks. *Within* a given class or racial category, women are worse off than men—as measured by jobs available, pay for the same jobs, etc., as Table 5–3 suggests.

an economic question, nor are its origins or its consequences to be measured in narrow economic ways. It has been calculated, for example, that well under $20 billion annually would eliminate all family money incomes below the poverty line. A society with a GNP well in excess of a trillion dollars whose governments spend in excess of three hundred billion dollars annually could not be economically strained by such a piddling amount. (Especially when we consider that other costs of government would thereby be reduced, and that other costs of government *should* be reduced.) That such a possibility is neither known about nor supported by most Americans is not a matter of economics or resources; it is a matter of attitudes and power.

The attitudes are those that look down upon the poor, and that despise and fear the nonwhite segment of the poor, which most white Americans would be surprised to learn constitute only one-third of the total officially described as poor. The power *not* to act along such lines is held at the top, but it is supported by the vast middle, who are mostly white, and mostly ordinary working people. Even were the money spent, to repeat, poverty would not be eliminated—not just because poverty is a relative matter, but because it is a social matter in the fullest sense. Its origins and its meanings are to be found in a complex pattern of inadequate education, health, and housing; in racial and sexual discrimination; in political powerlessness; in demoralization and a profound sense of hopelessness and disbelief. As Tussing says,

> [M]ost of the causes of poverty lie in the social and economic system as a whole, and not in the characteristics of the poor. . . [;] an economy or a society with a dominant majority of nonpoor persons and a minority of poor people has special characteristics, which are not perceived when one focuses only on the poor . . . [;] such economies in general, and the U.S. economy in particular exhibit a fundamental duality. Such economies adjust to the needs and behavior of the nonpoor majority, with subtle but harmful consequences for the poor.[26]

That such patterns are allowed and encouraged to exist in a society at once so rich and so proud of its watchwords of freedom and equality points to the profound dehumanization of the largest percentage of Americans. How has American capitalism managed to so dehumanize its people? We need only think through what has been said earlier in other connections. Americans from the beginning were told and were convinced that a capitalist economy would, when functioning successfully, achieve not only maximum incomes, but the freest (and best) of societies.

[26] *Poverty in a Dual Economy*, p. vii. Tussing goes on to point to the dual labor market, dual welfare system, and, among other matters, the dual housing system of the U.S.

The fact that this was believed while at the same time Native Americans were being killed and shoved aside, and Africans enslaved, means that racism, a virus carried over from Europe, had found a particularly receptive host in the United States. The success of American capitalism relied upon many things, of course, but, most relevant here, such success depended upon a single-minded concern with economic gain. This single-mindedness was made possible by a society that led its people to believe that other matters would somehow take care of themselves, or that they would be taken care of by others, in a government in which all would be represented by periodic voting.

For those at or near the top of society, the social context thus contained only one serious obstacle to their search for money and power—the competition of others also at the top. For those on the bottom, the simple struggle to eke out a tolerable level of life was all-consuming. Competition in markets came to mean competition of one segment of society against the other, as people became commodities, and both subjects and objects of gain. People as well as products have price tags. Life becomes commercial life; life becomes commercialized; it becomes dehumanized, quantified, trivialized—alienated.

Such talk has become common these days, as we now hear of the need to think of "the quality of life"—although it is difficult to conceive why what is obvious to most people must now be worked up as though it were a complicated new problem. Withal, the social scientists continue to think and work in quantitative terms, to seek to quantify the qualitative; and because quantification can never be the starting point of social analysis, the quantitative data and measures that are employed have themselves become part of the problem. The history of the "war on poverty" in the United States is a case in point.

Poverty Amidst Plenty

The degree to which so many Americans have walled themselves off from the ugly side of our reality was captured well by Michael Harrington, when he spoke of "the invisible poor." [27] In 1962, when the United States was congratulating itself on having to face the problems of affluence, there were by a highly conservative estimate (see Wilcox's quote below) nine million families plus five million unrelated individuals living at annual incomes below the official poverty line—that is, about one-fifth of the nation. Poverty cannot be understood, let alone eliminated, by thinking of it in purely quantitative terms; but it would be a step in the

[27] In his *The Other America* * (Baltimore, Penguin, 1962).

right direction to use accurate and meaningful quantitative definitions, at the very least. Because the government's definitions have become *the* definitions, it is important to show just how inadequate—some would say ludicrous, others obscene—those definitions are.

It was in 1964 that the government, responding to Harrington's book and the civil rights turmoil of the time, developed an estimate of the number of poor in America. This was done by the Council of Economic Advisers, at President Johnson's order. It is worth quoting a respected textbook on how that estimate was accomplished:

> The Council's estimate was based upon a study by the Social Security Administration of the income needed to support a nonfarm family of four. The SSA had established two standards for such a family, both based on estimates of dietary costs prepared by the Department of Agriculture: [1] a "low-cost" budget, permitting the minimum diet consistent with the food preferences of the lowest third of the population and adequate to avoid basic nutritional deficiencies. . . . The resulting budget stood at $3,995. This called for a far higher level of expenditure than welfare agencies were allowing for families receiving public assistance. *To meet the administrative need of these bodies*, the SSA prepared . . . [2] an "economy budget" based on a *deficiency diet designed for temporary or emergency use* . . . set[ting] the total budget at $3,165. On the basis of this figure, the CEA adopted $3,000 as its family poverty line . . ., [and] $1,500 as the line for a single individual. It thus found . . . some 35,000,000 people, a fifth of the nation, to be in poverty in 1962.[28]

Poverty must be "defined" by someone; as things go these days that someone means the government. Inadequate though the definitions have been, both qualitatively and quantitatively, they may seem less so in the future if recent plans materialize. The *New York Times* reported on April 4, 1973, under the headline "U.S. to Redefine What 'Poverty' Is," that the Office of Management and Budget (directed by Roy Ash, formerly head of Litton Industries, one of the fancier conglomerates) is "quietly examining the possibility of doing away with federal use of the word 'poverty' and of changing the income figures used to define the poor, 'because current usage exaggerates the [rising] number of poor,'" Presumably the new definition will be well-established by 1984; until the dispensation is provided, we will go on with the Johnsonian style.

The $3,000 estimate of 1964, which increased by the rate of inflation to $5500 in 1975, still is the universally used criterion for estimating the extent of poverty in the United States. As we saw earlier, the Bureau of

[28] Clair Wilcox, *Toward Social Welfare* (Homewood, Ill.: Irwin, 1969), pp. 26–27. Italics mine. The "emergency use" diet was first concocted by the Office of Civil Defense for a post-nuclear attack period! The article by Donald Light, cited earlier, is useful for this section.

Labor Statistics—an agency with more of a civil service and less of a vulgarly political position than the Council of Economic Advisers, which is appointed by and serves the president—calculated $9,800 as necessary for a "minimum budget for food, clothing, and housing, with little left over," for 1975. If poverty is to be defined in quantitative income terms, that figure seems more compelling than one designed for "emergency" periods: poverty is not only an emergency but a persisting condition.

To understand its persistence requires going beyond figures and into relationships, which can be seen as a set of vicious circles. To be born poor is to live in inadequate housing in over-crowded neighborhoods with bad schools, and little or no recreational facilities; it is to be mired down in an atmosphere of hopelessness—to say nothing of poor health, of crime, of price-gouging in the stores, of job discrimination, and of political underrepresentation. The psychological impact of such living can only be imagined (or read about) by those who have not experienced it directly; but it takes little imagination to perceive that those who are born poor are likely to stay poor and to have children who will be poor— with here and there an exception that proves the rule. Why, in a rich society like the United States would poverty for tens of millions of people persist? Why would poverty be institutionalized?

One way to begin to answer such questions is to ask another question: Who benefits from the persistence of poverty? And who pays? The easy and the most widespread answer suggests that nobody—except the welfare recipient—benefits, and that the upper layers of the society pay. But analysis shows otherwise, which it will be worth pursuing here. Two recent essays will be cited, one from the liberal and the other from the radical quarter.

In an article entitled "The Uses of Poverty: The Poor Pay All," Professor Herbert Gans has listed and discussed thirteen "functions" of poverty. "Functions" refer to "those observed consequences of a phenomenon which make for the adaptation or adjustment of a given . . . set of interest groups, socio-economic classes, and other population aggregates with shared values that 'inhabit' a social system." In brief, the useful functions posited by Gans are: (1) The existence of poverty ensures that society's "dirty work" will be done; (2) The very low wages of the poor subsidize a variety of economic activities that benefit the affluent (as domestic servants, for instance), and the poor pay a disproportionate share of all taxes (see Chapter 8); (3) Poverty creates jobs for middle-income people who "serve" the poor, such as social workers, prison guards, and so on; (4) The poor buy goods that others wouldn't, which is profitable to those who produce and sell them. These four functions are *economic* uses of the poor; the remaining nine are social and political. They include the self-defined elevation in moral and social standing that middle-class attitudes toward the poor allow to the middle class; the absorption by the poor of the costs of socioeconomic change, being powerless to do otherwise (most vividly, these days, in being pushed out of their homes for freeways, urban renewal, and the like); their availability as cannon-fodder for wars; their utility as a basis for arguing against liberal or left social change.[29]

Howard Wachtel, a radical economist, does not dispute the kind of points made by Gans, but he seeks to explore the *causes* of poverty. He points out, quite rightly, that everything said about the *uses* of poverty is consistent with an attitude that places the *causes* in the poor's short-comings as individuals. Those shortcomings usually fall under the head-ings of laziness, shiftlessness, and the like. But most of the poor (1) work full-time but at wages that leave them (and their families) underneath the official poverty line, or half-time because they cannot gain full-time jobs; (2) are handicapped and unable to work; or (3) are retired, having worked at low incomes when younger.[30]

How people get into and get stuck in such a situation was suggested by the metaphor of the vicious circle, above. More concretely (and only in part), we may look at the relationship of education to jobs, and of the jobs of the poor to the existence of the "dual economy." And finally we may examine the role of the State in the perpetuation of poverty. By now everyone must be aware of the "tracking system" (which in the early years of schooling classifies children according to tests and per-formance that do not always accurately reflect cultural background, thus forcing them toward lower or upper income occupations by virtue of the curricula in which they are placed) in primary and secondary education, and the relationship between that and subsequent education, to say nothing of the wretched quality of the primary and secondary schools attended by most of the poor (whether white or nonwhite).[31]

[29] Herbert Gans is Professor of Sociology and Planning at M.I.T. This article will be found in *Social Policy* (July/August, 1971).

[30] Wachtel's analysis, "Capitalism and Poverty in America: Paradox or Contradic-tion?" is in *Monthly Review* (June, 1972), along with two other essays supplementing his views by David Gordon and Barry Bluestone. Bluestone's essay is a version of the Statement before the Joint Economic Committee of Congress, referred to earlier, on the dual economy. Wachtel and Bluestone, along with many others have articles in-cluded in the excellent collection by Pamela Roby, *The Poverty Establishment,* cited earlier, in my view the best of such books.

[31] For extended discussion of the general role of education in maintaining poverty and class distinctions, see Samuel Bowles, "Contradictions in U.S. Higher Education," in James Weaver, ed., *Modern Political Economy*, pp. 165–200, his "Unequal Educa-tion and the Social Division of Labor," *RRPE* (Fall/Winter, 1971), and Herb Gintis, "Education, Technology, and the Characteristics of Worker Productivity," *American Economic Review* (May, 1971). These articles have become part of an important book by Bowles and Gintis, *Schooling in Capitalist America* (New York: Basic Books, 1976). See also the fine book by Miriam Wasserman, *The School Fix, NYC, USA* (New York: Simon & Schuster, Clarion, 1970), for an intensive study of one school system in full display. Her *Demystifying School* (New York: Praeger, 1974) is a

Education, beginning at the very first years, can and should be a process in which the young not only realize their creative and practical possibilities in terms of their life's work, but also a process whereby human beings learn to appreciate and to understand nature, society, human culture, and themselves. Instead, and especially for the poor, schools have taken on the quality of disciplinary barracks (and, for the better off, as Maynard Hutchins once put it, "play pens"), disillusioning and and embittering both students and teachers, to say nothing of parents and taxpayers. Presumably, in a society as rich as ours something better is economically possible. Given the concentration of power that exists in the society, it may be assumed that if the powerful had the will to change the situation, they could find the way. That the educational system deteriorates, rather than improves, allows one to conclude that a system designed for human needs and possibilities is not high on the priority list of those with power, if it is on the list at all.

The young who are maleducated and miseducated quite naturally find themselves able to get only the meanest jobs once they drop out of school or graduate. They get jobs in what Bluestone and O'Connor call the competitive (or "peripheral and irregular") sector, where productivity, power, and incomes are low. What the State does to mitigate these conditions—through manpower training programs and the like—will be examined in Chapter 8. There we will see that at the very best, State programs do no more than hold the line, and that more often they contribute to making a bad situation worse.

Affluence and Reality

It seems appropriate now to recall our criticism of the notion of "prosperity" in the 1920's (discussed in Chapter 4), and to relate that to the current notion of "affluence." Like so much else in the way of judgment in America, the *judgment* of affluence originates in the upper middle class and has a quantitative basis; it depends upon the height of real per capita income, absolutely and in comparison with other *nations*. If affluence is meant to suggest more than that, the notion dissolves—if, that is, we assume that affluence has some reference to the well-being of the *society* as distinct from a small fraction of its people; if we define that well-being in quantitative terms that do not include the military

comprehensive anthology of fine essays treating of the many dimensions of the schooling system. See also David Smith, *Who Rules the University?* (New York: Monthly Review Press, 1974) and Martin Carnoy, *Education as Cultural Imperialism* * (New York: McKay, 1974).

and the mountains of wasteful and trivial (to say nothing of offensive) production; if we examine what is available to the population in terms of convenient transportation, clean air and water, health, educational and recreational facilities, as well as insurance against natural and manmade disasters. If we combine qualitative with quantitative judgments, in short, we may reckon our society as being closer to general impoverishment than to affluence.

Earlier, we pointed out that if (as is impossible in capitalist society) money income had been divided equally among all families in 1970, each would have about $11,000, and that in 1971 it took just about that amount for the average family to sustain a moderate budget in the average city. Only two-thirds of the population lives in cities, of course, and it costs less to live outside the city, generally. But that figure is a before-tax figure; and all taxes take about one-third of the GNP. If we were to deduct one-third from the $11,000 (or $12,000, taking account of GNP increases since 1971), the national average would be down to just about the amount needed for a *minimum* budget. Of course, some taxes are used for expenditures that are life-serving, but it stretches the imagination to believe that is the case with most governmental expenditures,[32] if one takes account of the military, the excessive highway system, interest payments on the national debt (which is accumulated mostly in or for war and going almost entirely to upper income groups), subsidies to upper income farmers and agricultural corporations, stockpiling corporations, and the like. Partisans of almost any viewpoint could quibble until doomsday about the arithmetic of such conjectures, but what would remain, after all was said and done, would not be a level or quality of life that would suggest "affluence."

Like the notion of the prosperity of the twenties, the affluence of the recent past is for most Americans a cruel joke. So was the "glory that was Rome" for most Romans, something other than glorious. The decline and fall of the Roman empire has been cited innumerable times by critics of western society, as though what happened there and then can happen here and now. It cannot, because the societies have more differences than similarities. Some of the similarities are nonetheless telling. One of the most respected of the historians of Rome, in a chapter entitled "The Disorganization of Public Service," wrote (in 1898) an analytical condemnation of Roman society that brought together the interaction of poverty, inequality of income and wealth, overweening power and rampant greed

---

[32] Including what have recently come to be called "tax expenditures," meaning "implicit transfer payments" brought about through tax laws which, in enabling deductions (almost always to property owners and their incomes) require an increase in others' taxes to finance the budget. They came to about $23 billion in 1971. See Tussing, *Poverty in a Dual Economy*, pp. 62–63.

that with only minor adjustments might have been written of our country today:

It will be seen that in a society in which poverty is almost branded with infamy, poverty is steadily increasing and wealth becoming more insolent and aggressive; that the disinherited, in the face of an omnipotent government, are carrying brigandage even up to the gates of Rome; that parents are selling their children into slavery; that public buildings are falling into decay; that the service on the great post roads is becoming disorganised. . . . [F]raud and greed are everywhere triumphant, . . . the rich are growing richer and more powerful, while the poor are becoming poorer and more helpless. . . .

The overwhelming tragedy of that age was the result not of violent and sudden calamities; it was prepared by the slow, merciless action of social and economic laws, and deepened by the perverse energy of government, and the cupidity and cruelty of the rich and highly-placed.[33]

Reading Suggestions

The history of labor has been treated only superficially above; those wishing to gain an adequate basis for judgment will find no shortage of books. No one book on such a controversial area can stand as sufficient. A good place to begin is with Len De Caux, *Labor Radicals** (Boston: Beacon Press, 1970), which takes the story from the Wobblies up to the very recent past by one who was part of it and a fine writer to boot—as is Sidney Lens, whose *The Labor Wars** (New York: Anchor, 1974) is important and revealing. The classic source book and compendium is John R. Commons, et al., *History of Labor in the United States*, 4 vols. (New York: Macmillan, 1918–1935). Of the several Marxist studies of labor history in America, the most comprehensive is the multivolume work of Philip Foner, *History of Labor in the United States** (New York: International Publishers, 1947 *et seq.*). See also the deservedly popular *Labor's Untold Story**, by Richard Boyer and Herbert Morais (New York: United Electrical, Radio, and Machine Workers of America, 1974). Much has been written of the colorful "Wobblies." The definitive study is probably Melvyn Dubofsky, *We Shall Be All** (Chicago: Quadrangle, 1969). A convenient survey is Patrick Renshaw, *The Wobblies** (New York: Doubleday; Anchor Books, 1968). The drama and vitality of the Wobblies is caught best in the anthology by Joyce L. Kornbluh, *Rebel Voices** (Ann Arbor: University of Michigan Press, 1964). The New England

[33] Samuel Dill, *Roman Society in the Last Century of the Western Empire* * (New York: Meridian, 1958), pp. 228–9, 244.

Free Press pamphlet, *A Guide to Working Class History* is very useful (60 Union Square, Somerville, Ma., 02143).

Turning to inequality, poverty, racism, and sexism: the most penetrating analysis of America poverty is that of Ben Seligman, *Permanent Poverty,* cited earlier. A useful book of readings is Robert E. Will and Harold G. Vatter, eds., *Poverty in Affluence** (New York: Harcourt Brace Jovanovich, 1970). An excellent analytical treatment of urban blacks' economic situation is William K. Tabb, *The Political Economy of the Black Ghetto** (New York: Norton, 1970). Two excellent studies of broader scope are Robert L. Allen, *Black Awakening in Capitalist America** (New York: Doubleday; Anchor Books, 1970), and Raymond S. Franklin and Solomon Resnik, *The Political Economy of Racism** (New York: Harper & Row, 1973). Patricia Cayo Sexton, *Spanish Harlem** (New York: Harper & Row, 1965), studies the conditions of Spanish-speaking Americans. G. Osofsky, *Harlem: The Making of a Ghetto** (New York: Harper & Row, 1966) examines the history of black people in New York City through the 19th century and up to about 1930; in doing so he reveals how pressures and policies have worked to create and maintain patterns of discrimination from the very beginning. Arthur M. Ford, *Political Economics of Rural Poverty in the South* (Cambridge, Mass.: Ballinger, 1973) and David M. Gordon, *Theories of Poverty and Under-employment* (Boston: D. C. Heath & Co., 1972) are instructive and original analyses, as is Tussing, cited earlier.

A profound recent work on inequality and the context within which it is created and accepted is William Ryan, *Blaming the Victim** (New York: Vintage, 1971), wherein the author attempts the most difficult of tasks: trying to show people the ideological and mythological fog within which their attitudes move. (Some of this is excerpted in Roby, cited earlier).

References to works on sexism could be multiplied as each day passes, for the literature is growing rapidly. A book of readings that makes a good starting-place is Robin Morgan, ed., *Sisterhood is Powerful** (New York: Random House, 1970). The economic aspects of sexism are explored in Margaret Benston, "The Political Economy of Women's Liberation," *Monthly Review* (September, 1969); M. and J. Roundtree, "More on the Political Economy . . . ," *Monthly Review* (January, 1970); Peggy Morton, "A Woman's Work is Never Done," *Leviathan* (May, 1970); and URPE in its *RRPE*, vol. 4, no. 3 (July, 1972), has an entire issue, *The Political Economy of Women*, with about twenty essays ranging over a broad range of relevant questions, as it does again in Vol. 8, No. 1 (Spring 1976), *Women and the Economy*. Eli Zaretsky, "Capitalism, the Family, and Personal Life: Part 1," *Socialist Revolution*, vol. 3, nos. 1 & 2 (January-April, 1973), after a cogent review of major analytical contributions of the Women's Movement, goes on to provide a penetrating and original historical analysis (a model of what Marxian analysis can be) of the development of sexism and the family under capitalist conditions. Zaretsky's entire group of essays in this area is now available as a pamphlet from *Socialist Revolution* (396 Sanchez St., San Francisco, Ca. 94114), by the title indicated above, at $1.25. A penetrating and wide-ranging collection of essays on various dimensions of women's struggles written by Juliet Mitchell is available as *Woman's Estate** (New York: Vintage, 1973).

The literature concerned with oppression of Native Americans is growing also. A powerful historical treatment (of the period 1860–1890) is Dee Brown, *Bury My Heart at Wounded Knee** (New York: Bantam, 1971). A study of contemporary conditions from a moderate standpoint, and perhaps therefore all the more shocking, is Edgar S. Cahn, ed., *Our Brother's Keeper: The Indian in White America** (New York: World, 1969). Also consult the bibliography of *To Serve the Devil* (cited earlier) for further readings on racism as it has affected all groups in the United States.

The term *class* (working class, ruling class) has been used frequently in the text. My own understanding of the origins and the meanings of class distinctions has been woven through the materials beginning with Chapter 1. For other viewpoints, and for definitional treatments of this vital and complicated matter, see T. B. Bottomore, *Classes in Modern Society** (New York: Vintage, 1966); R. H. Tawney, *Equality** (New York: Capricorn, 1961; originally published in 1929); G. William Domhoff, *Who Rules America?** (Englewood Cliffs N.J.: Prentice-Hall, Spectrum, 1967) and his *The Higher Circles** (New York: Vintage, 1971). *Power, Politics and People: The Collected Essays of C. Wright Mills,** edited by Irving Louis Horowitz (New York: Oxford University Press, 1963) contains many essays on class, power, ideology, education and other issues most relevant to many of the chapters of this book. Marx and Veblen use class analysis throughout their writings, and I won't attempt to cite particular works. Mention of the "new working class" was made early in this chapter; on that, see Herb Gintis, "The New Working Class and Revolutionary Youth," *Socialist Revolution,* vol. 1, no. 3 (May-June, 1970). See also the penetrating studies of Richard Sennett and Jonathan Cobb, *The Hidden Injuries of Class** (New York: Knopf, 1972) and of F. Piven and R. Cloward, *Regulating the Poor: The Functions of Public Welfare** (New York: Vintage, 1971), some of which is excerpted in Roby. Finally, Charles H. Anderson, *The Political Economy of Social Class* (Englewood Cliffs, N.J.: Prentice-Hall, 1974) is a valuable and comprehensive analytical survey of an immense literature by a radical sociologist.

6

Nature and Nurture;
Country and City

Black spruce and Norway pine,
Douglas fir and Red cedar,
Scarlet oak and Shagbark hickory.
We built a hundred cities and a thousand towns—
But at what a cost!
We cut the top off the Alleghenies and sent it down the river.
We cut the top off Minnesota and sent it down the river.
We cut the top off Wisconsin and sent it down the river.
We left the mountains and the hills slashed and burned,
And moved on. *

They are herding our hearts down freeways.
The architects of America say
This is how it will be in another century:
We will join with armies of geese
In the cities of weeds,
Living on grass, in love with our own dung.†

The problems we now face in our environment and in our cities are problems of whole systems in dynamic imbalance. These problems have existed in significant degree from our very first years; they are simultaneously physical and social, economic and political, psychological and historical and ideological, in their origins and in their continuation and worsening over time. Can conventional economics grapple successfully with such problems?

* Pare Lorentz, from the soundtrack of the film, *The River*. From *A New Anthology of Modern Poetry*, Selden Rodman, ed. Reprinted by permission of Stackpole Books.
† Floyce Alexander, *Los Angeles*. Reprinted with permission of the author.

Conventional economics is abstract; it is concerned with purely quantitative *market* relationships; it takes both nature and historical time as "given," as it does also with technology; it has both a limited and an incorrect view of human psychology; and it totally ignores ideological and developmental matters. Such an economics can provide little understanding of either the nature or the origins of what now mounts to the crisis stage. Indeed, it is precisely what economists consider most necessary and most desirable—that is, maximization—that, in America's historical development, accounts for much of what has "gone wrong." Those who have exploited our natural resources, whether farmers, mineral or timber companies, or whatever, and those who have "developed" and ravaged our cities, have been businessmen or have moved in tandem with them. To provide a society dominated by such motivations with a market economics of maximization is like providing an alcoholic with directions to the nearest bar.

In the nineteenth century and the first part of the twentieth there was already awareness of both environmental and urban problems, and around the turn of the century movements to urge reforms emerged in both areas: the "conservation movement" and the "progressive movement." Their views as to the nature and the resolution of these problems did not lead them to examine basic institutions or to question the processes fostered by those institutions. They were reformers who, though often idealistic, were concerned with the economic and social inefficiency of rapacious resource use and of teeming and unsightly cities. They were concerned with making the existing system work better, more efficiently, and less turbulently, over time.[1]

The conservationists and urban progessives, who were often the same people, sought to bring order out of the chaos induced by the rapid and pervasive industrialization and urbanization of the turn of the century. Their contemporary counterparts are the liberal ecologists and urban planners. Their viewpoint is partially, but only partially, valid. They seek to eliminate dangerous and destructive resource utilization and deep inadequacies in urban existence, an aim entirely praiseworthy. But they view these problems as *extrinsic* to the American system. Quite correctly, they assume that American capitalism does not *need* blighted cities, polluted air, cut-over land, and wasted resources. Yet they fail to see that for capitalist development to proceed satisfactorily in its own

---

[1] See Faulkner, *The Decline of Laissez-Faire*, Chapter 15 ("The Era of Reform"), and also his *Quest for Social Justice* (New York: Macmillan, 1931), a social history of the progressive period. The best treatment of the conservation movement is Samuel P. Hays, *Conservation and the Gospel of Efficiency* (Cambridge: Harvard University Press, 1959). James Ridgeway, *The Politics of Ecology* (New York: Dutton, 1971), traces the development back to the English Industrial Revolution, through the pre-World War I period, and up to the present.

terms—as distinct from human terms—the economy cannot be constrained so as to *forestall* blighted cities, polluted air, and the rest. This analytical failing means that mainstream-liberal policy recommendations must be at best inadequate and at worst damaging. The problem of the inaccurate compass being worse than none at all, once more.

To repeat an important point: the prime reason for the *economic* dynamism of American capitalism has been precisely that it has been *socially* unconstrained. Now, when discussion is no longer about problems, as earlier in the century, but about crises, the universe of discourse must alter to meet our sense that time is running out.

Economists and other social scientists, once in the background of such discussions, have today moved more to the fore. Whether economists have anything to contribute depends upon whether or not economics moves toward the dynamic perspective of political economy (and similarly, in the appropriate ways, for the rest of social science). If it does so, and as it does so, it will have to be informed by some firm idea of the continuity of our development, of what brought us to where we are today, and of the manner in which business impulses have meshed with social and political developments to push us ever more rapidly to our critical present. The story begins with farmers, and their much idealized "way of life."

Farming as a Way of Business

The United States is the most industrialized of all societies. Yet, our social nature remains inexplicable if we ignore the dominating role played by farmers in the shaping of our history, our outlook, and our domestic and foreign policies. The first settlers came here for many reasons, but they all found themselves exploiting the land (and shoving aside or slaughtering its original inhabitants). Up to the end of the nineteenth century, and despite the great surge of industrialization that began around 1850, the numbers, the prestige, the economic importance, and the social outlook of farmers continued to take a leading role in setting the tone of American life. The tone was businesslike, and it was expansionist.

It began that way. Farming is, of course, "a way of life," as its proponents so often say. But American agriculture has been given its qualities and direction by those who are best at making money from the cultivation of and speculation in land. Less than a decade after the first settlers set foot at what became Jamestown, Virginia, their livelihood was dependent upon tobacco exports to England. So intense was their concentration on the marketing of tobacco that the Governor of Virginia (in

1616) had to *require* that each colonist plant at least two acres of corn for himself and each male servant, to avoid starvation.[2]

There were of course great differences in the agriculture of the southern and northern regions of the American colonies. But the differences were in the meanness or generosity of climate and soil, not in intentions. For those who set the tone of farming, the intention was to make money, not subsistence, from the land. The South was by far the most productive region, with its rich soils and long growing seasons. Beginning with tobacco in the seventeenth century, the South went on to raise indigo (for dyeing), rice, cotton, and sugar. Slaves were used in tobacco cultivation; but large-scale slavery awaited large-scale cultivation: plantations. Plantations began with rice and indigo, but became most characteristic with sugar, and, of course, cotton. Cotton became king as three developments merged: the British industrial revolution (whose leading sector was cotton textiles), competition from Mexican long-staple cotton, and the invention of the cotton gin in 1793 (which made practicable the use of short-staple cotton, the variety best-suited to the southern lands). The entire range of southern agriculture was commercialized, and dependent upon foreign markets—entirely dependent before the Revolution, and critically so thereafter.

The economics of southern farming kept the plantation owner and the small farmer alike in debt, as they responded to market conditions and unfavorable bargaining terms set by powerful brokers, shippers, and financiers in (usually) London. Indebtedness combined with the rapid exhaustion of the soil (especially in tobacco and cotton cultivation) to make the southern agriculturist an expansionist in two ways. He had to keep moving westward in search of more fertile lands; his marketing focus was necessarily international.[3]

In the North, nature was less generous than in the South, but still very generous indeed by comparison with, say, typical European conditions. The colonies in New York, Pennsylvania, and New Jersey raised grains and livestock, for domestic but also for export sale mostly to the Caribbean and the Mediterranean. The harsh climate and rocky soils of New England made those settlers into part-time farmers, and into part-time loggers or handicraftsmen, whalers and fishermen, until commerce and

---

[2] These "indentured servants" were before long outnumbered by African slaves. A useful overall history of American agriculture is U.S. Department of Agriculture, *Farmers in a Changing World* (Washington: USGPO, 1940), especially the first three hundred pages or so. Like many governmental studies written in the Roosevelt years, this book is remarkably objective, which can not usually be said of those issued today.

[3] See Eugene Genovese, *The Political Economy of Slavery** (New York: Pantheon, 1965), especially Chapter 4. The title is an accurate indication of this important book's contents. Subsequently, Genovese has produced the rich and probably definitive "political sociology" of slavery, in his *Roll, Jordan, Roll: The World the Slaves Made* * (New York: Pantheon, 1974).

manufacturers took hold enough to create urban markets for their diversified farms. But, like their counterparts in the so-called Middle Colonies and in the South, the New England farmers were always looking westward, and were always tied into foreign markets, directly or indirectly, for their economic well-being.

There was always a multiplicity of reasons for westward expansion from all the Colonies, and there continued to be long after independence. But tied to those other reasons—exhausted soils, excessive competition, a simple restless itch to move on—was one constant: land speculation. We cannot know the degree to which the westward movement would have been slowed without land speculation, but we may be sure it would have been a significant reduction quantitatively, and that the whole quality of the process would have been much altered. On that score, there is no disagreement among historians. Veblen put it in his own way:

> Habitually and with singular uniformity the American farmers have aimed to acquire real estate at the same time that they have worked at their trade as husbandmen. . . . They have habitually "carried" valuable real estate at the same time that they have worked the soil of so much of their land as they could take care of, in as effectual a manner as they could under these circumstances. They have been cultivators of the main chance as well as of the fertile soil. . . .[4]

Farmers, Politics, and Power

The passion for increasingly more land, in a country predominantly agricultural in its functions and outlook, meant that the political issues roiling American life in the century before the Civil War would revolve around the land, its value, and its uses. And so it was. *Land policy*—the accessibility, the size, and the price of western lands—persisted as a boiling issue. And, since the ownership of lands always required access to money and credit, monetary policy and control over banking were also destined to be a continuous source of political controversy. Because the market value of lands was, in important part, a function of their earning power, and because that in turn was vitally dependent upon the foreign trade of the United States, tariff policy was a key issue. Finally, to enhance and to realize the possibilities of real estate speculation and the marketing of commodities, an adequate transportation network (canals and railroads) was essential. It was around these issues that power struggles took place in the century before the Civil War. They contributed to the War for Independence and they were decisive for the

[4] *Absentee Ownership,* p. 135.

outbreak of the Civil War. The farmers won on all of them; or, so it seemed.

In 1763, the British "drew a line" the length of the Appalachian range—the "Proclamation Line"—beyond which American colonists were forbidden to invest, trap, or farm. Probably no single act of the British was more unanimously opposed throughout the Colonies than this. It brought together northern and southern farmers, merchants, frontiersmen, and financiers, and revealed to the colonists that a century and a half of westward movement, for them, would have to be halted. This in turn meant that their economic hopes and even their solvency were doomed, to the advantage of British capitalists. The resistance of agriculturists to that order found its more positive counterpart immediately after the Revolution, in the Land Ordinances of 1785 and 1787 establishing the procedures for settling the West; in their steady pressure to reduce the minimum size of land purchase, and the cost per acre; in their pressure on local, state, and federal agencies to build canals and railroads; in the successful battle (in Jackson's regime) to destroy the credit-controlling Second Bank of the United States; in the movement toward free trade of the 1840's; and in the ability of northern industrialists and financiers to persuade western farmers to join in the battle against the southerners in the Civil War. This last was with the inducement of a more generous land and transportation policy, and the fear that unless southern power could be displaced, western lands would fall under an unfavorable political dispensation.[5]

If farmers were winning all these battles, they were doing so, increasingly after mid-century, as unwitting tools of what Veblen calls the "massive vested interests" of the rising industrial state. Farmers found themselves after the Civil War faced with sharply falling prices, with monopolistic railroads and commission merchants, and with monetary and tariff policies cut to the needs not of farmers but of industrialists and financiers. The farmers were becoming, in short, an internal colony of the United States—they who had been the ideal, the presumably incontrovertible source of American virtue.

Before the Civil War, farmers had been political but, because of their pervasive strength, loosely so. After the Civil War, they began to organize. The last quarter-century was dominated by the political struggle that ensued. The manner in which the farmers both won and lost had consequences reaching far beyond anything they sought or, except in an occasional nightmare, dreamed of. The farmers sought only to maintain and expand the value of their lands and an ever-expanding market for their livestock and their crops. To gain those limited ends, they wittingly and unwittingly greased the skids for a vicious speed-up in

[5] The controversies affecting the evolution of the American State, and the meaning of, for example, the Second Bank, are examined on pp. 283–85.

racism, for what has become an American empire, and for an agriculture less of farmers than of corporations.[6]

More Corn, More Hell

It will be recalled that the several decades after the Civil War were marked by worldwide industrialization, by marked improvements in technology, in transportation and in communications, by pervasive national and international trade and competition, and by a tidal wave of economic imperialism. One of the innumerable consequences of those processes was falling prices, whose obverse side was rising production. The bushel price of wheat in 1871 was $1.24; in 1894 it was 49 cents; the production of wheat rose from 173 million bushels in 1859 to 468 million bushels in 1884. But all production and all prices were moving along such lines: the wholesale price index for *all* commodities fell from 135 in 1872 to 69 in 1896.[7]

In that context, the classic rule of American economic life kept its hold: survival of the fittest. The "fittest" in farming were those whose lands could enlarge, whose technology could improve, and whose marketing and financial arrangements could be arranged most efficiently and least expensively. But whether large or small, the farmers joined in a campaign from the late 1860's until the end of the century to alter the setting in which that contest would be fought out. This era of agrarian discontent, or the "Agrarian Uprising," took shape first as a national movement, with the founding of The Patrons of Husbandry ("The Grange"), in 1867. Soon one woman coined the slogan by which the movement came to be identified: "Raise less corn and more Hell." The farmers raised more of both.

Along with falling prices (beginning in the early 1870's), which was the result of impersonal forces working in the national and world economies, there were developments that were by no means impersonal, and the farmers fought all of them. In 1873, silver had been "demonetized." That act, passed by the powerful Republican Party, meant that the United States went on a gold standard, and that its supply of circulating

---

[6] See, for part of the story, C. Vann Woodward, *The Strange Career of Jim Crow** (New York: Oxford University Press, 1966), and his *Tom Watson: Agrarian Rebel** (New York: Oxford University Press, 1963), which clarify the dual nature of populism, moving between reform and racism. The treatment of farmers and foreign policy that follows is derived largely from the conclusive study of William Appleman Williams, *The Roots of the Modern American Empire** (New York: Random House, 1969).

[7] See Shannon, *Farmer's Last Frontier,* for the history of this period.

money was reduced; this exacerbated already severe deflationary trends. "Remonetization" emerged as a searing issue, uniting farmers with urban workers; it joined easily with anti-big business, anti-railroad, anti-tariff, and other comparable issues. Sitting at the center of all this was, however, an effort on the part of farmers to find "a new frontier," which could compensate for the slowing of westward expansion[8] and the deterioration of prices (always a problem, whether severe or moderate, for debtors, which farmers always are). In the decades before the mid-1890's, the farmers sought solutions in an expanding *foreign* trade, which they sought to facilitate by lowered tariffs, cheaper and better transportation, and a return to silver. Later, when these measures, too, proved inadequate they encouraged and supported the overseas imperialist ventures of the United States, to serve the same purposes.

In the first stage of those overseas developments, farmers received aid and comfort due to conditions entirely out of their range of influence: agricultural hardships in Europe, brought about by the spread of disease and a long period of unfavorable weather. In the midst of the unprecedented and severe depression that began in 1873, exports of crude foodstuffs began to increase spectacularly, strengthening the entire economy.[9] It was then also that the American trade balance shifted decisively from being "unfavorable" (that is, an excess of imports over exports) to "favorable."

If the meaning of those years, when the United States was lifted out of depression and into a new balance of trade position, was not lost on the farmers, neither was it lost on industrialists. The United States had from its very first years depended on foreign markets for its expansion; now it was dependent on them for resolving what became a recurring problem: excess productive capacity, both agricultural and industrial. The next chapter, which is concerned with the United States in the world economy, will examine this development more closely. Here it will suffice to say merely that the 1870's taught both Americans and Europeans for the first time what became a full understanding in the

[8] New lands were of course still being settled in the 1870's, and 1880's; but the slowing down of the process was quantitatively real, as suggested by the "closing of the frontier" which was announced by the Census Bureau in 1890. The qualitative deterioration of the frontier movement was bound up with the fact that the available lands were relatively arid and more suited to large grazing than to small cultivated tracts, and that the Homestead Act of 1862 (whose stated intention was to encourage small-scale settlement and ownership: in effect, 160 acres of land free with five years of settlement and cultivation) had come to benefit large timber, mineral, and railroad corporations almost exclusively.

[9] Exports of crude foodstuffs: 1875, $79 million; 1876, $94 million; 1877, $155 million; 1880, $266 million; 1881, $242 million. Exports of manufactured foodstuffs: 1875, $110 million; 1877, $150 million; 1880, $193 million; 1881, $226 million. Williams, *The Roots of the Modern American Empire*, p. 20.

years to come: "The United States," as Williams puts it, "was rapidly becoming the most powerful nation on earth." [p. 22]

When the agricultural crisis of Europe subsided, the Europeans, for the first time but by no means for the last, saw that they would have to raise barriers and find alternatives to the American export invasion. Alternative sources of supply in Argentina, in Russia, and in India were encouraged, all under the direct or indirect control of the European imperial powers; and, especially in France and Germany, the path toward effective tariff barriers on both agricultural and industrial products was pursued with increasing haste. By 1892, the French had climbed the first steps along that path, with the famous Méline Tariff; the Germans had arrived a few years earlier. With slight variations since then, the course of European tariff policy has been consistently protectionist, and increasingly designed to protect against American imports. The American Marshall Plan (1948–1952) had as an important component its design to find expanded markets for American exports, and not least among them agicultural exports. In addition to drawing American farmers once more into support of an expansionist foreign policy, this development has helped to make farm products the hot center of protectionism in the Common Market countries.

The System Joined

It is customary to point out that after 1896 the farmers' revolt subsided, to be replaced in the twentieth century by farmers' pressure groups, the key transforming development being the rise of farm prices after 1896 (and especially during World War I). But this leaves out an important point, a point given short shrift in most histories of the United States: the whys and wherefores of our turn toward overseas imperialism at the turn of the century. Farmers were very much part of that turn, and among its conscious beneficiaries.

The discontent of farmers beginning to be voiced in the late 1860's developed into the Populist Movement (and the People's Party) by 1892—combining in the process urban worker with rural discontent and active cooperation between black and white farmers. It was the first vigorous coalition of that sort, and apart from some small labor and socialist groupings in earlier years, the first, and perhaps unwitting, attempt to find an *internal* rather than an *external* resolution of America's economic and social problems. The response of northern business and southern white leaders was to mount vigorous anti-liberal, anti-left, and contrived racist programs. Undercut by internal divisions and external pressures, Populism shifted to the right and dissolved, and both racism and overseas expansionism were propelled into new strength.

In the heyday of nineteenth-century Populism, almost all farmers (and their allies) were ranged against big business; today, the dominating elements in agriculture *are* big business. The rural and urban contingents of Populism sought to bend State power to the needs of the common people; today, Big Agriculture and Big Labor work with Big Business and Big Government to defend themselves *against* the common people. In 1892, Populism stood for a broad range of social and economic issues; by the election of 1896 most of its leaders could be satisfied with the promise of rising prices and land values and expanding foreign markets even if that meant finding allies among previous business enemies and embarking upon a new form of colonialism. As Williams says:

> The farmers who were quasi-colonials in the domestic economy thus became anti-colonial imperialists in foreign affairs, as a strategy of becoming equals at home.[10]

The farmers already in 1895 were agitating to have the United States support the Cuban struggle against Spain, and then to guarantee that Americans would have enlarged access to Cuban markets, investment possibilities, and the like. Although American farmers had no similar interest in Asia at that time, they found it possible to support the logic of those who did—the processors (of cotton, meat, and flour) and manufacturers who had visions of an endless Asian market.[11] Nor were they indifferent to the meaning of an isthmian canal—initially in Nicaragua, but ultimately in Panama (a "nation" the U.S. created out of Colombia for that purpose).

Like the years that first produced the farmers' revolt, the mid-1890's were years of serious depression. The response laid down then has served as a template for American foreign policy ever since:

> The economic impact of the depression, and its effect in producing a real fear of extensive social unrest or even revolution, had completed the long and gradual acceptance by metropolitan leaders of the traditional farm

[10] Ibid., p. 25. "Anti-colonial imperialism" as a political stance for farmers meant (1) opposition to colonialism, which in turn meant (2) contesting for power in colonial areas against European powers (e.g., Spain), and seeking (3) to gain equal access to all markets in the world on a basis of free competition. In practice, given the already-established technological superiority of both American industry and agriculture, this meant a growing economic empire for the United States without the traditional political institutions of colonialism. Thus, "anti-colonial imperialism."

[11] That such "visions" were largely groundless, and given their force by a larger nationalist-expansionist drive, is well-argued by Marilyn Blatt Young, "American Expansion, 1870–1890: The Far East," in *Towards a New Past.*

emphasis on overseas market expansion as the strategic solution to the nation's economic and social problems.[12]

The farmers did not *want* war in 1898, nor did they expect it; they did not want war in the repetitive years of military intervention and gunboat diplomacy in the Caribbean, Central America, and Asia that carried us up to World War I. But they did want expanding markets and agricultural prosperity. From the very beginning, when anything stood in the way of economic aims—whether it was the rights or the lives of Native Americans or blacks, or the possibilities of peace—it was relegated to a secondary consideration by most white farmers. After due habituation, people can find justifications for victimizing others in the presumed characteristics of their victims, rather than in their own purposes.

American farmers did not invent American racism or American imperialism. But at a critical moment in our history, the last years of the 19th century, farmers lent their great prestige and their numbers to the forces that were moving along those lines. It was a turning point for American history, as much as it was for American farmers. The indifferent slaughter of buffaloes and of Native Americans became a habit easily applied to the slaughter of Filipinos (at least 500,000); the precedents for genocide in Indochina were established long ago.

The American agricultural sector lost what life it could call its own as the twentieth century moved on; but the idealized picture and many of the ways of the farmer persist. It is these that are probably called to mind when "the silent majority" is invoked. Not all that is thereby suggested is good and not all of it bad. Much of what Americans value, and much of how they calculate, is derived from the fact or the myth of the farm and the country town that was the social, political, and economic center of the farmer's life when he wasn't tilling the soil. As Veblen (who grew up on farms in Wisconsin and Minnesota) pointed out:

> It has come to be recognized that the country town situation of the nineteenth century is now by way of being left behind; and so it is now recognized, or at least acted on, that the salvation of twentieth-century democracy is best to be worked out by making the world safe for Big Business and then let Big Business take care of the interests of the retail trade and the country town, together with much else. But it should not be overlooked that in and through all this it is the soul of the country town that goes marching on.[13]

[12] Williams, p. 41.

[13] *Absentee Ownership*, pp. 152–53. And see Sinclair Lewis, *Main Street*, for a vivid example of Veblen's point.

The "country town" mentality Veblen refers to is that of Harry Truman, of Eisenhower, of Nixon—and of George Wallace, LBJ, McGovern, Ford, and Carter. Saying this suggests that there is and has been a division of thinking and attitudes among farmers, as well as other Americans, throughout our history. Those who won out have become part of the system of calculation and expansion that is the warp and woof of American history. There were and are others: farmers who love the land, and what it grows, and the pleasures of living on it; farmers who helped to swell the socialist and anti-imperialist movement led by Eugene Debs; farmers who are black and brown and yellow; and so on. Since the collapse of the People's Party in the mid-1890's, that other side of farmers has been moved far from the levers of agricultural power and influence, plays only a minor role in overall farm production, and even less than that in the larger life of the nation.

Agriculture and Agribusiness

Throughout the nineteenth century, the farmer was socially, politically, and statistically a predominating force; by the end of the century he was losing out in all but the statistical category. The numbers of farms and farmers continued to increase up to 1935 in absolute terms, while falling in relative terms as the economy came to depend increasingly on industrial production and the growth of services (finance, distribution, etc.). After 1935, farming and farms went into an absolute decline. Long before the numbers began to turn downward, the role of farming had undergone a transformation in the American political economy.

The last great effort of farmers to affect broad American policies was embodied in their impact on foreign policy around the turn of the century. Afterwards, although farmers would intermittently and diversely join in national political movements, their principal political activities would be as a particular interest pressure group, lobbying for price supports, output controls, favorable tariff policies, and government-subsidized research. The decline in their numbers tells part of the story why; their success as a pressure group did much to facilitate that decline.

In 1870, over half of the American people were engaged in agriculture. By 1930, fewer than a quarter were. Today the number is well under 5 percent. There were about one-and-a-half million farms in 1850. The number rose to four million by 1890, and reached a high point in 1935, with about seven million farms. By 1940, the number had dropped below six million; now there are fewer than three million, the lowest number in the past century. Fewer than a tenth of today's farms produce well over half of all agricultural output. One percent of all farms (mostly corporations) produced 25 percent of total farm output in 1972. As elsewhere in the American economy, there is a "dual economy" in agriculture, with over a million very small and poor farms at one end, and a few hundred thousand large or very large farms at the other. (When farm income rose at least 20 percent between 1972 and 1973, in connection with rapidly rising food prices, it was estimated that 90 percent of the increase went to 200,000 giant farms.)

The effectiveness of farmers as a pressure group began to take hold in the 1920's, and especially under President Hoover. Those first steps led directly to the present close cooperation between large farms, government, and agricultural colleges, and to the industrialization of agriculture. Since 1950, farm productivity has risen twice that of manufacturing industry, the gains going to the very largest farms while the small idealized farmer has been squeezed out of farming and into the cities.

In the long history of American farming, to have been a tenant farmer was a sign not of failure but of first steps toward ownership. But after World War I, as agriculture industrialized in the midst of widespread over-capacity, farm tenancy and share-cropping became virtually indistinguishable: it was the way *down*, or out. The mass exodus from farming was accelerated by the Depression and the Dust Bowl tragedies accompanying it; the exodus was pushed toward completion by the great step up in electrification, mechanization, and chemicalization in farming after World War II. Millions of farmers went bankrupt and were "tractored out" in the 1930's, and became part of a migratory labor force or of the unemployed. The military and production needs of World War II came just in time.[14]

Beginning in the Hoover Administration, a set of policies has evolved which seeks to prevent low prices and market instability for a broad range of farm products—keeping prices up through government loans and purchases, and supply down through production controls. The largest farms are the prime beneficiaries of these governmental programs. Thus, in 1967, the poorest *20* percent of farmers received 1.1 percent of government payments; the richest *5* percent of farmers (often corporations)

---

[14] The squeezing out process of the poorest farmers continues, even more tragically The affected people become part of the "migrant" labor force in the East for a few years, and then settle in the northern slums—the last of the tenant farmers. The "Dust Bowl" was a product of the misuse of the arid lands west of the Mississippi, which should not have been used for grain or cotton cultivation. See the important article by Paul W. Gates, "The Homestead Law in an Incongruous Land System," reprinted in Scheiber, *United States Economic History*, Chapter 10, which shows the misuse of the land and the manner in which a law presumably designed to foster widespread ownership did much to deliver the public domain to large land, mineral, railroad, and timber companies. Steinbeck's *Grapes of Wrath* is an unforgettable portrait of the Depression/Dust Bowl exodus of the small farmer.

received 42.4 percent of government payments. Total governmental payments in that year were over $3 billion. It could not be otherwise, for farm policies have been tied to output: the larger the output, the more the gains from the program, and vice versa. Though carried out in the name of the small farmer, these programs have been pushed through and administered by representatives of the farm pressure groups representing the largest farmers. The result is a program that makes the rich richer and allows the poor to stay poor, or forces them to get out of farming.[15]

In 1973, in the face of what was called a food shortage, of dramatic increases in food exports, and rapidly rising prices of food, the farm price support policies were shelved, at least temporarily. Like the energy shortage (to be discussed below) the food shortage is an institutional creation; like the more than doubled increase in energy prices that has occurred since 1973, the increase of about 50 percent (on the average) of food prices is deceptive. Farmers received the same prices in 1976 as they did in 1973; but the incomes of those who transport, process, and sell food had risen. Thus, three companies sell 82 percent of our breakfast cereal, four sell 70 percent of dairy products and 80 percent of canned goods; two to four chains sell the vast bulk of the food in almost every one of our metropolitan areas. In 1974 Safeway's profits rose by 51 percent; Del Monte's 43 percent; American Can's 52 percent; Amstar's (the sugar giant) profits rose 250 percent. Middlemen take almost 58 percent of the food dollar.[16]

Agricultural controls and subsidies are of course paid for the general public through taxation. If the public thinks about the matter at all, it finds some satisfaction in its belief that the programs are helping "the little guy." Meanwhile, the small farmer goes out of existence, as the policies work themselves out:

> Thus, the total number of farms dropped from 5.9 million in 1947 to 2.9 million in 1970, while the average number of acres per farm doubled (rising from 196 to 387 acres). In 1959, large farms with sales amounting to $20,000 or more per year represented 13 percent of all commercial farms and accounted for 52 percent of total sales of farm products; by 1969 19 percent of all farms with 73 percent of total products sales were

[15] The data are drawn from "The Effect of Taxes and Government Spending on Inequality," in Edwards et al., *The Capitalist System*, p. 243, put together by James T. Bonnen. For a long overview, see Murray Benedict, *Farm Policies of the United States, 1790–1950* (New York: Twentieth Century Fund, 1953). Edward Higbee, *Farms and Farmers in an Urban Age* ° (New York: Twentieth Century Fund, 1963) shows the inequities of programs within agriculture and as between some farmers and all city-dwellers.

[16] For a penetrating analysis of this question on the global scale, see Nick Eberstadt, "Myths of the Food Crisis," *New York Review of Books*, February 19, 1976.

in this category. . . . The number of small farms with less than 100 acres has declined precipitately (from 3.0 to 1.4 million) between 1950 and 1964. . . . Among the farmers squeezed out were about 500,000 crop-share tenants in the South, largely from cotton plantations. . . . [which] means not only cutting off cash income but also loss of housing and of the minimal security derived from having a plot of land.[17]

Little known to the general public, but of great importance to the large farmers, have been governmental programs financed by federal and state funds that undertake research on the whole range of matters affecting agricultural productivity. These programs have done much over the years to stimulate and improve mechanization, seeds, soil management, and the like; they have also been prime movers in the general chemicalization of farming. Chemicalization, which undoubtedly has had an extraordinary impact in raising the productivity of farm land, has an equally extraordinary impact on the destruction of the environment— and not a few human beings. The case of DDT is only the best known example of a long list of chemicals which have poisoned the soil, the waters, and surrounding foliage in such fashion as to unhinge the balance of nature, a balance that depends upon insects, birds, and small animals who are poisoned by presently-used chemicals.

The contemporary ecological imbalance is tipped most drastically in dangerous directions by *industrial* production and the use of industrial products, and most especially the automobile and petroleum products. But there is, in the contemporary agricultural pattern, a specially disturbing quality to the problem, for agriculture provides our food. That our food should be provided in ways that poison as well as sustain us, and that it should be produced in ways that destroy as well as replenish natural forces is frightening; that all this is the direct result of governmental subsidies for research in the Department of Agriculture and in the land-grant universities is shocking. At a U.S. Senate hearing in the summer of 1972, the current status of these relationships was summarized as follows:

> . . . a land-grant complex, a system composed of Federal research agencies and big universities in each state created in the last century with endowments of public lands or their monetary equivalent . . . , whose research was originally intended to serve consumers as well as rural communities, [but is] now focused largely on the development of big machines for vast farming enterprises, the breeding of crops for mechanized harvests and studies of chemicals for big corporations and big producers . . . with little regard for the quality or safety of products for the consumer or

[17] U.S. Dept. of Labor, *Manpower Report of the President* * (Washington: USGPO, 1971), p. 119. This is a valuable source of data on a broad range of problems affecting the labor force, poverty, etc.

the small farmer. One result . . . has been to drive farmers and workers off the land and into the crowded cities.[18]

The land-grant universities referred to all have Schools of Agriculture, and they in turn have Departments of Agricultural Economics. The methodology of agricultural economics is, like its parent's, neoclassical, and its purposes are also to show how efficiency and profits can be enhanced. There are, however, some differences: (1) "ag econ" has more of an empirical component than "econ"; (2) it is designed explicitly to serve the agricultural community, whereas general economists believe they are serving either nobody or everybody; and (3) the understanding that agricultural economists have of their role is provided to them by an annual reminder from state legislatures (and/or the Department of Agriculture), which pays their salaries and provides their research grants.

There is also at least one matter other than neoclassicism that the two groups of economists have in common: they are addicted to what E. J. Mishan calls "growthmania." That is, they are responding wittingly or not to the omnipresent need of a capitalist economy to expand, and to continue to expand. As Mishan puts it, "They continue to give expression to the basic doctrines of their fathers and spin rhetoric out of the growth theme in blithe unconcern of the spreading jungle of problems stemming directly from the material prosperity of the last decade or so." [19]

For farmers, as for capitalist businessmen in general, expansion of markets was essential. Economic expansion was aided critically all along the way by attendant geographic expansion—across the continent, first, and over the seas, later. It is unnecessary to recount here the laudable achievements that were part of that process in American history; our history books do little else. It is necessary, however, to underscore what is generally neglected. What were looked upon as aberrations or excesses, regarding the treatment of both human and nonhuman resources, were intrinsic to the process of American growth and development. And, if we wish to understand the pervasiveness and intractability of today's range of "problems," we must see them as the more severe contemporary manifestation of what has existed all along.

Since over two-thirds of all Americans now live in cities, most of the

---

[18] Reported in the *New York Times*, June 20, 1972.

[19] E. J. Mishan, *Technology and Growth: The Price We Pay** (New York: Praeger, 1969), p. xv. Mishan goes on to say that for such people, "any doubt that, say, a four percent growth rate, as revealed by the index, is better than a three percent growth rate is near-heresy; is tantamount to a doubt that four is greater than three." (Ibid.) Mishan was one of the very first of the mainstream economists to question the sacrosanct quality of growth, and his analysis is useful. It is also, however, limited, in that he sees "growthmania" *as* a mania; that is, as being irrational, rather than as intrinsic to the system.

problems afflicting America today show themselves in the cities. Racism, poverty, pollution, violence, transportation mess, urban sprawl, health and housing and educational deprivation—all these and more swirl around in tight and deadly embrace in our cities; all are explicable in their current as in their historical conditions as "by-products" of a process of development in which profit and power—not natural balance, not human needs and possibilities, not social balance—were the guiding criteria. The deterioration of nature has been relatively silent, and hidden unless studied; it is quite the opposite with the deterioration of daily life in our cities. That the exploitation of *all* of nature would go hand in hand with exploitation of the *human* component of nature was foreseen by Marx, long ago:

> In modern agriculture, as in the urban industries, the increased productiveness and quantity of the labor set in motion are bought at the cost of laying waste and consuming by disease labor-power itself. Moreover, all progress in capitalistic agriculture is a progress in the art, not only of robbing the laborer, but of robbing the soil; all progress in increasing the fertility of the soil for a given time, is a progress towards ruining the lasting sources of that fertility. The more a country starts its development on the foundation of modern industry, like the United States, for example, the more rapid is this process of destruction. Capitalist production, therefore, develops technology, and the combining together of various processes into a social whole, only by sapping the original sources of all wealth—the soil and the laborer.[20]

The great and rich land space of continental United States was swept over and conquered in a process so swift and violent that it has been called "the rape of the land." Heedless of any natural balance or of human beings standing in the way, the exploiters of the land moved for greed more than need, for power more than for satisfaction. So it has been too with the way our cities have grown and changed and deteriorated, in one wave after another. So too with the poisoning of our air and water. What land speculators were to farming, real estate and urban development interests were and are to our cities; as in farming, the entrance of government into the picture in this century has meant not a mitigation but an intensification of a long-existent process. The more rapid and more pervasive economic expansion of this century has brought with it more misuse of the land, more deadly cities, and an environmental condition so severe that to most it is terrifying.

The Jeffersonian dream of an agrarian democracy is not even remembered these days; the nightmare of urban decay and suffocation has taken its place. How did the city get that way, and how does it continue to move?

[20] *Capital*, vol. I, pp. 506–7.

Civilization and its Discontents

There was, not so long ago, a firmly-held notion that cities were the repository of all that is most precious in western social development. If that was a belief held too carelessly, there is even less to support the one that now spreads and grows: the cities embody all that is to be avoided. Furthermore, as this view spreads, it becomes a self-fulfilling prophecy.

American cities at their best were never, for a majority of their inhabitants, fit places to live, whether in the nineteenth or the twentieth century. But apart from a small handful of people, mostly young, who can find ways to experiment with rural living, the alternative to *making* our cities fit places to live is quite probably the disintegration of what we mean by civilization. That we have done so little, and done it so badly, on that score testifies to how very slender the civilized base has been for our social development.

A careful analysis of how our cities came to be, how they have changed over time, and how they have sunk into their current desperate state, if combined with an analysis of how all that related to our overall socioeconomic development, would quite probably tell us that a complete reorganization of our cities *and* of our society is necessary to make either livable or, in an acceptable sense of the term, civilized.[21]

Recorded history begins with cities, at that stage of social development when production and productivity had advanced to the point where a significant number of the population could be sustained even though they did not produce their own food; when a relatively complicated division of labor had emerged, requiring government and writing. All this (and much else involved) appears to have come forth a millennium or two before Christ in the rich river valleys of the Indus, the Tigris and Euphrates, and the Nile. In the ancient period, cities were of course serving commercial purposes; but their religious, military, and administrative functions seem more frequently to have been dominant. During the medieval period, cities emerged and grew primarily because of their locations, which favored the development of commerce. In the capitalist epoch, cities have arisen, expanded, and decayed almost entirely in response to economic needs and possibilities.[22]

[21] Larry Sawers, "Urban Form and Mode of Production," *RRPE*, Vol. 7, No. 1 (Spring, 1975) has attempted the sort of analysis called for here, showing how U.S. cities were shaped by being capitalist, and most of all in this century by the products and powers of the auto industry; he has also compared this with socialist developments.

[22] In the United States, the principal exception to the last generalization would be Washington, D. C., which was, however, a quite minor city until the political economy of the U.S., around the turn of the century, required an explicitly strong central government. The best introduction to the historical and current development of cities is

In the United States, the cities of the eastern seaboard—most notably Boston, New York, Philadelphia, Baltimore, Charleston, and Atlanta—waxed or waned as the changing patterns of agriculture, manufacture, foreign and domestic trade, finance, and transportation altered. They, and the cities that grew up in the trans-Appalachian West, fought strenuously and self-consciously to place roads, canals, and railroads in such manner as to become magnets for the trade, the industry, and the finance that could not otherwise flourish. In the early nineteenth century the competition along these lines between towns and cities was intense. If the emergence of Manhattan, for example, from a small village to becoming the nation's most populous city is to be understood, the story must begin with its advantages as a trading center: it was on the edge of the Atlantic, connected to the interior by the Erie Canal, and favorably located between New England and the South.

The same factors also affected other cities throughout the U.S.: Chicago, Omaha, Cincinnati (which was vulgarly known as "Porkopolis"), New Orleans, St. Louis, Detroit, Los Angeles, San Francisco, or Seattle. Transportation advantages, due to location near water routes, or emergence as a railroad center, made towns into commercial centers; then they emerged as centers of industry and finance, and in the process, as large population centers.

The reasons why the cities grew give important clues as to the criteria employed—and neglected—along the way regarding the quantity and quality of what we may call human services: housing, transportation, health, educational, and cultural-recreational facilities. These services came into being as responses to essentially market rather than human criteria, the sole exception being, in some cities, cultural facilities.[23]

The medieval European city often tended to develop in rings, moving outward from the initial walled city to "suburbs," one ring after another; or, it was controlled in its design from the beginning, as were many Central European cities. By comparison, the spatial development of American cities was haphazard. As the structure of the economy, both locally and nationally, changed, new patterns of production and new inflows of people ensued. What began as commercial districts became industrial, or financial; initially residential districts became commercial or industrial; initially suburban areas became part of the "central city."

Lewis Mumford, *The City in History* ° (New York: Harcourt Brace Jovanovich, 1961). A narrower and controversial economic interpretation is Jane Jacobs, *The Economy of Cities*° (New York: Random House, 1965).

[23] They responded to the "market," also; but museums, concert halls, libraries, parks, and the like, were more often created for non-market reasons: the tastes (vulgar or cultivated) of the rich; the complicated social convictions of an Andrew Carnegie (who financed innumerable public libraries in America); the strong European influences on Americans that diluted the pure American fluid of commercialism.

Perhaps the most vivid example of the latter development is Harlem, once a village separated from the bustle of New York by miles of "country." [24]

Cities and Suburbs; Sprawl and Decay

American urban development can be viewed as having three reasonably clear-cut stages: (1) most of the nineteenth century, (2) the forty years or so ending just before World War II, and (3) from World War II to the present. The earliest period covers the growth of cities proper; the second sees the emergence of malignant growth including the significant expansion of suburbs; the latest brings us megalopolis, urban sprawl, and the dying city.

Throughout the nineteenth century, American cities multiplied and grew; but it was in some kind of rhythmic balance with the growing economy. Immigration became a river and then a torrent after 1850; agriculture was becoming relatively less important (although it was producing more and more, with its rising productivity); and industrialization became the prime creator of urbanization. It was not until the turn of the century, however, that the kinds of urban problems now familiar to us began to become obvious—widespread slums, rampant health problems, poverty, blatant corruption, and the like. What Lincoln Steffens had to say about St. Louis at the time of its World's Fair (1904) might have been written yesterday:

> The visitor is told of the wealth of the residents, of the financial strength of the banks, and of the growing importance of the industries, yet he sees poorly-paved, refuse-burdened streets and dusty or mud-covered alleys; he passes a ramshackle fire-trap, crowded with the sick, and learns that it is the City Hospital. . . . Finally, he turns a tap in the hotel, to see liquid mud flow into wash basin or bath tub.[25]

[24] Gilbert Osofsky, *Harlem: The Making of a Ghetto,* cited earlier, in tracing out the long-standing oppression of black people in New York (from the city's earliest years to 1930), incidentally provides a useful view of the process of urban development. See also Robert G. Albion, *The Rise of New York Port* (New York: Scribner's, 1939), and, for a more general history, Taylor, *Transportation Revolution.*

[25] *The Shame of the Cities* * (New York: McClure, 1904), p. 31. Even earlier conditions are described by Jacob Riis, *How the Other Half Lives* * (New York: Hill and Wang, 1962), originally published in 1890. On this and related matters, see the essay by Stephen Thernstrom, "Urbanization, Migration, and Social Mobility in Late Nineteenth-Century America," in Barton Bernstein, ed., *Towards A New Past,* cited earlier.

Immigration and industrialization both speeded up substantially after 1900, and a net migration from rural to urban locations became a constant. In 1920, for the first time, there were more people in our cities than in the countryside.[26] The cities that grew fastest were those already largest. Into these rapidly expanding metropoli in every region of the country streamed people who would take up the lowest-paying and dirtiest jobs. They were from the poorer areas of Europe and Asia, and they were black and Spanish-speaking Americans moving from country to city. Their cheap labor was much desired, but they were in attitude despised and in fact neglected by the "WASP" power structures which ruled almost all American cities. They were despised as Catholics or Jews, as poor, as black, brown, yellow, or "swarthy"; for them, the cities, never well-planned and only partially attractive and pleasant, were sink-holes.

Much sentimental claptrap has been written about how the poor and oppressed of the cities after the turn of the century were "taken care of" by the political bosses and machines then dominant; even today respectable opinion not infrequently lauds a Mayor Daley of Chicago as the last of an unfortunately vanishing breed. The machines did have a function, of course, a function much like that a bandage has for a running sore. There is reason for nostalgia among the respectable people today concerning our cities of half a century or more ago, but it is not because they were livable. Rather, it is because the cities then *seemed* tractable and manageable; they were still growing, still serving indispensable economic functions.

Since World War II, it is megalopoli, not cities, that grow; many of the functions performed in and by cities are now taken care of in once suburban *residential* areas that are now also "suburban" *industrial* areas; and the cities have been filled by a forced migration of rural people, who are heavily nonwhite. This process has been occurring even with fewer and fewer industrial jobs to be found; with fewer jobs of *any* kind to be found. In order to be manageable today, the cities would have to be managed in critical part *for* and *by* the despised poor and nonwhite residents who constitute their largest segments. Such a politics goes against the American grain.

A few American suburbs developed in conjunction with the steam railroad after 1850. But the first significant suburban development went along with the electric urban, interurban, suburban railway, as the twentieth century began. What continental railroad developers were to westward expansion, electric railway (including subway) developers and their real-estate cohorts were to urban-suburban development.

In the years just before World War I, automobiles began to be mass-

---

[26] See Faulkner, *Decline of Laissez-Faire: 1897–1917*, especially Chapter 5.

produced, and that brought about the next major suburban movement. The possibilities associated with the electric railway and the automobile were fairly well exhausted before World War II, especially under the negative impact of the Depression. Since 1945, population has risen by more than fifty million; there has been a whole generation of high and sustained national income; the automobile (one for every two Americans) has become almost a universal possession; and the nation's industrialization, urbanization, and suburbanization have moved to levels of apparent saturation although doubtless there is more on the way. In the process, both the causes and the consequences of suburbanization have altered.

Suburban development prior to the 1930's was made possible by transportation developments that were taken advantage of by predominantly upper income families. The suburb, typically, was separated from the city by open stretches of country, and provided an opportunity to combine the advantages of city with country life. The suburban railway made its few stops, providing a leisurely and even a pleasant interlude; and some few drove to work and back. There were no "freeways." [27]

All that began to change as we moved into and out of World War II. The changes were first evident in and around Los Angeles, a "city" that drew people from all over the nation, but especially from the Midwest and South, as its oil wells, its aircraft production, its light and cheap labor manufactures, its warm climate and its glamor provided both jobs and dreams. The model it established for the rest of the country is well-captured by Mumford:

> Los Angeles has now become an undifferentiated mass of houses, walled off into sectors by many-laned expressways, with ramps and viaducts that create special bottlenecks of their own. These expressways move but a small fraction of the traffic per hour once carried by public transportation, at a much lower speed, in an environment befouled by smog, itself produced by the lethal exhaust of the technologically backward motor cars. More than a third of the Los Angeles area is consumed by these grotesque transportation facilities; *two-thirds* of central Los Angeles are occupied by streets, freeways, parking facilities, and garages. This is space-eating with a vengeance. The last stage of the process already beckons truly progressive minds—to evict the remaining inhabitants and turn the entire area over to automatically propelled vehicles, completely emancipated from any rational human purpose.[28]

[27] Except as rare pheonmena, such as the Bronx River Parkway, connecting the then richest county in the nation (Westchester) with the most populous city, New York. See Sweezy, "Cars and Cities," cited earlier.

[28] *The City in History*, p. 510. In 1907, horsedrawn vehicles in New York City moved at an average speed of 11.5 miles per hour; cars move at 6 miles per hour

How the horrors portrayed by Mumford came to be is explained by Bradford Snell, who adds some details of his own:

Thirty-five years ago Los Angeles was a beautiful city of lush palm trees, fragrant orange groves and ocean-clean air. It was served then by the world's largest electric railway network. In the late 1930's General Motors and allied highway interests acquired the local transit companies, scrapped their pollution-free electric trains, tore down their power transmission lines, ripped up their tracks, and placed GM buses on already congested Los Angeles streets. The noisy, foul-smelling buses turned earlier patrons of the high-speed rail system away from public transit and, in effect, sold millions of private automobiles. Largely as a result, this city is today an ecological wasteland: the palm trees are dying of petrochemical smog; the orange groves have been paved over by 300 miles of freeways; the air is a septic tank into which four million cars, half of them built by General Motors, pump 13,000 tons of pollutants daily. Furthermore, a shortage of motor vehicle fuel and an absence of adequate public transport now threatens to disrupt the entire auto-dependent region.[29]

There are still American cities that do not fit that model; but most that do not are racing madly to catch up with those that do. Greater Boston, Greater New York, Greater Cleveland, Greater Atlanta, Greater Houston, and of course Greater Los Angeles, all vie with each for growth, come what may. The San Francisco Bay Area, thought by many, as recently as a decade ago, to be exempt from such deterioration has instead come to

---

today. It is generally recognized that the Los Angeles style of one day becomes the national style soon thereafter. Nathaniel West's novel, *The Day of the Locust*, written in 1940, evoked that style exactly. The novel ends suddenly, with a race riot at a movie première.

[29] Bradford Snell, "American Ground Transport," in *Hearings* before the Subcommittee on Antitrust and Monopoly, 93rd Congress, 2nd Session, U.S. Senate (Washington, D.C.: USGPO, 1974), pp. A–2 and A–3. Just preceding that quotation, Snell has argued that "GM has both the power and the economic incentive to maximize profits by suppressing rail and bus transportation. The economics are obvious: one bus can eliminate 35 automobiles; one streetcar, subway or rail transit vehicle can supplant 50 passenger cars; one train can displace 1,000 cars or a fleet of 150 cargo-laden trucks. The result was inevitable: a drive by GM to sell cars and trucks by displacing rail and bus systems." He then goes on to posit "GM's role in the destruction of more than 100 electric surface rail systems in 45 cities including New York, Philadelphia, Baltimore, St. Louis, Oakland, Salt Lake City and Los Angeles." (p. A–2) When the San Francisco Bay Bridge opened in 1939, on one of its levels ran an electric train system. This was bought up by National City Lines (a creation of GM) in the early 1950s; by the mid-1950s the trains had been replaced by buses, and the bridge became a steady home for massive traffic jams. The new BART system, built at the cost of many billions, tunnels under the bay to serve the purposes of the destroyed train system. And the autos go inching along on the bridge.

stand as perhaps a pluperfect example of how very strong the drives are to "catch up" in the race. The Bay, enormous and convolute, ringed by hills in turn sloping into graceful valleys, is presently shrinking and dying as a body of water. Over 40 percent of the water area of the Bay has been filled in during this century. Steadily increasing amounts of effluent from the Navy, private industry, and residences have combined with intermittent oil spills to kill off much of the underwater life of the Bay, and to render its waters dangerous to humans. In addition, its valleys have seen orchards replaced by residential and industrial sprawl, now suffocating beneath smog. That all this is not yet enough is suggested by a two-page advertisement in the *New York Times* of April 25, 1972: "Metro San Jose" (south of San Francisco), whose population has risen more than ten times since 1940, boasts in the ad of its "runaway construction," its airline passengers, its new car sales—with the ad asking for more of the same.

The personal automobile has almost entirely replaced the dilapidated and expensive interurban railway; the suburbs have developed their own ghettoes,[30] their own smog, indeed their own suburbs. Industry has accompanied the automobile to the suburb, and the city has lost its ability both to provide a decent livelihood for a high and growing percentage of its residents, as well as to pay for its needed services.

All major American cities now lurch from one fiscal crisis to the next. The daily news announces school closings today, cessation of bus service the week after. Firemen, policemen, refuse collectors, teachers, and hospital workers organize and strike for better incomes and working conditions, attempting to stave off the city's slashes, rising taxes, and the rising cost of living.

In 1971, the Urban Coalition predicted that most major and many minor American cities by 1976 would be bankrupt—unable to pay off existing obligations and unable to borrow further. Doubtless the announcement was in part for dramatic effect, nor could the thinkers of the Urban Coalition, the largest percentage of whom are from the financial and business offices of New York, have anticipated the seriocomic antics of New York City, New York State, and Washington, D. C. from mid-1975 on, when the city of New York was at the brink of default. To hear President Ford and his treasury secretary tell it, the problems of New York City were those arising from iniquity, perversity, stupidity, and self-indulgence. Unquestionably all those characteristics exist in some measure in New York City, as they do in Washington, D. C. But New York's troubles arose principally out of what most of those who rule this nation consider to be the considerable triumphs of the post-

---

[30] Westchester County, N.Y., still one of the richest in the nation, also has the highest percentage of welfare poor (per capita) in the nation.

World War II era: massive building and highway projects—and the associated disruption of whole chunks of the city (leading to loss of jobs and of taxpayers)—plus New York's share of the costs and wastes of U. S. militarism. If there was one group that could be identified as having continuing and high power over New York in that period, it would be the "construction complex"—the banks, the builders and associated unions, the autonomous agencies, the federal and state bureaucracies, the politicians getting and dispensing patronage in the late twentieth-century version of "the Great Barbecue."[31] New York City has avoided bankruptcy for a while, but not yet with means possessed of solidity. Meanwhile, other cities move toward New York's fate, lagging not because of their greater fiscal rectitude in the past but because New York has had certain special characteristics which, if anything, should have occasioned pride more than castigation. New York has been more alert to the educational, cultural, and basic economic needs of its denizens than the other cities of the U.S.[32]

The Agony of the Cities: Nothing Fails Like Success

The listing of America's urban afflictions has become a persisting drone in the background of daily existence, like the whine of mosquitoes. We have already been bitten, and we know more bites will come. The

[31] I am here paraphrasing the words of Jason Epstein, in his astute and useful essay "The Last Days of New York," in *New York Review of Books*, February 19, 1976. For a thorough study, see Robert A. Caro, *The Power Broker: Robert Moses and the Fall of New York*° (New York: Random House, 1975). A government analysis that counters the banalities of the White House and shows the larger spread of the problem is *New York City's Financial Crisis*° "A Study Prepared for the Use of the Joint Economic Committee," 94th Congress, 1st Session (USGPO, 1975).

[32] There is insufficient space here to treat meaningfully the range of urban crises now pervading the whole nation. But each of them—jobs, housing, education, poverty, crime, health, transportation, and the environment—is taken up systematically in terms of analysis and proposals, by "conservative, liberal, and radical" analysts, in the book of readings edited by David M. Gordon, *Problems in Political Economy: An Urban Perspective*, cited earlier. Each section concludes with a comprehensive bibliography and suggestions for further reading. The book constitutes an efficient starting-point for serious students of these questions. A succinct economic analysis may be found in Daniel Fusfeld, "The Basic Economics of the Urban and Racial Crisis," URPE Conference Papers (December, 1968), available also as URPE *Reprint No. 2*. The essay presenting the most illuminating historical and contemporary analysis of the present and developing plight of U.S. cities is John H. Mollenkopf, "The Fragile Giant: The Crisis of the Public Sector in American Cities," *Socialist Revolution*, No. 29 (Vol. 6, No. 3), July-September 1976.

items on the list are by now all too familiar: housing problems that regularly combine insane, ugly, and costly urban construction with a steady worsening of a lifelong housing shortage; maddeningly inadequate public transportation; schools bursting with tensions while the hope of learning drains away; spreading drug addiction and crime and intensifying police brutality; increasing costs for decreasing medical care; welfare needs that are met by "workfare" laws and falling welfare budgets, as the cost of living rises; a "serious" level of unemployment in over sixty cities in 1976; a slow but steady increase of those officially classified as "poor," despite—or because of?—a War on Poverty. And smog, and power blackouts, and. . . .

The crisis of the cities is another way of describing a serious deterioration in the way people live; for people live—work, reside, go to school, get addicted, busted and pushed around—mostly in the cities. Over two-thirds of the population live in the 224 "metropolitan areas" of the nation. Many of the separate states also suffer from fiscal crisis; but theirs derives in large part from the cities'. Cities and states wait impatiently for Washington to bail them out; President Nixon proudly proclaimed his "sharing" of five billion dollars of annual federal revenue with the regions, while simultaneously cutting back federally-funded urban programs in amounts equal or greater to the "sharing," and while raising arms expenditures—processes that have continued since his removal from office: "defense" spending rose from $85 billion in fiscal 1974, to $88 billion in fiscal 1975, $98 billion in fiscal 1976 and $113 billion in fiscal 1977 (October 1, 1976 to Sept. 30, 1977). Whatever American mayors may think, seldom a voice is heard wondering if perhaps the over $1.5 trillion spent on arms over the past twenty-five years might not have a central responsibility for the cities' persisting fiscal crisis.

The rash of emergency announcements of recent years suggesting that the living conditions and fiscal mechanisms of urban life have come unstuck are of course accurate. But the inadequacy of living conditions in our cities is not new. It would be difficult to match the squalor and brutality found in 1900 Chicago as depicted by Sinclair in *The Jungle*, or their continuation as vividly described by O'Farrell in *Studs Lonigan*. The inadequacies have been there all along. But the new emigrants who mostly filled the cities tolerated what no longer is tolerated; what they found intolerable could be camouflaged or pacified by petty handouts, or hidden from view in ways no longer possible. The camouflage has peeled away under the hot blast of an unsuccessful war; belief in the basic beneficence of the system for tens of millions of Americans has shriveled in the same period. The system no longer delivers hope to the poor.

But it has not been the *failure* of the system that has caused these rude awakenings; it has been its *success*, as success is defined in this system. For the past generation (to look back no further) American capitalism has flourished as never before: real income per capita up more than 60 percent since 1946, an average rate of real growth of 3.5 percent, one or more automobiles and TV sets in almost every house, and many more houses than ever. That all this has been accompanied by militarization, imperialist expansion, war, large-scale corruption, waste and trivialization, is of course true. Withal, the economic system has been at its very best in the one way that is counted in our system as most important: it has done what it is designed to do, which is to produce goods—any old goods—and to yield profits and luxurious living to those within the top 10 percent of the population. When they can breathe, the 20 percent or so in the next layers down, moreover, have done better than that many people have ever done in other times or places. The system has succeeded; it can do no better. GNP, after all, is over one-and-a-half trillion dollars.

The problems of the cities are now acute not only for those who live and work in them (and less directly, for those in the larger metropolitan areas surrounding the cities) but also for those who own city real estate, and whose plants, offices, and stores are still located in the cities. Industrial and commercial firms may move to the suburbs as fast as decorum and costs will allow, but there are certain limits to that process, as there are limits to the exodus of middle American homeowners. Apart from considerations of human misery, there are billions to be lost if the cities are not "saved."

This threat, which has placed the urban crisis on the front pages for the past few years, has been made more vivid by the turbulence also seen on the front pages. The Urban Coalition has sought to enlist the voluntary cooperation of businessmen in bringing new life to the cities. The federal government has joined with local governments to renew and redevelop the decayed central cities. These and other programs have done both a lot and a little. Slums have been wiped out and replaced by shiny new buildings; but they have been office buildings, stores, or middle and high income apartment houses. Urban renewal, as the saying goes, has been urban removal for the former residents of the slums—removal, that is, to still other slums—thus increasing rents while compressing the population. Black people call the process "Negro removal."

The intensity of the urban problem guarantees that its existence is known to all; its social, political, and economic dangers to those at the top of the society have guaranteed that all levels of business and government have initiated or become part of innumerable programs with the stated intentions of eliminating poverty, slums, mess, and sprawl. Many of the programs died on paper. Those that have been implemented have been accompanied by a worsening of the problems they have sought to cure, sometimes because of the programs, sometimes despite them. Why?

Certainly a key part of an answer to what has gone wrong must begin with a fundamental reality: remedial programs are run by those who have been responsible for the problems they seek to cure. The programs are run by those at the top—the top of federal, state, or local governments, or of the appropriate bureaus; the top of the economy, or their accepted representatives on the national, regional, and local levels. Whether the reference is to manpower training programs where resistant unions as well as businessmen have a say; to urban development and renewal where real estate developers, banks, and construction companies move into decision-making positions; or to transportation and environmental reform where *all* power groups move in; whether in these or other instances, "the vested interests" have the largest say.

Take urban renewal. In the shaping of federal urban housing and renewal programs, the process normally begins with the best of intentions, in or out of Congress. Immediately a variety of pressures comes to bear: to place administration and control of programs on the local level, which means under the control of those in power, not those with the need; *not* to allocate adequate funds; *not* to compete with existing housing. One study sums up the resulting situation as follows:

> Our survey has shown that the men and women who make basic public housing policy at the local level are in no sense representative of the client group the programs are intended to serve. A substantial proportion of the commissioners do not favor adding to the stock of publicly subsidized housing, nor use of newer forms of public housing, nor many of the "liberalization" trends, including increased tenant participation. . . . [The authority] inserts, at a critical level of internal decision-making, an intervening layer of part-time, lay commissioners who act as a brake on the program by failing to keep abreast of new trends and techniques and by representing a microcosm of middle-class white views about the poor, their housing, and the responsibilities of government.[33]

Urban renewal does not make cities a better place to live for their residents, whose housing continues to deteriorate, who find jobs increasingly difficult to find, and so on. But it does help the construction industry, the banking industry, the real estate industry. It does so by

---

[33] Chester Hartman and Gregg Carr, "Housing Authorities Reconsidered," *Journal of the American Institute of Planners* (January, 1969). Quoted in David Gordon, *Problems in Political Economy*, p. 361. The entire section on housing in Gordon's book is worth reading for this matter. For an equally critical but conservative viewpoint see Martin Anderson, *The Federal Bulldozer* * (Cambridge: The M.I.T. Press, 1964).

building high-rise office buildings, shopping centers, and freeways cutting through the residential areas of the very people who are supposed to be benefitting. The scandals associated with the development run the gamut—for example, disclosures of extensive corruption of the Chicago Federal Housing Authority in 1972, the same year a multi-million dollar housing development in St. Louis was *torn down*, after only a few years' existence—but they are not to be seen as scandalous. This is the way the "development of our cities" takes place. The essentially private power structure that built our cities in the past in response to speculative and market stimuli is now a complex private-public structure that "rebuilds" our cities, in response still to the lure of profits, still buttressed by "cooperative" politicians. The process is not new; what gives it the smell of scandal is that it is carried out in the name of those who are in fact harmed by it. But that is scarcely new, either.

Meanwhile, and with no improvement in sight, the mosquito drone intensifies, and not a few are carrying malaria. Intense concern with the urban crisis began in the Kennedy Administration. It continued in the Johnson Administration, but as the War in Indochina deepened, the War on Poverty and Urban Blight devolved into skirmishes. Under Nixon, the rhetoric of urban rescue found its principle in Daniel Moynihan's "benign neglect"—which had the virtue, at least, of bringing rhetoric and reality closer together.

The Effluent Society

So goes the American city, with millions of Americans living badly and many dying prematurely. And then we have the problems of the environment—our air and water especially, in the cities and the countryside. The scope and spread of industrialism in America are regularly hailed as totems of our success. The equally extensive existence of environmental damage is viewed much as a drunken hangover might be—the unfortunate by-product of a great spree. But hangovers go away, normally; ecological imbalance worsens dynamically, affecting even, indeed especially, those who gain the least from its causes. The causes are deep-seated in our society. "What is at stake in the ecological crisis we face today," says Murray Bookchin,

> . . . is the very capacity of the earth to sustain advanced forms of life. The crisis is being drawn together by massive increases in "typical" forms of air and water pollution; by a mounting accumulation of nondegradable wastes, lead residues, pesticide residues and toxic additives in food; by the expansion of cities into vast urban belts; by increasing stresses due to congestion, noise and mass living; by the wanton scarring of the earth as

a result of mining operations, lumbering, and real estate speculation. The result of all this is that the earth within a few decades has been despoiled on a scale that is unprecedented in the entire history of human habitation on the planet.[34]

The ecological crisis, as Bookchin points out above, has many facets: the spoliation and waste of resources; the poisoning of our food and the sources of our food; what is coming to be called visual and aural pollution; and, of course, the pollution of air and water. The causes of each and all of these are found in the normal operations of our economy; here we will examine only pollution as it most directly affects urban life— air, water, and solid waste pollution.

Air, water, and solid waste pollution were familiar problems to the cities of England in the early nineteenth century. Sewage, garbage, foul drinking water, noxious air, and heedless expansion combined to produce intermittent cholera, sewer explosions and consequent fires, as well as significant reductions of productive efficiency.[35] It was to the self-interest of those with the most power in England then (and especially in London) to eliminate such problems. What is interesting is not that they made the attempt to do so, but that it took decades for substantial progress to be made, and that as the twentieth century arrived the progress was still lagging behind the problem. The problems today are considerably more intense. They are by no means confined to the United States (if anything, they are more intense in Japan); but the United States, as the largest industrial power, the largest user of raw materials, of electric energy, of automobiles—of everything—sits at the center of the problem not only for itself, but for the world. (We comprise 6 percent of world population; we use 33 percent of the world's energy.)

Air pollution presses most noticeably and painfully on urban-suburban dwellers. Threatening though it quite clearly is, whether in oncoming years it will be more deadly than poisoned water and waste pollution only time will tell—as time will also tell us, too late for damage to be undone, just how correct the scientists are who convincingly argue that the freon gas emitted from aerosol spray cans (for deodorants, shaving cream, and so on) is irrevocably destroying the ozone layer of the atmosphere, thus increasing not only the probability of skin cancer but also of permanent damage to agriculture over the whole globe. All forms are connected, in any case. Let us begin with water and waste pollution.[36]

[34] "Towards an Ecological Solution," *Ramparts* (May, 1970). Excerpts are reprinted in *The Capitalist System*, pp. 388–92.

[35] Ridgeway, *The Politics of Ecology*, discusses both causes and attempted reforms in that period, and relates them to our present.

[36] Gordon provides a concise summary of forms and causes of urban pollution, pp. 458–59.

The means, or attempted means, of maintaining our production and our cleanliness are among the principal causes of water pollution: the disposal of industrial and bodily wastes, of our soaps, and the washing away of insecticides and pesticides. Yet in every case, alternative ways can be and must be found. Additional factors are the increased runoff of water brought about by filled-in swamps and denuded hillsides, the closing off of local for distant water supplies as the major cities expand and reach out for "reliable" water, the increased use of water by industry and the resulting pollution of major rivers and lakes. Add it all together, and it may be understood why, as President Johnson pointed out in 1967, "every major river system in the country is polluted." So are most of the lakes and bays, and even parts of the oceans.

Quite simply, through organic and inorganic chemical residues, through sewage and heat and algae, clean water is rapidly becoming an increasingly scarce resource. In the economics textbooks over the past century, water, like air, has been classified as a "free" good. Free to business, perhaps; for American society it will cost billions of dollars for tens of years to get us back to the point where our water resources are safely usable, let alone free. Business made the profits from our reckless development; the entire population will have to finance the remedies—if there are remedies.

In a socioeconomic system as highly interdependent as ours, no single activity can be isolated in terms of its meaning. But we can point to complexes of activities and the relationships and processes within which they spin. Let us look at *paper* (and containers), first, and then go on to examine the most central of all complexes in the American economy, *automobiles* and *petroleum*.

Road Map to Disaster

Most of *solid waste* pollution does not emanate directly from the cities. But that which does is mostly composed of paper, plastic, and throwaway bottles and cans. The average trash disposal per person per day in the United States is seven pounds, which adds up to over three billion *tons* per year. Some of this helps to pollute the water; some of it takes up land space; some of it is dumped into the ocean. Ecology reformers urge us—regarding air and water and solid waste pollution—to use biodegradable soap, white (instead of colored) tissues, and returnable bottles; they urge us not to use the car, not to use the air conditioner or the TV on hot days; and buy a bike.

Meanwhile, the economic system has its needs if it is to continue without basic change. Reformers urge self-restraint on us all; yet business must continue to sell its products. Whatever else that means, it involves the *increased* use of packaging, paper, automobiles and gasoline. The automobile-petroleum complex is of course the major air polluter; but it connects with the pollution associated with paper, packaging, and consumerism in general, as it does with the growth of bureaucracy.

The bureaucracy of business is and has for long been more pervasive and substantial than that of much (and deservedly) maligned government; it is necessary if accounts and records are to be kept and profits to be made. Consumerism is just as much a product of advanced industrial capitalism. Modern industry must have mass markets, even with high military production. Mass markets mean, increasingly, advertising, sales promotion, credit, and packaging. Paper and plastic production is, of course, one of the major polluters of our waters through poisonous chemical wastes, and one of the great destroyers of forests which are in turn the natural preservers of both air and water. No matter what individual consumers do about disposing of their own waste, they will continue to see an increase in packaging, advertising, and useless printed materials—and pollution. The situation is even less susceptible to mitigation regarding the automobile-petroleum complex.

Four-fifths of all American families own automobiles; about one-third have two or more cars. About 60 percent of urban air pollution is due to the *use* of motor vehicles (varying widely from city to city, of course). If car users were to cut their driving by half, that would surely have a beneficial effect on the air, which would remain polluted, however. But more important, we may believe that the auto and oil companies would find ways to bring us back to normal. That is their business. In all the advertising of the auto and oil companies (GM alone spent over $300 million on advertising in 1971), there is nary a word about buying fewer cars, or driving less; nor are there suggestions as to ways of finding alternative modes of transport. "Earth Day," the nation-wide demonstration of concern over the environment, took place in 1970; in 1973 car sales broke all records, as did gasoline consumption. And when, in the slump of 1974 and 1975, car sales plummeted (by about one-third), the process was received as a national disaster, the only efforts made being those to somehow increase car sales once more. By 1976 they were up to "normal" and the sale of larger cars was increasing as a percentage of total sales. Larger cars use more resources, more than twice as much labor (50 versus 19 hours, on the average), and yield much higher profit than smaller cars, and they use more gasoline, of course.

Barry Weisberg has formulated the importance of the automobile-petroleum complex succinctly:

> No other factor has exercised such a predominant influence upon the direction and definition of the American industrial empire. In terms of

capital formation, patterns of employment, the extent of marketing penetration, transportation, energy, urbanization, ecological imbalance and American foreign policy, they are unrivaled in influence. The impact of their economic priorities upon the public policy of the United States is unsurpassed by any other lobby or combination of lobbies. The network of subsidiaries, affiliates, and joint ventures runs into the tens of thousands and affects the political economy of virtually every nation. Automobiles and petroleum determine the political composition of governments and the chemical composition of the atmosphere.[37]

As we saw in Chapter 4, the emergence of the automobile as a widely-owned commodity in the 1920's was the principal developmental growth factor in the prosperity of that period. Setting aside its importance for the petroleum and construction industries (of buildings, suburbs, roads, shopping centers, and so on) consider the sales other industries enjoy because of the automobile. It accounts for these percentages of the gross market consumption of the following products: malleable iron, 48 percent; steel, 21 percent; aluminum, 12 percent; lead, 65 percent; nickel, 15 percent; natural rubber, 69 percent; synthetic rubber, 34 percent; copper, 8 percent. Automobiles represent about one-quarter of *all* retail sales. The industry estimates that one out of every six jobs in the U.S. is dependent upon the automobile—it is responsible for employing 16 percent of the labor force, about 15 percent of GNP, involving more than eight hundred thousand *businesses*. There are more automobile mechanics per car than physicians per person. GM alone accounts for over half of all passenger cars produced in the U.S. and it directly employs almost eight hundred thousand people. Its sales in 1975 were over $35 billion. As noted in Chapter 3, EXXON's sales were over $45 billion in that year, with profits after taxes of over $2.5 billion. Ten auto-related corporations take about 23 percent of *all* corporate profits.

Dependence upon this pattern of production, jobs, consumption, and transportation has become an addiction in American society (and is rapidly moving in that direction in other industrial capitalist societies). The American people never decided that this dominating characteristic of their lives should be so, or that private transport should so fully displace public transport; nor is it likely, as Sawers expresses it below, that people (given the opportunity) would have decided to so afflict themselves:

If, in 1910, one asked, "A new form of individualized transportation—the automobile—has been devised. It is terribly convenient, but within 60 years it will directly kill 60,000 people each year and injure millions of

---

[37] *Beyond Repair: The Ecology of Capitalism,* cited earlier, Chapter 5. The foregoing quotation appears on p. 98; much of the data to follow are also drawn from this excellent study of these two industries.

others. Untold millions will suffer from heart and lung diseases that it causes; and because of it our cities will fall into decay, perpetuating and exacerbating racial and other social antagonisms, etc. Would you prefer an automobile-based transportation system or a public transportation system that does not have these noxious side effects?" it is inconceivable that many would have answered affirmatively. It is not a matter of lack of foresight; no mechanism existed for allowing any foresight to affect the decision about urban transportation.[38]

The process of "automobilization" of U.S. society did not create itself, nor is it perpetrated without the aid of pushers. There are, of course, as the foregoing data show, thousands upon thousands of street and road contractors, motel operators, repair shops, suburban shopping centers, fast-food shops, gas station operators, mechanics, salesmen, etc., etc., whose profits, incomes, and lives would be substantially disrupted were this complex to be lessened in our lives by, say, the proliferation of mass urban transit systems. But if they are among the dependent beneficiaries of the status quo, it is the auto, oil, and major construction companies who are its most powerful supporters. Up to very recently, they have been almost unopposed in the use of their power and influence both to expand the use of the automobile and to hinder even the maintenance of public transport.

These groups have also been the moving force behind the Highway Trust Fund, which has spent $32 billion on highways since 1956. (Its supporters claim another $300 billion will be needed over the next fifteen years, ten times the rate since 1956. For every $50 spent on highways, the federal government has spent one dollar on mass transit.) This lobby is also among the principal combatants of effective pollution controls, as revealed in the initiative campaign for and against the so-called Clean Environment Act in California in 1972.[39] Nationally the lobby has been successful in relaxing and postponing emission controls, and in preventing Highway Trust Funds to be used for mass transit projects.

Quite apart from the air pollution provided by motorists is that provided by the industries which are producing the stuff of pollution (not least of which are the auto and oil industries). In the San Francisco Bay Area, for example, official estimates state that industry is responsible for 54 percent of the visible air pollutants; and that ten corporations (four petroleum, four chemical) alone were responsible for 70 percent of all industrial pollution. The same ten corporations contributed about one-seventh of the $1.5 million used to defeat the Clean Environment Act.

The corporations that pollute the environment with their production,

[38] Sawers, "Urban Form and Mode of Production," p. 54n.

[39] See Weisberg, *Beyond Repair*, pp. 128–32, and the San Francisco *Bay Guardian*, July-August, 1972. Which lost two-to-one, as did the so-called "anti-Nuclear Initiative," seeking to control nuclear power plant construction in California (1976).

that induce us to use their products so that we do likewise, and that use their power to derail serious efforts to reverse these processes, are doing what is natural and necessary for them. They grow or decline as the system they now control grows or declines; and the law of growth to which all have become habituated knows only quantitative expression: *More!* As Mumford says, "the internal problems of the metropolis and its subsidiary areas are reflections of a whole civilization geared to expansion by strictly rational and scientific means for purposes that have become progressively more empty and trivial, more infantile and primitive, more barbarous and massively irrational."[40]

As if all this were not enough, in 1973 public clamor arose, or was created, about an "energy crisis." Since then, despite overwhelming evidence from both private and public quarters that there is not now, nor has there ever been, a *shortage* of energy, the public has been steadily reminded of the continuing "crisis"—as the prices of gasoline, heating oil, heavy fuel oil, and natural gas have more than doubled, as the major oil companies have seen spectacular increases in their profits and put up many thousands of new service stations while the smaller companies have been forced to the wall. But there was more to it than that. It is already easy to forget that the oil companies were very much on the defensive after the numerous oil spills of the late 1960's and early 1970's; but since 1973 the Santa Barbara channel has been re-opened for exploitation, the Alaska pipeline is almost a reality as a completed project (accompanied by innumerable dangers and scandals), and the public is becoming accustomed to repeated calls for allowing the profits of oil companies to be increased further (through still higher prices and decreased taxation) to encourage exploration. Also, the power of the United States in the capitalist world-economy has increased, for of the capitalist industrial nations we alone have any sizable share of our needs met by domestic supplies: the increased costs of petroleum products meant greater cost increases for Europe and Japan than for the U.S., lowering U.S. prices in world competition; and U.S. oil companies took the profits.

This development was made possible by the great dependence of the major countries and regions of the world upon petroleum, a dependence engineered artfully and deliberately (as we shall see in Chapter 7) by the major oil companies in conjunction with the U.S. government: as Tanzer points out,

> . . . even as late as 1952, the percentage of total energy consumed which was supplied by indigenous production [of coal, e.g.] was as follows: United States, 99 percent; Western Europe, 86 percent; Far East, 97 percent; Communist countries, 101 percent (i.e., net exports). . . . [But]

[40] *The City in History,* p. 554.

by 1972 the proportion of total energy supplies provided by indigenous production was as follows: United States, 85 percent; Western Europe, 41 percent; Japan, 13 percent; Communist countries, 104 percent.[41]

But surely there is an energy shortage, or if not now there will be soon?

A recent comprehensive study by Yale professor William Nordhaus presents the following picture of world reserves. Recoverable coal reserves have been estimated at over six trillion tons, or enough to fill all of the world's energy needs, at today's consumption rates, for well over 500 years. Total recoverable petroleum reserves have been estimated at more than 200 billion tons, or over seventy times current annual consumption. Similarly, the world's estimated reserves of natural gas are over 150 trillion cubic meters, or more than 150 years worth at today's consumption rates. The world's hitherto largely unexploited oil shale reserves are believed to be on the order of 200 times larger than conventional oil reserves. Finally, with the breeder reactor, which is expected to be perfected before the end of the century, estimated uranium reserves would contain more than a million times the energy of all fossil fuels. . . . And, of course, none of this takes into account the vast possibilities of non-polluting energy sources such as the sun, winds, tides, and hot springs, use of which may be preferable for environmental reasons.[42]

There is indeed an energy *"crisis,"* but not necessarily a *shortage* of energy. The crisis has been created by the most powerful companies in the history of the world, in league with the U.S. government, and the oil-producing (OPEC) countries. The nature of the crisis is a very different matter depending upon the viewer: from the standpoint of the general public, it is the latest and most spectacular instance of the use of concentrated economic and political power, employing all the techniques of modern mind management and chicanery; from the viewpoint of the oil companies the crisis has been one that combines recent and substantial over-supply with the political pressures of the environmentalists. The tumult and the shouting since 1973 appear to be an attempt—successful so far—on the part of the major energy suppliers to shape the future so that *potential* (if any) real shortages can be turned to their advantage, in the form of greater profits and greater power. As James Ridgeway points out:

[41] Michael Tanzer, *The Energy Crisis: World Struggle for Power and Wealth* * (New York: Monthly Review Press, 1974), p. 16. This book and Ridgeway's *Last Play* (cited below) are indispensable sources of data and analysis for grasping the ways and means of corporate/State power, and the great costs and dangers associated with them.

[42] Tanzer, p. 20.

These companies know, as the average citizen does not, that the energy crisis could be the most important political and economic issue of the last quarter of the twentieth century. Not only does the production, distribution, and use of energy underlie the entire environmental movement, but also energy is the foundation of the modern industrial state.[43]

Over two-thirds of the world's oil is controlled by seven companies, five of them American. As known oil reserves in the United States run out, dependence grows daily on oil found either in political hotspots such as the Middle East and Southeast Asia (of which more in the next chapter), or in areas such as Alaska where environmental damage is a high probability. The major oil companies, knowing this better than anyone else, naturally choose to make their investment decisions without interference from environmentalists or others. The "energy crisis" facilitates an increase in the *political* power of the oil companies, as the demand for their products becomes ever more desperate. This is all the more likely because the same companies have increasingly gained control over fuels other than oil: coal, uranium, and gas. EXXON, for example, is the single largest owner of *coal* deposits in the United States. As Ridgeway shows in meticulous detail, the oil companies have worked out an effective pattern of ownership and cooperation over competing fuels, and with those companies and facilities that transport (tankers and pipelines), accommodate (seaports), finance and own energy and other companies (banks, insurance companies, foundations and universities), are major users (nonferrous metal and power producers for example)—and, of course, with the agencies that regulate (the Federal Power Commission, and various state agencies).

Against such patterns of ownership, control, influence, and cooperation, the environmental movement seems a very small David with poor aim, pitted against an enormous and agile Goliath. Oil is the single most powerful industry in the United States and in the world; along with the automobile industry (and both are tied in closely with the most powerful financial institutions), its power is both unprecedented and unmatched, in the market and in politics.[44]

Environmental imbalance is systemic, the result of our system running at its necessary speed in ways that suit the system's criteria. It is not the result of self-indulgence, of people driving to work instead of biking, walking, or taking nonexistent mass transit facilities, for example. The

[43] James Ridgeway, *The Last Play: The Struggle to Monopolize the World's Energy Resources* * (New York: Dutton, 1973), p. 3.

[44] The relationship between the oil industry and Presidents Kennedy and Johnson is discussed briefly in Chapter 7; here we may refer to a bright survey of Nixon's connections with oil, and with other powerful supporters in what the author calls "the Southern-rim." See Kirkpatrick Sale, "The World Behind Watergate," *New York Review of Books*, May 3, 1973.

environmental costs have been very high up to now; they have only just begun to mount.

The Bell Tolls

What most people know about environmental imbalance is that if we don't take care, people might die. But even casual students of this question know that people have died from poisoned air in Belgium in the 1930's, that over 4,000 deaths in London in the 1950's were authoritatively attributed to "smog," and that deaths related to pollution are now reported regularly in Europe, the United States, and Japan. The people who die are those who have emphysema, or a heart condition, or who are otherwise weak—the poisoned air finishes them off. And there are the deaths due to poisoned water, or from fish poisoned by poisoned water, or . . . something. The cause of all this is well-known: the uncontrolled process of industrialization and consumerism. What is the cure?

The cure dwells in the halls of power. But the halls of power are presently filled with killers of the environment, even though they may soothe us with TV commercials showing either that there is *no* problem, or that if there is, it isn't *their* fault. Legislation, when passed over the substantial and well-financed opposition of the polluters, is soon diluted and controlled by their representatives. Cry the beloved country though we may, either singly or in massive crowds such as those on Earth Day, public action is the only means by which ecological imbalance can be replaced by ecological balance. But public action is presently dominated by local, regional, state, and federal bodies whose criteria center first around profit and power, and then, perhaps, on the preservation of life. That those with power are toying with their own lives as well as ours simply tells us that not only the powerless are dehumanized by this society.

It speaks volumes that it should be necessary through great effort to place an initiative for a "Clean Environment" on a state ballot, something any legislature could and should do without the powerless having to spend time and money to push such legislation. When such ballot measures are defeated by massive scare advertising, paid for by the very companies whose TV ads seek to soothe us, that tells us something more—about the companies and about the deluded voters.

This kind of threatening situation led Veblen, on the eve of World War I and after suggesting what had to be done, to go on and say, "But history records more frequent and more spectacular instances of the triumph of imbecile institutions over life and culture than of peoples who have by force of instinctive insight saved themselves alive out of a desperately precarious institutional situation, such, for instance, as now faces the people of Christendom." [45]

Setting modern war aside, one cannot imagine a more effective system for destroying life than that within which we now function; except that war cannot be set aside. It grows from the same social matrix as the destruction of the environment and the death of our cities; the principal difference is that the destruction by war is deliberate whereas that coming from our economic system is a "by-product." The social outlook guiding both disasters is the same, as is the technology. Growth for its own sake, production for its own sake, consumption for its own sake, and power for the sake of continuing the rest—these are the drives that have shaped the modern world, whose leader is presently the United States.

Human beings can do better on this continent, and they have. The civilization of the Native Americans, before we crushed it, was a marvel of balance between human beings and nature, and among themselves. Listen to this Chief as he speaks to a French officer in the early days of settlement:

As to us, we find all our riches and all our conveniences among ourselves, without troubles, without exposing our lives to the dangers in which you find yourselves constantly through your long voyages; and whilst feeling compassion for you in the sweetness of our repose, we wonder at the anxieties and cares which you give yourselves, night and day, in order to load your ships. . . . Now tell me this one little thing, if thou hast any sense, which of these two is the wisest and happiest? He who labours without ceasing and only obtains with great trouble enough to live on, or he who rests in comfort and finds all he needs in the pleasure of hunting and fishing?[46]

We cannot return to that condition of easy and natural balance, nor are there many Americans who would even if it were possible. But we can seek to live at peace with our environment, our fellow human beings, and ourselves in an urban and industrial civilization. We can, but not so long as the bulk of Americans continue to strive for profit and power and an overflowing cornucopia of increasingly contrived and expensive consumer goods—strive as donkeys strive for carrots fixed beyond their noses. The bulk of Americans cannot achieve what they seek.

The time has come to take thought, to reflect on what the genuine needs and pleasures of life are, and to find some symmetry between our ends and our means. Those ends are not mysterious, or the province of a few: we wish ourselves and our loved ones to eat well, to be comfort-

[45] *Instinct of Workmanship*, p. 25. By 1914, everyone expected war; however, its length, spread, and endless disastrous consequences were not expected by the "respectable people" who brought it about.

[46] Quoted in *To Serve the Devil*, vol. 1, pp. 43–4.

ably clothed and housed, to learn through education what we can become and do, to be healthy, to enjoy nature and the works of the species; to have control over our lives. Each of these ends moves away from us, not closer, with each passing year. We count as our treasures what we have been socialized to count as treasures, though they defile our lives and make robots of us all: the automobile, the TV, the encapsulated suburban existence, the gleaming high buildings, the ever-rising GNP, "fast" food. We are moving in the wrong direction for human beings.

Cities at their worst in the past had valuable qualities to them that our planners now rush to obliterate. They had neighborhoods, they were disorderly, they bustled with the diversities of our ethnic and religious backgrounds, they had some life of their own, and the people in them knew them as homes, not as way stations to the next job, or as places with airports, motels, freeways, and ghettoes. There is in our present processes a dynamic which guarantees its intensification—unless the people take hold. "We must," as Lincoln said in the midst of another crisis, "disenthrall ourselves." [47]

Reading Suggestions

We have glimpsed only the surface of the issues raised in this chapter, although many of the references footnoted will take the reader below that surface. Here are a few more suggestions. Theodore Lowi, in his *End of Liberalism** (New York: Norton, 1969), shows the deep inadequacies of present ways and means of liberal policies and politics, and most effectively in his discussions of urban reforms—not least because he speaks as a liberal. Among Mumford's many fine books, his *The Highway and the City* (New York: Harcourt Brace Jovanovich, 1958) is a profound study of the relationships suggested by the title. Health and education are among the critical problems of our cities. Barbara and John Ehrenreich, *The American Health Empire** (New York: Random House; Vintage, 1971) help us to understand why that is so regarding medical care. Educational problems and possibilities have called forth many fine books in recent years; I have found two of the most illuminating to have been Jonathan Kozol, *Death at an Early Age**and *The Night is Dark and I am Far From Home* (Boston: Houghton Mifflin, 1967 and 1975, re-

[47] What cities have been in America is discussed systematically and humanely by Jane Jacobs, in her *Death and Life of Great American Cities* * (New York: Random House, 1961). See especially the first chapter. Richard Sennett, *The Uses of Disorder* * (New York: Random House; Vintage, 1970) provides a penetrating analysis of the psychological dangers of the artificial order of urban/suburban existence, and offers some wise proposals for change.

spectively) and George Dennison, *The Lives of Children** (New York: Random House, 1969). Miriam Wasserman's *School Fix,** cited earlier, is valuable for understanding city politics as well as education. Studies of how cities "work" are badly needed. Two that commend themselves are Mike Royko, *Boss** (New York: New American Library, 1971), an easy-reading treatment of Chicago's Mayor Daley; a more penetrating study is by Edward C. Hayes, *Power Structure and Urban Policy: Who Rules in Oakland?** (New York: McGraw-Hill, 1972). A useful book of readings, ranging broadly in both focus and viewpoint, is Joe R. Feagin, ed., *The Urban Scene** (New York: Random House, 1973). The Steffens essay on St. Louis is included in an excellent anthology of the "Muckrakers'" writings—critical attacks on corruption, monopoly, poverty, etc., in the first years of this century—edited by Harvey Swados, *Years of Conscience: The Muckrakers* (New York: World, 1962). A useful mainstream analysis of the urban transportation mess is Wilbert Owens, *The Accessible City* (Washington, D. C.: The Brookings Institution, 1972). The automobile industry and much of its meaning is dealt with readably and well in Emma Rothschild, *Paradise Lost: The Decline of the Auto-Industrial Age** (New York: Vintage, 1973).

In *The Human Prospect** (New York: Norton, 1974), Robert L. Heilbroner develops a gloomy socio-politico-economic analysis of population and environmental developments, gloomy in part (I believe) because of the generally conventional approach he takes; gloomy in part also because the degree of social change necessary to allow such developments to be resolved is revolutionary in scope. The eminent biologist Barry Commoner helped to initiate deep concern with the environment in his *The Closing Circle** (New York: Knopf, 1971); in his latest book *The Poverty of Power: Energy and the Economic Crisis* (New York: Knopf, 1976) he too is much alarmed, but argues that the "problem" can be resolved by moving toward socialism, while showing that there is no need for either a food or an energy shortage.

7

Imperialism, American-Style

While this America settles in the mould of its vulgarity,
heavily thickening to empire,
And protest, only a bubble in the molten mass, pops and
sighs out, and the mass hardens,

I sadly remember that the flower fades to make fruit,
the fruit rots to make earth.
Out of the mother; and through the spring exultances,
ripeness and decadence; and home to the mother.*

Peoples of all nations live in part by myths; the hardiest of these, and probably the most dangerous, have to do with their nation's foreign relationships. Two such myths stand out for Americans: we have been a self-sufficient national economy; and our external relationships have been benign.

By comparison with other capitalist nations we have been, of course, relatively self-sufficient: Great Britain, for instance, must import half of its food and four-fifths of its raw materials, whereas our total foreign trade seldom rises above 5 percent of our GNP. In this, as in other social relationships, however, quantitative measures taken alone are misleading. From the beginning, our economic development has been critically dependent upon our foreign economic dealings. In the last century that dependence has steadily increased, until today the American economy is dependent not just for its health, but for its very functioning, on its commodity exports, resource imports, and foreign investments. That de-

* Robinson Jeffers, *Shine, Perishing Republic.* From *Selected Poems* by Robinson Jeffers. Copyright 1925 and renewed 1953 by Robinson Jeffers. Reprinted by permission of Random House, Inc.

pendence has grown along with the growth of an American empire, seldom seen as benign by those who live under its controls.

Nobody would dispute the generalization regarding dependence upon external economic relationships in our colonial period, of course. When we achieved our independence, it was the terms not the importance of those relationships that changed. America's foreign economic relationships and policies have been in a state of constant flux, from Independence to the present; both ends and means have changed—a necessity for a society whose economic structure is changing rapidly, in a rapidly changing world. The one constant in that history, however, is the conscious dependence of the United States on the rest of the world.

Those who have argued otherwise have been transfixed by the natural wealth and great size of the United States, which has of course set it apart from other nations. What has made us *like* other capitalist nations is that we have been a large and wealthy *capitalist* society. Capitalist societies have everywhere and always been vitally dependent upon their external relationships, have always functioned critically within an international setting. This has been much obscured, however, because almost all history is written and seen as *national* history, abetted by patriotic sentiments, education, and the sheer availability of such historical materials. And most history has been as superficial concerning capitalism as a system as it has been concerning the global setting within which national capitalist économies have functioned.

Capitalist economies must continually expand, as we have seen. The cutting edge of expansion often moves more easily and more profitably abroad than at home; yet it would be as unwise to attempt to isolate foreign from domestic functioning as to ignore one or the other, in what is a system of dynamic interdependence. At any one time one capitalist nation is dominant in the world economy. The very use of its dominance, however, leads to the emergence of a new leading power. Furthermore, the most powerful capitalist economy is not only the vital center of world capitalist expansion (or contraction); it is also the leading imperialist power. All these generalizations will now be examined in greater detail.

Americans quite generally see the United States as the leading capitalist, or "free world," power, and take great pride in our status as Number One. Most Americans do not see the United States as imperialist *at all*, let alone as the world's leading imperialist nation.[1] Yet the United States

[1] Typically, historians see the United States as having begun and swiftly ended its imperialist career in the years between the Spanish-American War and World War I, with a few pieces left to tidy up in the Caribbean in the 1920's. For a representative position, see Faulkner, *The Decline of Laissez-Faire*, Chapter 4. For a more realistic view, see Williams, *Contours of American History*, throughout, and the fundamental study of Walter La Feber, *New Empire: An Interpretation of American Expansionism, 1860–1898* ° (Ithaca: Cornell University Press, 1970).

is that nation, not only in the minds of radicals but also in the view of many spokesmen in the other capitalist powers (themselves the second-level imperialist nations), to say nothing of the views of Third World countries. Most Americans would choke on terms like "the American Empire"; yet, the British Empire, the French Empire, and Imperial Germany were terms bringing pride to most of the citizens of those countries. Anger and consternation ensued as their empires began to decline, and the United States, directly or indirectly, took over.

One reason Americans so quickly deny our imperial status is the pervasive lack of understanding of what imperialism is and does; another reason for the denial (for most Americans) is a systematic miseducation—what Veblen called "a trained incapacity"—regarding American history and American capitalism. Preceding chapters have sought to shed light on the latter; now we must explore the development and the nature of imperialism.

Imperialism is an historical process; to attempt a one-line definition of it (for instance, "the extension of political power by one state over another")[2] is to promote more confusion than enlightenment. As we now seek to show what imperialism has been and is, our discussion will move within a framework of several questions. *When* and *why* does a society expand its influence and control over other areas? *Where* is it likely to do so? *What* does the relationship mean to the imperialist and to the imperialized society? *How* are the relationships developed and maintained, and *how* and *why* do they change in nature and in meaning over time? *Who* benefits and *who* pays, at either end of the relationship? In seeking to answer these questions we shall first set forth a very general statement, and then explore the specific historical developments preceding and accompanying the emergence of the U. S. as Number One.

Imperialism: Becoming and Being

The seeds of both capitalism and nationalism are to be found in the medieval trading cities, such as Florence, Milan, Lübeck, and Bruges. So are the seeds of mercantilism and *modern* imperialism, which is sometimes called "the New Mercantilism."

"Buy cheap and sell dear" was the slogan emblazoned on the medi-

---

[2] Quoted critically by James O'Connor in "The Meaning of Economic Imperialism," in a collection of his essays, *The Corporations and the State* * (New York: Harper & Row, 1974), p. 153. The subtitle "Essays in the Theory of Capitalism and Imperialism" is aptly descriptive of these penetrating articles. The essay just mentioned is also collected in Robert I. Rhodes, ed., *Imperialism and Underdevelopment: A Reader* * (New York: Monthly Review Press, 1970), a very useful compendium.

eval merchant's escutcheon. The implementation of that policy abroad had two sides to it: *protection* and *privilege*. Internally for the towns it required a third policy, what the great historian of mercantilism Eli Heckscher called *"provisioning."* [3] "Mercantilism," Heckscher states, "is medieval town policy writ large." In an important sense, that is so; it is also useful to say that modern imperialism is "mercantilism writ large." But there are important differences between town economy, mercantilism, and imperialism—and of the meanings of protection, privilege and provisioning for each—differences given by the development of capitalism and of accompanying industrialism. The similarities and the differences both deserve comment.

The medieval trading town functioned very much as a unit in facing the external world. Surrounding it was the countryside, the source of its foodstuffs (and sometimes of its fibers and ores, used in medieval industry and trade). The provisioning policy of the towns had as its aim the guarantee of a steady and cheap supply of what the towns needed to consume and produce, an aim that placed the ruling merchant class in opposition to the surrounding feudal nobility and that ultimately brought the merchant into alliance with the rising monarchs who were also in conflict with the nobility. When those alliances were effective, the modern nation-state was the result. The merchants sought a united front in their dealings with other medieval traders in far-flung towns; Italians, Germans, and Flemings dealing with England, for example. The Italians and the Flemings in the twelfth, thirteenth, and fourteenth centuries were most powerful, and could function effectively in a pattern resembling "free trade." In the fourteenth century, the individually weaker German towns banded together in the Hanseatic League, a grouping of about seventy towns acting as a powerful unit in their trading activities over the face of Northern Europe and England.

In their own towns, the merchants sought price and wage policies that provided stability and a supply of exportable products at costs that would allow profits. The famous "just wage and just price" policies of the medieval towns were "just" up to the point only where the ruling merchants could flourish in their inter-regional activities. Much of what was "bought cheap" was a result of exploitative relationships outside and within the towns; what was "sold dear" was a function of the strength of the merchants elsewhere and that strength was enhanced whenever and wherever possible by trading privileges and by both economic and military protection. By the fourteenth and fifteenth centuries, the degree to which the necessary protection and privileges were forthcoming was

[3] Eli Heckscher, *Mercantilism* (London: Allen & Unwin, 1935), 2 vols., is the basic work. See his brief discussion "Mercantilism," in the *Encyclopaedia of the Social Sciences*. Perry Anderson's *Lineages of the Absolute State*, cited earlier, is indispensable for these developments.

becoming a matter of national or quasi-national power at both ends of the relationship.

While nation-states replaced trading cities as the focus of commerce and industry, the aims of foreign policy remained much the same, although means could and had to change: the scope of affairs had enlarged, and so had the power of the contestants. Provisioning policy now meant the assurance of domestic and external sources of food and raw materials; in turn this led to a colonial policy whose aim was to control the trade and resources flowing from the colonies and to prevent rival states from having access to those same areas. There were great gains to be made from success, and great losses to be suffered from the success of others—losses measured in profits, and in national economic and military strength. The medieval town policy of "buy cheap and sell dear" became a national policy; it became "beggar thy neighbor." One nation's strength was seen as inversely related to the strength of the others.

This was all pre-industrial, in the early years of capitalism, from the sixteenth into the eighteenth centuries. As the eighteenth century melted into the nineteenth, means changed. Both needs and possibilities were stronger; the developing changes were reflected in a new meaning for provisioning, privilege, and protection. Summed up, the new meanings created modern imperialism. At this point it becomes necessary to draw the distinctions between mercantilism and imperialism.

Capitalism in the days of mercantilism was not industrial. Colonial policies tended to have seaports and coastlines as their geographic locus. The great gains in trade were typically made from high value-low bulk commodities: pepper and tea, sugar and slaves, gold and silver. This might be expected in an era of long, slow, and dangerous voyages. As modern industry developed, the patterns changed. Steamships and railroads tied continents together, allowing and requiring hinterlands to be penetrated. Bulkier, lower-value commodities were needed to supply growing industry and industrial populations with raw materials and foodstuffs. The relatively short-term commercial investments of the earlier period were added to by necessary long-term investments—in expanded harbor facilities, in railroads, in mines and in plantations. The political impact of *mercantilist* colonial policy was typically manifested in effective relationships with *local* rulers and the regulation of privileged and protected trade between colony and metropolis. The new *imperialism* required,

> . . . as the colonial system of earlier centuries did not, a large measure of political control over the *internal* relations and structure of the colonial economy. This it requires, not merely to "protect property" and to ensure that the profit of the investment is not offset by political risks, but actually to create the essential conditions for the profitable investment of capital.

Among these conditions is the existence of a proletariat sufficient to provide a plentiful and cheap labour-supply; and where this does not exist, suitable modifications of pre-existent social forms will need to be enforced (of which the reduction of tribal land-reserves and the introduction of differential taxation on natives living in the tribal reserve in East and South Africa are examples).

Thus the "political logic of imperialism" is

to graduate from "economic penetration" to "spheres of influence," from "spheres of influence" to protectorates or indirect control, and from protectorates *via* military occupation to annexation.[4]

There has been much discussion of which comes first, political/military or economic expansion: Does trade follow the flag, or does the flag follow trade? Both happen, and they also walked hand in hand from the beginning. The gains and the rivalries associated with mercantilism and imperialism were handmaidens of colonial and imperial *strategies*—for instance, control of seaports and coaling stations, the development of naval stations for refueling and battle readiness—if for no other reason than to keep them from rivals. There was a graceful interaction: strategic considerations facilitated economic advance; economic advance required strategic considerations. Chickens and eggs.

The late nineteenth century wave of imperialism swept the globe; the sun never set on the British flag; next door, in some contiguous colony European flags also waved in the sun. Imperialism became direct, and control became direct. Colonial governments were *colonial*, and their "legal" masters were in the metropoli. Thus did the nineteenth century end and the twentieth century begin.

After World War I, the seams began to give; after World War II, the seams tore apart. Earlier, mercantilism had given way to imperialism; after World War II, imperialism gave way to *neocolonialism*, sometimes called "welfare imperialism." The strain on traditional imperial ties—those of England and France, of Holland, Italy, Germany, and Japan—had first appeared after World War I, in conjunction with strains developing *within* these major capitalist powers. The depression of the 1930's greatly increased the strains; World War II gave the *coup de grâce* to traditional imperialism. The older imperialist powers lacked the financial and military resources necessary to hold on to their territories, whether they knew it or not. Britain knew it better than some others, loosing its hold on India and most of its other colonies. France was less prudent; it spent much of its treasure and let the blood of Frenchmen and the peo-

---

[4] Maurice Dobb, *Political Economy and Capitalism* (London: Routledge, 1937), pp. 239–40. This analysis is in Chapter VII, "Imperialism," one of the most astute analyses of the development, emphasizing the differences between the earlier and later stages of capitalist expansion.

ples of North Africa and Indochina flow for years before it let go, almost bringing itself down in the process.

The United States stood waiting. As the only major capitalist power strengthened by World War II, the United States was able and eager to move into the "vacua" created by European and Japanese collapse. Our movement was in the name of preserving freedom and of promoting economic development. With these slogans on our banner, we strode forth to create the largest, the most profitable, and the most costly imperialist network in world history, as befitted the most powerful nation in the world's history. Our style was not to control ports or nations, directly, as in days of yore; we controlled only the finances, the economies, and the military of our neocolonial empire—ways we had learned in our prep school days after the Spanish-American war.

America's expansion overseas after World War II was not confined to hitherto colonial areas. Our hegemony was global: inroads into Europe, Canada, Central and South America, the Caribbean, the Middle East, South and Southeast Asia and Japan, and steel rings around the USSR and China. But our impact on the world was substantially diverse, depending upon whether the affected area was developed or underdeveloped when we took a strong hand: in Western Europe, Canada, and Japan, our influence helped to rescue and to speed up economic growth and development; in the rest of the capitalist world, our impact continued that of the earlier pattern—we deepened its *under*development.[5]

With the 1970's, a dramatic and uncertain new era opened up, both in the developed and in the underdeveloped sectors of the globe, as well as between them. The developed capitalist nations of Canada, Western Europe and Japan came increasingly into conflict and competition with the United States; the underdeveloped countries moved into one degree or another of resistance. They did so because of their own great needs, and encouraged by the Vietnamese, who had raised the costs and exposed the limits of American expansionism. Adding to the growing uncertainty has been the emergence of the multinational corporation—which, we shall see, lessens the power of national governments while increasing the power of international capitalism.

Up to now we have put forth a string of heady generalizations, which merely point to answers to our questions regarding imperialism—when and why, where, what and how, and who?—but which do not as such constitute adequate answers. The when and the why move in terms of needs and possibilities; the where in terms of what is useful and necessary and possible, regarding relative strength; what imperialism means is profit and power for the strong, exploitation and increased weakness

---

[5] Following André Gunder Frank, we shall argue that capitalist control of what became colonial areas transformed *un*development into *under*development—i.e., a relatively stable into a retrogressive process—later in this chapter.

for the already vulnerable, development for the advanced and under-development for the underdeveloped. In this chapter and earlier we have also seen that geographic expansion is critically encouraged and abetted by *economic* motivations, but that it is more complex than that. We shall also see that although the growth of advanced technology and monopo-listic structures of industry speeds up imperialist expansion, such expansion has clearly taken place before and without such structures. Great Britain and the United States were prime examples of that in the nineteenth century, before monopoly developed in either nation—Great Britain with its overseas empire and the U.S. with its continental expansion.

All these generalizations require much in the way of support and elaboration. Let us begin first with a central question: Does capitalism *require* imperialism? And, a somewhat different question: Where there has been imperialism, has there always been capitalism?

Capitalism and Imperialism

Empires litter the pages of history—Persian, Phoenician, Greek, Roman, Carthaginian, Holy Roman, to mention only a few. Although commercialism was an important part of the lives of some of these societies, only by misusing the term could we classify them as capitalist. And, on the other hand, the modern Swiss are surely capitalist, but, internationalist though they and their connections are, it would stretch the term to call them imperialistic. Still, as a world economic system capitalism has always *been* imperialist; or such, at least, is our argument. How and why is this so? [6]

The most persuasive argument stating that capitalism does *not* require imperialism—indeed, that capitalism and imperialism are *opposed* in their general features—was that put forth by Joseph A. Schumpeter. His definition of imperialism, one of those troublesome one-liners, helps to obscure the problem from the beginning. "Imperialism," Schumpeter says, "is the objectless disposition on the part of a state to unlimited forcible expansion." [7] By "objectless" Schumpeter means expansion for

[6] We shall find it convenient and appropriate here to follow closely the position taken by James O'Connor, in his article "The Meaning of Economic Imperialism," cited earlier. Our compressed summary should not be taken as an adequate substitute for the fuller position put forth by O'Connor. The analytical framework of Waller-stein, that of the global division of labor of the capitalist world-economy, is most use-ful to keep in mind in this connection. See his *The Modern World-System* (cited earlier), esp. pp. 36–63 and his "Theoretical Reprise," pp. 347–57.

[7] Joseph A. Schumpeter, *Imperialism and Social Classes* (New York: Kelley, 1951), p. 7. Edited and with an introduction by Paul M. Sweezy, a former student of Schumpeter's, and also his respectful critic. The original essay was written in 1919.

its own sake, and he observes that "objectless tendencies toward forcible expansion, without definite, utilitarian limits—that is, non-rational and irrational, purely instinctual inclinations toward war and conquest—play a very large role in the history of mankind." [8] Probably that was true in the past, and doubtless such inclinations persist in the present. What is at issue, however, is whether and when such inclinations become "objectful" and useful, indeed necessary for the maintenance of a social system such as capitalism, quite apart from whatever role expansionism might have played where *not* necessary. Here O'Connor is apt. "In connection with economic expansionism," he says,

> . . . pre-capitalist and capitalist societies differ in five general ways: First, in pre-capitalist societies economic expansion was irregular, unsystematic, not integral to normal economic activity. In capitalist societies, foreign trade and investment are rightly considered to be the "engines of growth." . . . Second, in pre-capitalist societies the economic gains from expansion were windfall gains, frequently taking the form of sporadic plunder. In capitalist societies, profits from overseas trade and investment are an integral part of national income, and considered in a matter-of-fact manner. Third, in pre-capitalist societies plunder . . . was often consumed in the field by the conquering armies. . . . In capitalist societies, exploited territories are fragmented and integrated into the structure of the metropolitan economy. . . . Fourth, in pre-capitalist societies debates within the ruling class ordinarily revolved around the question whether or not to expand. In capitalist societies, ruling-class debates normally turn on the issue of what is the best way to expand. Last, in relation to colonialism . . . , land seizure, colonist settlement, or both was the only mode of control which the metropolitan power could effectively exercise over the satellite region . . . ; capitalist societies have developed alternative, indirect, and more complex forms of control. [9]

A basic reason for the inability or refusal of Schumpeter and of other conventional social scientists to see the connection between capitalism and imperialism is their inability or refusal to see the role played by expansion and exploitation in capitalist development; or, to put it more accurately, their belief that the necessary expansion will take place under benign circumstances. For Schumpeter, expansion abroad is necessary, but it takes place through the "rational" mode of free trade; expansion at home takes place through the turbulent but effective impact of technological development on the growth and the institutions of capitalism. But capitalism's entire history has been characterized by obstacles placed in the way of free trade, apart from the exceptional decades of the late nineteenth century, which were decades also of raging im-

[8] Ibid., p. 83.
[9] O'Connor, "The Meaning of Economic Imperialism," pp. 155–6.

perialist expansion. Technological development, far from breaking down monopolies, as Schumpeter hoped, facilitated their entrenchment.

Growth and development are socially difficult to initiate and to sustain: they require expanding markets and resources and a docile labor force; they entail change throughout the society, not just in its economic institutions. In comparison, markets, resources, and cheap labor are readily obtainable abroad. What might take decades and much civil conflict to achieve at home can be achieved abroad more quickly, with less or no domestic conflict. Granted that it has been a relatively common matter for the populations of the powerful societies to become excited over foreign dangers and possibilities, real or imagined. But why do they become excited? What induces them to pay taxes, to make sacrifices, even of their blood? Whatever may be said of the precapitalist world, and whatever may be said of the "common man's" inclination to "go West," what may and must be said of the modern capitalist world is that the business community has seen the butter for its bread—and sometimes the bread itself—in what have become the colonial and neocolonial areas of the world. That the major share of profits and trade derive from relationships among and between the *developed* countries seems to contradict this assertion, but only if we fail to see the capitalist system as a *global* division of labor, and the crucial role played by the natural resources (especially oil) in the underdeveloped countries.

In Great Britain and the United States, the two leading imperialist powers of the last century, and also the two leading capitalist powers in their time, the principal voice shaping public policy both at home and abroad, directly and through the channels of public opinion, has been that of business. As Veblen said:

> Representative government means, chiefly, representation of business interests. The government commonly works in the interest of the business man with a fairly consistent singleness of purpose. And in its solicitude for the business men's interests it is borne out by current public sentiment, for there is a naive, unquestioning persuasion abroad among the body of the people to the effect that, in some occult way, the material interests of the populace coincide with the pecuniary interests of those business men. . . . It seldom happens, if at all, that the government of a civilized nation will persist in a course of action detrimental or not ostensibly subservient to the interests of the more conspicuous body of the community's business men.[10]

But even assuming that the imperializing process has been at the behest—or at the very least with the acquiescence of—business, has it

[10] *The Theory of Business Enterprise*, pp. 286–87. Veblen's attention to such matters is most intense in his *An Inquiry Into the Nature of Peace* . . . * (New York: Macmillan, 1917).

been necessary, *required?* There is finally no way of finding an unequivocal answer to that question; we can only point to constant associations and explain why the associations have occurred, still leaving open whether or not they *had* to occur. Perhaps, for example, capitalism could have existed without poverty; it has not, so we must explain why poverty exists in the midst of riches. Similarly (although I doubt it very much) capitalism *might* have grown and been sustained without overseas expansion and control; but what would have taken the place of the stimuli and gains from that expansion and control has never been explained. Professor Tom Kemp has put this point exactly:

> To claim that "imperialism" was not a necessary stage in capitalist development is to imagine that the colossal development of the productive forces which took place in the nineteenth century could have proceeded without the bringing into being of a world-wide economy dominated by the leading capitalist powers. It is to imagine that somehow the characteristics of early industrial capitalism could have become permanent, without the growth of combines and monopolies, as an atomized collection of owner-financed firms. It is to assert that there was no relation between the politics of states and the dominant economic interests within them. It is to assume that the powerful economic forces released by capitalism were kept in tow by old-line statesmen, demagogues and ideologues. It is to argue, with Schumpeter, the most clear-sighted and consistent representative of this school, that the characteristics of "imperialism" were atavistic survivals foreign to the true nature of capitalism, adopted by the bourgeoisie only as a result of a betrayal.[11]

Some readers will have been persuaded of the hand-in-glove relationship between capitalism and imperialism by now; some others never could be. Let us conclude this general part of the discussion with an observation of Harry Magdoff's on the same question:

> Imperialism . . . is so intertwined with the history and the resulting structure of modern capitalist society—with its economics, politics, and ruling ideas—that this kind of question is in the some category as, for example, "Is it necessary for the United States to keep Texas and New Mexico?" We could, after all, return these territories to the Mexican people and still maintain a high-production and high-standard-of-living economy. . . . Or one might ask, "Is Manhattan necessary for the United States?" It would surely be equitable to return land obtained from the Indians in a sharp deal. . . . Such a move to wipe out a terrible blot on the conscience of white America could be socially useful. Moreover, a new financial headquarters of the United States (and the capitalist world) could be designed

---

[11] Tom Kemp, *Theories of Imperialism* (London: Dobson, 1967), pp. 165–66. As the book's title suggests, this is a survey of various theories. It is by far the very best study of its kind.

to avoid slums, smog, pollution, and traffic crises. . . . The relevant question is not whether imperialism is necessary for the United States, but to discover the "rationality" of the historic process itself: why the United States and other leading capitalist nations persistently and recurringly acted in the imperialist fashion for at least three-quarters of a century.[12]

The foregoing has been an attempt to provide a skeletal framework for understanding what led to imperialism and what it is and means. Now let us flesh out that framework with historical matter.

The Baton of Economic Power

Capitalism and nationalism emerged together in world history, and induced comparable attitudes and behavior. Economic individualism and competition have their counterpart in nationalism and national rivalries. It would be foolish to believe that any one merchant, industrialist, or financier could attribute his economic successes entirely, or even mostly, to his own doings, independent of the larger economic context within which he makes his gains; similarly, it would be foolish to attribute the economic "successes" of a particular nation to *its* own doings, independent of the world economy. In the past several hundred years, there has always been one country in the lead. It has been economically strongest, and supreme in the technology, and dominated the patterns of trade, finance, and production of the time. And it has had its way in shaping and using the political and military forms of the time.[13]

In the early dawn of capitalism and nationalism, before either existed as such, Venice and Florence—both territorial states, not nations—carried the baton of leadership. In the late medieval and early renaissance periods, Venice ruled the Mediterranean; Florence, not a naval power, drew its strength from its trans-alpine relationships. Florentine capital and trade stimulated what became the more dynamic northern rim of Europe—principally Antwerp, Holland, and later England—at the cost,

[12] *Social Policy* (September/October, 1970) in an exchange between Magdoff and S.M. Miller, Roy Bennett, and Cyril Alapatt, "Does the U.S. Economy Require Imperialism?" Magdoff's portion of the exchange, "The Logic of Imperialism," is reproduced in *Monthly Review* (October and November, 1970). For a systematic and coherent analysis also moving along these lines, see Thomas Weisskopf, "Theories of American Imperialism: A Critical Evaluation," *RRPE*, Vol. 6, no. 3 (Fall, 1974).

[13] France in the eighteenth century (and Spain in the sixteenth) constitute partial exceptions to the generalization. Compared to either the Dutch or British economies, the French was institutionally and technologically retarded; yet France (like Spain, earlier) was seemingly "the leader," by virtue of military effort—but at the cost of distorting the more (in the long-run) rewarding economic relationships.

finally, of Florentine collapse in the fourteenth century, as a result of growth elsewhere.

Economic advance in the medieval period was principally a result of growing inter-regional trade, which in turn stimulated and required urban industry and finance. The dynamic process that has characterized world economic history ever since worked slowly but inexorably even then: the leading area benefited from its dominant relationships with lesser trading partners; the latter, transformed in the process, ultimately took over the lead. The nature of that process persists in the present; the scope and content have changed: national/international in scope, industrial in content.

The sixteenth century brought rapid overseas expansion, newly-found resources, and the need for expensive military forces on both land and sea. Traditional political and social patterns broke down, giving way chaotically to the emergence of new nations, new religious institutions, and the beginnings of capitalism. The Italians had brought Western Europe to that point; for centuries the Italians did not go beyond it, but the earlier "backward areas" did.

Beginning as cities, the Venetians, Milanese, Florentines, and Genoese grew into territorial states, and spent much of their time and resources fighting each other while extending their economic relationships to the east, west, and north. The scope of these relationships required an alteration in the traditional medieval pattern of inter-regional politics, a pattern given its nature and its sweep by the pervasive Church. In the fifteenth century, the Italian states invented diplomacy, as a means of undertaking and securing their negotiations abroad. In doing so, they hastened the birth of the nation-states that came to exist in strength in the sixteenth century, and whose rivalries would provide the massive and enduring conflicts that brought us to the present. It was a new world. As Mattingly has said,

> Our modern notion of an international society composed of a heterogeneous collection of fictitious entities called states, all supposed to be equal, sovereign and completely independent, would have shocked both the idealism and the common sense of the fifteenth century. Such a society would have seemed to philosophers a repulsive anarchy . . . ; and the concept would have been equally uncomfortable to practical statesmen.[14]

The transformation from medieval to modern economies took centuries; it took longest of all for the Italians. Benefiting for centuries from

---

[14] Garrett Mattingly, *Renaissance Diplomacy* * (London: Cape, 1955; Penguin, 1965), p. 24. Up until about 1400, he points out, the West "still thought of itself as one society. Christendom was torn by the gravest internal conflicts, by religious schism, doctrinal dispute, and the endemic warfare of class against class. . . . But Latin Christendom still knew itself to be one." (p. 16)

their location in the Mediterranean, central both for trade with the rich Near East and the emerging trans-alpine North, the Italians had little inclination to seek greener pastures. Columbus was hired by Spain; Cabot, also an Italian, was hired by England. The hinge on which the door opened for modern economies—that is, larger in scope, industrial in production—was the exploration and exploitation of overseas territories. Marx put it vividly:

> The discovery of gold and silver in America, the extirpation, enslavement and entombment in mines of the aboriginal population, the beginning of the conquest and looting of the East Indies, the turning of Africa into a warren for the commercial hunting of black-skins, signalised the rosy dawn of the era of capitalist production. These idyllic proceedings are the chief momenta of primitive accumulation. On their heels treads the commercial war of the European nations, with the globe for a theatre. It begins with the revolt of the Netherlands from Spain, assumes giant dimensions in England's anti-jacobin war, and is still going on in the opium wars against China, etc.[15]

In the fifteenth and sixteenth centuries, Portugal and Spain swept over the Far East and the New World. Their social and economic institutions were anachronistic; their gains drained away into Northern Europe, and especially into the hands of those who busied themselves in Antwerp—"a center of unbridled capitalism." Antwerp's location was central to the sea and overland trade of the North; it was granted a monopoly over the Portuguese spice trade first, and of the Spanish trade later (under Charles V). It was a glorious period, and a short one; it ended when Spanish largesse became Spanish destruction. Antwerp's typical figure, Tawney remarks, "was the international financier," serving the hustling merchants and princes who fattened on this enlarged world.[16]

---

[15] *Capital*, vol. I., p. 751.

[16] Tawney, *Religion and the Rise of Capitalism*, p. 67. His discussion of the rise of Antwerp, pp. 67–9, ends with a characterization which with only a few alterations, fits today's world all too closely: "Nourished by the growth of peaceful commerce, the financial capitalism of the age fared not less sumptuously, if more dangerously, at the courts of princes. Mankind, it seems, hates nothing so much as its own prosperity. Menaced with an accession of riches which would lighten its toil, it makes haste to redouble its labors, and to pour away the perilous stuff, which might deprive of plausibility the complaint that it is poor. Applied to the arts of peace, the new resources commanded by Europe during the first half of the sixteenth century might have done something to exorcise the specters of pestilence and famine, and to raise the material fabric of civilization to undreamed-of heights. Its rulers, secular and ecclesiastical alike, thought otherwise. When pestilence and famine were ceasing to be necessities imposed by nature, they reestablished them by political art" (pp. 69–70).

Trade War, War of Trade

The fall of Antwerp after the mid-sixteenth century, due to religious and civil strife and the depredations of the Hapsburgs, was followed by the rise, not of a city—which for centuries had been the centers of economic strength—but of a region: the United Provinces, with Holland at their lead, and Amsterdam at the center of Holland. It was the first approximation to an economically viable *national* unit. Though tiny in population (perhaps two million), and bereft of the normal run of soils, minerals, timber, and the like (and with much of its "soil," the so-called polders, built up out of the sea, and protected by dikes), the Dutch rose to heights never before reached economically. Industry, trade, and finance combined with an enormous fleet to allow the Dutch to rule the world in the seventeenth century, and to remain financially strong throughout the eighteenth century. France and England struggled in that century to wrest the baton from the Dutch, and from each other.[17]

Until the seventeenth century, the colonization of the world was in the hands of the Portuguese and the Spanish, while the Italians continued their hold on the Mediterranean although increasingly with competition from English and French merchants. In the seventeenth century, the Dutch gained control over whole areas (such as the Netherlands East Indies) or unique trading privileges (as in Japan). Their trade branched out from Holland to Scandinavia, to Africa, to all of the Americas, and to Asia. The Dutch East India Company was quite probably the most powerful single economic organization the world had seen up to that time, the General Motors of its day. Its intra-Asian trade was more profitable than its Asian-European trade, which was very profitable indeed. Some idea of the relative economic strength of the Dutch (and, as well, of the nature of "mercantilist" thinking) is given by a famous argument of Colbert (first minister of King Louis XIV of France) in 1669:

Commerce is carried on by 20,000 vessels and that number cannot be increased. Each nation strives to have its fair share and to get ahead of the others. The Dutch now fight this war [of trade] with 15,000 to 16,000 vessels, the English with 3,000 to 4,000 and the French with 500 to 600. The last two countries can improve their commerce only by increasing the number of their vessels and can increase the number only by paring away from the 15,000 to 16,000 Dutch ships. . . . It must be added that trade causes perpetual strife both in time of war and in time of peace between

---

[17] Excellent histories of the period of Iberian and Dutch dominance are J. H. Parry, *The Spanish Seaborne Empire* (New York: Knopf, 1966) and C. R. Boxer, *The Dutch Seaborne Empire* (New York: Knopf, 1965).

all the nations of Europe to decide which of them shall have the greatest share.[18]

The Dutch, lacking natural resources of their own, imported them from all over the world, processed them, and sold the higher-value product, once more, all over the world. They had begun to do that in the medieval period, with fish from the North Sea and the Baltic. That led to shipbuilding; to enhanced trade; to industries processing the grain (into gin, as well as flour), the cocoa, the coffee, the tobacco, the diamonds, the fibers, etc. From it all, the Dutch became the leading trading, industrial, financial, and shipping nation. In finding its way to that eminence, the Dutch—like the Italians before them—opened up and stimulated other areas.

The other areas included France and England, both larger in population and richer in natural resources than the Dutch; both were able also to copy, or to reproduce, the economic sources of Dutch strength. The English became much better at it than the French, although, at the opening of the eighteenth century if there seemed to be any serious rival for Dutch power, it was the French. As the eighteenth century wore on, it increasingly became the scene of an Anglo-French struggle on land and sea, in Asia (especially India), in the Caribbean and North America, and on the Continent. When the French were finally defeated at Waterloo, the underlying economic strength of the British had been decisive.

British economic strength was given its critical edge over the French by the trading proclivities and abilities of the British, derided by the French as "a nation of shopkeepers." In the eighteenth century, France was by far the richer (for the benefit of a small fraction of its people) of the two nations, as it was twice England in population, and blessed with the best and broadest agricultural resources of any European nation. But in the emerging capitalist world where trade was vital, the natural riches of France, requiring little foreign trade, turned out to be dynamic disadvantages. Recall Colbert's calculation of the relative number of English and French vessels: England, although it had a much smaller population, had at least five times as many ships. Ships, shipbuilding, and sailors strengthened fighting as well as trading capacities.

France, rich and the dominant military power of Europe, was continually involved in continental warfare. The splendor of its Court had another side to it: its power, its corruption, and its taxes bled France dry, and influenced the pattern of French production toward the elegant. The economic power of the future lay with those who moved toward the mass production of the mundane. While France was achieving cultural and military supremacy in the seventeenth and eighteenth centuries,

[18] Quoted in Heckscher, *Mercantilism*, vol. 2, pp. 26–27.

England was improving its technology and spreading its trade. In England, there was a bourgeois revolution in the seventeenth century, and an industrial revolution in the eighteenth century; in France, the consolidation of absolute monarchy in the seventeenth century, and a weak bourgeois revolution in the eighteenth century. In England, Adam Smith; in France, Napoleon.

World Economy and Imperialism

The nineteenth century belonged to Great Britain. The Dutch, although economically supreme in the seventeenth century, presided over a string quartet by comparison with the symphony orchestrated by Great Britain in the nineteenth century. The Dutch scrambled continuously, in and between wars; the strength of Britain achieved the *Pax Britannica*. Industrialism and modern technology made the difference: it was a difference in scale and penetration, entailing differences in all aspects of social existence. The sixteenth through the eighteenth centuries were given their dynamism by trade, and overseas relationships were mercantilist; the nineteenth century was industrial in its dynamic, and imperialist overseas. These contrasts require further emphasis.

Industrialism means many things; England, as the first industrial nation, was characterized by: increasing specialization within the economy, and the sharp decline of agricultural sufficiency; increasing use of coal and iron in production, and for transportation; increasingly capital-intensive production (that is, the use of machinery, with high fixed costs) and the consequent need for mass markets; the need to guarantee that no part of this increasingly interdependent system would break loose and bring it all down. For England especially, the new industrialism meant the need to import the major portion of its foodstuffs and raw materials. These were not produced, generally, at ports or coastal strips, but in the hinterland. The iron steamship made it possible to carry bulky and low-priced commodities more cheaply and more reliably than sailing ships; the railroad made it possible to penetrate whole continents. The process of realizing these needs and possibilities led to the annexation of whole territories. In addition to privileged trade, there was privileged investment; instead of colonial outposts, an empire; instead of forts, occupying armies; instead of dots on a map, whole areas colored pink.

The British were not alone, either in need or in possibility. But they were strongest in both. The last part of the nineteenth century saw them in rising competition with the other "Great Powers"—being part of that competition is what *made* a nation a "Great Power"—and, by its very end, with Japan and the United States. In turn, control over overseas areas was necessary to keep others out, as well as to make what gains there were from getting in, oneself. Control of the high seas was sufficient to this end in the nineteenth century (sea power playing the role that air power and nuclear missiles do in this century). To say that the nineteenth century was the century of the *Pax Britannica* is to say that Britain's navy was without serious competition; there was not even a close second. Apart from a few abortive maneuvers toward overseas expansion by the French and the Americans in the 1860's, Britain's role as world ruler was unchallenged until the 1890's. The umbrella of control was based on a virtual monopoly of naval and mercantile sea power; under that umbrella, British business thrived overseas, and a period of the freest international trade and most unified international monetary system in capitalist history was created. Nor is it unimportant that the peace established by Britain allowed American development to proceed unhampered by foreign violence or the necessity to sustain a significant army and navy. As will be seen later, American hegemony after World War II created a similar worldwide condition for the capitalist system— but now with something Britain did not have: competitors of great strength with a different and, now, also of the same ideology.[19]

The period of 1815–1915 is usually described as "a century of peace." It was, if by peace is meant no war between "the great powers." But it was a century of desperately sought alliances, of scrambling for coaling stations and, toward the very last years of the century, of an arms race.

Britain's economic well-being in the nineteenth century depended squarely on buying, selling, and investing all over the world. The relationships developed with the United States and with Germany are most informative in showing how the very process of British success in these economic activities meant the creation of even mightier rivals, as had been the case with those who had carried the baton of power in earlier times.

Britain's two principal customers for consumer and capital goods, and loans were Germany and the United States. In return, Britain took in foodstuffs and raw materials, gold, commissions, profits, and interest. But the importation of goods and capital for the United States and Germany meant an enhanced ability to develop their own economies, and a movement toward industrialization. Doubtless the British rela-

---

[19] A most illuminating analytical approach to this question has been provided by Frederic C. Lane, the great economic historian of (especially) the Mediterranean world, in the four essays that comprise Part Three of his *Venice and History: The Collected Papers of Frederic C. Lane* (Baltimore: Johns Hopkins Press, 1966). The leading concept in Lane's analysis is "protection rents and costs," where rent (as used by economists) is a return to monopoly—in this case the monopoly of organized violence—and the costs are those of military supremacy.

tionship was more necessary for Germany than for the richer United States; in both cases, however, Britain was creating rivals in trade, industry, finance, and for imperial space. In the 1890's, voices were already being raised in England to curb its free trading policies in favor of protection and to anticipate an open conflict with Germany, which was expanding its navy, competing with increasing effectiveness in world markets, and seeking to catch up in the race for empire.[20]

Like Father, Like Son

While America was a colony of the British, American foreign trade moved within a complicated and extensive system of restrictions, prohibitions, requirements, and subsidies, all designed to enhance British profits and power. Initially this model of mercantilist policy worked to the mutual benefit of Britain and the colonists; by the mid-eighteenth century, the same system harmed the Americans and benefited the British.

The first policies toward America taken by the British (in the seventeenth century) had two main designs in mind: to strengthen British trade and shipping at the expense of the Dutch, and to strengthen the colonies (through subsidies and guaranteed markets) as potentially strong economic and strategic assets. It was classic mercantilism, and the Americans had almost two centuries of habituation to such policies, before breaking loose from Great Britain.[21]

Among our very first steps after Independence was the creation of our own mercantilist system. Alexander Hamilton was the most productive economic thinker in those first years, issuing one *Report* after another. His *Report on Manufactures* (1791), revolving around the need to develop industry and to protect it in its "infant" stages, set the stage for a coherent and tight protectionist trading policy, with subsidies mixed in. Like the European experience on which it was modeled, American protectionism recognized the importance of foreign trade: protectionism was designed not to reduce its volume but, through selectivity, to minimize its costs and enhance its gains. The mercantilism of Hamilton has appeared and reappeared in our history, interspersed with movements seemingly going in the opposite direction; it continues today.

[20] See Ross J. S. Hoffman, *Great Britain and the German Trade Rivalry, 1875–1914* (Philadelphia: University of Pennsylvania, 1933), Alfred E. Kahn, *Great Britain in the World Economy* (New York: N.Y.U. Press, 1946), and Albert Imlah, *Economic Elements in the Pax Britannica* ° (Cambridge: Harvard University Press, 1958). The classic work describing and analyzing the overall financial network is Herbert Feis, *Europe: The World's Banker* ° (New Haven: Yale University Press, 1930).

[21] The nature and intensity of the rivalry between the Dutch and the English is definitively treated by Charles Wilson, *Profit and Power* (New York: Macmillan, 1957).

Daniel Webster's career, involving a complete turnaround on foreign economic policy, reflects the changing position of the New England economy. As a Congressman from New Hampshire (1813–1817), and Massachusetts (1823–1827), Webster represented the trading center of the United States and was an ardent free trader, an antiprotectionist. Later, as a Senator from Massachusetts and U.S. Secretary of State (both in the 1840's), Webster utilized his orator's talents on behalf of protectionism. New England was becoming the home of American "infant" industries. In the 1820's, he was an opponent of protectionist Henry Clay, whose "American system" was designed to give American farmers a "home market" composed of buyers earning incomes from manufactures in America; a decade or so later, he and Clay were protectionist allies, leaders of the "Whigs," a party whose explicit business concerns foreshadowed the Republican Party that emerged just before the Civil War.

After the death of Clay and Webster (both in 1852), the Whig Party disappeared; it had been split earlier over the question of tariffs (as well as over the extension of slavery), with the Northern Whigs supporting tariffs, and the Southern Whigs pushing for freer trade. The latter won out, in 1846, with the Walker Tariff, which reduced protective tariffs while seeking to increase revenues through high tariffs on domestically non-competing goods (such tariffs are called "revenue tariffs"—for example, on coffee). Those who opposed the Walker Tariff favored increasing trade also, so long as the trade that took place did not injure American industry.

Nobody then doubted the critical quality of American foreign economic relationships which, in that early period, involved borrowing steadily from Britain, and paying back through the rising exports of (almost entirely) agricultural products, and especially cotton. When the conflict between southern and northern interests brought the nation to the edge of civil war, the South assumed that the importance of the relationship between cotton exports and British textiles was such that Britain would actively and effectively intervene on the South's side. That Britain did not testifies to the less evident but nonetheless more powerful relationships already existing for trade and investments in the North; however, the South's assumption testifies to the acknowledged importance of trade in the United States at that time. It grew more important in succeeding decades.

From Youth to Maturity

The United States, as the first colony to be exploited in a modern way and the first to rebel, had very early on begun to view the Western Hemisphere as its backyard. We could not expel the British from Canada; but from the rest of North America, the Spanish, the French, the Russians, the Dutch and the English were bought out or pushed out. The Monroe Doctrine set the tone as early as 1823: there would be no further European colonization or attempts to implant monarchy in this hemisphere; the United States would not meddle with existing colonies nor in internal European affairs. By the end of the century, we had begun to meddle in others' colonies; after World War I we began to take a hand in European affairs.

The Republican victory that brought Lincoln to the presidency also set the stage for a set of foreign economic policies suited to emerging industrialism. Strong protective tariffs were passed in 1862, and immigration was stepped up through the revival of indentured labor. In 1873, with the "Crime of '73," silver was demonetized so as to integrate the American economy with the emerging international gold standard. And, as we saw in Chapter 6, American exports of unfinished and processed agricultural commodities expanded substantially in the late 1870's, deepening a dependence on exports for that production which continues to this day.[22] In that respect, as also with our international financial, trading, and industrial relationships abroad after the Civil War, the American economy transformed itself from one that was relatively passive and dependent upon foreign economic relationships for its health, to an increasingly aggressive economy upon whose health most of the world became dependent. That transformation was all but accomplished in the 1920's; it was obvious to all by the 1950's. The data which follow suggest some of the quantitative signs of the process.

Up until the 1870's, the United States was in the category of an "immature debtor" nation: it owed other countries (mostly England) on net balance, and it imported more than it exported. That stage was changed into "mature debtor" (that is, it was still in debt, but was now exporting more than importing) in the 1870's, due in large part to the upsurge in agricultural exports. But when Europe's agricultural crisis ended, our exports continued to exceed our imports for an entire century, except for three years, 1888, 1889, and 1893. In 1971–1972, the balance reversed, for the first but not the last time in this century.

In the midst of World War I, we became an "immature creditor" nation, as our rising export of capital brought us to a position of being owed by the world on net balance, and as we continued to export more than we imported. A "mature creditor" country presumably imports more than it exports, and pays for it with earnings in addition to those from merchandise exports (from investments, shipping and insurance services, and so on). When our balance of trade went negative (that is, our

[22] Apart from war years, and those of the Depression of the 1930's, agricultural exports normally have provided at least one-sixth of farm income. For example: 1910, 16 percent; 1963, 17 percent.

TABLE 7–1   U.S. Exports and Imports, Selected Years 1820–1970 (Million $)

| | Finished Manufactures | | Crude Materials | |
	Exports	Imports	Exports	Imports
1850	$ 17	$ 95	$ 84	$ 13
1870	56	174	214	57
1880	93	197	243	142
1890	133	231	309	180
1910	499	368	574	578
1930	1,898	757	829	1,002
1940	2,330	409	464	1,011
1950	5,741	1,504	1,886	2,465
1957	11,786	3,527	3,109	3,186
1965	15,220	8,876	2,888	3,653
1970	26,001	22,463	4,492	3,474

SOURCE: Adapted from *Historical Statistics of the U. S.*, Part 2, p. 839. Between 1930 and 1950, figures are much distorted by the impact of depression, trade restrictions, and war and postwar phenomena.

imports exceeded exports) in 1971, we became a mature creditor nation, but we did so with a widespread feeling of uneasiness that in some quarters verged on panic. Let us now examine some of the tendencies underlying these changes.

Our transition from immature to mature debtor was accompanied by our growing productive—and therefore exporting—power; this in turn meant a changing economic structure. From being an exporter chiefly of crude raw materials and foodstuffs (e.g., cotton and wheat), we became an exporter *also* of semi-finished and finished manufactures (e.g., steel and machinery). Table 7–1 shows how the absolute amounts grew over time, and how their relative positions changed.

Note that between 1890 and 1910 the United States had changed from a net importer to a net exporter of finished manufactures; and in the same period it changed from being a net exporter to a net importer of crude materials. More recently, as the figures for 1970 show, there has been a tendency toward an even-ing up, for both manufactures and crude materials. Table 7–2 shows the rising importance of the United States in total world exports and in the export of manufactures. As in Table 7–1 the absolute amounts traded rose substantially over these years. The figures for 1950 are misleadingly high, because all industrial countries other than the United States had yet to recover from the impact of World War II. Since 1957, U.S. percentages have declined (in 1969 our percentage of world exports was down to 16 percent) but absolute amounts have more than doubled.

TABLE 7-2

	U.S. Exports as % of World Exports	U.S. Exports of Mfrs. as % of World Exports of Mfrs.
1899	20.5%	11.6%
1913	22.1	13.0
1929	27.0	20.4
1950	32.0	26.6
1957	30.0	25.3

SOURCE: Data calculated from A. Maizels, *Industrial Growth and World Trade* (Cambridge: Cambridge University Press, 1965), pp. 426–27 and p. 434. An abridged paperback edition appeared in 1970: *Growth and Trade** (same publisher).

The notion that the United States has only a slight dependency on its foreign economic relationships stems directly from the percentage that exports and imports bear to our GNP. Except for the war-affected years between 1915 and 1920, exports have been at or below 5 percent of our GNP in this century; imports have been at or below 4 percent. Table 7–3 indicates how this compares for other industrial countries.

That handful of countries is responsible for 90 percent or more of all industrial production in capitalist countries; and the U.S. produces at least half of that. The U.S. exports and imports about one-sixth of all exports and imports in the world, with one-sixteenth of world population. The ten countries listed in Table 7–3 export and import about two-thirds of all exports and imports (in the nonsocialist world). Finally, the best customers for the leading trading and industrial nations are each other, as they have been throughout the industrialization period of the past century or so. Since the late 1940's, for example, the countries to which we export and from which we import most are Canada, Great Britain, West Germany, and Japan. As in the internal relationships of

TABLE 7-3 Exports as a Percentage of GNP, 1968

U.S.	4
West Germany	23
United Kingdom	18
France	14
Japan	10
Canada	24
Italy	18
Netherlands	43
Belgium-Luxembourg	38–76

SOURCE: see *Fortune* (August, 1971), pp. 144–49.

each capitalist society, those at the top buy and sell most to each other; those at the bottom, whether depressed income groups or depressed nations, see the gap between themselves and the rich steadily widening over time. The dual economy phenomenon is pervasive, nationally and internationally.[23]

Adolescent Giant

When World War I broke out, the United States was $3 billion in debt to the rest of the world; when the war ended, the rest of the world was $6 billion in debt to us (exclusive of war debts). The United States had taken over Britain's place as the industrial, commercial, and financial center of the world. For better and for worse, the reality of our new position was not matched by a suitable or a coherent foreign policy for several decades. When, after World War II, that policy fell into shape, its very success would be our undoing; this process had been true of Britain and of the Netherlands, earlier.

The "immature creditor" status of the United States after 1918 was more than an economist's dry classification; it describes well our state of mind, and the immature policies with which we related to the rest of the world.

A creditor nation is a net exporter of capital, a net lender to private parties and governments abroad. Debtor nations can only maintain a healthy balance in *their* external relationships if they can sell in the markets of the lending countries (and earn foreign exchange)—as, for example, the United States could when, in the nineteenth century, it was able to export increasing amounts of its production to Europe (and as the underdeveloped countries today cannot). The United States, from the Civil War on, was a high protective tariff nation with only an occasional deviation. That was perhaps understandable up to World War I; from then on it stood in conflict with our creditor position. Nonetheless, our tariffs rose again in the 1920's, and were jacked up to their highest levels ever in 1930. If the free trade policies of Great Britain in the nineteenth century were taken as the proper standard for the world leader, the United States was breaking the rules of the game. In the fragile world

---

[23] The bases for the generalizations regarding world trade were first developed by Folke Hilgerdt, in two studies for the League of Nations, *The Network of World Trade* (1942) and *Industrialization and Foreign Trade* (1946). His studies were extended in the massive book by Maizels, cited above. Ingvar Svennilson, *Growth and Stagnation in Europe* (Geneva: United Nations, 1954) contains much additional data. It also offers an at least partially effective analysis of the stagnation of European economies between the two world wars—the main focus of his book.

economy after World War I, for the economic leader to break the rules meant that the game would be lost by everyone.[24]

But Great Britain could *not* be taken as the standard for foreign economic policy after World War I, nor was it by the United States, despite the entreaties of liberal economists from 1920 on. Why not?

First, when Britain began to rule the world economy, there were no other significantly industrialized economies. A free trade policy maximized both exports and imports, and the imports did not constitute a threat to British industry. Ricardo had advocated such a position decades before Britain adopted it; it made sense for that economy. Subsequently, economists transformed Ricardian notions into eternal verities, good for all times and places; Ricardo had been concerned with one time and one place, and he had assumed away foreign competition. When the United States moved into dominance it faced Great Britain, Germany, Japan, and a handful of lesser industrial countries as competitors. All were hungry for markets, all were bristling with protective devices.

Second, when Britain forged its international policies, the major powers had been and would remain at peace with each other. Britain ruled the sea lanes, as both merchant and naval power. The United States came into supremacy in the midst of world war, itself a result of great instability and conflict. The years after World War I were merely a resting period until World War II. In that resting period, the world was rocked by revolution in Russia, and outbreaks of revolutionary and counterrevolutionary developments in the fragments of the broken Hapsburg empire; by a frenzied inflation in Germany; by fascism in Germany and Italy; by worldwide depression, and the collapse of colonial economies. Had the United States pursued a set of "mature" foreign economic policies from 1920 on, some of these developments *might* have been averted; however, most of them would have been untouched by anything the U.S. might do. It was no longer the nineteenth century. Different trading policies were needed; different policies to run an empire were needed, also. The United States *after* World War II—for better and for worse, once more—developed those policies. They will be analyzed shortly.

Something else made our possibilities quite different from those of Great Britain in the nineteenth century: the internal balance of power and the social outlook of Americans concerning power and influence. The United States could not reproduce the experience or adopt the principles of nineteenth century Great Britain, merely because the U.S. was domi-

---

[24] American policies and the relevant economic data for the 1920's and 1930's are thoroughly examined in Hal Lary et al., *The United States in the World Economy* * (Washington: Department of Commerce, 1943). The study is in effect a call for the United States to grow up, essentially along earlier British lines. As such, it has a quaint ring to it.

nant in the world economy. Our behavior as world economic leader is not explicable solely in terms of the differences between the nineteenth and the twentieth centuries; much of the explanation lies in the nature of American politics. In part because our independence was won through war, the United States—despite its perennial dependence on the world economy—is nationalist in its mood and in its policies; always, and now as a nationalistic empire.

From the Embargo Act of 1807, through the "Buy American" campaigns of the 1830's, the 1890's and the 1930's; from the geographic expansion that has characterized our history from its first moments up to the present; from Secretary of the Treasury Alexander Hamilton to Nixon's Secretary of the Treasury John Connally, the United States—in moods varying from buoyant to desperate to arrogant—has shaped its internal and external policies on the steady assumption that this country has special qualities that give it special rights. Other countries also use their power to advance their national interests, of course. The United States has assumed that *its* national interests, after all is said and done, are to the interest of other countries; and if that is less clear to others than to Americans, so much the worse for them.

Thus, protective tariffs for "infant industries" can easily be justified, but their continuation to "protect" monopolistic industries whose size and efficiency is unrivalled in the world (as was the case, for example, with steel since the late nineteenth century, and until recently) has no justification except the power that continues them and the profits that ensue. Thus, it is understandable that older industries (such as cotton textiles and shoes) have resisted being phased out by cheaper imports, but it is quite another matter for protection to work the miracle of allowing such industries to *expand* over time, which has curtailed the possibilities of repayment of debt by developing countries where the cheaper product is made. Thus, it is not strange that financial investment follows the highest returns; but it is more than irresponsible, it is dangerous when lenders turn away from renewing and extending loans to pursue the will-o'-the-wisp of a ballooning stock market, as happened with Latin American loans when Wall Street boomed away in 1927 and 1928 (facilitating the collapse of those already weak economies). Finally, protectionism was by no means the exclusive possession of the United States, but for the leading national economy to break all world records in the critical year of 1930 was sheer recklessness.

During the Depression, the world broke out with a rash of economic nationalism, marked by import quotas, export subsidies, increased tariffs, competitive devaluation, exchange controls, and the like, to the accompaniment of a steadily falling volume of world trade and rising international hostility.

In 1933, a "World Economic Conference" was convened, in the hope that the mutual throat-cutting accompanying the Depression could be halted, or even reversed. The key nation in strength and influence was the United States, but President Roosevelt, "after a brief interval in which it seemed that he would throw his force into the World Economic Conference, abandoned international responsibility, even disparaged it by fostering nationalist devices, though not without the face-saving afterthought that a prosperous America would do most to produce a prosperous world." [25]

New Frontiers: The Muscles Flex

When Great Britain moved to full free trade in the mid-nineteenth century, it did so knowing it had nothing to fear from foreign competitors. The United States has never made such a fulsome move toward free trade in its period of preeminence. But in 1934 we took a small step in that direction, with the Reciprocal Trade Agreements Act (RTAA) and the Export-Import Bank (Eximbank); other steps of the same limited sort have been taken in subsequent years. Our conscious needs for expanded foreign markets, taken together with confidence in the ability of our production to compete effectively in an open market (the basis for our "Open Door" policy for China, decades before) made for the institutionalization of a new world trade position.

It is often said that the United States had thus finally abandoned its long "isolationist" stance for a new "internationalism." It is more appropriate to see the earlier position as nationalism with an inferiority complex, and our developing position since the 1930's, our rising interventionism, as nationalism with a superiority complex. Be that as it may, the RTAA was designed to increase trade through negotiated, bilateral, mutual tariff reductions, between the United States and one nation at a time; the Eximbank was aimed at increasing exports to Latin America (primarily), through loans to governments to finance purchases from American companies. In the context of the Depression, neither of these measures had much effect; the effects have been more substantial since World War II, in these as also for domestic New Deal measures, as we saw in Chapter 4.

When World War II began, it abruptly shoved aside the Depression and transformed the context within which foreign economic policies would and could be made. But the war did not prevent plans from being made, some of them aired in the 1930's, all of them aimed at market expansion. The nature of the problem was seen clearly by Dean Acheson

[25] Broadus Mitchell, *Depression Decade*, p. 57.

in 1944, when as Assistant Secretary of State he told a congressional hearing:

> We cannot go through another ten years like the ten years at the end of the twenties and the beginning of the thirties, without having the most far-reaching consequences upon our economic and social system. When we look at that problem, we may say it is a problem of markets. . . . We have got to see that what the country produces is used and sold under financial arrangements which make its production possible. . . . You must look to foreign markets.

But couldn't the United States consume everything it produces?

> That would completely change our Constitution, our relations to property, human liberty, our very conceptions of law. And nobody contemplates that. Therefore, you find you must look to other markets and those markets are abroad.[26]

Soon an impressive collection of men from the world of corporate industry and finance began to construct programs that mixed economic expansion with the politics of Cold War. Their names, in addition to Acheson's, are very familiar by now: John Foster Dulles, Averill Harriman, James Forrestal, John J. McCloy, A. A. Berle, Jr., Robert Lovett, Douglas Dillon, Dean Rusk, Christian Herter, George Ball. . . . Most of these men were associated with both the Council on Foreign Relations and the State Department, the Department of Defense, and the CIA, moving back and forth between corporate offices, the Council, and governmental position with ease. The journal of the Council, *Foreign Affairs*, is generally conceded to be the most influential journal of its kind.[27]

Beginning in 1941 with the Atlantic Charter (constructed by Churchill and Roosevelt) and coming to fruition in the Dumbarton Oaks and Bretton Woods conferences of 1944 (both with widespread international representation), the United States used its power to shape the new international organizations that were institutionalized in 1945 and 1946: the United Nations, the International Monetary Fund (IMF), and the International Bank for Reconstruction and Development (IBRD, or World Bank). All these organizations were to be dominated by the lop-

[26] Quoted by William A. Williams, "The Large Corporation and American Foreign Policy," in David Horowitz, ed., *The Corporations and the Cold War* * (New York: Monthly Review Press, 1969), pp. 95–96. Lloyd C. Gardner's essay in that same collection, "The New Deal, New Frontiers, and the Cold War," is very useful, as is his book *Economic Aspects of New Deal Diplomacy* (Madison: University of Wisconsin, 1964).

[27] For an extended discussion of this matter, see G. William Domhoff, "Who Made American Foreign Policy, 1945–1963," in Horowitz's volume.

sided power—military, political, and economic—of the United States in the postwar world. The IMF was designed to stabilize the international monetary situation over time (and to function as a substitute for the "automatic gold standard" which had served the same function before 1914.) The World Bank was designed to lend for capital projects. The assets of both institutions were dominantly American from the beginning; and the United States has been the prime decision-making power in both organizations—as it has been in the Inter-American Development Bank, a later development.

In the decade following 1945, the United States created a whole new framework within which its entire foreign policy would move. Unlike the UN, the IMF, and the IBRD, which were all international in their construction (no matter how dependent on the U.S. they may have been), the next steps were devised by and for the United States. The drama began with Winston Churchill's famous "Iron Curtain" speech at Fulton, Missouri, in 1946. In the next year a whirlwind of institutional innovations began to form:

1947 *The Truman (Greece-Turkey) Doctrine.* Truman asked for and received $400 million from Congress "to help free peoples to maintain . . . their national integrity against aggressive movements that seek to impose upon them totalitarian regimes." Control of the Balkan area before World War II had been in British hands, now too weak to continue.

The National Security Act. Created the "National Military Establishment," incorporating the preexisting Department of the Navy with the new Department of the Air Force and Department of the Army under the Department of Defense. (The latter had more candidly been called the War Department since 1789.) This Act also created the Central Intelligence Agency and, of course, the National Security Council, the pivotal center of policy-making.

1948 *The Marshall Plan.* At a commencement address at Harvard in June, 1947, General George Marshall (then Secretary of State) proposed what became in 1948 the European Recovery Program. In its four years of operation, the program gave $13 billion to eighteen Western European nations (including Greece and Turkey) for a broad variety of investment projects. Over 70 percent of the amount was spent for American goods. The program was sold to Congress on those grounds and as a means of "rolling back the tide of Communism." [28]

[28] And it was sold to the American people as just more of the milk of U.S. kindness. But it was more oil than milk, and the shrewd use of economic and State power. As Tanzer writes, "Since war-torn Europe and Japan were heavily dependent upon

Organization of American States (OAS). All nations but Canada in this hemisphere were charter members. Its purpose, according to our State Department, is to protect the hemisphere from "the interventionist and aggressive designs of international communism."

Selective Service Act. The United States had had a military draft only during the Civil War, World War I, and, beginning in 1940, for World War II. The Selective Service Act of 1948 built the draft into our postwar history.

1949 *North Atlantic Treaty Organization* (NATO). The military counterpart of the Marshall Plan.

Point Four Program. Announced in Truman's inaugural address, it was a program of technical assistance to "underdeveloped areas." It has continued to the present in one form or another.

1950 *Subversive Activities Control Board.* Created by the McCarran Internal Security Act, aimed at controlling and restricting "domestic communism." In the same year Senator Joe McCarthy and the Korean War joined in, creating some kind of symmetry between domestic and foreign affairs.

American Military Assistance Advisory Group (MAAG). Created to assist and advise the French in Indochina. In 1951 we began to assist France in financing the war; by 1952 we were paying three-quarters of the bill.

1951 *Japanese-American Treaty.* A mutual security pact, one of whose provisions allowed the U.S. to "administer" Okinawa, one of our principal military bases in Asia. The treaty was renewed in 1960 and 1970. The U.S. has now agreed to phase out of Okinawa, but the military bases remain.

1954 *Southeast Asia Treaty Organization* (SEATO). The counterpart in Asia of NATO.

1955 *Middle East Treaty Organization.* Another NATO counterpart, made up originally of Iraq, Iran, Turkey, Pakistan and Great

---

U.S. assistance for reconstruction, the [U.S.] oil companies and the U.S. government used this opportunity to virtually ram American-controlled oil down the throats of the world to replace coal. Thus, Walter Levy, head of the Marshall Plan's oil division, and previously an economist for Mobil, noted in 1949 that 'without ECA (the Marshall Plan) American oil business in Europe would already have been shot to pieces,' and commented that 'ECA does not believe that Europe should save dollars or even foreign exchange by driving American oil from the European market.' Some $2 billion of total Marshall Plan assistance of $13 billion was for oil imports, while the Marshall Plan blocked projects for European crude oil production and helped American oil companies to gain control of Europe's refineries." Tanzer, pp. 17–18.

Britain, with a participating American military mission. Iraq withdrew in 1959, and METO became CENTO *(Central Treaty Organization)*.

The United States, in a very few years, had jumped headlong into the international arena, armed with both economic and military supremacy. There was some vocal opposition in the first few years; for example, from the conservative and influential Senator Robert A. Taft, and from the liberal-left, whose numbers peaked in the period surrounding the 1948 election.

The trade union movement, existing as the separate AFL and CIO (until 1955, when they merged), provided both opposition to and support for growing American intervention around the world: opposition from left-wing unions in the CIO (all of which were expelled between 1949 and 1950), and substantial and growing support from the non-left CIO unions and the entire AFL.[29] In 1947, organized labor was skeptical of the Marshall Plan; at its convention in 1948, the CIO endorsed it. In 1949 both the AFL and the CIO cooperated in the creation of the explicitly anti-Communist International Confederation of Free Trade Unions; in the 1950's, labor officials were accepting funds from the CIA (secretly) for anti-Communist activities abroad. And so the web of cooperation between organized labor, the cold warriors of Washington, and corporate leaders became tighter and tighter until, in 1966, George Meany (then President of the AFL-CIO) could proclaim that criticism of the war in Vietnam "can only pollute and poison the bloodstream of our democracy."[30]

Dollar Shortage to Dollar Glut

The election of 1952 brought General Eisenhower and Richard Nixon to the White House. The old-fashioned "isolationist" wing of the Republican Party had been suppressed and a working consensus on anti-communism abroad and at home had been created between the GOP and the Democrats. Organized labor and agriculture worked in harmony with organized business on the highest levels; the gains made from

[29] The unions expelled were the United Electrical Workers, the Mine, Mill, and Smelter Workers, the Fur and Leather Workers, the Food, Tobacco and Allied Workers, the Marine Cooks and Stewards, the Fishermen, the International Longshoremen's and Warehousemen's Union, and the American Communications Association. See Ronald Radosh, *American Labor and United States Foreign Policy* * (New York: Random House; Vintage, 1969), pp. 435–36.

[30] Ibid., p. 4. Pages 3–29 and 435–52 provide a summary and an evaluation of organized labor's contribution to the Cold War, including secret cooperation with the CIA.

rising exports and arms production assured that almost any conflict could be ironed out with minimal trouble—at least, for those at the top of business, farming, labor, and government.

Foreign economic affairs approached the euphoric for the United States. The American economy had to find expanding markets abroad for its extraordinary productive capacity, and additional outlets for capital. After World War II, the rest of the world was desperately short of productive capacity. The condition after 1945 came to be known as a "dollar shortage"; that is, the world wanted more from us than it could sell to the dollar area (principally the U.S., but including Canada and much of Latin America). Our economic strength in that period was the basis for our ability to create the American-dominated political framework suggested by the list above. Within that framework, our strength increased; and so, after the mid-sixties, did others'. To many in the world, that Germany and Japan now lead the parade of our competitors provides wry amusement.

Already in the Truman Administration, one matter in addition to markets and investment outlets was seen as vital: America's increasing and (in the popular view) surprising dependency on raw materials imports—of small quantities of strategic materials such as tungsten, chromium, columbium, and the like, and, looming in the near future, of large quantities of petroleum, iron ore, and similar materials.

In 1951, the International Development Advisory Board's *Partners in Progress* ("The Rockefeller Report") made the connection between raw materials dependency and foreign policy explicit. In 1952, the President's Materials Policy Commission issued a five-volume report ("the Paley Commission Report") entitled *Resources for Freedom*. In the report, past, present, and future supplies of raw materials were studied, evaluated, and measured against new demands and technology. The conclusion was twofold: by the 1970's, the United States would be vitally dependent upon imported raw materials, qualitatively and quantitatively; and its foreign policies must reflect and fulfill that need. Our policies had begun to do so in the years immediately preceding the Paley Report; they did do considerably more in the years to follow. The means adopted turned on American investments in the countries possessing the needed resources, and on political/military arrangements suited to assuring secure flows of both profits and the raw materials themselves. The geographic framework entailed was imperial in its scope; the policies were imperialist in their nature. The Cold War provided the rationale for those policies, in the name of defending the entire "Free World" against Communist aggression.[31]

[31] See Harry Magdoff, *The Age of Imperialism: The Economics of U.S. Foreign Policy* * (New York: Monthly Review Press, 1969). His data on the importance of foreign trade and raw materials imports, in Chaper 2, are an excellent example of

The fifteen or so years following 1945 were of course marked by upsets large and small, at home and abroad: the Chinese Revolution, the Cold War, and the semi-defeat in Korea; and there were four recessions between 1948 and 1961 (despite the enormous amounts of production going into arms and abroad). But in general, that period was one of optimism and confidence; indeed it was one of complacency regarding American economic and military strength. Problems arose, and would continue to do so; but with the whole world seeking American consumer and capital goods and accepting our leadership, what's to worry?

The Troubles of the Pax Americana

When the 1960's began, the United States seemed unchallengeable in the world, and few indeed were challenging the American system at home. By the end of the sixties, doubts and turbulence at home had become widespread, due to racial unrest, to intractable poverty, to the Indochina War, to a growing malaise and alienation. In the same years, power grew elsewhere: the other industrial capitalist countries had gone beyond recovery to bursting strength. Third World countries were finding ways to resist and to show independence—Tanzania, Cuba and Vietnam in their ways, Peru and Chile in theirs, the oil exporting countries (through the Organization of Petroleum Exporting Countries [OPEC]) in theirs. And the Soviet Union and China were now major and stable powers. If, as emperor, the United States was by no means yet naked, neither were its clothes dazzling.

From the 1940's on, American governmental and private activities abroad provided a high and rising demand for American production and thus stability and growth for the economy, while simultaneously enhancing and protecting the empire and the gains from it. Both deliberately and unwittingly, however, these activities sped up the transformation of preexisting industrial economies in Europe, Canada, and Japan, as well as the processes of social change in the dependent nonindustrial economies in Asia, the Middle East, Africa, and Latin America. By the mid-sixties,

---

how what seem to be insignificant quantities are in fact qualitatively critical. In the past few years, many fine books have exploded the Cold War rationale, and shown the conscious duplicity involved in its propagation. Some of those will appear in the Reading Suggestions at the end of this chapter; here the most readable will be noted: Carl Oglesby and Richard Shaull, *Containment and Change* * (New York: Macmillan, 1967), Part One. Written by Oglesby, this traces the Cold War up from its beginnings in the years surrounding the Soviet Revolution into its full savage consequences in Indochina. Without perhaps wishing to do so, Halberstam's *Best and the Brightest* goes far to underpin Oglesby's and others' critiques of the Cold War.

the consequences of all these changes were appearing: economically in the worsening of America's balance of trade and payments position, and politically/militarily in the softening of our alliances and, most notably, in the Indochinese military disaster. The first postwar administration to sense the possibility of these difficulties was that of John F. Kennedy.

Kennedy's advisors knew the American empire was already well along by 1960; they also knew it could not function in the same terms as its predecessor, the British Empire—economically, politically, or militarily. For us to adopt the status of "mature creditor," different means were necessary, as they were also if we were to hold down challenges to existing and vital patterns of dependency. The contrasts between Britain in its heyday and the threats and possibilities facing the United States were noted generally above; some elaboration is now appropriate.

In Britain's day, "internationalism" could and did mean free trade. Britain's competitors did not appear until the end of the nineteenth century, and then as *newly*-industrialized nations. The United States came to eminence in the midst of already existent industrialized and highly nationalistic nations. By 1960, as a result of American policies of investment and encouragement, these other nations—and especially Germany and Japan—were becoming technologically competitive or even superior to us, in ways not so in 1934, the year of the RTAA. American loans and investments facilitated the modernization of foreign industries, and as a condition of Marshall Plan aid we pushed the Europeans into patterns of cooperation—most noticeably the European Common Market—which strengthened the separate economies and enabled them ultimately to stand against us in a united front relating to, say, tariffs. Comparable steps stimulated the Japanese economy.

Our export surplus rose to over \$7 billion in 1964, and then began to drop; it became negative in 1971 for the first time in this century, stayed there in 1972, rose to a little over \$1 billion surplus in 1973, and was negative again in 1974. The Trade Expansion Act of 1962, usually seen as the legislation that headed Kennedy's priority list, aimed to prevent that; it was designed to encourage the necessary expansion of European and Japanese exports, but *only* insofar as our own exports could expand at least as fast, thereby maintaining and increasing our export surplus. But not even the Number One capitalist power is omnipotent, let alone able to eat its cake and have it too. As we discussed in Chapter 4, the very developments that expanded production, investment, and trade, and that so much stimulated the U. S. economy after World War II also produced what have become our main competitors. The process of global economic expansion had to slow down, as it always must; when it did, after 1973, the policies of the New American Emipre had begun to sputter. But in 1975, once more, the U. S. ran an enormous trade surplus of over $11 billion. What had intervened (apart from inflation) were energy and food "shortages." In 1975–1976, the U.S. underwent what was temporarily seen as a "recovery" from the worst economic contraction since the 1930's; but its giant trading partners in the world did not. Between 1974 and the present, Britain, Germany, Italy, Canada, Japan, and France all have had unemployment and inflation rates breaking all records for the period after World War II and which for most are likely to persist.

In a different guise and with a more attractive rhetoric, the U.S. was returning to some approximation of its go-it-alone behavior of the 1920's. That was dangerous enough in the 1920's, but is even more so in the 1970's: the difference is that in the earlier period the capitalist world-economy was already fractured and so our behavior only slightly worsened an already bad condition; the "prosperity" of the major economies since the 1950's has depended quite closely upon their tight integration and it still does. As Joyce Kolko has shown in her valuable study of this process, the economies of the major powers are now "synchronized," for movements both up and down.[32]

Britain could accommodate an import surplus without internal damage, in its day; policy-makers for the United States believe we cannot. Why not?

Britain's import surplus was "paid for" by the returns from its overseas investments; that is, on balance, inflow from overseas investments exceeded capital outflow, as is also true for the United States now: for example, in 1971, the net excess of interest and dividends from foreign investments over new capital outflow was $4.8 billion. On balance, therefore, it is not American investment abroad that exacerbates our balance of payments problem; quite the contrary. Until 1971, our trade balance was also positive. Setting aside net tourist expenditures by Americans, and also setting aside the exacerbating effect on our payments deficit of short-term and speculative capital outflows (caused by the troubles of the American economy at home and associated instability in the world monetary system), there has been one major source of trouble for our balance of payments: what Lane would call the "protection costs" of empire. U.S. governmental expenditures abroad (gifts, loans, and military—which were $6.2 billion in 1971, for example—create and maintain the world hegemony allowing the world capitalist system to function, and provide the foundation for the net inflow of "protection rents." However, as Sweezy and Magdoff point out, this entails a "vicious spiral:

[32] Joyce Kolko, *America and the Crisis of World Capitalism* (Boston: Beacon Press, 1974). On this matter, see especially her Chapter One; but the whole book is relevant.

direct investment income is essential to pay the costs of empire, but the costs of empire are basically determined by the need to protect the investment income and this is certain to grow as time goes by." [33]

Given our enormous governmental expenditures abroad and our domestic habituation to and dependence on an export surplus, the United States can only function as a secure Number One power if *we* find ways to initiate a substantial and persistent expansion of *world* trade. Only thus can our exports keep ahead of our imports *and* can other countries find adequate export markets for ourselves, and all rest easy with a persistent American payments deficit. Failing the requisite rate of worldwide economic expansion, the United States faces an insoluble contradiction (within the framework of maintaining its empire): domestic considerations require a trade surplus while global considerations require us to run a trade deficit. In the words of an economist for the First National City Bank, "it is politically difficult for the U.S. to maintain a liberal [that is, relatively free trade] import policy unless we also run a trade surplus." [34] That is what Marx called a "contradiction."

Why did Britain's empire not entail the kinds of problems that ours does? Britain's empire was global, as ours is. But the costs of empire in the nineteenth century (after all adjustments for prices, size, and so forth) were much lower than today, and they occurred within a simpler domestic and international context. The technology of nineteenth century imperial order was minimal for Britain, which relied on naval power almost exclusively, and seldom had to use it. By contrast, the United States had three and a half million men and women under arms in the late 1960's, and over two thousand bases spread-eagling the globe. [35]

Britain presided over a balance of power in the heyday of advancing imperialism and easy subjugation of weak countries; the United States

[33] "Balance of Payments and Empire," *Monthly Review* (December, 1972).

[34] Quoted in *Fortune* (August, 1971) in the article "U.S. Foreign Trade: There's No Need to Panic," p. 186. *Fortune's* optimism seems misplaced, for the analysis in that article did not anticipate the trade reversal of 1971, let alone its worsening in 1972: "In the *late* 1970's the trade balance may well turn negative—and stay negative for many years thereafter." (My emphasis.)

[35] Writing in 1970, Colonel James A. Donovan stated, "In addition to the 600,000 military men in Southeast Asia, there are 300,000 U.S. Ground and Air Forces stationed in Europe and South Korea. Tens of thousands of Americans serve in warships on the high seas. There are over 1,200,000 U.S. fighting men stationed overseas at 2,270 locations in 119 countries. Additional divisions, air forces, and fleets stand by in the continental United States prepared to execute numerous contingency plans for every area in the world deemed to be of interest to the defense and welfare of the United States and its allies." *Militarism, U.S.A.* * (New York: Scribner's, 1970), p. 2. Donovan is now retired from the Marine Corps. The most penetrating factual and analytical study of contemporary American militarism as a counter-revolutionary force is Michael T. Klare, *War Without End: American Planning for the Next Vietnams* * (New York: Knopf, 1972).

seeks to preside over a world with accomplished and threatening revolutions in Asia, the Middle East, Latin America, and Africa, and has to do so with something less than enthusiastic support at home. The costs of empire today are staggering, in dollars and in political strains. The increasing competitiveness of Europe and Japan began to nibble away at our trade surplus in the early 1960's; the Indochina War fed a domestic inflation that finally tore great chunks of our surplus away; more recently a new force—the multinational corporation—has acted to reduce our *national* economic competitiveness, to destabilize the international currency system, and to place further pressure on our trade and payments position. But that is by no means the end of what this giant new force means. It requires separate examination.[36]

Bigger Than a Breadbox: The Multinational Corporation

The twentieth century is earthquake country: war, revolution, vast changes in social behavior, wildly contrasting periods of economic expansion and contraction, a widening gap between rich and poor, and a constant reshuffling of political forms and relationships all over the globe recall the extraordinary turbulence of the seventeenth century, except that both the pace and the spread of change in this era have been considerably more substantial. Into this already highly unstable world a new and exceptionally powerful business institution has entered: the multinational corporation (MNC).

Whether the MNC will function so as to strengthen world capitalism— or the power of any particular nation within the world structure—or tend to make things come unstuck is presently impossible to know; the fate and the meaning of the MNC will be determined by the major currents of world economic and political life over the next decade or two. What is certain, however, is that the MNC will be one of the major currents

[36] The trade deficit was over $2 billion in 1971, and three times that in 1972. The payments deficit rose from $4 billion in 1970, to about $30 billion in 1971; it fell to about $12 billion in 1972. Our gold stock, which was over $24 billion in 1949, had declined to $10 billion by 1972. Further than that it will not drop, because President Nixon "closed the gold window"—i.e., ceased to allow dollars to exchange for gold— in 1971. For a useful analysis and much data on this process, see Frank Ackerman and Arthur MacEwan, "Inflation, Recession and Crisis . . . ," in *RRPE* (August, 1972). Those wishing to explore the mysteries of devaluation, gold, and the like, will be helped by Richard Du Boff, "Dollar Evaluation and Foreign Trade," and Jacob Morris, "Monetary Crisis of World Capitalism," in *Monthly Review* (March and January, 1972, respectively). See also Ernest Mandel, *Decline of the Dollar: A Marxist View of the Monetary Crisis** (New York: Pathfinder Press, 1972) for a series of illuminating essays written over the period 1964 to 1972. Joyce Kolko, *America and the Crisis of World Capitalism,* Chapter Three is also helpful.

in that process; it is the most dynamic force now at work in the world economy, and it has done much to add to the power of private corporations in the leading capitalist nations.

As we saw in Chapter 3, a few hundred MNC's already control over 15 percent of world *production,* and they are growing at a rate of 10 percent a year. What is an MNC? Why are they? What do they do, why do they grow, with what means and consequences?

All MNC's are international corporations, but the reverse is not so. By definition, an international corporation has operations, with sales outlets (or mineral production, for example) in more than one country; such international operations provide the long background for the emergence of the true MNC. But the MNC is more complicated than that, both in its bases and its meaning. As suggested by Hymer (in Chapter 3), the MNC can be understood by comparing it with the *national* corporation as it evolved in the United States at the end of the nineteenth century, and subsequently. Indeed, one way to find the most apt comparison is to note the behavior of those corporations that moved their operations from the New England area to the South, especially during and after the 1920's—in response to cheaper labor, resource availability (for example, cotton or timber), tax advantages, and favorable marketing conditions. The MNC operates in all its facets—manufacturing, marketing, finance—over the face of the world as though the world were one nation. The 1960's technology of communications and transportation was one basis for this development; as we shall see, economic and political questions (such as rapid growth rates, lower labor costs, the need to avoid protective tariffs) were the propelling causes. The American giant corporations took the lead in the process, as they sought new outlets for their great capital, and rising profits from extended operations; the giant corporations of Europe and Japan soon joined the parade. The latest phase of the process is the rapid upsurge of European and Japanese investment, production, and banking in the United States (as well as in other areas).

When the truly *national* corporation developed in the United States in the late nineteenth century, it broke through local and regional political controls and its rising power transformed the private-public political structure to the advantage of the corporations, which at first sought a laissez-faire setting and subsequently (just before World War I) began to move toward centralized controls suitable to their needs. Up to now, the MNC has had something of the same effects: freed from politically-imposed limitations in their headquarters country, able to bring effective pressures to bear on their host countries, and increasingly seeking to create a *world* structure of relationships suited to their needs, while simultaneously acting as both an expansive *and* a destabilizing force in the world economy.

American corporations began to control manufacturing production facilities in Europe as early as the 1920's—for instance, General Motors' take-over of Opel in Germany and Vauxhall in England. Today's process is different. In the earlier period, the relationship meant that the American firm controlled and profited from the production of German or British autos. "But by 1970 General Motors [was] turning Vauxhall and Opel into two integrated components of an international production machine." [37]

The first major wave of American direct investment in postwar Europe was as a means of moving along with the rapid growth of their economies, *inside* European tariff and other obstacles. "Between 1958 and 1963, over 3,000 American companies either set up subsidiaries in the European Common Market countries, or gained control over already existing firms within it." [38] This says nothing of American investment in Britain, or in other non–Common Market countries in the same years. In the space of a few years, the MNC's in the U.S. had begun to preside over the global economy in much the same fashion as the "Fortune 500" (or fewer) do over the American economy. Kolko is worth quoting at length on this question:

> By 1965 there were 3,300 American multinational corporations controlling approximately 23,000 subsidiaries around the world, and the larger the corporation the more important were their overseas interests to their total profit and sales. Although this number has grown rapidly since 1964, more importantly in 1972 only 187 held three-fourths the total assets of U.S. investment abroad. At the same time there was a sharp acceleration in the concentration of capital in the U.S. itself. Between 1950 and 1968 the top 200 corporations' control of all manufacturing assets increased from 46 to 66 percent. It is these same 200 that control the preponderant sector of the overseas investment. Of the 1969 net earnings of all U.S. industrial corporations, the share of the top 87 was 50 percent or equal to that shared by the remaining 194,000 U.S. corporations. Of these top 87 corporations, only three do not have major overseas interests. And all the figures on assets and profits, according to the FTC report of 1969, were "greatly understated"—many corporations did not include their full foreign holdings. [39]

As the new technology of transportation, communications, and control improved—and it improved at increasing rates—the original motivations

[37] Hugh Stephenson, *The Coming Clash: The Impact of Multinational Corporations on National States* (New York: Saturday Review Press, 1972), p. 22. Stephenson is editor of the (London) *Times Business News*. His book is an excellent source of information on this development.

[38] Ernest Mandel, *Europe vs. America*° (New York: Monthly Review Press, 1970), pp. 22–23. The Common Market began in 1957.

[39] Kolko, *America and the Crisis of World Capitalism*, p. 30.

for the MNC were added to. What had first been seen as a necessity for political reasons (including getting in "under" tariffs) was transformed into a new possibility for economic reasons. The European giants joined in—although leaving the U.S. MNC's with 60 percent of all direct foreign investment in the world as the 1970's began. Some of the Europeans, especially the oil companies, were also long-experienced in multinationalism. Now, as Hymer points out, "the multinational corporate system is no longer an American system, but is, at the very least, a North Atlantic system both in the sense that Europeans have joined the ranks and in the sense that American firms have become less tied to the United States." [40] Let us look at some representative and important facts concerning the MNC's.[41]

1. Among these giants, the very largest are the Americans: EXXON, ITT, GM, GE, IBM, Ford Chrysler, et al. The largest American corporations are also the largest MNC's. In almost all the established industries, the largest European MNC is smaller than any of the top *three* companies in that industry based in the United States. Petroleum is an exception: of the seven largest oil companies, the second largest is Royal-Dutch Shell.

2. Many of the largest American companies have around half or more of their fixed assets outside the United States: EXXON, ITT, Singer, Colgate-Palmolive, Mobil Oil, National Cash, Corn Products, Goodyear, Sperry Rand. The same is true for many smaller companies, such as International Packers, Burroughs, Heinz, Pfizer, and Gillette.

3. Profits for many giant American corporations depend for as much as a third, a half, or more on foreign operations—for example, Eastman Kodak, International Harvester, Minnesota Mining and Manufacturing.

4. Seventy percent of ITT's employment is in mid-Europe.

5. Forty percent of all American direct investment in France, West Germany and the United Kingdom is owned by EXXON, Ford, and General Motors.

6. American companies control 95 percent of European production of integrated circuits; 80 percent of electronic computers (IBM alone has 65 percent); 30 percent of European car and vehicle production.

7. About half of the largest 500 American corporations now have substantial manufacturing interests outside the United States. Forty of these have more than one-third of their total physical assets abroad. One consequence is a steady decline of American exports of finished manufactures (by 29 percent between 1955 and 1964) and an increase in the exports of semifinished goods, that is, of components and materials (an increase of 326 percent between 1955 and 1964).

[40] Op. cit.
[41] Derived from Stephenson, *The Coming Clash, passim,* and Joyce Kolko.

8. In 1970, 298 U.S. MNC's accounted for 51 percent of *all* U.S. manufactured exports, and imported 34 percent of *total* imports. Much of this trade to and from the U.S. and between other countries involves transfers between various divisions of a given corporation, which greatly facilitates the juggling of costs and profits and the reduction of tax liabilities.

9. The largest private employer in Formosa (Taiwan) is the General Instrument Corporation (of the U.S.).

10. In 1970, half of the largest three hundred American corporations had subsidiaries in Spain.

11. Japan, though much affected by American military and trading relationships, was almost totally without American investment. In 1970 Japan began to undo its restrictions on foreign capital. In 1971, Chrysler, Ford, and GM all set up joint-venture companies in Japan. The process continues, because Japanese companies have begun to join the multinational parade and must give a *quid pro quo* in order to do so. In 1973, Sumitomo gave $2 million to Yale University; Mitsubishi gave $1 million to Harvard Law School. (How multinational can you get?)

12. Not only American companies are involved, of course. Between 1962 and 1972 British investment in the U.S. doubled, to over $2 billion, and to something more than that in the Common Market countries. In turn, over 15 percent of all British manufacturing industry was owned by foreigners, and over two-thirds of that by Americans. Over two-thirds of Canadian industry is foreign-owned, mostly by Americans.

These, and similar facts, are impressive indications of a major change in the structure and functioning of the capitalist world economy. This is all the more so when we recognize that the corporations are among the most powerful within their own societies *and* in the other societies where they operate; that what they produce—whether consumer goods, such as TV's or autos, or capital goods, such as computers—are among the most valued commodities today, and that their financial strength and flexibility guarantee that there will be increasing difficulties for those not already giants to join the race or to keep from being beaten down by those who win it.

It may be seen that what is now taking place through the MNC is a global replaying of what happened in the American economy with the rise of the giant national corporation. In the United States in this century, the main dynamics of both economic and political life have been provided by the giant corporation. Much of what has happened has been a result of their direct needs and desires; very little has happened that they saw as incompatible with their own interests. Labor policy, monetary and trade policy, tax policies, resource policies, and the like, have changed in complicated ways throughout this century; they have never veered very far, for very long, from the ways found acceptable by Big Business. Is it likely that the consequences of monopoly/oligopoly in a national economy will be reproduced on a global scale by the MNC? Of necessity, because the scale *is* global, there are important differences; because the power is great and concentrated and capitalist, there are important similarities. At least one major difference between the dynamics of domestic and global concentrated power is just now becoming evident: the rise of monopoly capitalism at home brought with it, of necessity, the expansion of the State (as the next chapter shows); the expansion of the State at home was also a primary means by which the large U.S. corporation could, in having its way eased abroad, become the MNC, in industry, mining, trade, and finance, as the U.S. empire took hold in both the rich and the poor nations. The power of the MNC is now so great that it needs the State less and less: the global economy is becoming "privatized" in its relationships as, for example, private banks take the place of U.S. government lending, as private military sales take the place of U.S. "military assistance." The implications of this development are several, not least in importance being those that point to increased international economic instability, and to an even more remote possibility that the people of this country—who, after all, do have the formal possibility of influencing their government's foreign policies, but no rights to influence those of the MNC's— might have any say whatsoever about the global role of U.S. economic power.[42]

The MNC is too new a phenomenon for us to understand its full meaning; the best we can do now is to conclude the discussion with a series of questions pointing to important areas of its operations.

1. What does this "interpenetration and international concentration of capital," as Mandel calls it, mean for jobs and wages in the advanced capitalist nations? The MNC is the ultimate in capitalist strength and flexibility. It moves in and out of areas, products, and techniques with an ease hitherto unknown. Its flexibility is labor's weakness. Labor's greatest weapon has always been the striking union. MNC's can redistribute production in the face of a strike; they do so even without the threat of a strike. One aim of the MNC is to find the geographic area of maximum labor advantage in terms of some optimum combination of wages, skills, and labor strength. Sometimes this means East Asia (wages in Taiwan in electronics are one twentieth of those in the U.S.), sometimes Northern Scotland; sometimes, even, the United States. The MNC rapidly moves out of reach of the *national* trade union. A telling example: in 1971, Ford (U.K.) decided to resist wage-demands of the well-organized British auto workers. Henry Ford II met with the British Prime Minister (Heath), who agreed that even at the cost of major labor unrest, such resistance was desirable. Ford switched some of its produc-

[42] For a useful review of the financial aspects of this "privatization" process, and some of its accomplished and expected consequences for the indebted Third World

tion to its Cologne factory, whose work force consisted most of newly-recruited, non-union, *Turkish* migrant workers. They had recently replaced *Italian* migrant workers who had slowly become unionized, and whose work contracts were allowed to lapse. Such workers have few rights in the host country. Ford won out in the British dispute, unsurprisingly.[43]

If organized labor has any possibilities of fighting against that kind of power, it is at the moment dependent upon its ability to organize *international* trade union cooperation; that is, between American, British, and German (and perhaps other nations') autoworkers, in the foregoing case. Steps along those lines in a few industries have been attempted, and others may be expected to follow. The prospects for American unions being able to take such steps effectively are significantly reduced by their membership in the International Congress of Free Trade Unions (ICFTU), a Cold War creation which places barriers even to *discussions* with many of the most relevant (Communist, or presumed to be Communist) unions abroad. The principal trade union federations in both Italy and France, for example, are Communist-dominated. Quite apart from that self-inflicted weakness, however, American organized labor is likely to find its strength effectively and steadily reduced as that of the MNC grows.

2. What will the MNC mean to tariff policy? Or, a variation on that question, is it likely that either smaller business *or* labor can hope for tariff protection to protect sales and jobs at home? Tariffs lose their meaning when production takes place *within* the national boundaries, a fact that was one of the principal stimuli to the initial growth of the MNC. What becomes necessary, therefore, are barriers to the flow of *capital* across national boundaries or, given the already substantial existence of MNC's in the world, even the forcible expulsion or expropriation of MNC capital. Anything can happen, of course; as matters now stand, it seems most unlikely that the most powerful corporations in the world, corporations whose sense of business identity appears to be stronger than their sense of national identity, but whose power within their own and other nations' governments is high and rising, would allow such developments to get very far. The kind of political pressure required to make such an eventuality probable would have to be substantial and broad-based, and nationalistic in its orientation; the future may see such a movement, but at present none is in sight. Organized labor is the most likely spearhead of such pressure, but that would seem to conflict with its need to organize internationally.

3. What are the effects of the MNC on the international monetary

---

countries, see the two-part essay of Emma Rothschild, "Banks: The Politics of Debt," in *New York Review of Books*, May 27 and June 24, 1976.

[43] The full story is given in Stephenson, pp. 157–58, along with other similar incidents.

system, and on the balance of payments and trade conditions for individual nations? The MNC's include almost all of the very largest corporations in the world. They are giant producers, with sales amounting to about half a trillion dollars annually. They have and must have large financial reserves. They are constantly shuttling investment and working capital from nation to nation, and taking in flows of profits and interest. To quote Stephenson on part of this picture:

> International corporations may at any given moment have an overall balance sheet in a dozen or more currencies. This gives them both the commercial *need* and the commercial *means* to protect their interests by "speculating," or (more politely) "taking positions" in the foreign-exchange markets.[44]

Among the most active and largest of the involved MNC's are the international oil companies. Stephenson quotes an oil-company treasurer as saying "when I write a cheque, it is the bank that bounces." [45] Giant national corporations *in* the United States have the same kind of importance in the financial situation; but there are of course no balance of trade and payments or foreign-exchange rate problems directly entailed by domestic operations. It is Stephenson's considered opinion that the international monetary crisis of 1971, which led to the U.S. going off the gold standard, to dollar devaluation, and to the Nixon wage-price freeze, was due to "the increasing monetary freedom of the international company" (p. 138). In 1973, the U.S. Tariff Commission came to the same conclusion. "In August of 1973, influential British opinion had it that 'America is at the centre of what is potentially the most dangerous monetary and trading crisis since 1931.'" [46] Now a new international monetary system is presumably in the making. One major reason for its necessity is the MNC; its shaping will be largely determined by the MNC.

4. Other questions concerning the MNC are being raised as the world becomes conscious of its existence and its importance. Here we shall end with our final question: What does the great and growing strength of the MNC mean to the relationships between the leading capitalist countries and the dependent economies of the Third World? Our answer will stress that the historical relationships between these two sets of countries—comprehended in the terms mercantilism, colonialism, imperialism, and neocolonialism—have meant retrogressive development for the Third World, and that the MNC intensifies that cruel process.[47]

[44] Ibid., p. 123.

[45] Ibid., p. 126.

[46] Editorial Comment, *Manchester Guardian Weekly,* August 25, 1973.

[47] For further general discussion of the MNC, see the two part essay in the *Monthly Review,* "Notes on the Multinational Corporation" (October and November, 1969). For general discussion but with special emphasis on the meaning of the MNC

Backward into Underdevelopment

There are just about four billion people in the world. The distribution of income within the capitalist portion of the world (which contains over two-thirds of world population) is very much like that within each capitalist country, except more so. If we divide the countries of the world into "rich" and "poor," 69 percent of the people live in poor countries. In 1965 they received 15.5 percent of capitalist world income. The *average* annual per capita income in the poor countries was $167; in the rich countries it was $2,040. Two additional facts: (1) most of the people received much less than the average in both rich and poor countries (that is, the median is lower than the average) for the distribution of income is highly unequal in both; (2) the gap between rich and poor countries has widened since 1965.[48]

The gap that widens today has been widening since the first penetration of Europeans into these areas; nor are the West's lamentations and worries about the gap new. Both the sorry facts and the attitudes of *noblesse oblige* are constants of this history from the beginning. Not until this century did the attempt grow to explain the whys and wherefores of the relationship: why the capitalist powers systematically penetrate the rest of the world and what the consequences are for both ends of the relationship.

The first attempt was made by J. A. Hobson in 1902. Hobson was a radical critic (but not a socialist); he sought to show that Great Britain benefited little from its empire, and argued that the impulse to empire (at least in his day) was due to the inability of Britain's own population to consume what it produced: "The taproot of imperialism," Hobson said, "is the unequal distribution of income." [49]

Hobson's analysis was picked up and transformed by Lenin. Writing in the midst of World War I, and using Germany as the basis of his analysis, Lenin saw imperialism—"the highest stage of capitalism"—as having its "economic quintessence" in monopoly capitalism. The growth of giant industry, its organization along monopolistic lines, its inter-

---

for the Third World, see R. J. Barnet, and Ronald Müller, *Global Reach: The Power of the Multinational Corporations* ° (New York: Simon & Schuster, 1975). O'Connor, "International Corporations and Economic Underdevelopment," in his *Corporations . . .* is a succinct and strong analysis.

[48] Between 1960 and 1970, per capita output in the rich countries increased 43 percent; in the poor countries 27 percent. See *New York Times*, July 10, 1972, in its summary of data in the latest *Statistical Yearbook* (for 1971) of the United Nations. The income figures above are taken from "Capitalism and Underdevelopment in the Modern World," by Thomas E. Weisskopf, in *The Capitalist System* (cited earlier), p. 444.

[49] See J. A. Hobson, *Imperialism* (London. Allen & Unwin, 1902), p. 81.

mingling of industry and high finance, its needs for investment outlets, markets, and raw materials, its competition with other capitalist states, and its control over State power all combine to push advanced capitalist states inexorably over the globe—and into conflict with each other.[50]

Lenin's analysis of imperialism has been central to the development of anti-imperialist analysis, despite the general recognition that the spread of imperialism was substantial (e.g., by Great Britain) *before* the stage of "monopoly capitalism," and that the specific conditions of German capitalism formed too narrow a base for an understanding of imperialism in the twentieth century. The further development of this analysis has been swift since World War II.

The key contributions have been those of Paul Baran, Harry Magdoff, André Gunder Frank, and Samir Amin. Baran, in his *Political Economy of Growth** (New York: Monthly Review Press, 1957), modernized and broadened Lenin's analysis and went on to analyze not only the imperialist *impulse* but its *consequences* on the "backward areas," including his assessment of the possibilities of their freeing themselves from capitalist domination. Harry Magdoff's *Age of Imperialism* focuses especially on the American empire in its contemporary phase. Frank, in a series of essays shortly to be commented on, centers his attention on the meaning of "dependency" for the underdeveloped areas. Samir Amin, beginning independently of Frank, has produced a massive historical-theoretical work in two volumes, *Accumulation on a World Scale: A Critique of the Theory of Underdevelopment* (New York: Monthly Review Press, 1974) which brings all this together and presses further still, arguing that "everything in this field still remains to be done." Not "everything," perhaps, but much indeed.[51]

For a summary understanding of the gap between rich and poor nations, the widening of that gap, and the systematic worsening of conditions for the peoples of the underdeveloped countries, Frank's analysis is compelling. It moves within several "hypotheses": *First,* "in contrast to the development of the world metropolis, which is no one's satellite, the development of the national and other subordinate metropoles is limited by their satellite status." The "satellites" are the underdeveloped countries. *Second,* "the satellites experience their greatest economic development and their most classically capitalist industrial development

---

[50] V. I. Lenin, *Imperialism** (New York: International Publishers, 1939). Written in 1916, and published first in 1917. Lenin's contemporary and associate Nikolai Bukharin probably contributed to Lenin's views; he also took a view less restricted to German conditions. See his *Imperialism and the Accumulation of Capital** (New York: Monthly Review Press, 1972, written in 1914).

[51] Here it is worth recalling the excellent survey and analysis by Tom Kemp, *Theories of Imperialism,* cited above, a study of which will show that our own presentation of the development is cursory—and deliberately so.

if and when their ties to their metropolis are weakest." (As, for example, during the Depression of the 1930's, or during World War II.) When the ties grow strong again, Frank argues, *under*development, that is, retrogressive development, once more ensues. *Third,* "the regions which are the most underdeveloped and feudal-seeming today are the ones that had the closest ties to the metropolis in the past." Related to these hypotheses are two more: *Fourth,* what are thought of as latifundia or haciendas today (the "feudal-seeming" plantations) were born as *commercial* enterprises in the dim past; and, *fifth,* that the decline of these plantations as viable institutions is due to a decline in the demand for their products. Putting all these arguments together, Frank concludes that the economies and the societies of the Third World (and his focus is primarily Latin America) have undergone a process of deterioration and distortion because of their coerced relationships with the developed countries. They have gone backward into underdevelopment.[52]

It has been customary among American historians to believe that the United States, because of its great domestic market and abundant resources, did not *need* the overseas empire it began to develop in the years just before and after 1900; from that observation, conventional observers have gone on to see us as having gradually abandoned what we picked up. The great resurgence of American interventionism after World War II is seen as an attempt by the United States to defend freedom and to help the weak to become strong. The facts can be seen otherwise.

American overseas experience began to take on its current shape with the Spanish-American (more accurately, the Spanish-Cuban-American) War. From then on, we developed strong relationships with a growing number of countries spreading out from Cuba to the Caribbean and Central America, from the Philippines into the Pacific. All this was before World War I.

The period after 1914 was hectic and without a persisting pattern. World War I, the Depression, and World War II had massive disruptive effects. The hold of the traditional imperial countries (Great Britain, France, Belgium, Holland, Germany, and Italy) was shaken by World War I and the Depression; World War II almost totally transformed their colonial relationships. Into that shambles strode the United States—because it could, and because, to maintain order in the world capitalist system, it had to.

---

[52] Frank is a prolific writer. The argument above may be found in his essay "The Development of Underdevelopment," in Rhodes, *Imperialism and Underdevelopment,* Chapter 1; as Chapter 1 in James D. Cockcroft, André Gunder Frank and Dale L. Johnson, *Dependence and Underdevelopment* ° (New York: Doubleday; Anchor, 1972); and as Chapter 1 in his own *Latin America: Under-Development or Revolution* ° (New York: Monthly Review Press, 1969). His other works support his hypotheses.

Academic economists, encouraged and prodded by corporate and governmental needs and funds, made the study of "the development of the underdeveloped" into a recognized area of economics.

Unsurprisingly, American mainstream economists transported both their economics and their attitudes into the new field; so did business and government leaders. All these uncritically assumed: (1) the aims of the United States regarding the Third World countries are benign, and generously so; (2) if our activities' consequences have been in any respects negative, let alone unsuccessful, in producing development, that is accidental or due to the shortcomings of the poor countries; (3) "pragmatism and moderation" (in the phrase of W. W. Rostow) are the appropriate means to development and independence and that revolutionary movements act as destructive obstacles; (4) the methodology of conventional economics is sufficient to the end of understanding and specifying developmental processes.

What de Tocqueville said of political institutions applies with full force to the whole range of imperialistic relationships—and, as well, to the comic-tragic qualities of development economics:

> The physiognomy of a government may best be judged in its colonies, for there its features are magnified and rendered more conspicuous. When I wish to study the merits of the administration of Louis XIV, I must go to Canada; its deformity is there seen as through a microscope.[53]

When American postwar intervention in the underdeveloped areas became institutionalized, beginning with Truman's Point Four program in 1949, the economic and political characteristics of the affected countries were already desperate: deep poverty, dangerously high rates of population growth, oppressive governments, illiteracy, malnutrition and disease, and a long list of social traits that added up to human misery. A generation later all these characteristics have continued and intensified. Our intervention, like that of the Europeans before us, far from "developing the underdeveloped," has produced and speeded up a process of underdevelopment.

Charity Begins at Home

We have seen that the expansionist drives of the United States are, so to speak, congenital traits; that this country has always been sensitive to the gains to be made from expansion, and, over time, has quite con-

---

[53] Quoted by Baran, op. cit., p. 249. This compares with the famous utterance of Lyndon Johnson: "Foreign policy is merely the extension of domestic policy."

sciously seen expansion as a means of resolving domestic problems—
economic, political, and social. After World War II, our inclinations
along these lines were given more force, and provided more opportunities. Business and government leaders knew that we would require
expanding markets and investment outlets abroad, and that our raw
materials requirements would depend increasingly on external sources
for their satisfaction. Add to that the collapse of European power in the
colonial areas due to war-wrought weakness, an upsurge of independence movements in the colonial areas, and the existence of established
revolutions in the Soviet Union and (by 1949) in China. The stage was
set for a swift and pervasive expansion of American hegemony. It took
somewhat different forms than European colonialism and imperialism,
and was all the more effective for having done so. Because of the relatively greater power of the U.S., both the gains and the damage were
greater.

In 1950, U.S. direct foreign private investment was $11.8 billion; by
1971 the figure had risen by almost eight times that amount (cumula-
tively) to $86 billion. It doubled between 1950 and 1956, doubled again
by 1964, and doubled again by 1971. By 1974 it was ten times the amount
of 1950: $119 billion. By far the largest share (about 80 percent) of this
investment was in the developed countries, and half of that was in manufacturing facilities. Of the $23 billion invested in underdeveloped coun-
tries, almost all was in raw materials extraction, and the greatest part of
that was in petroleum. The investments in the developed countries are
vital for enhancing competitive strength and profits, the investments in
the underdeveloped countries are vital as guarantees of precious raw
materials, for global strategy and, of course, for profits.[54]

The direct investments of American corporations in the poor countries
are less than a third of total direct investment abroad, but they bring in
about half of all profits from foreign direct investments. They bring them
in to the very largest corporations; mostly, the big oil companies. The
largest, EXXON, in 1965 had stated foreign assets of $4.5 billion, or 52
percent of all its assets. Its foreign sales were 68 percent of all its sales,
and yielded 60 percent of its total earnings.

A useful sense of the comparative magnitudes of the giant corporations in the world is given by a 1973 compilation of the Library of
Congress (reported in the general press), ranking the 100 largest entities
in the world—countries and companies—for the years 1960, 1965 and

---

[54] The figures above and immediately following are taken from *International Economic Report of the President* * (Washington: USGPO, 1976) and from the comprehensive article by Thomas E. Weisskopf, "U.S. Foreign Private Investment: An
Empirical Survey," in *The Capitalist System*, pp. 427 ff. Weisskopf points out that
the investment in *non*-raw materials facilities in the underdeveloped countries has
recently begun to rise rapidly.

1970, ranking countries by GNP and companies by annual sales volume. (The comparison of production with sales is technically inexact, but valid nonetheless.) In 1960 there were 59 countries and 41 companies on the list; in 1965, 57 countries and 43 companies; in 1970, 49 countries and 51 companies. The companies are almost all MNC's. In 1970, GM was the 24th largest entity in the world, its sales higher than the GNP of Yugoslavia, Pakistan, and South Africa (25, 26, and 27, respectively). Then came AT&T. Then EXXON. Then Denmark. Then Ford. The largest non-American company, Royal Dutch Shell, was 36th, a bit smaller than Norway, a bit larger than Venezuela (much of whose economy Shell controls). In 1960 there were neither Japanese nor German companies in the top 100; in 1970, there were two Japanese (Hitachi and Nippon Steel), and six German companies (VW, Siemens, Farbwerke Hoechst, Daimler-Benz, August Theyssen-Hutte, and BASF).

The "Seven Sisters," the oil companies that control the world's petroleum (and much of its other energy supplies)—EXXON, Mobil Oil, Texaco, Gulf Oil, Standard of California, Royal Dutch Shell, and British Petroleum—were all in the top 100 "entities," and they are of course among the top MNC's in the world. EXXON, the largest of these, functions in ways similar to the others. Its operations are mostly outside the U.S., and (apart from its crude oil production) mostly in the developed countries. In 1972, EXXON had "36,420 retail outlets in 14 European countries, pumping more gasoline than EXXON sells in the U.S." (*Business Week*, July 29, 1972). But its oil reserves (and some of its refineries) are in the underdeveloped countries, and two-thirds have been in the Middle East. It would be very surprising indeed if EXXON and its "Sisters" did not take a strong interest in the "political stability" of these source countries. Given the power of the oil corporations in their own nations' politics and the vital importance of oil not just for profits but for day-to-day private and industrial life in modern economies and the military, it would be even more surprising if national policies deviated from the policies desired by the oil giants. The oil companies have complex interests and a long-term vision, in keeping with their power. They negotiate with nations, and their decisions must be ratified by their own nations—as in the case of the Tehran and Tripoli Agreements of 1971, between the oil companies and OPEC (representing eleven oil *countries* in North Africa, the Middle East, Southeast Asia, Africa, and South America), which raised the take per barrel of the petroleum exporting countries. The companies can and do pass on such increases in the form of higher prices to buyers while also gaining tax reductions in the U.S. because of their increased "royalties," and acquiesce for a variety of reasons (including the delicate military and political conditions in some of these areas, and the potential profits to be gained through higher prices not only for oil but for coal, gas, and nuclear energy supplies which they own).

TABLE 7–4   Selected Minerals: Net U.S. Imports as a Percent of Domestic Mine or Well Production

	1937–1939 Average Percentages	1966 Average Percentages
Iron Ore	3	43
Copper	−13	18
Lead	0	131
Zinc	7	140
Bauxite	113	638
Petroleum	−4	31

The oil companies are likely to make policy in the future, as they have in the past. What the companies want and decide they need in the future is no more likely to coincide with what the peoples of either the consuming or the producing countries need than it has in the past.[55] The United States, once overflowing with oil, abused and misused its resources (abused with irrational pumping practices by engineering standards, and misused by selling petroleum products for uneconomic purposes—such as heating oil). By 1966 we were already importing (net) an amount of oil equal to 31 percent of our domestic production. What is true of oil is generally true of other raw materials that are used in bulk (as compared with, say, molybdenum, used as an alloy). Table 7–4 indicates this trend.

Magdoff also shows (p. 47), that in the relationship between net mineral imports and consumption up to 1919, we were net exporters; after 1940 our position as a net importer of all minerals (except gold) rose steadily, from about 5 percent of consumption in 1940–1944 to 14 percent in 1961.

The United States had to expand its power in the underdeveloped areas if they were to be kept in the capitalist orbit as sources of raw materials and of high profits; that it was able to do so is dramatically revealed by comparing its position in the Middle East just before World War II with the present. (See Table 7–5.)

The importance of oil to the functioning of the economy, and the power of the oil corporations in domestic politics, achieves a consensus

[55] Two books that go far toward providing understanding of how the oil companies work abroad and at home are Michael Tanzer, *The Political Economy of International Oil and the Underdeveloped Countries*° (Boston: Beacon Press, 1969) and Robert Engler, *The Politics of Oil* ° (Chicago: University of Chicago Press, 1961). Anthony Sampson, *The Seven Sisters*° (New York: Viking, 1975) is a useful supplement to Tanzer and Engler. A conservative economist's view of the current market conditions for oil, which sees claims of shortage as nonsense, is M. A. Adelman, *The World Petroleum Market* (Baltimore, Johns Hopkins Press, 1973).

TABLE 7–5   Oil Reserves in the Middle East

	Amount	% of total	Amount	% of total
	Estimates of Reserves Controlled (billions of barrels)			
	1940		*1967*	
Great Britain	4.3	72.0	73.0	29.3
United States	0.6	9.8	146.0	58.6
Other	1.1	18.2	30.0	12.1

in our domestic politics at the highest levels, even where differences exist on other matters, just as the consensus is broader on foreign than on domestic affairs. The trade magazine *World Petroleum* illustrated this in its comments on Presidents Kennedy and Johnson:

> The USA oil industry finds little to complain about in the Kennedy Administration. . . . The president even went out of his way to write a nice letter to the National Petroleum Council, an industry advisory group of 95 top oil and gas executives, a letter almost without precedent in the 18-year-old history of the council. . . . (Sept., 1963) Lyndon Baines Johnson . . . has the interests of the industry at heart, as shown many times during his career of 31 years in political life in Washington. . . . (Jan., 1964)[56]

What is true of international oil in the Middle East finds its counterpart wherever oil reserves are located—for example, in Venezuela and in Southeast Asia, where at least some of the doggedness of the American war is to be understood in terms of estimated oil reserves which, according to one petroleum expert, make the Louisiana oil resources "look like a postage stamp on an elephant's ass."[57]

What is true of oil is true of other vital raw materials; for example, a shortage of chromium in 1972 (except for supplies from the USSR) was critical enough to cause our foreign policy to defy the UN ban on imports of chromium from Rhodesia as a means of bringing pressure to bear on Rhodesia's blatant racist policies. So it goes, with tungsten (from South Korea), columbium (from Brazil and Mozambique), cobalt (from Zaire), and so on.

All this strengthens American corporations and supplies important needs for the American economy, as it presently operates. What does it mean for the underdeveloped countries?

---

[56] Quoted in Michael Tanzer, *The Political Economy of International Oil and the Underdeveloped Countries*, pp. 57–8.

[57] This is discussed in my article "The Political Economy of War," *The Nation*, June 28, 1971, with an accompanying article by Michael Tanzer, "Offshore Oil Sweepstakes." The "offshore" area curves around Indochina.

Bad to Worse

There was, until recently, a broad consensus that the internationalization and militarization of the American economy—whether or not those were the terms used—was good for Americans. The results were jobs, profits, and national security. As domestic tensions and social and economic troubles have multiplied in recent years, however, what were formerly seen as blessings are increasingly seen as disasters in disguise, and not only by radicals. This change in attitudes has made it easier to understand the calamity that the United States and other powerful nations have imposed on the underdeveloped countries. If their conditions before our policies took hold were bad, their present conditions are worse. The choice facing most of these countries is to allow this tragic path to continue to unfold, or to find ways to break the hold of the powerful countries; in Frank's words, "underdevelopment or revolution." Both the powerful nations and the underdeveloped ones realize the truth of this ultimate choice.

Most observers of the changes taking place in the underdeveloped areas find it difficult to understand why their economies steadily deteriorate, and why their governments—presiding over increasing hardships for the majority—move toward increasing coercion. It is the same kind of puzzlement that middle class people express about the continuation of poverty among the poor, despite all the help given them by the middle class. For such observers, the cause is sooner or later found as shortcomings of the victims. And victim is the appropriate term.

The continuing poverty of poor countries compares on many counts with the continuing poverty here at home. Both take place in a world whose already great riches increase by the day. Both occur within the context of the dual economy: the rich get richer; the poor get poorer, and are accused of an innate capacity for bringing misfortune on themselves. Finally, in attitudes mixing exasperation with pity, the better-off conclude that, after all, some people *are* better than others.

Economists normally cite a list of "factors" which, in combination, enhance the possibilities of growth and development: resources, entrepreneurship, the quantities and skills of the labor force, the availability of capital, markets, and a State that contributes to (or at least does not detract from) the developmental process; and some economists argue that the process will move more rapidly if the development is "balanced" (all industries moving together) and others if it is "unbalanced" (a few strategic industries taking the lead). Thus, as the underdeveloped economies find themselves in increasing difficulties, the quite natural response is to pinpoint the manner in which any factor is not satisfied: their resources are poor (but so were Japan's and Germany's, among others); they lack a lively entrepreneurial group (although Asians and Middle

Easterners, for instance, are also known as crafty and aggressive businessmen); their labor force is inadequate in its skill composition, and disposed to be inadequately responsive to market stimuli (as was also said to be true of the British workers during the Industrial Revolution); they are short of investment capital (as were all capitalist countries in their industrializing stages); their domestic markets are too skimpy to absorb industrial production and they cannot compete in world markets, except with their raw materials (as was true of all but the leading nations over time); their governments are corrupt, or ill-advised; their development is too balanced, or too unbalanced. And, on top of everything else, their populations grow too fast. Why can't they be more like, say, us?

The conventional explanation of why development fails in the poor countries has many inadequacies; the most commanding concern the profoundly unhistorical quality of those explanations, and with their studious avoidance of acknowledging the degree to which the plight of the underdeveloped economies is to the benefit of the rich countries. Every industrial capitalist nation depended critically upon its own geographic expansion, or upon the buoyant world markets created by others' expansion. The expansion, of course, was into the lands of the presently underdeveloped countries. Setting morality, politics, and warfare aside, there is simply no space left into which the poor countries can expand— except, perhaps, space already controlled by the rich countries. Apart from any other consideration, therefore, the underdeveloped countries today must develop without the ease provided by the external possibilities of expansion. Indeed, quite the opposite is the case: the external relationships of the underdeveloped countries press down on them, and are negative. They are negative regarding their worsening terms of trade. Their productive facilities are owned by outsiders or, when owned by their own nationals, owned by those who function at a level and in a way subservient to the outsiders, as a kept and servile business class. When they do produce manufactures, they find themselves walled out of the rich markets by protective tariffs, import quotas, and the like. As for their domestic markets, the duality of their economies means that, even more so than in the rich countries, the overwhelming proportion of the people are abysmally poor, and the small high-income group finds its satisfactions in luxury goods or bank accounts abroad.[58]

But what about all the aid given to the poor countries by the rich, and especially by the United States? And of the private investment by outsiders? Shouldn't those flows of capital have made a difference? They did: they made a bad situation worse. In the frequent international

[58] See Arghiri Emmanuel, *Unequal Exchange: A Study of the Imperialism of Trade* * (New York: Monthly Review Press, 1972), for a penetrating and original analysis of these relationships.

meetings attended by representatives of both rich and poor countries—such as UNCTAD (the UN Commission for Trade and Development)—representatives of the poor countries regularly complain of the tariff barriers erected against their manufactures, and about the deterioration in their terms of trade, that is, the purchasing power of their exports. The deterioration, serious in the 1920's and 1930's, set in again about 1958, and has gone on since.

The terms of trade are more easily controllable by the rich countries than by the poor; just as an oligopolist or monopolist can set prices, but a competitive producer cannot. The rich countries give aid: but normally there is a high proportion of military grants buried in dollar aid. The usual custom is to tie aid to purchases in the granting country, and aid has always been considerably less than private investment from abroad (and has been decreasing since 1966). What results is a stark fact relating aid and the terms of trade (the meanings of both of which are dominated by the rich countries): the poor countries lose a considerable amount of what they receive because of the deterioration in the terms of trade. UNCTAD calculated that losses due to worsening terms of trade were 36.5 percent of official aid in 1961, and rose to 42.8 percent by 1966. They have risen since.[59]

The rich countries invest in the poor countries in their own self-interest, of course. Corporations do so for profits; they receive the support of their governments (in subsidies, investment guarantees, and policies designed to maintain a "friendly climate for investment") because that's what governments are for, and because the governments have interests that coincide with those of the corporations, on both economic and strategic grounds. The impact of private foreign investment is harmful to the poor nations; its net effect is to yield an income inflow to the rich, not to the poor. The U.S. Department of Commerce found that for the period 1956–1961, the ratio of inflow of profits and interest to the United States to outflow of investment from the United States with the under-developed countries was 164 percent; that is, in those years more came back to the U.S. than went out. For the years 1950–1961, the Department found (for Argentina, Chile, Peru, Venezuela, Colombia and Mexico) that remittances of profit and interest to U.S. investors exceeded new private U.S. investment by $3.9 billion. In 1970, the earnings of the

---

[59] See Magdoff, p. 158. His chapter on "aid and trade" is informative on this and other relationships. What we have just stated about the terms of trade does not take into account (as Magdoff does), the increasing indebtedness forced upon the under-developed countries by their worsening position, which in turn reduces their net earnings from exports, and leads to further indebtedness. The question of aid is treated in a fascinating manner by Teresa Hayter, *Aid as Imperialism* * (London and New York: Penguin, 1971). Working as a professional in a major aid agency, she discovered the differences between the rhetoric and the reality of aid.

foreign affiliates of American firms, amounted to about one-quarter of the total of *all* U.S. corporate profits after taxes.[60]

Expansion into the underdeveloped countries, and exploitation of their people and of their resources have provided the critical *margin* of dynamic capitalist development for the developed countries. They act as if they knew it, all along. In the mercantilist period, no bones were made about it; in the past century or so, exploitation is done in the name of the "white man's burden," "*la mission civilisatrice*," or, for the United States, "the preservation of the free world, and the development of the underdeveloped."

The free world seems to be free only for private investment. It is difficult to know what other kind of freedom is or was meant in places like Greece, South Korea, Thieu's South Vietnam, the Union of South Africa, Brazil, Chiang's Taiwan, the Dominican Republic, Guatemala, and Iran, among other cherished diadems of the free world. Except for a few small societies that have fought their way out of it, that "free world" has been preserved. Saved for freedom, it continues to underdevelop backward into a perverse and ever more repressive form of capitalism, displaying all of its evils but none of its virtues.

The developments of the past half-century would have passed comprehension for Schumpeter and Hobson, the only two mainstream economists who set about to analyze imperialism with any seriousness. Both thought capitalism to be rational in its essence, and both thought imperialism to be irrational—as well as immoral. Seeing it in its best light, Schumpeter prized capitalism; Hobson was not opposed to the system as such, only to its excrescences. Imperialism was one such, and he saw

---

[60] This pattern is characteristic, and the figures have, if anything, increased in recent years. In 1966, Chase Manhattan Bank, seeking a relaxation of the restrictions on overseas investment demanded by Johnson's 1965 "Voluntary Balance of Payments Program" (itself brought about by the payments crisis associated with the Indochina War), issued a brochure stating the facts about petroleum investments and urging that oil companies give "complete reporting" in order that the government would see that such investments reduced rather than increased the payments deficit, because of the "quick payback" period. Some of their facts are worth quoting at length: ". . . these investments have yielded dollar inflows that are considerably larger, year by year, than the new investment outflows. In balance of payments terms the petroleum industry is more profitable than the average U.S. foreign investment: in 1964 it accounted for about a third of net U.S. overseas investment, yet produced over 50% of total U.S. direct investment income." *Balance of Payments of the Petroleum Industry*, Chase Manhattan Bank, 1966, p. 4. They add that the "paycheck period" is three years; i.e., the rate of profit is 33-1/3% per annum. Every year since 1957 has shown a rising excess of inflow over outflow. The Bank addressed this brochure to the petroleum companies to enhance their truthfulness, and to the government to enhance its understanding. The data from the Department of Commerce are cited in Frank, *Latin America . . .*, pp. 49, 151, and 162–63 and in Joyce Kolko, *America and the Crisis of World Capitalism*, pp. 33–34.

it as due to the other main excrescence, a highly unequal distribution of income. Rid the society of the latter and there would be no need for the former: "The only safety of nations lies in removing the unearned increments of income from the possessing classes, and adding to the wage-income of the working classes or to the public income, in order that they may be spent in raising the standard of consumption." [61]

Schumpeter counted on free trade, the rational way, to be the hall-mark of capitalist development. There has been less of it since he wrote (1919) than before. Hobson's hope for a redistribution of income "from the possessing classes" has not been met, although the "public income" has risen from what was little in his day to hundreds of billions annually now. But it has accompanied the spread not the decline of imperialism.

Schumpeter's and Hobson's ideas have an attractive quality to them, much as do idealizations about the relationships between men and women; like the latter, their analyses have served all too frequently as a means of obscuring or rationalizing ugly realities. In both cases it has been possible for confusion (or worse) to spread (and take hold) because the relationships—between imperialist and imperialized, as between men and women—are many-sided and complex; that is, if either set of relationships were simply and clearly one of *sheer* exploitation and/or oppression, rationalizations, no matter how ingenious, would not "sell." But just as the relationships between men and women vary substantially in degree and kind of oppression and exploitation—from raw brutality to "babying" or to what Veblen called "vicarious consumption" (husbands using their wives to show off their own wealth, for example)—so it is that the processes of imperialism have in them varying degrees and kinds of exploitation and oppression, and carry with them varying degrees of material gain and loss for diverse portions of the dependent country's population—which remains exploited, oppressed, and dependent.

Just as Schumpeter and Hobson failed to see the role at all of exploitation in capitalist development, and as men virtually always have the same lack of understanding regarding the extent or the nature of their dominance over women, so also in both cases is there a lack of consciousness as to how those with relative power *always* formulate ideas and policies which, though seemingly rational for themselves and for what they wish to defend, are irrational and destructive for those relatively powerless—and, finally, for *all* concerned.

Schumpeter and Hobson have not been alone in framing "attractive" analyses, nor are they alone in having their ideas buffeted by cruel winds. They and other well-intentioned social thinkers have failed to develop a theory of power, a theory of the State, that would support their leading ideas, whose validity depends upon their compatibility

---

[61] Hobson, *Imperialism*, p. 89.

with how power is developed and by whom, how it is used and by whom, and for what purposes. Such questions take us now to an examination of the State.

Reading Suggestions

This chapter, despite its length, has only scratched the surface of what needs to be known. In addition to looking further at many of the works cited in this and other chapters—such as *Monopoly Capital* and *Contours of American History*—serious readers will find some of the following books especially helpful.

William Ashworth, *A Short History of the International Economy Since 1850* (London: Longmans, 1964) is an unexciting but useful summary and analysis of major institutional, technological, and economic developments. The literature on imperialism is expanding rapidly. URPE has put together a very useful bibliographical collection on all geographic areas and many analytical topics in its *Case Studies in Imperialism and Underdevelopment, RRPE* (Spring, 1971). See also its *Dependency and Foreign Domination in the Third World, RRPE* (Winter, 1972), and *Capitalism and World Economic Integration: Perspectives on Modern Imperialism, RRPE* (Spring, 1973). An extraordinarily comprehensive bibliography (well over 200 pages in length) on MNC's and the Third World is Harry Strharsky and Mary Riesch, eds., *The Transnational Corporations and the Third World* (Washington, D.C.: CoDoC International Secretariat, 1975). Their address is 1500 Farragut St., N.W., and their document invaluable for those doing serious work in the area.

A generally neglected but vital aspect of the current situation both at home and abroad is treated comprehensively and strongly by Herbert Schiller in three of his books: *Mass Communications and American Empire** and *The Mind Managers** (Boston: Beacon Press, 1971 and 1973) and *Communication and Cultural Domination** (White Plains; N.Y.: International Arts & Sciences Press, 1976). The book of readings by Rhodes has been cited; another such collection (which overlaps a bit) is K. T. Fann and Donald Hodges, eds., *Readings in U.S. Imperialism** (Boston: Porter Sargent, 1971). William A. Williams, *Tragedy of American Diplomacy** (New York: Dell, 1962) provides a strong analytical summary of the major directions of American foreign policy, especially since the 1890's. Joyce and Gabriel Kolko, *The Limits of Power** (New York: Harper & Row, 1972) is an intense examination of the crucial period 1945–1954. David Horowitz, *Empire and Revolution** (New York: Random House; Vintage, 1969), emphasizes U.S.-USSR relationships, real and concocted. An interesting collection of Marx's many mostly journalistic pieces on these matters is Shlomo Avineri, ed., *Karl Marx on Colonialism and Modernization** (New York: Doubleday Anchor, 1969).

There is an enormous amount of literature on underdeveloped areas. One of the useful books is David E. Novack and Robert Lekachman, eds., *Development and Society: The Dynamics of Economic Change** (New York: St. Martins, 1964). Pierre Jalée, *The Third World in World Economy** (New York: Monthly Review Press, 1969), has put together facts and figures otherwise difficult to find, within a sound analysis. Chandler Morse et al., *Modernization by Design* (Ithaca: Cornell University Press, 1969), is an attempt from several social disciplines to achieve a realistic appraisal of problems of development; Morse's chapter relates "economic" and "non-economic" matters scientifically, in the best sense of that much-abused term.

Finally, some books of a different sort. Felix Greene, *The Enemy** (New York: Random House; Vintage, 1970) is a powerful and most readable attempt to explain to us that we *are* an imperialist power and what that means to those whom we oppress *and* to ourselves, as a nation and as individuals. A marvelously written and powerful analysis of the fictional literature of British imperialism (of Joyce Cary, Joseph Conrad, E. M. Forster, et al.), which serves much the same function as Greene's book (and not just for British imperialism) is Jonah Raskin, *The Mythology of Imperialism** (New York: Dell, 1971). One of the bloodiest meanings is detailed in the so-called Cornell Study, *The Air War in Indochina** (Boston: Beacon Press, 1971), edited by Raphael Littauer and Norman Uphoff. Its lowkeyed and heavily statistical analysis is overwhelming and horrifying. Without saying the words, it shows that the final result of imperialism, unless overthrown, is genocide. *The Pentagon Papers** (New York: Bantam, 1971) show clearly (if not fully) how and why the government deceived us as the process took shape. Noam Chomsky in his *American Power and the New Mandarins** (New York: Vintage, 1969) and *At War with Asia** (New York: Vintage, 1970) provides a penetrating and horrifying historical analysis of the process. His *For Reasons of State** (New York: Vintage, 1973) contains essays mostly sparked by the Indochina war, but with an importance going beyond the war and into the nature of contemporary American social tensions and power. His analysis of the Pentagon Papers (Chapters 1 and 2) shows how very limited those Papers' contents are, by comparison with the full story of aggression and deception. Daniel Ellsberg's *Papers on the War** (New York: Simon & Schuster, 1972) is a one-time insider's discussion and analysis that takes us further into the jungle of U.S. government, to help us understand how very far from the ideal it strayed—as regards lying, illegality, brutality, and corruption—as it took the U.S. into and through what Ellsberg properly calls a criminal war.

8

The State

Was it for this our fathers kept the law?
This crown shall crown their struggle and their ruth?
Are we the eagle nation Milton saw
Mewing its mighty youth,
Soon to possess the mountain winds of truth,
And be a swift familiar of the sun
Where aye before God's face his trumpets run?
Or have we but the talons and the maw,
And for the abject likeness of our heart
Shall some less lordly bird be set apart?
Some gross-billed wader where the swamps are fat?
Some gorger in the sun? Some prowler with the bat? *

All agree that what the State has or has not done has been of great importance in the social and economic development of modern societies. But beyond that simple statement, disagreement sets in and soon becomes sharp. When has the State's role been beneficial and when harmful? When vital and when of small consequence? How does one measure the State's importance, and within what temporal and functional framework? How does the State relate to private groups, at any time and over time?

Asking these or other questions places an examination of the role of the State in a context of ideological and theoretical dispute. It also raises still another question: to what degree and in what ways does the relationship of the State to economic development manifest and in what ways does it conceal the changing structure and functions of *power* in modern capitalist societies? [1]

*William Vaughn Moody, *An Ode in Time of Hesitation*. From his *Poems and Plays*. Reprinted by permission of Houghton Mifflin, Inc.

[1] A good part of these introductory pages follows closely my position in "The State,

The activities of governments have been much studied by historians, but very much as though "government" and "State" are the same entities. The larger and more decisive meaning of the State and, therefore, the role of *power,* remains a vast *terra incognita*. It is power that informs and is informed by the complex relationships between public and private institutions; at the center of that complex will be found the State system, supported by and maintaining the political and social system over which it rules. To explore and map out the ground that comprehends power, socioeconomic stability and change, and the State is slippery work; if we are to understand our past and have any say whatsoever in our future, that effort is essential.[2]

The Easy Way

Historians and social scientists of the mainstream who have dealt with the government, the State, and power in capitalist society customarily have been motivated by a particular tension and have operated with a particular assumption. Typically, neither the tension nor the assumption has been explicit. The tension has been between those who thought it desirable to minimize the role of the government and those who wished to see its powers broadened. The assumption has been the *pluralist* notion that government in capitalist societies, like the functioning of the economy, is a response to the forces of competition. Some elaboration of both these points is necessary.

For example, Great Britain is seen to have had a "weak State" in the nineteenth century, Germany a strong one. The terms of the historical discussion are confined to easily discernible, hotly debated, and explicit policies: statutes, regulations, fiscal, monetary, and commercial policies, subsidies, and the like. Seldom is there an analysis of what governments did *not* do, or what *ceased* to be done (for example, in the way of social and human protection), let alone what the State was responsible for that did not appear in specific actions or that did not "appear" at all.

This last-mentioned role of the State, what we may call its nonactions, is by its nature the most obscure. When understood it is among the most

---

Power and the Industrial Revolution, 1750–1914," *URPE Occasional Paper No. 4* (Spring, 1971), concerned with Great Britain, France, and Germany.

[2] In the past decade or so there has been a major upsurge of analytical effort among Western Marxists in this area. A good part of that is summarized, evaluated, and used as a starting point for further work in an excellent two-part essay by David A. Gold, Clarence Y. H. Lo, and Erik Olin Wright, "Recent Developments in Marxist Theories of the State," *Monthly Review* (October and November, 1975). The openness, seriousness, clarity, and strength of these essays are models for radical analysis.

revealing of the relationships between private power, governmental activities, and social conditions. Put together with the more obvious manifestations of power, this aspect of social existence allows a long step to be taken toward an understanding of the State. An absence of such understanding encourages the following kind of misleading observation concerning social conditions in industrializing Britain; the statement is made, it should be noted, by a respected economic historian who has done more than others to study "the State":

> . . . in the age of laissez-faire the role of government in economic affairs was largely a passive one. . . . The social evils in town and countryside that followed in the wake of the Industrial Revolution might have been alleviated at an earlier date if the governing classes had been better informed about the great changes that were taking place in the mines and factories. . . . The government was inactive because it saw no good reason why it should do anything.[3]

"The governing classes," it may be assumed, contained men who were the creators and beneficiaries of the very conditions of which the author thinks they were ignorant, ready in a trice to employ the coercive power of the State to subdue those who sought to change these conditions, power that had been used to abolish social protections at "an earlier date" (as discussed in Chapter 2).

The "social evils" mentioned by Henderson were due to the absence of social controls at the time, as the "self-regulating market economy" held full sway. Given their earlier abolition, their continuing absence can be explained in good part by "non-decision making," a phenomenon analyzed explicitly in a recent study:

> . . . non-decision making is a means by which demands for change in the existing allocation of benefits and privileges in the community can be suffocated before they are even voiced; or kept covert; or killed before they gain access to the relevant decision-making arena; or, failing all these things, maimed or destroyed in the decision-implementing stage of the policy process.[4]

This is close to what Claus Offe calls "negative selection," the ways in which "anti-capitalist" interests (whether self-consciously so or not) are systematically rebuffed or excluded from the processes and policies of

[3] W. O. Henderson, *The State and the Industrial Revolution in Prussia, 1740–1870* (Liverpool: University Press, 1958), pp. xiii–xiv. The reference in the quote is to Britain.

[4] Peter Bachrach and Morton S. Baratz, *Power and Poverty: Theory and Practice** (New York: Oxford University Press, 1970), p. 44. Both the theory and the practice discussed in this excellent work are significant additions to what we have known. The empirical focus is Baltimore.

the State.[5] Those involved in protest activities (among others) in recent years have experienced all these deflecting techniques in full measure; indeed, it is the success of such techniques in maintaining the status quo that has led many to an enhanced interest in the way power works.

Non-decision making is a principal means of maintaining the status quo, or of slowing and guiding the changes away from it. It is the monopoly of those who have great power in society; those who are deflected, ignored, suffocated, and whose proposals are "maimed or destroyed" are those with much less or no power. In capitalist democracies the guiding assumption of conventional social theorists, the assumption on which their "theory of the State" is founded, is *pluralism*. The pervasiveness of this assumption, and the confusions surrounding it, require that it be looked at critically. After doing so, we shall attempt an analysis of power, and of the nature and role of the State in the United States.

Few economists have a "theory of the State," or are even conscious of the need for one. In the fragmentation characteristic of the social sciences, economists who might feel that need can, so it is believed, turn to the political scientists. The latter would be much offended at the suggestions above that the State has been neglected. They do have a theory of the State: pluralism. The only thing wrong with it is that it takes for granted the very matter most requiring examination: power. In this neglect, the political scientists have matched their economist counterparts who take private property and basic capitalist institutions for granted. But, as Ralph Miliband points out,

> A theory of the state is also a theory of society and of the distribution of power in that society. But most Western "students of politics" tend to start, judging from their work, with the assumption that power, in Western societies, is competitive, fragmented and diffused: everybody, directly or through organized groups, has some power and nobody has or can have too much of it. In these societies, citizens enjoy universal suffrage, free and regular elections, representative institutions, effective citizen rights, including the right of free speech, association and opposition; and both individuals and groups take ample advantage of these rights, under the protection of the law, an independent judiciary and a free political culture. As a result, the argument goes, no government, acting on behalf of the state, can fail, in the not very long run, to respond to the wishes and demands of competing interests. In the end, everybody, including those at the end of the queue, gets served.[6]

[5] Offe is one of those whose creative theoretical work is reviewed succinctly and well in the Gold et al. essays just noted, Part 2. References to Offe's and others' works are usefully collected in the two-part essay.

[6] Ralph Miliband, *The State in Capitalist Society* (New York: Basic Books, 1969), p. 2. Harold J. Laski, *The State in Theory and Practice* (New York: Viking, 1935) is an earlier, modern, and still relevant attempt by a Marxian political philosopher to understand the modern State. A most useful critique of "liberal" theories of the State

Pluralism as the basis for thinking about the State assumes that sovereignty resides in the voter and that political outcomes depend upon competition among those vying for those votes. Neoclassical economics, the body of theory that guides economists' thinking, has its parallel assumptions. Not the voter, but the consumer is sovereign; business firms vie with each other for the consumer's vote—that is, the consumer's dollar. Economic demand determines economic supply; political demand determines political supply. It is a comforting set of beliefs for those who accept it; all that is ignored is the underlying reality in society that makes some considerably more equal than others. All that is ignored is power, who has it, how it is obtained, how used, how distributed, how lost. A theory of the State without a theory of power is, in the old saying, like Hamlet without the Dane.

Power, Power, Who Has the Power?

What *is* power? It is the ability to act effectively, to make things go one's way, or to keep them so. The Latin root for the noun *power* and the verb *to be able* is the same. Power is the ability, for present purposes, to make or to influence decisions and non-decisions. Where does it come from? Most simply, power is held by those who control what is valued in their society; what has been valued; what is coming to be valued. What is valued may be tangible (productive assets or weaponry) or intangible (the ability to formulate or represent cherished beliefs or aspirations).

Control over the means of material survival places its possessors at the center of power in any society, although the forms and functions associated with such control have differed quite substantially in history— a priesthood in Ancient Egypt, the Church and warriors in medieval Europe, for example. Control over productive wealth in a capitalist society as *a* source of power comes closest to being *the* source of power. This characteristic is one way of defining capitalism; it also helps to explain the great dynamism of capitalist economic development.

Still, complexity in the structures of power exists in a capitalist as in any other kind of society; this complexity is substantial and, upon reflection, obvious. Power derives from different areas of society—economic, political, military, religious, cultural, social—and functions at different levels—local, national, international. Still, from this patterned and dynamic complexity, order may be derived; we may think of *structures* of

---

is C. B. Macpherson, "Politics: Post-Liberal Democracy," in Robin Blackburn, ed., *Ideology in Social Science,* cited earlier.

power. Visually, we may think of a many-sided pyramid, its sides representing the diverse sources of power and its shape, narrowing to a peak, representing the concentration of power. Power changes hands over time, which requires that this visual representation be thought of as a moving film, rather than as a diagram. Nor should it be forgotten that those who have power at lower levels of the pyramid (those who control education, or police, or medical facilities on the local level, for example) have power that for some purposes is just as vital as those who wield power at the top. Some examples are in order.

In medieval Europe, power was in the hands of those who ruled over religious and military affairs; they also controlled the productive land. Which came first, the chicken (religious and military power) or the egg (control of the land), need not detain us here; there were tangibles and intangibles involved. For the medieval serf, the locally-held power was most vital in determining the conditions of life.

Something concerning the chicken and egg argument seems worth saying. The simple Marxian view would argue that the "egg"—that is, control over the land—came first; a more complicated view would see the long and militarized anarchy of the so-called Dark Ages as having its unifying factor in the Roman Catholic Church and its stabilizing factor in unremitting military activities. Church functionaries were often fighters; together they comprised the aristocracy of medieval Europe; the serfs supported them from the land. The "middle class" was virtually nonexistent in the early Middle Ages; as it became more prominent through its expanding trading activities, it was leaned on increasingly by the feudal military and clerical nobility; the structure of power was altering in the process.[7]

The consequences of the successful discharge of the feudal military function included an increase both in political stability and in trade and industry; the unifying role of the Church began to break down, and to seem a hindrance. The Reformation of the sixteenth century had many sides to it, in as many countries; central to that struggle was a challenge that denied the fiscal and political prerogatives the Church had long possessed. In what had been an epoch whose deep attachment to religious belief is unintelligible to moderns, any major struggle for power had to revolve around the control of religious institutions and translate itself

---

[7] For the origins of feudalism, see F. L. Ganshof, *Feudalism* (London: Longmans, 1952). For the definitive view of the complexities of the period see Marc Bloch, *Feudal Society*° (Chicago: University of Chicago Press, 1964) 2 vols. A simpler Marxian view is well-put in Marion Gibbs, *Feudal Order* (London: Cobbett Press, 1949). This treats only English society, which explains what I take to be the undue simplicity of the treatment. Both Perry Anderson's two volumes and Immanuel Wallerstein's *Modern World System* are of great importance for full understanding of the transformation of medieval and the emergence of early modern social formations.

into religious categories: the confessional, the role of the priest, faith and works, and the like.

When the Church lost its hegemony in Europe, its place was taken by the descendants of those militarists who once walked hand in glove with the Church; as secular dynasties they now ruled over nations in a time of substantially larger and more expensive conflict. Merchants and financiers were quite frequently the handmaidens of this transition; they were required to finance the now mercenary (once feudal) fighting forces, and their trade and industry gave strength to the new nations.[8]

The stage was set for yet another struggle for power. From the viewpoint of capitalist development, its most decisive manifestation was in seventeenth century England: a struggle between what has been called "the divine right of kings" and "the divine right of capital." It was not a clear-cut struggle to its participants, nor would its eventual outcome— laissez-faire capitalism—be entirely clear for over a century after the dust settled. The age was still religious: thus, "the Puritan Revolution." It was the age of mercantilism, and of a class of merchants and financiers whose strength had increased along with England's: thus, "the bourgeois revolution."

The English Civil War began in 1640 and ended in 1688. The motives of those involved were mixed, and any one of a particular religious, business, or military status might well be found on either side. But the bourgeois mentality was the most viable; by the close of the seventeenth century, the bourgeoisie had begun to move toward parity with the aristocracy (monarchy and hereditary peerage), even with the Established Church playing a subsidiary and supporting role to the latter. Thus the dynamic new economic forces and the more traditional political and social values came into an uneasy but workable balance, a balance that has yet to disappear totally in Great Britain. The structure of power had been decisively altered; the nation of shopkeepers had been born; capitalist control over production came to be valued *most* in the nexus of power.[9]

---

[8] The classic process had merchants and incipient monarchs working together against a feudal nobility. Where that did not occur, or where it faltered, the nation-state did not arise until centuries later. See, for example, G. Barraclough, *The Origins of Modern Germany* (New York: Putnam, 1963; originally published in 1949), esp. Part Four.

[9] The evolution of power structures was quite different elsewhere. In the United States the capitalist class, though its composition and base changed continually, started out on top, with no competitors from the past and the ability to sweep any potential competitors into its net or aside. The American businessman was able both to create and to control the political and social ("normative") sources of power—i.e., the system of government, the political system, and religious and educational institutions all accepted the directions and values established by business. The historically evolved patterns in Germany, Italy, Japan, and France were different from each other and from the United Kingdom and the U.S. See Barrington Moore, Jr., op. cit.,

The State as a System of Power

Who most valued this control over production? Not, surely the simple folk who found themselves swept off the land and into the brutal
conditions of the towns, the mines, mills, and factories, with increasing
tempo and ruthlessness; nor the women and children who pulled coal
carts deep in the mines or tended spindles for twelve or more hours a
day. What is valued and why does not tell us much about the acquisition of power; the *who* is always important, the who and their location
in the structure of power as society moves through time.

Except for revolutionary periods, alterations in the structure of power
are brought about by those already sitting fairly high in the structure;
the alteration allows them to move up even more. The Tudor and Stuart
dynasties that led England toward the civil war that in turn reduced the
power of the Crown did *not* value economic matters above all else; that
honor was reserved for their own noble attributes. But of necessity the
monarchs did value rising economic strength in England, without which
England would have been subdued by the feisty rivalries of the sixteenth
and seventeenth centuries. So men of trade, industry, and finance rose to
positions of influence and importance, each step making the next easier.[10]
Politics and opinion, education and literature, paid increasing homage—
and more criticism—to the new men of affairs; religious standards subtly
but surely altered in their favor (as Tawney shows brilliantly in his essay
introducing *The Discourse Upon Usury*, cited earlier). The English
Civil War signified that the complex of new structures had reached an
impasse; existing political institutions, the formal structure within which
power works, had to be revised. A new State system was needed, a
system suited to surging capitalism.

The modern capitalist *State system*, as Miliband sees it, has many
components: government; administration and bureaucracy; military,
paramilitary, and security forces; the judiciary; lesser (local and state)
governments; and legislative assemblies (federal and other). But Nicos
Poulantzas, one of the most creative of recent Marxian theorists of the
State, transcends Miliband's definition of the State system as in the
following:

> The system of the State is composed of *several apparatuses* or *institu-
> tions* of which certain have a principally repressive role, in the strong

for some of the appropriate analysis. For the English Civil War as a process, see
Christopher Hill, *Reformation to Revolution*, and Michael Walzer, *The Revolution of
the Saints* (New York: Atheneum, 1968).

[10] An important and illuminating analysis of this process is Henri Pirenne, "The
Stages in the Social History of Capitalism," *American Historical Review*, Vol. XIX,
No. 3 (April, 1914), pp. 494–515.

sense, and others a principally ideological role. The former constitute the repressive apparatus of the State, that is to say the State apparatus in the classical Marxist sense of the term (government, army, police, tribunals and administration). The latter constitute the *ideological apparatuses of the State*, such as the Church, the political parties, the unions (with the exception, of course, of the *revolutionary* party or trade union organizations), the schools, the mass media (newspapers, radio, television), and, from a certain point of view, the family. This is so whether they are *public* or *private*. . . . This position is in a certain sense that of Gramsci himself, although one he did not sufficiently found and develop.[11]

Miliband's response to this analytical alteration is itself an important contribution, both to his own and the general understanding of the State. He says, in direct reply to Poulantzas:

I am extremely dubious about this. . . . [Just] as it is necessary to show that the institutions mentioned . . . *are* part of a system of power, and that they are, as Poulantzas says, increasingly linked to and buttressed by the state, so is it important not to blur the fact that they are not, in bourgeois democracies, part of the state but of the political system. These institutions *are* increasingly subject to a process of "statization"; and . . . that process is likely to be enhanced by the fact that the state must, in the conditions of permanent crisis of advanced capitalism, assume ever greater responsibility for political indoctrination and mystification.[12]

The debate between Miliband and Poulantzas, and the numerous other differences on the Left concerning the State, are of great importance both analytically and politically—one must, after all, understand the State if it is to be overthrown. While we cannot attempt either to pursue further or to settle those vital controversies, we can emphasize the importance of examining them carefully. Underlying those controversies is the epigrammatic Marxian view of the State as stated in the Communist Manifesto: "The executive of the modern state is but a

[11] Italics in original. The structure elucidated by Miliband is found in Chapter 3 of his *The State in Capitalist Society,* and it is much elaborated upon in Chapters 4 through 8. (What I call "lesser governments" Miliband classifies as "sub-central.") This quotation is taken from the important debate between Poulantzas and Miliband in Blackburn, *Ideology in Social Science* (pp. 238–62) in which Poulantzas, in keeping with his own major work, *Political Power and Social Classes* (London: New Left Books, 1973) furnishes a searching (and friendly) critique of Miliband's *The State in Capitalist Society,* and the latter replies. Some of this is well discussed in the Gold et al. essays noted above. It may be noted that Poulantzas raises the name of Gramsci, whose ideas have become fundamental to many on the Left both in Europe and the U.S., and concerning whom we shall have much to say subsequently.

[12] Ibid., pp. 261–62. His emphasis.

committee for managing the common affairs of the whole bourgeoisie." Whether that means that the State system, however defined, responds directly or indirectly ("instrumentally" or "structurally" or in terms of "consciousness and ideology") [13] is a matter for further research, debate, and analytical testing. Here we may at least state with great firmness that however that debate proceeds and concludes, it has already made the notions of "pluralists" seem almost comic in their cheerful banalities. Neither Marx nor Veblen developed a truly systematic understanding of the State; their observations on power and the State, however trenchant they may have been, left an enormous amount to be done. After a long hiatus in which little *was* done, the task has been taken up, in most hopeful ways, as suggested above. We already know that power is held and used in complex ways; those who would transform its present sources and uses and who seek to replace it with more human forces will have to work with all the necessary distinctions in mind.

The State system (whether narrowly or broadly defined) is the system though which power flows; within it power grows, for use within and outside the State system itself. The State system, like the larger social system which it represents, is oligarchic and pyramidal in structure: a powerful few at the top and people of some but not much power in the middle; the mass of participants in the State system (as in the economic system) are mere hirelings. Within each of the six categories noted by Miliband (and to be elaborated upon below) the pyramidal structure is reproduced. As between the categories there is a difference between higher and lower: top federal government positions are usually in the State elite; while top local positions usually are not, for example.

The *sources* of power are diverse, with control over the means of production the most important. The framework through which power is *used* to affect the State system is the framework of politics; the political system. The forms or institutions of politics, like the sources of power, are diverse: power is applied through *pressure*—in and through political parties, and directly on (or in) the agencies of the State through lobbies—whether industrial, agricultural, financial, labor, religious, or professional lobbies (such as the AMA or the ABA). Also, the more powerful interested groups can more directly affect the top layers of the State, and entrench its representatives there (for example, in the president's Cabinet). However, as Poulantzas states, ". . . the *direct* participation of members of the capitalist class in the State apparatus and in the government, even where it exists, is not the important side of the matter." [14]

---

[13] See Part 1 of the Gold et al. essays for these distinctions and a valuable discussion that centers upon them.

[14] In Blackburn, *Ideology in Social Science*, p. 245. His emphasis. The reasoning of Poulantzas on this matter is subsequently agreed with by Miliband, although in a complicated way. See *ibid.*, pp. 258–59.

These component parts of the political system are constantly seeking to bend the State system to their wills; they are also among the legitimators of that system and the larger society over which it presides. Let us examine in more detail these elements of State power.

Competition Among the Few

In the American State system, the *government* is the executive branch: the president, his cabinet, and his top aides. The government is not the State, but the government speaks for the State. As Miliband puts it,

> . . . the state . . . is a nebulous entity; and while men may choose to give their allegiance to it, it is to the government that they are required to give their obedience. A defiance of its orders is a defiance of the state, in whose name the government alone may speak and for whose actions it must assume ultimate responsibility.[15]

Electoral contests for control of the government are contests for who shall interpret and represent the interests of the State. Except in revolutionary or counterrevolutionary periods, however, these contests take place within narrow limits—narrow enough, *usually,* that the expression "Tweedledee and Tweedledum" has come to characterize them more often than not. However, in times of rapid social change, contests for power *within* the system, reflecting divisions of opinion between the most substantial groups, led to more important electoral choices. Ours are such times.[16]

The next sector of the State system, *administration* and *bureaucracy,* includes the numerous public and semipublic agencies (such as the Federal Trade Commission, which is a public agency, and the Federal Reserve System, which is semipublic). These agencies are presumed to work in harmony with government, and usually do. Whether they do or not is not a matter of statute; they are not necessarily responsible to the executive. Their heads are frequently appointed for periods that extend beyond the government of one term. (The seven directors of the Federal Reserve Board, for instance, are appointed for fourteen years, staggered

[15] *The State in Capitalist Society,* p. 50.

[16] Poulantzas is useful on this point when he refers to " . . . fractions of the capitalist class . . . [and] existent differences and relations under imperialism between comprador monopoly capital, national monopoly capital, non-monopoly capital, industrial capital, [and] financial capital. . . ." In Blackburn, op. cit., p. 244. "Comprador monopoly capital" refers to interests in an underdeveloped—i.e., imperialized—country's capitalist class—simultaneously a *dependent* and an *exploitive* group in the world-economic system.

over time.) The largest number of the working members of such agencies are civil servants, subject to neither appointment nor election. Although presumably devoid of "political" inclinations, in fact (and especially at the top) their political leanings are strong, and tend to be well-known when they come into conflict with the executive (for example, Arthur Burns, as Chairman of the Board of Governors of the Federal Reserve System, at one time or another under Nixon). The persistent tendency for these administrators, as for virtually everyone at the top levels of the State system, is to be conservative—which tends to mean "liberal" in today's usage—and to be drawn from the top business or professional levels of society.

The *military, paramilitary,* and *security forces* of the State will receive a separate treatment when, later, we seek to evaluate the role of the Pentagon in the current power structure; here they will merely be characterized. As the coercive elements of the State, they serve the government of the day and its foreign and domestic policies, although they are independent of executive control with regard to appointment for all but the very top positions. In the past thirty years or so, this coercive force has grown most. Again, Miliband:

> Nowhere has the inflation of the military establishment been more marked since the second world war than in the United States, a country which had previously been highly civilian-oriented. And much the same kind of inflation has also occurred in the forces of "internal security," not only in the United States; it is probably the case that never before in any capitalist country, save in Fascist Italy and Nazi Germany, has such a large proportion of people been employed on police and repressive duties of one kind or another.[17]

The *judicial* sector of the State system is presumed to be independent of the interests of the government; it is concerned with continuity and adherence to established law. The top federal judges are appointed for life by the president; such appointments are among the juiciest plums in the orchard of patronage that enhances the power of the presidency. Presidents are often in conflict with one or another of Supreme Court and other federal judges; and this is an additional reason why presidents cherish their right to appoint. Viewed over the long run, however, the range of conflict is narrow. The memory of man knoweth not the appointment of a federal judge who questioned the fundaments of the American capitalist system, least of all the sanctity of private property.

[17] Ibid., p. 52. That was written in 1969. In those days such statements about the scope of "internal security" forces (meaning, in the U.S., the CIA and the FBI) were pooh-poohed by the stalwarts of the mainstream. Little did we know, then, how very much more extensive, "illegal," intrusive, and repressive these forces have been—and remain, as the congressional inquiries of the mid-1970's have divulged.

Veblen puts it wryly: "In the nature of the case the [property] owner alone has any standing in court. All of which argues that there are probably very few courts that are in any degree corrupt or biased. . . . Efforts to corrupt them would be a work of supererogation, besides being immoral." [18]

What Miliband calls "sub-central government"—that is, local, county, and state governments—in the United States is a bewildering array that reproduces in form and function most of the State system, but at a lower level of power and importance. For day-to-day questions of life, however, this sub-central system may be and usually is critical, in the areas of education, health, welfare, police, housing, and transportation, for example. This welter of governments is the prime channel through which much of the power of the State runs; it also is the channel through which the voice of local and regional interests and attitudes is conveyed to the State élite. They are, as Miliband remarks, "power structures in their own right" (p. 53).

The final segment of the State system as defined by Miliband is the *legislative assembly:* the two branches of Congress (with their counterparts in state and local assemblies). Historically, Congress has provided both conflict and cooperation for the executive branch, although always within the narrowly-defined limits that characterize the behavior of the other elements of the State system. In this century, there has been a marked tendency toward concentration and centralization in the economy, as we have seen; that tendency has had its counterpart in the concentration and centralization of power in the State system. The power of the federal government vis-à-vis the separate states has grown to a disproportion that would have seemed incredible to Americans at the turn of the century; this is also true of the power of the executive branch vis-à-vis Congress.

These developments toward concentration and centralization in the economy and in the State system are both cause and result of the internationalization and militarization of the United States. Already in the 1930's respected voices were expressing alarm at how "dangerously slow and inefficient" the processes of representative government are when considerations of foreign policy are at stake. By 1952, when Eisenhower took office, "consensus" on foreign policy had been achieved between the two major parties; consensus on foreign and military policy would thenceforth mean that the executive branch would decide first and induce Congress to go through the formalities of granting what became automatic appropriations afterward. The path that led us to our present condition began to be cut out in the first years of this century; it was smoothed by the key processes of *legitimation,* now to be examined.

[18] *Theory of Business Enterprise,* p. 282n.

It's All Right . . .

Modern societies all use coercive devices of one sort or another to one degree or another; by far more important than coercion are the practices that bring about voluntary acquiescence.[19] These practices fall under the heading of legitimation. Taken together with the public and private institutions that they legitimate, the ways in which acquiescence is achieved make a grim joke of pluralistic notions of political competition, as oligopolistic economic power and modern advertising make a mockery of notions of economic competition. Whether or not the processes to be described constitute conscious *deception* to achieve their consequences is not important; indeed, the high probability that what the legitimators do they do out of principled conviction rather than guile makes their impact all the more powerful.

Politically, we grow up within a universe of discourse in which certain matters are taken for granted and others lie beyond the pale. We are socialized to be deaf and blind and dumb on a range of matters, the more so the more basic they are to the society's functioning. The process is not much different in its results from that which affects our tastes in food. Certain foods, enjoyed in other lands, are seen as repulsive or as non-foods; so it is with political questions.

Of course *anything* can be discussed. Whether or not an audience will assemble or listen, or, if it does, will move in suggested ways, is a matter of who is saying what to whom. At any time there is an undesigned apparatus that sustains the largest elements of the status quo. The constituent elements of that apparatus vary from time to time and place to place, of course. They include: the major political parties; the media; the educational system; religious institutions; popular cultural life (including TV and organized athletics); public relations and advertising; the family—in short, much of what Poulantzas refers to as the *ideological apparatus* of the State. From cradle to grave, we are enclosed within certain options and views presented as reasonable; contrary options and views are easily dismissed as "idealistic," "foolish," "alien," "juvenile," or "dangerous" with regard to job, to security, to virtue, to almost anything. Legitimation is one side of a conservative process whose other side is socialization.

Those who are heard most clearly and most frequently in and from the apparatus noted above are those at the top of its parts: political

[19] The relevant processes and relationships comprise and create what Antonio Gramsci called "the hegemony of the bourgeoisie." I shall discuss Gramsci at some length in the final chapter; until then it may be useful to point to an excellent introduction to his principal contributions: Eugene Genovese, "On Antonio Gramsci." in his *In Red and Black,* cited earlier. Genovese sees Gramsci as the "greatest Western Marxist theorist of our century," a judgment with which I would readily concur.

leaders; the major commentators in the media; the establishment in the universities and schools; religious leaders; the most popular figures in entertainment and sports; the largest corporations; our parents. Parents become so through the processes of nature (and become less so in modern society); social leaders rise to the top because they function effectively with the existing system. Few people ever come to doubt a system that allows them to rise to high levels of income and status; most, indeed, find totally praiseworthy a system that is able to recognize their special talents. They are believers when they begin; true believers as they rise. By comparison, dissenters are usually seen as scruffy; are usually of low income and status; are often angry, distraught, complaining; or worse. All this should be obvious; let us look at the news media for illustration.

The Pentagon Papers informed Americans of the conscious deception practiced by Administrations on both the media and the public with regard to the war in Indochina. The Papers tell us nothing of the systematic bias of the news media in presenting what they know regarding controversies over foreign policy, labor struggles, protest groups, and the like.[20] In the media, too, there has been a process of concentration and centralization, with most Americans now getting most of their ideas —insofar as they are gotten through the media—through one "local" newspaper (usually owned elsewhere), and three national TV networks and their star commentators.

Those who own and control the media are, of course, businessmen, who are in it for money, and naturally inclined to keep from rocking the boat. If that is not always true of the reporters who work for the distinctly conservative publishers and network executives, the pressure is great for it to become so. News that smells of criticism is modified, truncated, or, more frequently, not presented. Reporters who would make their way do not make it by filing unprinted stories. Advertisers complain; readers and viewers complain; presidents and vice-presidents complain. Reporters ship out or shape up. (Investigative reporter Daniel Schorr, for example, was removed from his post at CBS and brought before a Senate committee for his refusal to reveal sources on a CIA story.) The news takes on all the qualities of a rooting-section at a football game, with the newspeople rooting for our side—that is, the status quo. Our generals are brave, resourceful, even humane; theirs are sneaky, treacherous, cruel. Businessmen are responsible; strike leaders are reckless of the interests of the economy and of their rank and file. Police are

---

[20] Thus, the hundreds of pages detailing thousands of incidents involving deception (mostly about Vietnam), found in Halberstam's *Best and the Brightest*, necessarily depend upon information accumulated over many years—but not brought to light systematically by those who knew until years, too many years, later. Everyone at the top—of the government, the media, of business—is on the "team."

also brave, beleaguered, patient; protestors are violent, amoral, wild-eyed. Doubtless this systematic dichotomy in adjectives is for some commentators a matter of playing the game; for most it is a matter of developed conviction. The road to the top is a finishing school.[21]

Turning to the more general process of legitimation, there can be little doubt that the most insistent and respected voice in the United States is the voice of business. That is only partly because most "professionals"—doctors, lawyers, publishers, entertainers, and athletes—have a high regard for making money, whatever else they may take seriously. Mainly, it is because, as was noted in Chapter 3, a capitalist society depends for its health on a healthily functioning business sector. Policies that might militate against that would cause a "loss of confidence" among businessmen. For most people in the United States there is no lively awareness of or interest in an alternative to the capitalist economy; the possibility of such a loss of confidence is tantamount to the possibility of unspeakable economic disaster. In short, business has the open respect of the entire society, except for the few who criticize business, and who thus forfeit respect in the process.

The pressures brought to bear on the State system are therefore the pressures of business people or business-minded people; the people who occupy the top and middle posts of the State system are almost entirely people from the middle or upper class. Prior education, aspiration, and function prepare those who are called to be deserving of their responsibilities. The United States Senate, once known as a "rich man's club," still deserves that description for all but a very few; but so does the rest of the top drawer of the State system.[22]

---

[21] Despite the craven quality of most of the media, the few honorable exceptions have existed and have drawn the wrath of (especially) Presidents Johnson and Nixon, with the latter using the Federal Communications Commission and Spiro Agnew as weapons to achieve purification—unsuccessfully, Watergate allowed one to believe. An excellent survey of "How the news media use bias, distortion and censorship to manipulate public opinion" is Robert Cirino, *Don't Blame the People** (New York: Random House; Vintage, 1971). Cirino documents the charges contained in the foregoing subtitle, for a long list of issues: hunger, auto safety, smoking, pollution, the Indochinese war, and much else. An older, marvelously written and deeply-revealing book is the series of essays by A. J. Liebling, *The Press** (New York: Ballantine Books, 1961). See also James Aronson, *The Press and the Cold War** (Indianapolis: Bobbs-Merrill, 1970). The collection of essays by I. F. Stone, *In a Time of Torment* (New York: Random House, 1967) adds up to news that only Stone saw fit to print, which required his own *I. F. Stone's Weekly*. His *Hidden History of the Korean War** (New York: Monthly Review Press, 1952) also pertinent in this connection, is now coming to be seen as the authentic and damning explanation of that war. The book was assiduously ignored by journalists and scholars until recently; its lessons have yet to be absorbed.

[22] C. Wright Mills, in his *Power Elite*, cited earlier, in his *White Collar** (New York: Oxford University Press, 1951), and in his *New Men of Power: America's Labor Leaders* (New York: Harcourt Brace Jovanovich, 1948) analyzes all this gen-

From State to States to Superstate

The foregoing discussion applies as a sketch outline of the State system in the United States today. The nineteenth-century conditions were different both in form and content. An examination of three of the conflicts that marked that century will serve the twofold function of highlighting the differences while at the same time revealing the central role of power in the process of social change: 1) the so-called Bank War; 2) the Civil War; 3) the Populist uprising. These conflicts represent, respectively, the successful struggle for laissez-faire capitalism; the triumph of industry and finance over agriculture and commerce as the center of capitalist dynamism; and, finally, the last gasp of Jeffersonian democracy. Each sought to alter the State system or, as in the case of Populism, to restore an idealized past.

Bank War

One of the first achievements of the triumphant English bourgeoisie after their Glorious Revolution was the creation of the Bank of England; the First Bank of the United States, chartered for twenty years in 1791, was designed to serve much the same purposes for the United States. Both were "central banks"; that is, bankers' banks, endowed with the responsibility of influencing the supply of money and the rate of interest in the direction of the public interest. Mercantilist in their origins, central banks have become a key feature of all modern capitalist economies. The United States is unique in having created, allowed to lapse, re-created, and then destroyed its central bank. From the 1830's until the creation of the Federal Reserve System (our present central banking system) in 1913, the United States was the only major capitalist economy without a central bank, which was destroyed in the middle of Andrew Jackson's two terms as president.

The charter of the First Bank of the U.S. lapsed, amidst controversy, in 1811. The monetary chaos that followed encouraged the chartering of the Second Bank of the U.S. (1816–1836). One-fifth of the Bank's stock was owned by the federal government; the rest was in private hands. The Bank served as a repository for federal funds, most important of which were payments for public lands and customs collections. In that period, the latter amounted to about 90 percent of all governmental revenues. Currency at the time was in the form of banknotes; that is, promises to pay in specie to the bearer the face value of the bank-

---

erally and with specific application to businessmen, the professions, and labor. G. William Domhoff, following in Mill's tradition, relates these matters to the social and political setting in a definitive manner. See *Who Rules America?* (cited earlier) and *The Higher Circles** (New York: Random House; Vintage, 1971).

note. The issuing banks were predominantly private banks chartered by state governments, and the Second Bank issued its own banknotes, the soundest of the time. When a Kentucky bank paid, say, $1000 to the federal government for a land purchase, or when a New York bank paid $1000 in customs collections for an importer, those banks were placing their notes in the hands of the Second Bank. The Second Bank became their creditor; it could demand specie in return for the note. The notes of the various banks came into existence in response to loans to the banks' customers. The banks, creditors to their customers, were debtors of the Second Bank. The latter's ability to demand specie was the power to curtail the lending capacities of the banking community. In turn, that meant that the Bank had critical control over the uses of the economic surplus. Power over the extension of credit then as now also meant power to influence the nature and direction of economic activity.[23] Then as now, such power is among the most important political powers; then as now, the power rests in mostly private hands, or in the hands of those congenial to the banking community.

The Second Bank itself made loans; that was its principal business. It was a profit-making institution, as well as one having public purposes. Quite naturally, other banks saw the Second Bank as a competitor, and one with extraordinary power. The Second Bank's directors and owners tended to represent the older and more powerful mercantile and financial interests of the new nation, and especially those in Philadelphia. By the 1820's, New York City was rising in strength, Baltimore was seeking to do so, and the West was opening up rapidly. The bankers, land speculators, and merchants in those and comparable areas saw the Bank as "the monster of Chestnut Street." Andrew Jackson, vowing to destroy the Bank, made it the central issue of his re-election campaign of 1832.[24]

[23] Today, loans result in checking deposits for the borrower. Private banks no longer (since the 1930's) issue banknotes. The First and Second Banks of the United States were *creditors* of the banking community; the Federal Reserve System is a *debtor*. Member banks (about half of all banks, controlling about 85 percent of all deposits) must keep about one-fifth of their deposits on reserve in the Federal Reserve System. The latter exercises its influence on the supply of money and credit and the interest rate through means that alter the amount of reserves or the amount required. See any economics textbook for explanation.

[24] The Bank was located on Chestnut Street, in Philadelphia. The head of the Bank by the late 1820's was Nicholas Biddle, an astute and strong-minded banker in his own right. The best and most comprehensive discussion of the relevant issues is Bray Hammond, *Banks and Politics in America From the Revolution to the Civil War* (Princeton: Princeton University Press, 1957). The most popular book, which received the Pulitzer Prize, is Arthur Schlesinger, Jr., *The Age of Jackson*° (Boston: Little, Brown, 1946). It is a model of intensive scholarship combined with unsupportable interpretation, as Hammond shows, dominated by Schlesinger's attempt to find justification for elements of the New Deal. Hammond's own book is very much dominated by *his* contemporary concerns; namely, to support a strong Federal

Jackson, who had risen to the presidency because of his military exploits as the "Hero of New Orleans" (1815) and his campaigns against Indian tribes, was a planter and friend of the larger propertied interests in Tennessee. He was thought to speak for the common man. In his fight against Biddle and the Second Bank his most numerous supporters were the western farmers and the urban workers of the East. Standing less noisily behind them, however, were the bankers, merchants, manufacturers, and land speculators who saw the credit-restraining powers of the Second Bank as the last remaining obstacle to rapid increases in their fortunes. Jackson won re-election in 1832; the Second Bank, although its charter had four years left to run, was rendered ineffectual. The relatively concentrated financial and mercantile structure of power was displaced, pushed aside by a rapacious, rugged and uncontrolled laissez-faire capitalism. Politically, this meant that the jealousies of the individual states as against the federal government were institutionalized: the era of effective "states' rights" accelerated. In practice this meant that raw economic power was the almost pure representation of State power for the rest of the century. The "great barbecue" would shortly begin.

Civil War

The forces unleashed by the destruction of the Bank led to a great step-up in all forms of economic expansion: banks multiplied (there were over 10,000 separate banknotes by the 1850's); trade and industry spread from the Atlantic seaboard out to the Mississippi; canals and railroads tied the broad land together; soils, minerals, and forests were exploited with abandon. A new economic structure took shape; the political structure lagged behind.

We need only summarize briefly what was discussed earlier concerning the South: the South by the 1820's was the leading sector of the American economy, with its King Cotton. The South's economic needs and its social system gave it a viewpoint on matters of the State profoundly different from that coming to be held by the manufacturers, merchants, and financiers of the North. But up to the Civil War, the South held the largest part of the strategic posts in the State system.

The South used its rivers and its coasts for the bulk of its transportation needs; the North needed canals and railroads. The South exported its cotton and imported manufactures; the North wanted protection for its growing industries. The South had a labor supply over which it was both economically and politically unchallenged; the North was faced with labor short in supply and politically free. The South's needs for

Reserve System. History is seldom written by people without serious interests in their own present, which is a virtue, not a vice. But it is well for both the historians and their readers to be explicitly conscious of those interests.

westward expansion were modest as compared with the temptations and needs facing the North and West. In short, the South wanted a State system that was suited to planter capitalism; the North needed a system that would enhance industrial capitalism and rapid westward expansion.

Slavery was of course the major *public* issue of the Civil War. Whether it was the most important causal issue is another matter.[25] We can do little to reconstruct the inner motivation of those in the past. But one can gain useful insights into what those involved in a struggle wanted most by seeing what those who won did with their enhanced power. The slaves were freed, of course. But within a few years the promises of "forty acres and a mule" were shelved; more important, arrangements were made between the triumphant North and the defeated South to allow the latter to regain full sway over its internal politics in exchange for northern control of the federal government and easy access to the investment possibilities of the South—in railroads, timber, land speculation, and the like.[26] The new State system removed all obstacles to the full possibilities of industrial capitalism in the United States. All obstacles but one, that is; that one, the lingering belief in America's promises as a democracy, underlay the Populist struggle toward the end of the century.

Vox Populi

The Populist struggle, perhaps because it contained so much of the hopes and fears of Americans, has been misrepresented in histories from its own day (the 1890's) until now. It is seen generally as having its center in the Middle West; actually, the South, and especially the Deep South, was its stronghold. It is viewed as centering on money fanaticism, which may represent its midwestern spokesmen, but did not represent Populism. It is viewed as being inextricably mixed with racism; in fact, the Populist movement in the South brought the only years—and they were few—in which racial egalitarianism was practiced, and in which poor whites and blacks fought shoulder to shoulder, politically and physically.[27]

[25] For an informative analysis of this point, see Barrington Moore, "The American Civil War: The Last Capitalist Revolution," Chapter III of his *Social Origins*, cited earlier.

[26] C. Vann Woodward, *Reunion and Reaction**° (New York: Doubleday; Anchor, 1956) provides a definitive interpretation of the sordid "Compromise of 1877 and the End of Reconstruction," the consequences of which included the conservative-racist coalition still central to our social existence.

[27] C. Vann Woodward is probably the most astute and humane of leading historians on the South. His essay "The Populist Heritage and the Intellectual," in his collection *The Burden of Southern History*° (New York: Random House; Vintage, 1961) is a

The distinction must be made between populist tendencies and Populism. The former is a collection of conflicting notions which more often reflects the biases of those who recount them, rather than the nature of Populism. Populism was a movement based on the dire needs of its main participants and a nostalgic and hopeful view of what could be and was "supposed to be." It sought to reassert the hegemony of ordinary people, while not doubting the desirability of basic capitalist institutions. Small farmers, small businessmen, and workers were seen as the true heart and muscle of America; the State should be their instrument and their protector—against Big business, Big banks, Big railroads, and the misuse of government. Those were the Populists' wishes; their needs were the father of those wishes. They found themselves faced with ruinously falling prices and a shortage of credit; with extortionate rail rates and commission charges; with manipulated commodity exchanges; with state and even more federal legislatures, and especially the Senate, that responded to the direct pressures of the most powerful. By 1896 they also found that the leadership of their movement had come under the domination of a distorted view of their aims —"free silver"—and a Nebraskan, William Jennings Bryan, who represented not only what was slightest in Populism but worst in America. Whether Bryan revealed his ultimate essence when he became Secretary of State under Wilson or prosecutor of Scopes in the famous "monkey trial" is a matter of dispute; but his essence lay somewhere other than in the central position of the Populists.

Populism was dying well before the election of 1896 gave it the *coup de grâce*. Taking no chances, the massive GOP campaign of 1896 was the first truly modern political campaign. Master-minded by Marcus Hanna, a Cleveland shipping, banking, transportation, and newspaper magnate, the campaign made regular assessments on businesses, engaged in widely-publicized scare tactics, and effectively scattered the opponents of big business rule, the "communists" of the day. In the South the period saw a new and more intensified set of segregation ("Jim Crow") laws, accompanied by waves of lynchings. By then the popular heart of Populism was muffled, its racial egalitarianism had been replaced by confusion and hatred, its social and political goals had given way to narrow economic criteria, measured by the level of farm prices. The removal of Populism sped up even more the consolidation of economic power that Populism had resisted. The State system moved toward "political capitalism," as the economy moved toward monopoly capitalism. Institutionalized racism came to be as much a part of the urban North as slavery

balanced appraisal of Populism. See also Chapters 8 and 9 of his *Origins of the New South*, cited earlier. For black/white cooperation, see Jack Abramowitz, "The Negro in the Populist Movement," *Journal of Negro History*, vol. 38, no. 3 (July, 1953).

had been in the South;[28] white Americans went about their business and looked the other way. And, already in 1897, the drums of overseas imperialism had begun to sound for Americans who very soon would march to them, again and again. The present act of the American drama had begun; the mass of Americans became a background chorus to it, mixing laughs with screams, cheers with anger. Most stood silently, hoping for the best with their eye on the main chance—some seeking the big bonanza, most just trying to hold on.

Lost Democracy

The opening years of this century for many Americans seemed very much like our own times; it was an age of dislocation.

> The decline of political democracy and the rise of monopolies were not the only dark aspects of American civilization. Among those which called for remedy were the gross inequality of wealth, wide existence of poverty, racial inequality, the domination by big business of politics, religion, education, and the courts, the selfish and stupid waste of natural resources, carelessness of human life, exploitation of women and children. ... America's new rulers were the "robber barons" and her new God, Financial Success.[29]

The accompanying hue and cry of social criticism was begun by writers and reformers, conscious that things were getting out of joint; the policies that ultimately ensued were shaped and controlled by businessmen and the politicians who suited them. Reformers awakened business to the chaos of the time, threatening not least to business.

Able to organize their own kind, and powerful enough to move things, big business brought order out of that chaos. It was order cut to their needs and aims, cut to the needs of industrial capitalism. Thus the Progressive Movement, frequently seen as an anti-business reformist movement, resulted in a set of far-reaching changes which strengthened the hold of business on America. And the Progressives' "respectable reforms" also did much to take the steam out of popular discontent. For that to happen, the hold of business criteria had to extend itself deeply and consciously into the State system, which in turn had to be expanded and strengthened to assure domestic and international order.[30]

[28] Not without a firm foundation in the pre-Civil War past, however, as Osofsky, cited earlier, and Leon F. Litwack, *North of Slavery: The Negro in the Free States, 1790–1860** (Chicago: University of Chicago Press, 1961) both make crystal clear.

[29] Faulkner, *The Decline of Laissez Faire*, pp. 368 69.

[30] These generalizations, and many to follow, depend upon the important historical revisions about the period developed by Gabriel Kolko in *The Triumph of Conservatism*, and James Weinstein in *The Corporate Ideal in the Liberal State, 1900–1918*, both cited earlier. Probably without intending to do so, Robert H. Wiebe, *Business-*

In the days just before the Nazi seizure of power, a respected German economist noted:

> The animosity of German capitalism against the state does not rest upon fundamental theoretical foundations, but upon purely opportunistic considerations. It is opposed to the state when control is in the hands of a political majority whose permanent good will it doubts. German capitalism, which would like to be freed of the power of the state, and which seeks to push back state intervention as far as possible, is constructed exclusively upon the most thorough intervention of the state.[31]

German capitalists had worked steadily to devise a State system suited to their needs throughout most of the nineteenth century. American business, operating in a much less stringent social and natural context, needed only to be left alone: laissez-faire (plus tariffs and gifts) was just right. The rapid and pervasive industrial development that swept America at the end of the nineteenth century, however, created a set of problems that individual businesses, no matter how large, could not resolve by themselves. Public institutions were needed to provide the requisite scope. Advanced industrial capitalism, even in the United States, requires social institutions that will prevent its precarious and fruitful interdependencies from becoming a source of breakdown, whether economic, social, or political. In short, *rationalization* becomes a necessity.

The term rationalization is many-sided in its meaning, for it is designed to cope with diverse problems. Brady, in his massive study of the German rationalization movement of the 1920's, comments that:

> . . . rationalization was begun, and largely carried through, at a time when forces were converging to undermine the institutional framework of German capitalism. As the rationalization movement developed, it became increasingly clear that its progress was to be conditioned by the solution of numerous issues directly related to the radical and far-reaching changes that were taking place in the political, economic, and social institutions of the country. The drift to the two extreme wings, and the politicization of nearly the whole range of economic problems, meant that these issues were to be resolved, if at all, in an atmosphere of bitterness, struggle, and drawn compromise.[32]

*men and Reform** (Chicago: Quadrangle, 1968) presents data that allow the same conclusions. Kolko centers on the ability of the largest corporations to use the State to curb uncontrolled competition and to reduce instability; Weinstein emphasizes the role of the large corporations and their National Civic Federation in conscious displacement of laissez-faire, over the opposition of the smaller companies and the National Association of Manufacturers.

[31] Quoted in Robert A. Brady, *Business as a System of Power*, p. 294, from M. J. Bonn, *Das Schicksal des deutschen Kapitalismus* (1931).

[32] Robert A. Brady, *The Rationalization Movement in German Industry* (Berkeley: University of California Press, 1933), p. xiv. The "two extreme wings" were socialism and fascism.

Although both the timing and the content of the German movement were different from comparable developments in the United States, the impulses were fundamentally alike. In the U.S. their beginnings were in the Progressive Movement, in the decade or so preceding World War I. As Kolko notes:

> Progressivism was initially a movement for the political rationalization of business and industrial conditions, a movement that operated on the assumption that the general welfare of the community could be best served by satisfying the concrete needs of business. But the regulation itself was invariably controlled by leaders of the regulated industry, and directed toward ends they deemed acceptable or desirable. In part this came about because the regulatory movements were usually initiated by the dominant businesses to be regulated, but it also resulted from the nearly universal belief among political leaders in the basic justice of private property relations as they essentially existed, a belief that set the ultimate limits on the leaders' possible actions.[33]

The Burdens of Success

The problems that led to these new political needs ranged through the whole society. The absence of a central bank and other control institutions in the economy allowed normal fluctuations to translate into severe panics and depressions. The depression of the 1890's was unprecedentedly deep; the "Panic of 1907" was a panic in more than name. The giant corporations that emerged from the immense combination movement of 1897–1904 behaved with no more recklessness than businesses always had; now, however, they were no longer mice but bulls in a china shop. National markets for interdependent industries meant pervasive and deeper crises. Business competition had always been alarming to the businesses competed with; the heavy industrialization of the new century made alarm an inadequate reaction. Financial manipulation was a popular business sport throughout the nineteenth century; in the twentieth century it brought Wall Street and a host of other financial enclaves

---

[33] Kolko, op. cit., pp. 2–3. In another study, Kolko documents these generalizations about regulation for an industry interpreted quite differently by previous students. See his *Railroads and Regulation, 1877–1916*° (Princeton: Princeton University Press, 1965). His main point is that though the impulses for regulation may arise outside the industry to be regulated (farmers, in the case of railroads), the industry comes to see regulation in its own interests, and shapes the legislation to assure that outcome. The conclusion, in the light of the history of regulated industries, seems inescapable; however, most conventional observers, seeing each reaffirming instance as an aberration, have let the conclusion slip through their flimsy analytical nets.

crashing down. Business could no longer afford to cavort heedlessly; it had to settle down.

Much the same was true of the exploitation of our natural resources, as was noted earlier. Mining the soil, cutting over timber lands, and the spoliation of mineral resources had brought great profits: if continued in the same way and in greater amounts, such exploitation would dry up its sources. Resource management was necessary: resource management by business. Nor were human resources in a different category. Housing, labor conditions, and welfare had never been a matter of keen concern for those who built the cities and hired the workers, but the scope of such activities had never been as great as they suddenly appeared to be in the new century. Urban housing and welfare reform and some mitigation of harsh labor exploitation were put forth as necessities; they would not stop the running sores, but they might at least cover them. Mostly, not even that happened.

From the Spanish-Cuban-American War up through World War I, the presidency passed from McKinley to Roosevelt to Taft to Wilson. They were different types of men, and their reputations in history books emphasize those differences. But they had one characteristic in common: they provided unbroken continuity in the creation of the new "political capitalism." The solidifying developments within the State system took place in the first administration of Woodrow Wilson. The "New Nationalism" of Teddy Roosevelt translated easily into the "New Freedom" of Wilson. All four presidents found themselves occupied with foreign affairs more than any president since Jefferson: McKinley agonized into the Spanish-Cuban-American War; Roosevelt charged up San Juan Hill and created Panama and its canal; Taft served as the first American governor of the Philippine Islands; Wilson, promising to keep us out of war, sent troops to Mexico and got us into World War I. From then on public relations and manipulation developed into a high art.[34]

The continuity manifested itself in domestic as well as in imperial

---

[34] The media were blunter in the first days than since. By the time the U.S. had "pacified" the Filipinos (at the end of Taft's term as governor, 1901–04, from which he went to secretary of war, and then to president) over 300,000 had been slaughtered, not without the substantial encouragement of the leading San Francisco weekly of the time, *The Argonaut*, as exemplified by excerpts from an editorial of 1902: "There has been too much hypocrisy about this Philippine business—too much snivel—too much cant. Let us all be frank. WE DO NOT WANT THE FILIPINOS. WE WANT THE PHILIPPINES. All of our troubles in this annexation matter have been caused by the presence in the Philippine Islands of the Filipinos. . . . Touched by the wand of American enterprise, fertilized with American capital, these islands would speedily become richer than Golconda was of old. But, unfortunately, they are infested by Filipinos. . . . They are indolent . . . ; and they occupy land which might be utilized to much better advantage by Americans. Therefore the more of them killed, the better. . . ." The whole editorial is reproduced in Jacobs, et al., *To Serve the Devil*, Vol. 2 (cited earlier), pp. 335–37. The full caps are in the original.

policies: all busied themselves with conservation, with urban reform, with "trust-busting," and with financial and industrial reforms. They were the midwives of "political capitalism," which took hold after 1900, and which has been altered and strengthened from then up to the present.

Those who have come to consciousness since World War II are likely to take the ways and means of political capitalism as the "natural" state of affairs; those whose consciousness was formed in earlier decades will remember that the "normal" state of affairs for capitalist society was assumed to be one in which the State was unobtrusive in economic and other affairs. The State in the United States has always operated so as to provide an acceptable or favorable context for capitalist development; in the nineteenth century it did so largely through "non-decisions," that is, unobtrusively—except for railroad subsidies, protective tariffs, and a few other explicit policies noted above. But in the twentieth century the State's role became obtrusive, and explicit. The political outlets and institutions of the State had to be and came to be used to attain the desired conditions of stability, predictability, and security. Characterizing this development, Kolko says:

> *Stability* is the elimination of internecine competition and erratic fluctuations in the economy. *Predictability* is the ability, on the basis of politically stabilized and secured means, to plan future economic action on the basis of fairly calculable expectations. By *security* I mean protection from the political attacks latent in any formally democratic structure.[35]

There were many conflicts along the way, of course: between various aspects of the business community; between labor and business; between local and national politicians; between socialists, anti-business reformers, and those who represented business interests; between anti-imperialists and imperialists. There are always conflicts; more to the point is who wins out, and how; and one must remember that alongside those who seek what they get are those who, seeking something else, unwittingly assist those who win out.

Business criteria won out in these conflicts, but the criteria of *giant* business, not of business in general. As the century began, the giant corporations represented the most intense gathering of power in the society; because it was economic power, it translated into State power. These were the new monopolists; their breeding ground was the old competition. One of the consequences of the State system created in those years was that the movement from small to large to giant firm came to be more under control than in the nineteenth century: the new

---

[35] Kolko, *The Triumph of Conservatism*, p. 3. Italics in original.

laws and regulatory agencies put a curb on rapacious behavior within industries, much as Great Powers do with Lesser Powers in the world of Statesmanship, so that the large might be more secure against the possibilities of interlopers. It also meant a loss of whatever benefits the public may have derived from the uncontrolled warfare of business. The invisible hand that presumably transformed naked self-interest into society's well-being would have to find a different strength than price competition. The antitrust laws of the 1890's began by forbidding collusion and the "intent to monopolize." By the 1930's amendments made it illegal to engage in price competition. By the 1960's, except for curious exceptions, competition became "non-price competition," institutionalized to the point where laws against price competition were not needed.[36] In an economic world where advertising, product variation (such as, automobile model changes), sales promotion, research and development, and lobbying became the chief means of enhancing corporate strength, the battle went to the already strong, even more than it had earlier.

One of the closest students of the "era of reform," in intending to characterize the beneficent qualities of the period, says:

> By 1917 a change appeared evident in the entrepreneurial spirit and conduct of private business. The flush days of the "robber barons" had passed; leaders of business and of the larger institutions had begun to show some of the characteristics which distinguish them today [1951]. Risk and profit had become less important than security and power. . . .[37]

When the robber barons of feudal times passed from the scene, it was because their territories had come under the control of a count, a duke, a prince, or a king, with the financial assistance of the merchants upon whom the robber barons had preyed. The analogy therefore breaks down; in America the robber barons *became* the counts, dukes, and princes, and the king bent largely to their will. And, although the search for security and power is certainly what the "larger institutions" sought, they reduced risk and increased profits as a result.

The areas encompassed by these efforts cut through the entire economy, producing new laws and a new bureaucracy. Some examples:

[36] Laws forbidding price competition, such as the "Resale Price Maintenance Act" (1937), most generally called "fair trade" laws, emerged after the National Industrial Recovery Act was declared unconstitutional in 1935. The National Recovery Administration (NRA), a form of self-government in business, gave the power to fix prices (*inter alia*) to industry trade associations (in the form of "code authorities"); violators of these private agreements were punishable by law. The similarities between the provisions of the NRA and those for "self-management in industry" under the Nazis are, to say the very least, striking. See Robert A. Brady, *Spirit and Structure of German Fascism** (New York: Viking, 1937), Chapter X. A major difference is that the German laws were not declared unconstitutional.

[37] Faulkner, op. cit., p. 379.

Labor. The Clayton Antitrust Act (1914) exempted unions from the antitrust laws (although the exemption has been narrowed by judicial interpretation and subsequent legislation). The relevant parts of the Act are called "Labor's Magna Carta"; time has shown this label to be overly-effusive. In 1916, the Adamson Act provided for an eight-hour day for railway workers, the first such federal legislation. Their organization had made them among the most powerful unions (in a generally weak array) from the 1870's on; in 1926, the Railway Labor Act provided labor protections that were subsequently generalized in the Wagner Act (1935). The contest over the labor legislation of the Progressive Period well reveals the differences between "corporate liberalism" and the continuing raw laissez-faire attitudes of small business.[38]

Banking. The Glass-Owen Currency (Federal Reserve) Act of 1913 re-created the central bank for the United States. From the destruction of the Second Bank in 1832 until then, the country had been periodically rocked by banking collapse and financial panic. The National Bank Act of 1863, which passed for our national banking system until 1913, assured that when problems arose they would become more intense than without any "system" at all; this was not surprising, for the Act's original purpose was to help finance the Civil War. The Federal Reserve System was itself weak and ill-organized, as revealed by its contribution to the financial disasters of the 1920's. It was strengthened during the New Deal.

Taxation. The 16th Amendment was ratified in 1913, providing for an income tax. Although never very progressive, it was more so in 1913 than it is now (incomes below $4000 were exempt, and that was a large amount in 1913). Of taxation, more later.

Conservation. The Newlands Act of 1902 provided for the "reclamation" of arid lands through irrigation. What this meant was a bonanza for irrigation companies in gaining cheap access to the public domain, most of which was then arid. Teddy Roosevelt was an ardent conservationist.

Consumer Protection. Roosevelt was also an ardent supporter of good eating. Much impressed by Upton Sinclair's *The Jungle*, he joined reformers by creating the Pure Food and Drug Administration, and by passing the Meat Inspection Act (both 1906).

Business Regulation. The Federal Trade Act of 1914 added the Federal Trade Commission to the enforcing agency of the Justice De-

[38] See Weinstein, op. cit., Chapter Two, but also *passim.*

partment. Under Roosevelt the courts first used the Sherman Antitrust Act (1890) prohibiting collusion and the intent to monopolize against business (Northern Securities Case, 1904). In 1911, it was used to break Standard Oil into seven separate companies although the Rockefeller family was not ordered to divest itself of its ownership in the new structure. Most authorities agree that the step-up in antitrust enforcement led not to more competition, but to oligopoly—today's form of monopoly. The Hepburn Act of 1906 and the Mann-Elkins Act of 1910 gave new powers to the Interstate Commerce Commission (created in 1886) in railroad regulation. The long-run effect seems to have been that the railroads, though presumably competing with other transportation industries (truck, air, autobus), have been able to raise rates and maintain profitability despite declining and deteriorating service.

Foreign Trade. The Webb-Pomerene Export Trade Act (1918) allowed companies involved in foreign trade to form selling cartels (a means of achieving a uniform sales policy for different firms); that is, they were exempted from the antitrust laws, as a means of sharpening the already sharp edge of American competition in the world economy. As competition in the world economy revived and became severe in the early 1970's, pressures mounted to revive this policy.

In the Catbird Seat

Efforts by corporate liberals and their supporters to create a new State system after 1900 were halting, contradictory, and controversial; the onset of World War I speeded up the development, gave it coherence, and stilled controversy. The impact of the war on the economy was so beneficial, however, that in contributing to the upper echelon prosperity of the 1920's it also allowed a re-emergence of laissez-faire as the dominant business mood. The mood was one thing, the reality another.

The economic gains of the United States from the war need no further discussion; the institutional changes accompanying the sustained upsurge in production were equally significant. Businessmen, and especially those from the industries most closely connected with war production—metals, fuels, vehicles—were drawn into the councils of government as never before. They were predominantly from the large corporations. As occurred with even greater strength in World War II, the government sought to maximize production and minimize conflict in the economy. This entailed active and close cooperation between representatives of industry, agriculture, and labor, with industry as the dominant member. The Council of National Defense and the War Industries Board were the key agencies; their leading personnel were those who had also led in the creation of the new State system in the years leading up to the war.[39]

Subtly, but firmly, the easy use of State power by business became unchallenged and unchallengeable. The political habits of those who used that power and those who acquiesced in it were transformed. Those who might think differently were largely those who opposed the war and the system that presided over it: the Socialists (led by Eugene Debs). As has happened more than once, a general opposition to American involvement in a war was transformed into enthusiastic support when we became directly involved. The opposition was crushed, its leaders jailed, its ideas reviled.[40] The larger outcome was that is made possible the repression of the entire Left in the years after the war through the "Palmer raids" of 1919–1920 and the "Red Scare" that ensued (whose most famous instance was the Sacco-Vanzetti case[41]). In that period, as in the years after World War II, a major consequence of anti-Left campaigns was to remove whatever influence Left ideas had from the trade union movement, leaving the latter weak and docile. The "consensus" on foreign policy in the Cold War had its earlier counterpart in a "consensus" on domestic policy in the 1920's.

The mood of business could be laissez-faire in the 1920's because the reality was so firmly under their control as to require little in the way of explicit government intervention. The decade opened with Harding as president, followed by Coolidge and Hoover. If Harding had any distinction at all in the office, it was that he was a close competitor of Buchanan as the most mediocre of presidents, although as far as we know Buchanan lived at a somewhat higher moral leve'. Calvin Coolidge signified the temper of the times exactly. He gained the prominence he needed for presidential stature by helping to break a strike while he was Governor of Massachusetts. He was famous for saying little: "Silent Cal" was his affectionate nickname. What little he said

[39] See Soule, *Prosperity Decade*, Chapters I, II, and III.

[40] Even when, as in the case of the IWW, it took no stand against the war. For the cooperation of trade unions, the opposition by the Socialist Party, and the curious position of the IWW, see James Weinstein, *Decline of Socialism** (New York: Random House; Vintage, 1969), pp. 47–53, and his essay "The IWW and American Socialism," *Socialist Revolution*, vol. 1, no. 5 (Sept.–Oct., 1970), esp. p. 27.

[41] Wilson's Attorney General, A. Mitchell Palmer, organized raids on homes and offices of "suspected Communists." Thousands were arrested, hundreds jailed and deported. The socialist movement was still strong, the Russian Revolution was publicized as a direct threat to the U.S., immigration had been at its peak (almost a million in 1920), and strikes were numerous. Foreign-born people were most noticed among the radicals (and aliens could be deported by the Secretary of Labor if found to be "radical"). Sacco and Vanzetti were anarchist labor organizers accused and convicted in 1921 of a payroll murder in what is (and was) widely considered to be a frame-up. They were electrocuted in 1927.

was telling: "The business of America," as noted earlier, "is business." "The man who builds a factory builds a temple, the man who works there worships there, and to each is due not scorn and blame, but reverence and praise." [42]

As F. L. Allen notes in his entertaining evocation of the spirit of the twenties, *Only Yesterday*, "The great god business was supreme in the land and Calvin Coolidge was fortunate enough to become almost a demi-god by doing discreet obeisance before the altar" (p. 211). By some, the relationship between divinity and business was pushed explicitly. Bruce Barton, founder of one of the largest advertising agencies (BBD&O) wrote in 1924 what became perhaps the best-seller of the time, *The Man Nobody Knows: A Discovery of the Real Jesus*. Jesus, it appears, was "the founder of modern business."

> He picked up twelve men from the bottom ranks of business and forged them into an organization that conquered the world. . . . Nowhere is there such a startling example of executive success as the way in which that organization was brought together.[43]

The God That Failed

Hoover was a different breed of man. His critical view of the evolving State system has been misunderstood or neglected, largely because his reputation became bound up so tightly with the Depression that began in his term. Hoover was a committed adherent of capitalism; but he opposed the direct use of the State to advance the interests of capitalists. He knew, as president, that what he opposed was already a prominent feature of capitalist development. He believed in self-reliance, but self-reliance in voluntary cooperation with others with the same needs. W. A. Williams states Hoover's position as follows:

> . . . Hoover feared that the corporation leaders would produce an American form of fascism. If labor became predominant, on the other hand, the result would be socialism or some willy-nilly variation thereof. . . . If each broad interest group in the economy continued its evolving attitude of viewing the government as a marketplace in which to compete for its share of the gross wealth, then the system would ultimately be dominated

---

[42] Quoted in James W. Prothro, *Dollar Decade: Business Ideas in the 1920's* (Baton Rouge: Louisiana State University Press, 1954), p. 224. This is a revealing study of what businessmen thought at a time when they had the confidence to be candid about their social philosophy. When what is revealed is not frightening it is very funny.

[43] Quoted in Prothro, ibid., pp. 229–30. Judas Iscariot is viewed in that connection as being a bit overzealous, but of good spirit.

by a state bureaucracy which would lack even the distinguishing characteristic of a positive ideology. And wars engendered by struggles for predominance in the world marketplace threatened to produce a tyranny of even graver proportions because of the increased role and influence of the military.[44]

What Hoover feared from business was in place before he took office in 1928. Whatever cogency his ideas might have had was buried, as he was, by the avalanche of the Depression. The collapse of the economy was blamed on those who had taken credit for its achievements; everyone looked to the State for succor. As noted before, the effects of New Deal policies during the Depression were insubstantial; the major meaning of the New Deal was the manner in which it sought to flesh out the State system that has carried us into the present.

Sophisticated though corporate liberals were by comparison with small businessmen before World War I, they were not sophisticated enough to create a State system that would give any significant access to that system by those not in business. Their inclinations to do so were lessened by the roaring confidence of the 1920's. Business' fall from grace in the thirties allowed some kind of balance, however minimal, to be achieved—over the howls of rage and accusations of betrayal of some but by no means all business spokesmen. The State became explicitly interventionist in matters of the business cycle, monetary and fiscal controls, protection for labor and the aged, agriculture, and foreign trade. There were precedents for all these developments; the New Deal put them together in a new balance. The New Deal re-educated corporate leaders to what they had first begun to learn thirty years earlier; World War II and the Cold War showed them how valuable that education could be in profits, in social stability, in domestic and world power. The growth and developmental aspects of the years since the Depression were examined in Chapter 4. The stabilizing and tension-promoting aspects of the new State system will occupy the remainder of this chapter.

The Best Laid Plans . . .

The decade of the fifties comprised the years of the "great celebration," of the "silent generation," of the avuncular Eisenhower. The upsurge of left-wing attitudes and organizations from the thirties and forties had been squashed by spy scares, McCarthyism and the repression that gave it teeth, and by the often enthusiastic cooperation in these

[44] Williams, *Great Evasion*, p. 155.

endeavors by intellectual and labor leaders. Marx had become a four-letter word, Veblen a barely-known freak, the influence and power of the United States expanded all over the globe, and capitalism flourished at home.

In the midst of this quiet and complacency, C. Wright Mills wrote his *Power Élite* (1956), a biting appraisal of the State system at that time. Leading American liberals, meanwhile, were getting the materials together that allowed them to pronounce "the end of ideology," and that "the fundamental political problems of the industrial revolution have been solved. . . ."[45]

Mills was the first academic social scientist after World War II to recognize and explore the extraordinary role then being played by foreign policy and the military in the entire life of Americans and their foreign satellites. The original quality of his argument, to say nothing of its controversial nature, led to an immediate reaction from "liberal, radical, and highbrow critics." Almost all of the reaction was scornful.[46]

As Mills saw it, the "power élite" has three components: "the corporate rich," the "political directorate," and the "warlords." For Mills, as in our earlier discussion of the State system, the first two components overlap: the "political directorate" holds the top posts of the State system; those who occupy those posts are from the highest levels of business—in fact, in spirit, or in association (for instance, corporate lawyers). That is, the power élite reduces to two segments: corporate rulers and the warlords of the Pentagon. How much power the Pentagon has, and the degree of autonomy with which it can or could use that power is now a matter of substantial controversy; when Mills first made his argument about the military, it was dismissed out of hand in all quarters.

The final test of greatness for an analytical or theoretical contribution does not depend upon its being indubitably "correct," but whether or not it leads to substantial questioning, further research, and improved understanding. *The Power Élite* qualifies as such a work. The way in

---

[45] Daniel Bell, *The End of Ideology** (New York: Free Press, 1960), S. M. Lipset, *Political Man** (Garden City, N.Y.: Doubleday, 1960), p. 406. The ideas leading to these conclusions were developed earlier in the British journal of elegant liberal opinion *Encounter*, which was financed in part, it was subsequently shown and admitted, by CIA funds. Bell and Lipset are among the most noted pluralists.

[46] The classifications are those of G. William Domhoff and Hoyt B. Ballard, eds., *C. Wright Mills and The Power Elite** (Boston: Beacon Press, 1961), a very useful collection of the criticisms and of Mills' response to some of them. Miliband's book, cited earlier, is dedicated to Mills. Although among the most prolific and creative of American sociologists, Mills never rose above the rank of associate professor; nor, it might be added, did Veblen. For a useful if brief discussion of the whole notion of "élites," which is critical (largely implicitly) of Mills, also see Poulantzas in Blackburn, op. cit., esp. pp. 241–44, and Miliband, ibid., pp. 254–56.

which Mills made his case stimulated others to their own hypotheses and studies, which were also stimulated by the increasingly *obvious* growth of the State system and its military component then and later. Much of the discussion has moved along lines that over-simplify and distort the real problems suggested by Mills; it has taken place largely within the *liberal* universe of discourse and analysis. At the same time, other analyses are developing that seem more to the point, analytically more promising and also more frightening in their import, and *radical* in both discourse and analysis. Seymour Melman's work is representative of the former at its best; James O'Connor's of the latter. Let us examine each in turn.

Warfare State?

A professor of industrial management at Columbia University, Seymour Melman has emerged as the foremost liberal academic critic of the destructive tendencies of the U.S. Beginning (in 1965) as a critic of the military-related waste and the misuse of our entire range of resources he became a severe critic of the war in Indochina. Now he ranks as one of the most intensive students of the military-industrial complex in America. The opening words of his *Pentagon Capitalism* define his position clearly:

> An industrial management has been installed in the federal government, under the Secretary of Defense, to control the nation's largest network of industrial enterprises. With the characteristic managerial propensity for extending its power, limited only by its allocated share of the national product, the new state-management combines peak economic, political, and military decision-making.[47]

In 1974 Melman came forth with still another book in what he now sees as a series—*The Permanent War Economy: American Capitalism in Decline* (New York: Simon & Schuster)—which in his words "delineates the workings of a new economy—in the firm and in the aggregate —that has been spawned by the military system, and that has resulted

[47] Seymour Melman, *Pentagon Capitalism** (New York: McGraw-Hill, 1970), p. 1. See also the book of readings edited by him, *The War Economy of the United States** (New York: St. Martin's Press, 1971). The earlier book is *Our Depleted Society** (New York: Holt, Rinehart, and Winston, 1965), in which his present stance began to appear. Although it will be argued that Melman misses the main point of what he has studied, he stands out as one of a small handful of honorable and humane academics in a university establishment that generally works hand-in-glove with the military-industrial complex.

finally in a military form of state capitalism." (p. 12) Melman is quite explicitly antimilitarist, and just as clearly he is *not* anticapitalist. Indeed, however strong his humanitarian attitudes against war may be (and they appear to be very strong), he seems equally upset by his fervent belief that the multidimensional consequences of a "permanent war economy" will bring U.S. capitalism down:

> In the experience of many people during the thirty years after World War II, especially in the upper middle class and in the technical and administrative occupations, the expectation that war spending brings prosperity was borne out. What went unrecognized was that war economy produces other, unforeseen, effects with long-term destructive consequences. These include the formation of a new state-managed economy, deterioration of the productive competence of many industries, and finally, inflation—the destruction of the dollar as a reliable store of value.... [The] $1,500 billion spent on the military since World War II produced no economically useful products for the society.[48]

And, somewhat later:

> The permanent war economy, far from solving problems of capital and labor surplus in American economy, as suggested by the conventional wisdom, will be shown to perform as a prime generator of uninvestable capital, unemployable labor, and industrial inefficiency ... [and] to be a prime cause of the American inflation of the 1970's, a development that is inexplicable to those trained in contemporary economics that classifies military outlays as just another species of government spending.[49]

The data confronting Melman and all other students of the role of military production in the American economy make such characterizations plausible. A recent student of the matter, writing in 1970, has pointed out that:

> In the United States, 10 percent of our personal income and 20 percent of our manufacturing output are derived from this war industry. Indirectly, the livelihood of twelve to fourteen million Americans, including two-thirds to three-fourths of our scientists, now depends on this industry. The defense sector has had the fastest rate of growth of any area in the economy, and it accounts for more than half the research done in this country since the Cold War began.[50]

To which may be added, as Melman points out in *Permanent War*

[48] Ibid., p. 19.
[49] Ibid., p. 24.
[50] James L. Clayton, ed., *The Economic Impact of the Cold War* (New York: Harcourt Brace Jovanovich, 1970), p. 281. This quotation is from Clayton. The many essays in the collection are most informative in terms of background data.

Economy (p. 23), "the military element in 1971 was 73 percent of the $97 billion of total federal purchases for all uses . . . [;] the assets of the U. S. military establishment [in 1970] were 38 percent as much as the assets of all U. S. industry [$544 billion]."

The key to understanding is in knowing what questions to ask; it is a characteristic feature of liberal (but not only its) criticism that it starts with wrong-headed questions. In our previous discussion of imperialism, we asserted that such a wrong-headed question was "Does the U. S. Economy Require Imperialism?" The authors who asked that question concluded that imperialism was unnecessary and that there are other ways the American economy *could* flourish. A better question is, given that the United States *is* imperialist, why and how did it get that way, and what are its domestic and international consequences? Melman, concerned with the militarization of the U. S. economy, asks the same kind of question: his concluding chapter of *Permanent War Economy* is headed "Does American Capitalism Need a War Economy?" The whole chapter is an extended "No!" regarding not only U. S. capitalism but capitalism in general—when he shows, for example, that military spending as a percent of GNP was many times higher in the U. S. than in West Germany or Japan but their growth rates were some multiple of ours in the 1960's.[51]

In the conclusion of his latest book Melman proposes ways and means for the United States to "exit" from its condition of a "permanent war economy." His alternatives are unquestionably attractive and eloquently summarized:

> . . . instead of military nonproductive activity dominating public budgets, a concentration of public funds on reconstructing and improving vital areas of public economic responsibility; instead of operating on the assumption of a permanent war economy, thoughtful planning for conversion to other work; . . . instead of economic neglect and social decay for 30 million Americans, an effort to end poverty and economic underdevelopment. . . . (p. 299)

Melman is closely familiar with the failed attempts of recent years to move in the desired direction, and he knows that ". . . a movement to terminate the war economy requires competence to undo the web of ideological controls and challenge the political power of the war-economy chiefs" (p. 291). He sees this as possible only with major efforts over many years—and sees the only alternative, which he eschews,

[51] The picture had begun to change as the 1970's began. "By the end of 1971," *Der Spiegel* (the *Time* of West Germany) reported, "the German armaments industry had completed deliveries worth more than $24 billion to the West German armed forces alone and had expanded its market to include much of the rest of the world." (July, 1972) Similar trends are at work in Japan (and in other Western European nations) but such facts are not necessary to argue that Melman is asking the wrong question.

as socialist revolution (also, as we shall discuss in the next chapter, a matter of major efforts and many years).[52]

The question that then arises is not whether there are conceptual *capitalist* alternatives to the imperialism and militarization of the U. S. Conceptually, there are alternatives to *everything* that happens; but past and persisting realities also exist. Over the long history of global (and U.S.) capitalism, it is both possible and necessary to note that each new era of capitalist development perceives preceding eras as having held unique horrors—the cruel exploitation of children in the mines and mills of Britain during the Industrial Revolution, for example, or the unspeakable history of slavery and the slave trade, now viewed with relief as having passed into the dustbin of history. And then? And then the tidal waves of nineteenth-century imperialism, and the death, displacement, and social destruction all that meant to hundreds of millions over the globe. And then? And then World War I, and depression, and World War II, and Hiroshima, and Indochina, and . . . all that is now in the dustbins of history. And it all has a set of common characteristics: a systematic disregard for the human, social, and natural costs of economic "progress," and, as well, processes brought into being at the behest and to the advantage of a very few—here, there and elsewhere. Was that all due to *capitalism?* Have there not been, are there not still, horrors in the world where capitalism is not even the possible cause? Of course, but capitalism—nobody would deny—depends for its vitality on its *profitability*, and everything else is and must be secondary. For such a society to prevail, it must bring out the worst in us. A socialist society, by comparison, although it *may* display the whole spectrum of human misdeeds, *need* not: it is a society whose major virtue and whose major challenge is that it depends upon bringing out not the competitive and combative, but the cooperative side of us; and both "sides" are there to be brought out. The argument will be pursued in Chapter 9.

Since 1971, military expenditures have risen from $70 billion to more than $100 billion per annum.[53] The conceptual argument can be made that the replacement of military by peaceful governmental expenditures

[52] A systematic, highly informative, and extended discussion of the military-industrial complex and its functional relationships with the maintenance of capitalism is given by Michael Reich and David Finkelhor, "The Military Industrial Complex: No Way Out," in Tom Christoffel, David Finkelhor, and Dan Gilbarg, eds., *Up Against the American Myth°* (New York: Holt, Rinehart and Winston, 1970), a fine collection of critical essays touching on much of the material of this book.

[53] Military purchases peaked in 1968, at $76.9 billion. As they began to fall, the government, through its many agencies, began to facilitate the sale abroad of arms produced by U.S. companies, and to do so through undercutting other countries' sales, and various political/economic pressures, mostly in the underdeveloped world. Between 1961 and 1974, U.S. companies sold $37 billion of arms abroad, with 1974 (at $10.8 billion) the high point—so far. For a fine analysis, see Michael T. Klare, "Latin American Weapons Market: How to Trigger an Arms Race," *The Nation*, Aug. 30, 1975.

to that amount *could* sustain the economy as much as or more than the present pattern; or, that cutting both expenditures and taxes would release private purchasing power that *could* take up the slack in consumer and investment expenditures. Essentially this is the form Melman's hopes take.[54] In addition to being irrational and immoral in our military spree, he argues, we are living dangerously: we may bring on the war we seek to prevent, and we are undoing, not preserving, capitalism. "The New State" is growing, like a cancer in our midst. He sees the Pentagon as the "single social force . . . [with] a controlling influence in changing, swiftly, the character of life in a large and complex society. . . ." Thus,

> Failing decisive action to reverse the economic and other growth of these institutions, then the parent state, if it is saved from nuclear war, will surely become the guardian of a garrison-like society dominated by the Pentagon and its state-management.[55]

Melman no longer accepts the notion, if he ever did, that the growth of the Pentagon was necessary to counter an *external* threat. He sees it now as a self-fueling, self-directed "para-state," which "both breeds and needs foreign and domestic crises" (*Ibid.*, p. 226). His view of *why* all this happens is his Achilles heel: profit-seeking is incidental to it. He sees the personnel who run the Pentagon, both civilian and military, as growing directly out of the managerial outlook of the modern corporation. And what motivates the modern corporation?

> I have emphasized here the idea of enlarging decision-power as the occupational imperative, the operative end-in-view of modern corporate management—as against the more traditional idea that profit-making is the avowed central purpose of management. Profit-making, as a step in the recoupment of invested money, has diminished in importance as an independent measure of managerial performance.[56]

Despite this presumed insouciance toward profit-making, corporate profits since World War II have broken all records, *after* taxes. The highest rates ever were recorded in the first quarter of 1972, and then broken in the second quarter once more: ". . . second quarter profits [were] at better than a $52-billion annual rate—more money than U.S. business has earned in any quarter in history." (*Business Week*, August

---

[54] A lucid and compelling, if also general and abstract, argument as to why the only major expenditures to be expected from the federal government are on arms and on highways is provided by Evsey Domar, "Investment, Losses, and Monopolies," *Income, Employment, and Public Policy, Essays in Honor of Alvin H. Hansen* (New York: Norton, 1948).

[55] *Pentagon Capitalism*, p. 227.

[56] Ibid., p. 22. Viewing profit-making as a step in the "recoupment of invested money" makes investment sound like slipping on a banana peel.

12, 1972) and then, in 1973 all previous records were again broken—going down in the worst parts of the downturn of 1974 and 1975, of course, but up high again in 1976. What would happen if they really tried?

Melman is not taken in by Cold War propaganda, but he gives no indication that he sees the *creative* connection between "the corporations and the Cold War." There was and is a high consciousness among the corporate leaders who served in or as advisors to the State of just what the alternatives were as between an American Empire or, failing that, "radical readjustments in our entire economic structure . . . , changes which could hardly be made under our democratic free enterprise system." [57]

Melman and other conscientious liberals may or may not have begun to see the role of the corporations in creating the current strength of the Pentagon; his fear, in any event, is that whoever and whatever created it, it has taken on a life of its own. It is, in his view, a Frankenstein monster. To date, the evidence is at best inconclusive for that view. The future is no doubt a precarious one; up to now, as the conduct of the Indochina War attests, the sober corporate heads are still capable of curbing the power of the military when it threatens to go too far. Thus, after essentially military advice was taken on that war in the Johnson Administration (the earlier penetration under Truman and Kennedy having been essentially nonmilitary in its guidance) and the military failed, serious steps were taken to cut back on American personnel and expenditures. That the number of casualties to the people of Indochina rose markedly under the impact of the enormously expanded air war is quite irrelevant to the argument about the decision-making process. Businessmen have never been noticeably tender about human life. Under Nixon the war became manageable and was attenuated, *and* military expenditures rose; limits were set to the further expansion of the Empire; the future would entail digging deeper within its shrunken boundaries.

Perhaps because the Pentagon itself finally saw the Indochina War as a disaster to themselves; perhaps, in addition, because the expanding military budgets (for fancy hardware) constituted a satisfactory meal for their appetites; or perhaps for other reasons, the Pentagon is functioning in ways satisfactory to the corporate world. The possibility always exists that corporate and military criteria *might* clash seriously; many Ameri-

[57] The argument is that of Will Clayton, out of Wall Street to vice-president of the Export-Import Bank, to Assistant Secretary of Commerce, to Undersecretary for Economic Affairs in the State Department, in the Roosevelt and Truman administrations. He was a key figure in the Committee for Economic Development, the organization which plays the same role now as that played by the National Civic Federation before World War I. The quotation is from an important article by David W. Eakins, "Business Planners and America's Postwar Expansion," in *Corporations and the Cold War*, cited earlier, p. 168.

cans envisage that, and envisage the corollary of an attempted, even a successful, *coup d'état*. Whether this possibility moves to the realm of probability depends not upon the kinds of fears expressed by Melman, but whether the present social crisis in the United States deepens. In short, and in anticipation of what will now be discussed, the present and probable future role of the military in the State system is a function not of *their* ambitions but of the nature and depth of the problems facing American capitalism. A movement toward a military *coup d'état* is as unlikely as it is unnecessary in the foreseeable future. Should it become likely it will be as part of something larger: a business-supported movement toward American-style fascism. The strategic feature of the present State system is not a struggle between the military and the business world; it is a division within the business world itself, along lines suggested by Poulantzas' "fractions."

Warfare-Welfare State

The major political tendencies in a society like ours cannot be evaluated without an analysis that centers on the power, the needs, and the modes of conduct of giant national and multinational corporations. Baran and Sweezy's *Monopoly Capital* sought to provide an analytical framework within which the key processes and relationships can be investigated and understood. The theoretical center of their analysis is "the tendency for the surplus to rise." What is the "surplus" and why does it tend to rise?

> The economic surplus . . . is the difference between what a society produces and the costs of producing it. The size of the surplus is an index of productivity and wealth, of how much freedom a society has to accomplish whatever goals it may set for itself. The composition of the surplus shows how it uses that freedom: how much it invests in expanding its productive capacity, how much it consumes in various forms, how much it wastes and in what ways.[58]

[58] *Monopoly Capital*, pp. 9–10. In a valuable appendix to this book, Professor Joseph D. Phillips has made analytical and statistical estimates of the components and behavior of the surplus, pp. 369ff. The major components of the surplus are property income, the wastes of distribution, advertising, and selling, the incomes of those in the financial/legal sector, and, largest of all, government expenditures. These are defined as elements of the "surplus" in the sense that the incomes and expenditures involved are not necessary to maintain current levels of production and life. O'Connor, as we shall see momentarily, modifies this conception, showing the government to be a generator as well as an absorber of surplus. I have tried to clarify the applicability of the concept of the "economic surplus" to contemporary radical concerns in "Social Commitment and Social Analysis: The Contribution of Paul Baran," *Politics & Society*, Vol. 5, No. 2 (1975).

Baran and Sweezy posit that the surplus as a percentage of GNP has risen from just under 50 percent in 1929 to a figure closer to 60 percent in the 1960's; the State (on all levels) absorbs over half of that surplus. Clearly an analysis of the State becomes critical for understanding the behavior of the society, whether or not one accepts fully the foregoing conception and estimates.

The characteristic feature of *all* modern industrial capitalist nations is not only that they are monopolistic in their economic structures but that the State system has become central to their life processes. James O'Connor's ongoing work is foremost among that which seeks to explicate this modern political economy in the U.S. What follows depends basically on his efforts.[59]

O'Connor posits three sectors in the economy: (1) the monopolistic sector, (2) the competitive sector, and (3) the State sector. He assumes that the economy is marked by surplus capital and surplus labor. It is the interaction of all these characteristics that gives the economy and the State their quality and direction. The quality is that of a monopoly capital warfare-welfare State; the direction has combined imperialism, militarization, racism and sexism to bring us to our present condition; the future direction is problematic. Now, some elaboration.

The monopolistic sector is the pride of the American economy. It is where productivity, high profits and the highest wages are found. It is the world of the big corporation—such as GE, GM, IBM, ITT, EXXON —and of the most powerful unions (the teamsters and construction unions being notable exceptions). It is where the greatest concentration of business and labor power exists, and where productive capacity is in surplus.

The competitive sector is where most businesses, and as many workers as in the monopolistic sector, function. Unlike the monopolistic sector, productivity is low and technology nondynamic; profits are low; wages do not allow livelihood; and labor is in surplus. This sector comprises small retailers, small manufacturers, real estate operators, and the like. Competitive business firms often have substantial power on *local* issues; their power on the national level is confined to their influence on the two major political parties.

[59] Brady's *Business as a System of Power* (1943) was the first study to show the similarity of tendencies among all leading capitalist economies toward both monopoly and "political capitalism." Andrew Schonfield, *Modern Capitalism*, cited earlier, covers some of the same ground for the years since World War II, from a conventional standpoint. O'Connor's analyses have appeared as essays in *Socialist Revolution*, vol. 1, nos. 1 and 2, and vol. 2, no. 2, as "The Fiscal Crisis of the State," I and II, and "Inflation, Fiscal Crisis, and the Working Class," respectively. *The Fiscal Crisis of the State* is an expanded and revised version of these early essays. Some of this is reproduced in his collection *The Corporations and the State* (cited earlier), along with other pertinent essays.

The State sector (federal, state, and local) is responsible for State expenditures and activities. The nature and importance of that responsibility is well-clarified by O'Connor and warrants lengthy quotation:

> State expenditures have a twofold character corresponding to the capitalist state's two basic functions [accumulation and legitimization]: social capital and social expenses. *Social capital* is expenditures required for profitable accumulation; it is indirectly productive. . . . There are two kinds of social capital: social investment and social consumption. . . . *Social investment* consists of projects and services that increase the productivity of a given amount of labor-power and, other factors being equal, increase the rate of profit. A good example is state-financed industrial-development parks. *Social consumption* consists of projects and services that lower the reproduction costs of labor and, other factors being equal, increase the rate of profit. An example of this is social insurance, which expands the reproductive powers of the work force while simultaneously lowering labor costs. The second category, *social expenses*, consists of projects and services which are required to maintain social harmony—to fulfill the state's "legitimization" function. They are not even indirectly productive. . . . The best example is the welfare system, which is designed chiefly to keep social peace among unemployed workers.[60]

In the process the State indirectly generates as well as absorbs and redirects a growing part of the economic surplus. It is the most rapidly growing sector. Although its function is to provide economic stimulus and social stability it has been both source and mitigator of the tensions accompanying the American social crisis. Its ways of doing both now deepen the crisis.

Surplus capital is a way of characterizing the excess productive capacity and the corollary supply of investment funds which, in the absence of the State sector, would have brought down American capitalism long ago. The key role of the State has been to use up and to create outlets for capital, in the military, in nonmilitary goods and services, and abroad. Given that fundamental development, American business has been able through advertising and sales promotion to develop the "consumerism" that propels Americans to spend more than they earn whenever possible, on almost anything.

Surplus labor in a capitalist economy is the other side of the coin of surplus productive capacity. In a rational society there would be neither; in a society where marketability and profitability are the criteria of

---

[60] O'Connor, *Fiscal Crisis of the State*, pp. 6–7. His italics. A clear and concise summary and critique of O'Connor's work is provided in "Review: The Fiscal Crisis of the State," *Kapitalistate*, No. 3 (1975), a journal begun in 1973 as an international effort by Marxists to strengthen the theory of the State—a group of which O'Connor has been a leading figure, as have Gold, Lo, and Wright, cited above.

production and of employment there must be both. Surplus labor was seen as a "problem" in vivid terms in the 1930's. One of the most widely-read authors at that time was Walter B. Pitkin, best-known for his *Life Begins at Forty,* where he was speaking to the middle class. In another book, *Let's Get What We Want* (1935), Pitkin, then extremely popular in business circles, proclaimed:

> . . . most well-mannered debaters carry on with the White Lie of Democracy; and thus reach worthless conclusions. A land swarming with tens of millions of morons, perverts, culls, outcasts, criminals, and lesser breeds of low-grade humans cannot escape the evils all such cause. . . . So long as we have an underworld of 4,000,000 or more scoundrels willing to do anything for a price, and a twilight world of fully 40,000,000 people of profound stupidity or ignorance, or indifference, and a population of nearly 70,000,000 who cannot support themselves entirely and hence must think first of cost, whenever they buy things, we shall have a nasty mess on our hands.[61]

Liberal and radical critics of contemporary America usually join in one important error: they assume that military spending has risen to astronomical levels, which is true, but that nonmilitary government spending has increased only slightly, which is *not* true. The basis for that error is a failure to appreciate the degree to which social sophistication is possessed by the corporate élite; put differently, it is failure to understand that the strongest impulse toward "liberalism" today is found in the largest corporations, the counterpart of what was true in the Progressive period. Before providing some of the relevant data on this score, the view of David Rockefeller of Chase Manhattan Bank can serve as a *leitmotiv:*

> In view of the emerging demands for revision of the social contract, a passive response on the part of the business community could be dangerous. Any adaptation of our system to the changing environment is far more likely to be workable if those who understand the system's problems share in designing the solutions. So it is up to businessmen to make common cause with other reformers . . . to prevent the unwise adoption of extreme and emotional remedies, but on the contrary to initiate necessary reforms that will make it possible for businessmen to continue to function in a new climate. . . . By acting promptly, business can assure itself a voice in deciding the form and content of the new social contract.[62]

[61] Quoted in Brady, *Business as a System of Power* p. 268 n. Brady cites Pitkin also in *Spirit and Structure of German Fascism,* pp. 395–96, to show that the Nazis were not alone in their views in the capitalist world. The U.S. population when Pitkin wrote was about 126 million. Adding his figures gives us 114 million more or less worthless types. Many are called but few are chosen.

[62] *Wall Street Journal,* December 21, 1971. Quoted in O'Connor's *Fiscal Crisis of the State,* p. 227.

The "new social contract" referred to by Rockefeller is a step beyond the present warfare-welfare State, an attempt to transform social expenses into social capital. To the so-called "military-industrial complex" it would add a "social-industrial complex." Some steps toward that "contract" have already been taken; as we shall see, the very factors making for that "progress" are now serving to obstruct its further movement. To build a warfare state has not been difficult; the attitudes necessary to that construction, however, tend to militate against the construction of the welfare state. Especially is that so when America's long adherence to a naive individualism is taken into account. Violence and raw patriotism run deep in the American grain; concern for social balance has at best been a veneer. Building the American empire has been like rolling off a log; the other task set by the corporate élite has been like trying to roll that log up a steep mountain. Today the mountain has become cliff-like in its angle. The energy that lies behind the effort accumulates in the surplus population of the State and the competitive sectors and the power of corporation leaders; the resistance to it comes from small business and organized labor in the competitive sector and some of the powerful in the State sector. If only, a Rockefeller must think, those who resist would try to understand what O'Connor makes clear:

> . . . both welfare spending and warfare spending have a two-fold nature: the welfare system not only politically contains the surplus population but also expands demand and domestic markets. And the warfare system not only keeps foreign rivals at bay and inhibits the development of world revolution (thus keeping laborpower, raw materials, and markets in the capitalist orbit) but also helps to stave off economic stagnation at home.[63]

What are the data supporting this development? Total government spending at all levels in the United States was 8 percent of GNP in 1890; in 1960 it was over 30 percent. Nonmilitary governmental expenditures rose from 5 percent to 18 percent of GNP in the same period. Military spending is almost exclusively done by the federal government. State and local government spending, almost entirely non-military, increased seventy-fold in this century. Local and state spending is in the area of social capital (transportation, education, health), income maintenance (such as, welfare), and fire and police forces. But the federal government also spends on nonmilitary social capital (for example, highways, education, housing and community development), on income maintenance, and various other forms of social consumption (food stamps, and so on). All categories of State spending rose in the 1960's. Although *federal* spending on the military rose by 75 percent, its income maintenance out-

---

[63] O'Connor, *Fiscal Crisis of the State*, pp. 150–51. For an extensive set of essays covering most aspects of tax, expenditure, and other policies, largely critical in nature, see the excellent collection of Robert D. Haveman and Robert D. Hamrin, eds., *The Political Economy of Federal Policy* (New York: Harper & Row, 1973).

lays rose by 100 percent. Local and state expenditures that fall under the heading of the welfare system rose even more. These data are taken from O'Connor, Chapter 4, as are Tables 8–1 and 8–2, which illustrate these tendencies for the federal government.

The State thus accomplishes many badly-needed functions for maintaining American capitalism: (1) the social capital provides facilities and skills (for example, highways and trained workers at all levels) that reduce the costs and increase the profits of business; (2) the social capital that takes the form of income maintenance enhances purchasing power; (3) military and paramilitary forces abroad and at home create and maintain a framework within which orderly business can be transacted; (4) the research and development associated with military production, an important part of social capital, enhances productivity and subsidizes investment in the monopoly sector; (5) jobs are provided: over 25 percent of the entire work force in the 1960's was estimated as owing its jobs directly or indirectly to State payrolls and contracts.[64]

It sounds like a fool-proof system; if it were criminal, it might be almost the perfect crime. The reasons why it is not fool-proof, why it

TABLE 8–1   Trends in Budget Outlays by Major Category, Fiscal Years 1960–71 (billions of dollars)

Category	Outlays				Average Annual Change in Outlays		
	1960	1965	1967	1969	1960– 1965	1965– 1967	1967– 1969
National defense	46.0	49.9	70.6	81.4	0.8	10.3	5.4
Space	0.4	5.1	5.4	4.2	0.9	0.1	–0.6
Income maintenance	24.5	34.2	43.9	56.8	1.9	4.9	6.5
Education, health, manpower	2.5	4.1	8.6	10.3	0.3	2.3	0.8
Housing and community development	0.7	1.5	2.6	3.3	0.2	0.6	0.4
Physical resources	6.4	10.2	10.3	10.8	0.8	0.0	0.2
Interest	6.9	8.6	10.3	12.7	0.3	0.8	1.2
Other outlays (net)	4.9	5.9	7.8	6.2	0.2	1.0	–0.8
Sales of assets	–0.1	–1.1	–1.2	–1.1	–0.2	0	0
Total	92.2	118.4	158.3	184.6	5.2	20.0	13.2
Total, nondefense adjusted for asset sales	46.3	69.6	88.9	104.3	4.7	9.6	7.7
Annual % increase	....	....	....	....	8.5	13.0	8.3

SOURCE: Charles L. Schultze (with Edward K. Hamilton and Allen Schick), *Setting National Priorities: The 1971 Budget* (Washington, D.C.: The Brookings Institution, 1970), pp. 11–12.

[64] Ibid. Nor can one overlook the inestimable difference that would be made for *all* jobs if those estimated were to be reduced or cease to exist.

TABLE 8–2 Program Composition of the 1965 Federal Budget (New Obligational Authority)

	Amount ($ millions)		Percent	
National Security Programs	$ 59,820		44%	
U.S. military forces		48,806		81.6
Scientific competition (NASA)		5,304		8.8
Foreign nonmilitary aid		2,826		4.7
Foreign military forces		2,325		3.9
U.S. passive defense		372		0.6
Political and psychological competition (USIA)		176		0.3
Arms control and disarmament		11		0.1
Public Welfare Programs	45,783		34	
Life insurance and retirement		23,402		51.1
Public assistance and welfare		5,976		13.0
Aid to farmers and rural areas		5,398		11.8
Unemployment insurance		4,059		8.9
Health		3,303		7.2
Veterans compensation		2,121		4.6
Urban housing and facilities		1,533		3.4
Economic Development Programs	14,386		11	
Transportation facilities*		5,154		35.8
Natural resources		4,278		29.7
Education, training and research		3,677		25.6
Aids and subsidies to business		1,277		8.9
Government Operations	15,616		11	
Interest payments		11,102		71.1
Housekeeping functions		3,299		21.1
Judicial and law enforcement		451		2.9
Conducting foreign relations		395		2.5
Regulatory programs		237		1.5
Legislative functions		132		0.9
Total	135,605		100	

* Transportation facilities consist of three major programs: land transportation ($3,980 millions), air transportation ($751 millions), and water transportation ($423 millions).

SOURCE: Murray L. Weidenbaum, "The Allocation of Government Funds," mimeographed paper based in part on a paper presented to the annual meeting of the Western Economic Association, Eugene, Oregon, August 27, 1964. Data computed from details in *The Budget of the United States Government for the Fiscal Year Ending June 30, 1965* (Washington, D.C.: U.S. Government Printing Office, 1964).

is, indeed, in great trouble, are why O'Connor writes of the "fiscal crisis of the State," which may be summed up as the tendency for *necessary* State expenditures to outrun politically *feasible* tax revenues. It all has to be paid for, through taxation of all kinds on all levels. And there is a tax revolt (or better, "counter-revolution") in the making, which arises not from careless construction or administration of the system, but from the very features that make the system necessary and that have made it possible. Veblen would say the system has the defects of its virtues; Marx would see it as the culminating set of inherent contradictions of capitalism.

The State system has exfoliated in all its parts; but some parts have grown more than others. They are the parts most satisfying and least controversial among those at the top and middle levels of power; the parts that hue most closely to America's long-standing love affair with money-making and with expansion (employing violence when necessary). The fuel of American dynamism has been the pattern of investment directed by profit and the work ethic accepted by the population. The resulting dualism in the economy has its corollary in the dualism of the State system. The nonmilitary grows, but it cannot keep up with the natural, normal, and powerful tendencies to create and maintain inequality in the distribution of income and wealth.[65] Without the expansion of the "welfare" side of the warfare-welfare State, the United States would have moved closer to a revolutionary *or* counterrevolutionary condition. Even with that expansion, however, the essentially half-hearted efforts made have produced a situation of slowly-increasing tension and polarization, exemplified by the success of super-patriots like Nixon, Reagan, and Wallace with implicitly antiblack, explicitly antiwelfare slogans. The clearest manifestations of this process are in the fiscal crisis of the State, the head-on collision of rising tax resistance with rising needs for State expenditures. When to this is added the necessity of keeping inflation down at home in order not to exacerbate an already serious international trade and payments problem, the directly conflicting needs of the warfare-welfare state become apparent.[66]

Arise, Ye Wretched Taxpayers

Everywhere and always, the State is supported by taxes—hidden or open, regressive or progressive. That is the same as saying that the status

[65] Bluestone's analysis along these lines is recommended again in this connection. *Monthly Review* (June, 1972), pp. 65–71.

[66] See the excellent analysis by E. S. Herman, "The Income 'Counter-Revolution,'" in *Commonweal*, 3, January, 1975. See also, along something of the same lines, William K. Tabb, "Whose Ox is Gored? Income Shares and Recovery," *The Nation*, October 4, 1975.

quo is supported by taxes; the burden of them is almost without exception *not* on those most able to pay. In the medieval world, the labor provided by serfs on the lord's domain was the principal tax of the time; the principal tax in nineteenth-century America took the form of tariffs, a tax on consumers. Local property taxes, sales and excise taxes, and payroll taxes now comprise the principal tax burden on Americans, and all such taxes are regressive. Income taxes, progressive in surface structure, are so widely-evaded by the well-off within the framework of the law that their effective progressiveness is minimal.

Tax grumbling does not occur simply because taxes are being paid, but when one or more developments occur: the percentage of income paid (in *all* taxes) rises to substantial levels; the uses to which taxes are put are objectionable; the distribution of the tax burden is seen as inequitable. All these developments come together in the United States today. Total taxes amount to about 30 percent of GNP; objections to non-military State expenditures are mounting rapidly; the tax burden is (as will be shown momentarily) highly inequitable. The upshot takes on the proportions of an incipient tax revolt.

Taken by itself, rising tax resistance would not constitute a fiscal crisis. The inexorable need for rising expenditures by the State, taken *together* with tax resistance, has produced the crisis. If expenditures continue to rise, resistance even to warfare spending (already beginning to surface) might become substantial.

Until very recently, the signs of today's fierce mood were hidden from sight. By the election of 1972, taxes had become a pervasive and heated issue. The objections to rising taxes grew as the taxes rose; and grew even more as knowledge spread and deepened about who was paying how much for what. The average taxpayer still has much to learn, but what is already becoming well-known is substantial.

The richer you are, the less likely you are to pay your full share of taxes. If you are rich enough, you may have to pay *no* direct taxes, and indirect (sales and excise, for instance) taxes are regressive—that is, the higher your income, the lower the percentage. Among the pleasanter and more time-consuming duties of Congress is to devise tax breaks for the top levels of corporate and individual taxpayers. The salaries of Congressmen place them in the top 5 percent of income recipients, which is why their duties in this respect are taken seriously. Corporate and personal income taxes have been steadily reduced in the past decade in nominal rates; loopholes through the lowered rates have widened.[67]

When the federal income tax was initiated in 1913, a single person had an exemption of $3,000; today it is $750, and of course a dollar bought considerably more in 1913. In 1913, the initial rate of tax was

[67] Unless otherwise indicated, the data on these matters are taken from O'Connor, *Fiscal Crisis*, Ch. 8.

1 percent on the first $20,000 of taxable income; now it is 20 percent. In 1916 only 400,000 tax returns were taxable; today it is over 55,000,000. The big jump was from 4,000,000 net taxable returns in 1939 to 32,000,000 in 1950, the period encompassing the later New Deal and World War II, in which the new State system came to flower.

The progressiveness of personal and corporate income taxes is mitigated by loopholes; the progressiveness of the tax system as a whole is eliminated by *non*-income taxes at all levels of government. Property taxes are passed on to tenants. Payroll taxes are paid for in part by workers and in part by employers; they are regressive for the worker (because the tax is only on the first $7,000–8,000) and even more so because the employer's contribution is passed on in the form of higher prices or lower wages. (See *Business Week*, July 15, 1972.) In the years since 1964, nominal personal income tax rates have been cut four times, from a maximum rate of 91 percent down to 50 percent; after 1966, payroll tax receipts began sharply to exceed corporate income tax receipts. Property taxes are the principal source of local receipts; state governments raise about two-thirds of their tax revenues from sales and gross receipts taxes. Income taxes on the state level account for only about 16 percent of revenues. Tax withholding, begun after World War II on the federal level and now spreading throughout the separate states, has overcome the lower-income population's ability to evade taxes, while legal loop-holes have increased the ability of the well-to-do. The resulting pattern is not surprising.[68]

Average tax rates for federal, state and local taxes for 1965 reveal a pattern defying the notion that government power is used to redistribute income. Table 8–3 indicates the tax pattern for 1965. John Gurley estimates that the 200,000 families with average incomes (including capital gains) in excess of $150,000 a year pay *income* taxes of about 20 percent of their true incomes.[69]

The best that can be said of the tax system—a system which, since

[68] If the latest proposals for "value-added" taxes are legislated, the pattern will be even more regressive; the value-added tax is a fancy name for a complicated federal sales tax.

[69] In "The Real Impact of Federal Tax Policy," in Gordon, *Problems in Political Economy*, op. cit. There are at least two hundred millionaires who in 1970 paid *no* income taxes. For this and similar data, see Philip Stern, *The Great Treasury Raid*, cited earlier. The number of known millionaires increased from 27,000 in 1953 to 200,000 in 1969, according to *U.S. News and World Report*, December 15, 1969. *Fortune* (May, 1968) estimated that there were 166 individuals with over $100,000,000, many of them having accumulated their income and wealth since World War II, the period in which popular fancy has it that such accumulation was made impossible by the tax laws; in September, 1973, *Fortune* reported that at least "39 men had amassed wealth of $50 million or more [6 from $200 to $700 million]" between 1968 and 1973, exclusive of inheritance.

TABLE 8–3   Taxes as a Percent of Income

Income Class	Federal Taxes	State and Local Taxes	Total Taxes
Under $2,000	19%	25%	44%
$2–4,000	16	11	27
$4–6,000	17	10	27
$6–8,000	17	9	26
$8–10,000	18	9	27
$10–15,000	19	9	27
$15,000 and over	32	7	38
Total	22	9	31

SOURCE: Joseph Pechman, "The Rich, the Poor and the Taxes They Pay," *The Public Interest* (Fall, 1969), quoted in Richard Parker, *The Myth of the Middle Class* (New York: Liveright, 1972), p. 216. This is a generally useful book on income and wealth. The Pechman essay is included in the Haveman & Hamrin collection, cited above.

the framing of our constitution has presumably been shaped in terms of ability to pay—is that it is proportional to income and not, as most believe, progressive (that is, a system where taxes rise both absolutely and relatively as income rises). It is proportional between $2,000 and $15,000 per annum; for the poorest and all others, it is regressive.

The highest effective tax rates are on the poorest segment of the population—44 percent for those with incomes under $2,000 per year, Income taxes are at about 5 percent for those in that group; most of what they pay is in the form of sales, excise, and payroll taxes, and hidden taxes passed on by landlords and corporations. About 40 percent of Americans receive annual incomes in the $6–15,000 range (see Tables 5–1 and 5–2, Chapter 5). They include workers from the monopolistic sector, small businessmen, and lesser professionals. The taxes they hate most are *not* hidden. This segment has been the largest purchasers of houses in the postwar years. Property taxes are now at about a $50 billion rate per annum; 60 percent of that is paid by homeowners, the rest by businesses. The rates have been rising: in California, for instance, "the property tax take has climbed by 147% in the past decade." (*Business Week*, February 12, 1972) Over half of federal income taxes are to finance the warfare state; most of local property taxes, taken together with sales and excise taxes, are to finance the welfare state.

The incipient tax revolt is aimed most heatedly and most effectively at the financing of the welfare state; it combines, of course, with hostile attitudes toward nonwhites and the young and, as well, with the traditional schizophrenic view of Americans toward education. It combines with something deeper: the naive individualism and Puritanism so much a part of the American tradition has made us a people deeply distrustful of all public agencies but the military, and especially distrustful of income maintenance programs. "You get what you deserve."

The middle-income income receivers and taxpayers (those in the $6,000–15,000 range) have entered the outer rings of the charmed circle of American opulence in the very years that the warfare state has grown; they see themselves and their tenuously-held possessions as being under dire threat, in order to assist a largely despised surplus population and an educational apparatus they see as being both costly and feckless. Their targets *should* be the military and the inequities of the tax system. Why aren't they?

Our history, our traditions and our non-social philosophy constitute the largest part of the explanation; much of that has been discussed in earlier chapters. It is also necessary to understand the culminating role played by the rise of the warfare state itself in shaping current attitudes, attitudes which militate against the acceptance by the "middle Americans" of the "welfare" side of the warfare-welfare State.

Shine, Perishing Republic

Overseas imperialism as a way of life for the United States is now at least three-quarters of a century along. For the past thirty years, militarism has joined with imperialism.

In my view and that of many others (those cited above, such as Oglesby, Kolko, Mills, I. F. Stone, Williams, Klare, Sweezy, Magdoff), American militarization has not been the result of external threats to our national safety but of a conscious and deliberate attempt to underpin economically and geographically expansionist policies, as outlined in Chapter 7. To achieve that, given the antimilitarist attitudes common in the United States between the two world wars, a massive and sustained propaganda effort was necessary. Doubtless some of the propagandists, both high and low in power, *believed* there was a threat; doubtless some still do. There was, of course, a problem; the spread of socialism in Europe and Asia could not be taken lightly by a capitalist world always needing exploitation and expansion. But that was a political/ideological problem; if, in the past thirty years, it has ever had a military tinge to it that was a happily self-fulfilling prophecy.

Moving into the geographic and economic soft spots allowed by the weakening of all the other capitalist powers after World War II, the United States gained two additional bonuses: the stimuli from military production and a virtual end to domestic dissent, at least until recently. Capitalism, the free enterprise system, and freedom became synonymous; dissenters at home were dupes or worse, opposition abroad was part of an international atheistic Communist conspiracy to overrun the world. Human attitudes toward public policies that would promote opportunities, jobs, and the amenities of life to the lower one-third of the population—that is, that would provide for social stability and higher overall productivity, the function of the welfare state—became suspect as "Communist" attitudes, adding to the long-standing resistance to social policies. Both the universe of acceptable discourse and the kind of person who could rise to high political levels shifted to the right. Why?

Education and popular discourse in the United States have done little to allow appropriate answers to that "why?", for they have tended to discourage widespread interest in social and historical analysis. The general inclination is to personalize historical processes, and to become attentive only in periods of great drama: we read and speak much of political figures, but study political relationships and what they represent very little. Thus, one can read through Halberstam's *Best and the Brightest* and learn an extraordinary amount about the individuals (Acheson, Rusk, Johnson, the Kennedys, Rostow, McNamara, the Bundys, Maxwell Taylor, Nixon et al.) who conspired to take the United States to war against the peoples of Indochina, and about how they lied to the people, the press, and to each other in the process. The discussions are generally astute, and the information we gain is valuable, but the reader is left with an interpretation of the period based upon the strengths and weaknesses of *personalities*—in the absence of any other analysis. Similarly, in commenting on the revelations of Watergate a portrait of substantial accuracy is made concerning President Nixon:

> In the end, his long reliance on playing upon the baser parts of people's nature, his professed conviction that they are children who must be disciplined before they can be trusted with responsibility, his readiness to resort to the most undemocratic means to retain and expand his control over them, and finally, his apparent belief that his personal interest is identical with the public interest together make up the character of the tyrant—the man who would assert himself by making his will the will of a nation.[70]

But Nixon's inclinations along each and every one of these lines were familiar to those who financed his campaigns and who voted for him from 1946 through 1972. Both his financial and his voter support increased

[70] "Talk of the Town," *The New Yorker* (June 23, 1973). It is worth adding that for several years preceding 1973, this magazine had come to be the most persistent voice opposing the war and criticizing the diminution of civil liberties, outside of radical publications, a tradition begun with its devotion of a full issue to the horrors of Hiroshima, in 1946 (written by John Hersey). Intentionally, consciously, or not, the magazine has come to stand for the urbane values of a confident bourgeois—but not an imperialist or totalitarian—society.

steadily over that period of 26 years (notwithstanding electoral setbacks in 1960 and 1962).

In those same years, almost insensibly, Americans were led to accept as plausible what in earlier years they had thought dangerous or laughable. Nixon was by no means the only such person who rose to high office or great power in that period. As military budgets and bases abroad rose to numbing levels, political contests were won increasingly (if never entirely) in terms of the patriotic strenuousness and vicarious bravery of the victors—making General Eisenhower first into a university president, and then a beloved but often befuddled president; making Joe McCarthy, a man of no evident scruples, into the most feared (and therefore one of the most powerful) of men; making Lyndon Johnson into a president, and potentially no worse than most and better than some from the past, but a president who was both able and inclined to continue our plunge into Indochina by presidential and governmental deceit both supported and prodded by the politics of the Cold War— and to do so while classifying his enemy as "a raggedy-ass little fourth-rate country," peopled by "little yellow dwarfs"; giving us, finally, Richard M. Nixon.

As a person, Nixon earned the criticisms he received; but something has to be explained about the society that elects and re-elects such a person. When Nixon began his political career in 1946, he did so on the basis of innuendo and a sneering anti-Communism. At first, he was viewed as a political aberration, at best. But he was a man moving with the times. As his power grew, he did not change, except that each step up the ladder, from Congressman to Senator to Vice-President to President, allowed him to delegate his gutter skills to others, while also bringing him that presumably un-American deference that Americans usually give to those in high office. Nixon stood in 1972 where he had always stood, off on the far Right; but the United States had moved over, making him a Centrist.

In changing so, Americans came to value what earlier they found valueless, or worse. It was not all a matter of ideas and fear-filled rhetoric. A very high percentage of Americans came to be dependent upon the militarized empire for their jobs and profits; or so they came to believe. As things have been, of course, the belief was correct, even though as things have stood more recently the real income and the jobs of Americans are in trouble *because* of our addiction to empire and militarism. From being the cutting edge of prosperity, America's imperial/ military basis of production has become a two-edged sword: our external (and militarized) relationships in becoming so important to the United States, now that they have run into a period of troubles, have become the cutting edge of worsening economic and political problems.

The winding down of the Cold War, signified by more congenial relationships with China and the Soviet Union, is now assumed to be under way; for the system within which Americans *now* live, however, that consummation so devoutly to be awaited poses a social challenge of enormous proportions: the centralized, intertwined, and powerful corporate and State bureaucracy that fed and was fed by the Cold War seems presently out of control.

The dogged manner in which the United States pursued its horrifying and finally self-destructive war against the Indochinese peoples continued long after it was perceived as irrational by important elements of the business community (as early as 1967), leading as it did to inflation at home, to a deterioration of our international economic strength, and to corrosion of the structure of American institutions; our involvement in Indochina, which began under Truman, was both consequence and partial cause of the centralized patterns of power that had their most recent effusion in the processes leading to Watergate. It was not coherent actions by the business community or government leaders that led to our withdrawal from Indochina; it was the military and political strength and determination of the Indochinese peoples (not least the critical Tet offensive of 1968) and an antiwar movement headed by the powerless that finally led the "respectable" people of power in this country seriously to seek ways out; similarly, the breaking of the Watergate conspiracies depended upon a handful of reporters, one judge, and the breaking of discipline among the conspirators themselves.

Whatever else this tells us, it shows that a simple theory of the State, whether that State policy represents a pluralist consensus or the decisions of "the executive committee of the ruling class," does not hold now, if it ever did. Some Marxists to the contrary notwithstanding, it is clear that Marx, at least, never held such a simple theory. He saw that under certain developmental conditions, and especially those under imperialism, a State bureaucracy could grow that would pervert and distort the power relations more normally arising from capitalist rule. Writing of the bureaucracy of France's Second Empire (1852–1860) under Napoleon III, his formulation might have characterized recent American history:

> Apparently the final victory of this governmental power over society, it was in fact the orgy of all the corrupt elements of that society. To the eye of the uninitiated it appeared only as the victory of the Executive over the Legislative, of the final defeat of the form of class rule pretending to be the autocracy of society, by its form pretending to be a superior power to the society. But in fact it was only the last degraded and the only possible form of that class ruling, as humiliating to those classes as to the working classes which they kept fettered by it.[71]

[71] Quoted by Shlomo Avineri, *The Social and Political Thought of Karl Marx*, pp. 50–51. This appeared in the original draft (but not today's published versions) of Marx's *The Civil War in France*.

The Indochina War was a savage and destructive experience for the peoples of Indochina, many millions of whom were killed, maimed, and displaced by it. Setting our own Civil War aside, it was probably the most dislocating and unsettling experience in American history, to which Watergate was a loud coda. The War served as lightning flashes do, providing intermittent heat and light on the American scene, and it burned away much of the mythology of the Cold War. It helped many Americans to identify the United States as imperialist; it added new emphasis to what racism means; and it along with the spate of social analyses directly and indirectly stimulated by the war, along with Watergate, have forced Americans to be somewhat less casual about the corruption they have always taken for granted.

One cannot judge now what the ultimate consequences of the growing re-appraisal of American reality will be. As of now, the facts of life for the State system in America must be part of that re-appraisal: (1) Militarism has come into existence with civilian support under the leadership of a corporate élite (with the greedy prodding of the military); (2) although the quality of life in America has deteriorated in many if not all areas—demonstrably in the areas of health, education, the environment, drugs and crime, transportation, the viability of our cities, and the morale especially of the young—the largest proportion of Americans still appears to place the blame for all this not on rampant capitalist imperialism and racism but, as is so often true, on its principal victims at home and abroad.

So it appears, at the moment. For the longer run, appearances may be deceptive.

Reading Suggestions

That the appearance of pluralist political competition, expressed customarily in electoral contests between the Democratic and Republican parties, is belied by a more carefully studied reality is the well-documented argument of Walter Karp, *Indispensable Enemies: The Politics of Misrule in America* (New York: Saturday Review Press, 1973). He shows the conscious and cynical cooperation between the two parties that has persisted and grown in this century, with the consequence of maintaining the power structure within those parties, and the rule of monopoly capital (to the gain also of their allies in the military and organized labor). Some of the details of these alliances are brought together in Morton Mintz and Jerry S. Cohen, *America, Inc.** (New York: Dell, 1971). See also, for a broader and more radical collection Maurice Zeitlin, *American Society, Inc.* (Chicago: Markham 1970). Two other books of readings illuminating in these respects are Herbert I. Schiller and Joseph D. Phillips, eds.,

Super* State: Readings in the Military-Industrial Complex* (Urbana: University of Illinois Press, 1972), and Robert B. Carson, Jerry Ingles and Douglas McLaud, eds., *Government in the American Economy: Conventional and Radical Studies on the Growth of State Economic Power** (Boston: D.C. Heath, 1973). Michael T. Klare, *War Without End*, cited earlier, shows how this works out regarding the political economy of American counter-insurgency, past, present, and future.

URPE has several publications relevant to this chapter: *RRPE* Special Issue (August, 1970), *The War and its Impact on the Economy; In Conference Papers* (December, 1968) the essay by Daniel Fusfeld, "Fascist Democracy in the United States," a view somewhat gloomier than that presented in this chapter; *RRPE* Special Issue (August, 1972), *On the New Economic Policy: The New Economics and the Contradictions of Keynesianism*, cited earlier, contains essays that range from domestic to international to methodological emphases, all concerned with the State in one way or another. "The New Economics: Handmaiden of Inspired Truth," by R. Du Boff and E. S. Herman is especially useful in showing how the mainstream ("brandname") economists have cooperated in selling the ugly policies of recent administrations. Brady's *Spirit and Structure of German Fascism*, cited earlier, and Franz Neumann's *Behemoth: The Structure and Practice of National Socialism, 1933–1944** (New York: Harper & Row, 1966; originally Oxford University Press, 1942) make good corollary reading in this connection.

A recent and powerful analysis that explores "the workings of the entire socioeconomic structure with particular attention to the relationship between American capitalism and politics" makes an invaluable addition to what has been attempted in this chapter: Ira Katznelson and Mark Kesselman, *The Politics of Power** (New York: Harcourt Brace Jovanovitch, 1975).

A useful collection of essays from the spectrum of opinion on power in the United States is Richard Gillam, ed., *Power in Postwar America: Interdisciplinary Perspectives on a Historical Problem** (Boston: Little, Brown, 1971). Dahl, the pluralist spokesman, can be compared with Sweezy, Mills, Eisenhower, and Kolko. The concluding essay by Robert Paul Wolff is especially useful. Many of Mills' essays have been collected in Irving Louis Horowitz, ed., *Power, Politics, and People** (New York: Oxford University Press, 1963) who has also put together a group of essays in honor of Mills, *The New Sociology* (New York: Oxford University Press, 1964) which is worth studying.

A careful and thoroughgoing presentation of Marxian views is Stanley W. Moore, *The Critique of Capitalist Democracy: An Introduction to the Theory of the State in Marx, Engels, and Lenin* (New York: Paine-Whitman, 1957). There is of course no substitute for reading Lenin's own *State and Revolution** (New York: International Publishers, many editions). Confusion over the role of the State, and the states, in early American life is rife; Carter Goodrich, ed., *The Government and the Economy: 1783–1861** (Indianapolis: Bobbs-Merrill, 1967) contains a group of essays that clarify the early period.

The manner in which the State's resources are misused from the viewpoint of those on the bottom of society is well-treated from a variety of angles in books cited earlier and worth recalling here: Pamela Roby, *The Poverty Establishment*, Dale Tussing, *Poverty in a Dual Economy*, Piven & Cloward, *Regulating the Poor*, and Ryan, *Blaming the Victim*.

Finally, those who wish to explore some of the depredations of the CIA as seen by an insider will find Philip Agee, *Inside the Company: CIA Diary** (Hammondsworth, Engl.: Penguin, 1975) one of many worth reading.

9

Epilogue:
The Future
Lies Ahead

These are transitional years and the dues will be heavy.
Change is quick but revolution will take a while.
America has not even begun as yet.
*This continent is seed.**

Neither knowledge of history nor of social analysis can tell us what the future holds; taken together, at best and at most they can tell us where we are, how we got there, what to look for in the unfolding present, and what questions to ask. Marx and Veblen, who most effectively combined historical analysis with social theory, differed greatly on what the developments they studied augured for the future; yet they shared a healthy respect for the shaping importance of the past. In a famous passage, Marx said it this way:

> Men make their own history, but they do not make it just as they please; they do not make it under circumstances chosen by themselves, but under circumstances directly encountered, given and transmitted from the past. The tradition of all the dead generations weighs like a nightmare on the brain of the living.[1]

Both men saw change as continuous, and marked always by conflict.

*Diane di Prima, *Revolutionary Letter #10.* Copyright © 1971, 1974 by Diane di Prima. Reprinted by permission of City Lights Books.

[1] This is part of the opening statement of *The Eighteenth Brumaire of Louis Bonaparte,** available in many editions. It is contained in *Selected Works,* cited earlier, pp. 97ff.

Veblen saw social evolution as a race between the life-giving and life-destroying, cooperative and predatory, elements in human nature and society, but he feared that "force and fraud" were more likely than love and reason to take the lead in that race. His final hope was his ironic reservation that to foresee the future was itself hopeless; it was a matter of "opaque cause and effect," of "blind drift."

Marx was more hopeful, about both our ability to foresee the future, and what the future held. His theory of social change saw capitalism creating both a final crisis for itself *and* creating its own gravediggers—the organized working class—who would replace capitalism with socialism.

What then of the future of the United States? "Blind drift"? More "force and fraud"? Or movement toward socialism? The history of the U.S. is the history of a capitalist democracy—unlimited capitalism and considerably limited democracy. From the beginning our political and social history has taken place in the stated terms of representative government, human equality, and social mobility. Glorious though these political and social ideals may have been, the historical realities were shaped predominantly by our economic development, by capitalism's integral needs for economic and geographic expansion and only barely constrained human and resource exploitation—white Americans treating nonwhites as subhumans or (along with women) as second-class citizens, most Americans treating our natural environment as something to conquer, and, in this century, viewing the rest of world as our particular oyster.

Our long history of technological advance and economic expansion made us the primary world power in a social process in which economic power was decisive. At home, *quantitative* economic achievement has encouraged and allowed the bulk of our population to be deflected from concern over the *quality* of their own and others' existence.

Will the future allow the continuation of all these long-standing and deep-seated processes and relationships? It does not seem so. Although it is impossible to foresee what shape the American future will take, and whether we will shape it actively or passively, we may be reasonably sure that it will be substantially different from our distant and recent past. We are in a period of transition; for better or for worse, it is likely that the near future will see changes in basic political, economic, and social institutions. Why is this so? Can anything be said of likely directions?

Troubles, Here and There

The decade of the 1960s was one of unprecedented searching and turbulence for the United States. Even though the 1970's have seen a calming of the surface turbulence, uneasiness and searching continue; and we may remember that the raucous sixties were preceded by the "silent fifties." In the perspective we have advanced, the explanation for such developments should be looked for in the changing conditions of expansion and exploitation.

The developmental changes for the United States that have shaped the past generation began during World War II and took their current forms shortly thereafter: internationalization, militarization, and related and dependent patterns of domestic investment and "consumerism." The sustained economic growth since 1941 was made possible by these developments, guided by a growing State in close cooperation with the business community. But each of these developments has created conditions that make it increasingly difficult for them to serve as continuing sources of sustained economic growth. Economic and geographic expansion and human and resource exploitation, which have for so long been sources of vitality for global and American capitalism, have now combined in their effects also to create a new time of troubles.

The nature of those troubles may be spelled out as a quick summary of what we have traced in preceding chapters: (1) the expansion of U.S. influence and investment in the rest of the industrial capitalist world has produced a growing source of effective competition for American products—in markets both at home and abroad—as well as increased demands and uncertainty in financial and resource terms; (2) the expansion of U.S. power into the Third World has become excessive in its costs and has quite probably reached its limits, from which we are now drawing back, and which is a new and potentially unsettling experience for the United States; (3) the militarization of American production has created economic stability, jobs, and profits, but also intensified corruption, an enlarged bureaucracy, and resistance; in addition, the slowed rate of *increase* in military expenditures (declining as a *rate* of GNP) reduces their effectiveness in supporting the economy; (4) "consumerism" finds its limits in the distribution and levels of purchasing power and the ability of business to manipulate tastes and encourage indebtedness, a combination that does not hold out endless promise unless a new boom in economic growth ensues, a process difficult to anticipate; (5) domestic private investment depends upon actual and expected increases in demand and profits, here and abroad, which takes us back to the tendencies to expand or contract coming from points (1) through (4) and which closes the circle.

But more is involved: the economic buoyancy and the policies and processes making for buoyancy since World War II have produced other developments that have been and are likely to remain sources of trouble within the system. The stimulating role of the State for expansion has required a rise of all taxes to a level (over 30 percent) that constitutes an already substantial and increasing drag on purchasing power; it has also meant the proliferation of bureaucracy in both the public and the private sectors; it has meant a growing dependence of the principal beneficiaries of State policies and also growing attention to the activities and *non*-activities of the State. In short, rightly or wrongly, the State is increasingly seen as the cause of what is both wanted *and* disliked in current society. With the emphasis on inflation and waste, the arguments mount, as conflicting groups point to each other's cherished desires as waste or worse: conservatives and reactionaries decrying expenditures on health, education, and welfare, as they argue for more military expenditures, liberals supporting all forms of expenditure, and those further to the left attacking military expenditures while advocating programs that will increase jobs and social services. The State, as it rises inexorably to play a vital role in the economy, has also become a political target in ways new to our history, and people at all levels and in all quarters of society have become increasingly political as a result. The turbulence of the sixties is likely to have been only the first round in that process of heightened politicization.

Much more could be said of the destabilizing consequences of American economic growth since World War II. Let us note only two more developments of as yet unascertainable but clearly momentous implications: (1) all the talk of affluence for the past years has underscored the relative deprivation endured by tens of millions of Americans, while the great wealth and productivity of our economy makes the continuation of such deprivation difficult to smooth over; (2) continued reliance upon rapid industrial growth as a solvent for social problems must be set against the widespread conviction that such growth must somehow be controlled if we are not to poison ourselves out of existence.

The upshot is a developing crisis. Economic and political in its roots, the crisis is not only social, but moral in its tensions; its ultimate resolution will have to comprehend all these dimensions, for better or for worse. If the United States is approaching a crisis, that means some basic alteration in American institutions is in the offing. Just when, just what, just how, is presently unknowable; but the tensions characterizing the totality of American existence seem unlikely to persist for long without some means being found of subduing or eliminating them.

The attempted resolutions of ongoing tensions *could* mean merely more drift, more shambles, year after year; at some time, however, they are likely to produce a process of dynamic polarization, and a substantial move either to the Right or to the Left—*toward* an American version of fascism or *toward* an American version of socialism. For most Americans, either possibility sounds outlandish; still, one or the other is likely before this century ends. We can only look briefly at the conditions that might lead to either. First, American-style fascism.

Waiting for Rightie [2]

A movement to the Right has been underway for some years now in the United States, assuming such a movement is defined by increasing power in the hands of a few and increasing powerlessness for the many; by the resort to physical and judicial coercion to solve domestic and international problems; by a growing resort to secrecy and manipulation in both private and public affairs; by a steady erosion of civil liberties; by a decline in policies seeking, however weakly, to set a floor to deprivation and oppression; by a growth of venality and corruption; by the emergence of authoritarian leaders.

All these developments have become part of our daily news in recent years. Do they add up to fascism? Some would say they do; but by fascism it seems more appropriate to mean not merely the emergence of such tendencies but their coming together in a new combination requiring a decisive closure on the traditional forms of political existence. To put it this way is not to encourage a relaxed view of obvious and ominous tendencies; it is to say that fascism is considerably more terrible in its reality than are the tendencies toward it.

When fascism emerged in other nations, such as Italy and Germany, it came in on the heels of a deep socioeconomic crisis, *and* in conjunction with a substantial threat from the Left. Other countries' histories are not likely to be repeated by the United States, nor to suggest the same preconditions for social change in the United States; our capitalist history has been significantly different from others' and our evolution toward either fascism or socialism is also likely to have its own qualities.[3]

Were the movement toward social crisis in America to become more pronounced, and were it to be joined by an actual or threatened economic collapse, it seems highly likely that American-style fascism would be attempted. It could be attempted in America even without economic collapse. Deepening racial fears and hostilities could threaten so much in the way of social chaos that only a strong authoritarian rule might promise any sort of stability; that, combined with increasing sociocultural disintegration, with declining moral sensitivity, with yearning for simpler,

---

[2] As the first edition of this book was in press, Alan Wolfe, in *RRPE*, Vol. 5 No. 3 (Fall 1973), coincidentally published his excellent essay "Waiting for Righty: A critique of the 'Fascism' Hypothesis." It is a penetrating discussion of fascism and a warning on the misuse (especially the overuse) of the term. See also, on this question and much more of relevance, his *The Seamy Side of Democracy** (New York: McKay, 1973). Both the essay and the book are rich in bibliographical references.

[3] Arno J. Mayer, *Dynamics of Counterrevolution in Europe, 1870–1956: An Analytic Framework** (New York: Harper Torchbooks, 1971) is an incisive and original analysis of great value for approaching the socio-psychological-political (but not the economic) dimensions of fascism.

more "virtuous" and less challenging days, could be used as an excuse to seize power and lead the nation back to a past imbued with fantasy. There are right-wing leaders who will do what they can to encourage such a development, as Watergate revealed.

Whether such leaders can move far in such directions depends not only upon the existence of crisis, but upon the existence of alternatives. That means the Left. Is the Left now or will it be in the foreseeable future able to muster an effective opposition to such tendencies, which are already very real? Or, even more, will it be able eventually to win out and create an American socialism?

Toward an American Revolution?

The emergence of fascism in the United States would require at most "only" a *political coup d'état;* there would be no need to alter basic *economic* institutions substantially, except to move *more* toward coordinated capitalist planning, *more* toward economic nationalism, *more* toward a regressive use of the State's taxing powers. But socialism would require a basic *revolution* of the whole range of institutions—economic, political, social, cultural—social ownership and control of the means of production, in turn enabling a structure of production and consumption suited to human needs and possibilities, a structure of power allowing and requiring democratic control of the society, and a social system (not least an educational system) that would stress equality and cooperation rather than privilege and competition.

To achieve a qualitative (systemic) change in the U.S. that also has staying power, whether it be a shift to an American version of socialism *or* fascism, will require the participation or at the least the conscious support of a *majority* of the politically attentive population. To bring about fascism (by comparison with socialism) is relatively easy: less would be involved, and there is more power at hand to do the job. Harold Laski called fascism "capitalism with the gloves off," by which he meant capitalism without the political democracy that historically has accompanied it. Fascism is *counter*revolutionary. Socialist *revolution* demands much more, especially if it is to be worthwhile.

For there to be a socialist society, there must be a socialist movement with the strength to cause and carry through a revolution. In turn, that requires an analysis that shows why socialism is *necessary,* and that convinces the largest percentage of the population of this need; a *program* that makes socialism attractive; a *strategy* that makes a socialist revolution possible. If that is what is meant by a revolutionary movement, the United States has "not even begun as yet." The United States does have large numbers of people of all ages, colors, sexes, and working conditions whose lives seem to them increasingly intolerable and alienating; it will seem so until the country undergoes a social reconstruction of revolutionary proportions.

In the preceding chapters I have sought to provide a valid analysis of U.S. capitalist development that can serve a variety of purposes. In showing the many ways in which capitalist development has been and remains destructive and dangerous to human beings and the rest of nature, and therefore crippling of the human potential, I have also been arguing implicitly the necessity for democratic socialism. But who could and might bring that about in the U.S.? How? When? And what would a democratic socialist society be? No individual or small group of people can give definitive answers to such questions; they will be answered, if at all, as the process works out through time. But *some* kinds of tentative answers are necessary *all* the time. First, let us consider *strategy*—which of course must be intertwined with both analysis and program.

In the recent past, although much revolutionary rhetoric and self-styled revolutionary tactics existed in the United States, a socialist movement has not appeared nor is there a discernible or organized political base for one. The need, therefore, is for American socialists to construct a socialist movement.[4] That political base remains nonexistent, except as a potential, both because of and despite the ways in which the present system horrifies, frightens, disaffects, and oppresses growing numbers of people, while demeaning and crippling the potentialities of the large majority. In one degree or another, this has been so throughout our history. Why, then, has the U.S. *now* begun to polarize in attitudes?

The key elements appear to have converged since the mid-sixties. In that period, the interactions of domestic and international developments flowing from the military triumph of World War II combined with (1) a rhetoric that revolved around peace, democracy, and equality; (2) an economy whose technology was widely hailed as making all things possible; and (3) a determined drive against "communism" abroad and at home that had the unexpected consequence of illuminating the inadequacies of American society. It was of course the young, both black and white, who most quickly noted the gap between the rhetoric and the reality, and whose customary impatience with temporizing first led them to seek ways to close the gap by bringing reality closer to rhetoric.

None of that was entirely new, although the convergence of disparate developments in a white glare of attention perhaps was. The aims of the

---

[4] See John Judis, "New American Movement, 1975," in *Socialist Revolution*, No. 26 (October–December, 1975), p. 119. This is a generally instructive discussion of (among other matters) strategy, as is his earlier essay, "From the New Left to a New Socialist Party," *Socialist Revolution*, No. 18 (November–December, 1973). Judis has been much influenced by Gramsci.

young were voiced pervasively by almost everyone else—politicians high and low, educators, businessmen, clerics, et al.—while at the same time the society became more bent on war, active racism intensified, poverty programs were abandoned and, among other things, the leadership of the nation became steadily more mediocre, to say the least. That was true at all levels; at the highest level, what seemed barely possible under Kennedy came to seem implausible under Johnson and impossible under Nixon and Ford. This tragic evolution was necessarily matched by an enhanced process of repression and further corruption of the judiciary, victimizing those who sought to realize the expressed ideals of America. And all the while the U.S. deteriorated even further: in the seventies, more poverty, more corruption, more economic troubles, more hypocrisy on racism—but less war.

It is vital to note and to understand that only a very small number of the young ever engaged in the political struggles of the sixties; it is equally vital to note how very great the attention and furor was that attended their efforts. In the United States that has always happened, whenever Left or radical movements seemed to be more than mere exercises in free speech. That this has been more true in the United States than elsewhere is a consequence of our uncompromising and uncontested capitalism. It is a matter of what Antonio Gramsci calls "hegemony," a concept worth exploring. Hegemony is:

> . . . an order in which a certain way of life and thought is dominant, in which one concept of reality is diffused throughout society in all its institutional and private manifestations, informing with its spirit all taste, morality, customs, religious and political principles, and all social relations, particularly in their intellectual and moral connotations.[5]

Gramsci developed the idea of hegemony as a means of understanding both the power of capitalism and the political needs of the working class if it were ever to gain power: "the working class, before it seizes State power, must establish its claims to be a ruling class in the political,

---

[5] Gwynn Williams, quoted in John M. Cammett, *Antonio Gramsci and the Origins of Italian Communism** (Stanford: Stanford University Press, 1967), p. 204. This book is fundamental to an understanding of Gramsci, leader of the Italian Communist Party in the 1920's, until imprisoned by Mussolini for 11 years (until just before his death in 1937). See also the excellent essays by Carl Boggs on Gramsci in *Socialist Revolution*, Nos. 11 and 12 (1972), now much expanded into his book, *Gramsci's Marxism** (London: Pluto Press, 1976). Gramsci's writings are now easily available. See his *The Modern Prince and Other Writings** (New York: New World Paperbacks, 1967) and the larger selection in Quintin Hoare and G. N. Smith, eds., *Selections from the Prison Notebooks of Antonio Gramsci** (London: Lawrence and Wishart, 1971). Although Gramsci's analyses are treated briefly here, they are of substantial relevance for American conditions.

cultural, and 'ethical' fields."[6] This contrasts sharply with the inclination of some Marxists to speak of "smashing the State," and to see that as possible in a short-term and almost apocalyptic process—using (however mistakenly) Lenin as guide and the Soviet Revolution as model. This ascribes to the State a nature, role, and power which it may have had in Czarist Russia, but which it does not have in the advanced capitalist nations of the West. As Gramsci says,

> In Russia the State was everything, civil society was primordial and gelatinous; in the West, there was a proper relation between State and and civil society, and when the State trembled a sturdy structure of civil society was at once revealed. The State was only an outer ditch, behind which there stood a powerful system of fortresses and earthworks: more or less numerous from one State to the next, it goes without saying. . . .[7]

A vital point in the understanding of capitalism and in the development of a socialist strategy revolves around the question of *force:* What is the role of force in maintaining capitalism through time, especially in advanced industrial societies? And what must or could be the role of force in bringing about socialist revolution? These questions take us back to Gramsci's notion of hegemony. The term has close links with the function of "leadership" in societies: the class that has (or that could have) hegemony in the society is the class for whose leadership there is (or could be) effective and pervasive support—ranging from enthusiasm to passive acquiescence; naked force plays a minor, and usually an implicit, role. As Boggs says:

> The traditional Marxist theory of the State—including Lenin's own concept of hegemony—was, according to Gramsci, limited in the exclusive attention it paid to the role of force as the basis of ruling class domination; there was no understanding of the subtle but pervasive forms of ideological control, manipulation, and domination—a crippling legacy that led to the impoverishment of revolutionary strategy in virtually every socialist movement. No regime, regardless of how coercive or authoritarian it might be, could sustain itself through organized state power alone, for in the long run its scope of popular support or "legitimacy" was bound to be crucial, particularly in moments of crisis. In differentiating these two types of control, Gramsci contrasted the functions of "domination" (direct political coercion) with those of "hegemony" or "direction" (consent, ideological control) . . . correspond[ing] roughly to the . . . distinction between state and civil society. It was obvious to

---

[6] Cammett, op. cit., p. 205.

[7] *Prison Notebooks,* p. 238. Gramsci is not always consistent in his meaning of "civil society," sometimes meaning by it the realm of ideology, politics, religion (see the discussion between Miliband and Poulantzas in Chapter 8, above), and at other times almost equating it with "mode of economic behavior." See ibid., pp. 206–208.

Gramsci that Marxism, as an expression of the vast majority of the people, would have to take account of both spheres of control in order to press its claim as a viable political force.[8]

It would be difficult to find an industrial capitalist nation in which the "hegemony" of the ruling class is as thoroughgoing in its spread as in the United States; as we approach crisis, it is that hegemony which is showing the first signs of beginning to give way. But we shall move through that crisis into fascism unless an alternative vision of society is created, and unless those who would bring socialism educate and organize around that vision. The hegemony of the ruling class is not simply economic, nor simply anything; it is the consenting acceptance of the main elements of social existence by the mass of the population. That hegemony will not be effectively displaced by an economic crisis;[9] quite the contrary, in the absence of a strong socialist movement working with a socialist program of coherence and comprehensiveness, an economic crisis would hasten fascism.

It is widely accepted that revolutionary periods are preceded by developments in which those who subsequently make the revolution see their hopes become raised within the system, but then without chance of realization within that same system. But revolutionaries alone do not make a revolution. The revolutions that have occurred in the past have occurred only during or after a *crisis*, which itself results from the system's own normal, interacting ("dialectical") processes and relationships. Revolutionaries have been able to seize the opportunities presented by the social crisis. An "historical" crisis of the system is thus a necessary condition for revolution. But it is not sufficient unto itself, as the American Depression of the thirties shows.

When a capitalist system's "natural" evolution leads through crisis to institutional discontinuity, the stage begins to be set for revolution *or* counterrevolution, that is, fascism. It is not enough to believe that fascism is deeply contrary to basic human needs, that reason and decency and well-being in our well-informed and productive world *should* vitiate the possibilities of fascism and enhance the possibilities of democratic socialism; that, in short, fascism "can't work," and would therefore mean the later emergence of a still larger crisis. Fascism has happened frequently in this century; it can still happen here. Should it, in an age of nuclear weapons, faith in the "ultimate" triumph of socialism becomes a cruel

---

[8] Carl Boggs, "Gramsci's Prison Notebooks," in *Socialist Revolution*, No. 11, p. 97.

[9] Gramsci: "It may be ruled out that immediate economic crises of themselves produce fundamental historical events; they can simply create a terrain more favorable to the dissemination of certain modes of thought, and certain ways of posing and resolving questions involving the entire subsequent development of national life." *Prison Notebooks*, p. 184; quoted in Boggs, *op. cit.*, 108.

figure of speech, a dangerous delusion. Fascism must and can be prevented only by simultaneous efforts on two fronts: struggles *against* its lurking potential and *toward* democratic socialism.

Although many of those who participated in the protest movements of the sixties thought and acted as though they were then in the midst of a revolutionary process, it is probably true that most today would agree that despite the rhetoric, the furor, and the great heights of emotion and activity of that period, it was a period of revelation, not of revolution. The leading edge of that process was provided by young blacks, at least partially stimulated by minor institutional changes and a pleasing language of racial equality that began to be publicized—for the first time in our history, it is important to note—in the late fifties. The young blacks were joined by young whites who, unburdened by considerations of material striving, and later horrified or threatened by the Indochinese War, began to request and later to demand that this society live up to its fundamental promises. There was no excuse for not doing so, if their elders could be taken at their word. Both young blacks and young whites believed and acted, for a while, as though reason and the setting of virtuous examples would move society to fundamental change, almost as though they were priming a pump. Within a decade they had learned and others had been taught that the well is dry—or poisoned.

The process of revelation in the United States has been remarkable, not only in its swiftness—and its belated appearance both explicable *and* remarkable—but also in the way in which the uncovering of one layer of oppression helped to reveal one after another layer of oppression, injustice, violence, material and spiritual deprivation, and repression, as though the United States were an onion.

Still another remarkable feature of the last decade was that the impetus for change did not come from its expected sources, economic interest groups, but instead from those who, seeking to make America realize its promises, fought principally on grounds of morality rather than economic interest. The "Movement" thus lacked an adequate theoretical base, initially a perverse source of its strength. It is worth noting that the simultaneous existence of formal political democracy and economic autocracy, on the one hand, and widespread naïveté as to the manner in which the latter vitiates the former, on the other, raises interesting possibilities for the future, as it did in the sixties. A people that does not know it is *de facto* powerless can, by acting on mistaken assumptions, both improve its understanding and push further and more vigorously than it might otherwise do—for a while. At some point, in other words, the myth of American democracy could turn out to be a building block for a struggle to make the myth into a reality. And something else is vital to note here: "faith" in the U.S. began to crumble while its economy was strong, indeed at its strongest; small and then large numbers of Americans began to reject the "hegemony of ruling class." The faith that was lost in the 1960's is quite unlikely to be regained; and the 1970's have brought more and different troubles—cessation or slowing of *economic* expansion, in the midst of disillusionment, and the continuation of so much that was fought against in the 1960's.

To become a Movement that is also a revolutionary movement, the moral and the analytical bases must be strengthened and combined, and these views will have to comprehend the numerous interests that are now and that remain to be articulated into both an analysis and a program. But morality and understanding only facilitate social change; they do not bring it about. That requires power.

Earlier it was noted that power arises from control over both intangibles and tangibles. The intangibles—morality, ideals, and understanding —are necessary if the nature of our developing crisis is to be grasped and in any sense dealt with. We may think of these as the normative sources of power. But unless the American crisis ushers in a complete breakdown of the existing power structure (as happened in Russia in 1917, but which is not presently foreseeable in the United States), a socialist movement must have a non-normative source of power: it must have control over tangibles. In our society that means some control over the means of production.

Clearly, that in turn cannot refer to ownership, so it must mean control gained by the organization of the working class, defined in its contemporary and broadened sense. The working class has its sheer numbers to shut down production as its *potential* source of power; at the present time and in the foreseeable future, the potential has no counterpart in reality. Nor can it have until and unless the Left begins to operate in terms substantially different from its past.

This is another way of saying that the American Left must be both more and less American. Both the Old Left and New Left have adopted all too much of capitalist America's ways—individualist power drives, imagistic appeals, the search for simple or quick solutions, over-emphasis on narrow economic programs—and neither Old nor New have acted as though they understood the strength of American capitalism, or the degree to which the social system it has created has been accepted as natural and desirable by most Americans. Such shortcomings have been entirely understandable; but to continue with them is entirely too dangerous.[10]

[10] For a prolonged discussion of Left movements in the U.S. throughout this century by one who has been and remains part of some of them, see James Weinstein, *Ambiguous Legacy: The Left in American Politics* (New York: New Viewpoints [Watts], 1975). Peter Clecak, *Radical Paradoxes: Dilemmas of the American Left, 1945–1970* (New York: Harper & Row, 1973) covers less time and views *theoretical* rather than political processes, through the writings of Marcuse, C. Wright Mills, and Baran and Sweezy.

Who and How and When and Where

What more can we say about the components of a strategy to develop a socialist movement and a socialist society in the U.S.? Gramsci's general conviction that "the seizure of power by a new class is unlikely to succeed without a prior victory in the area of civil society," connotes a protracted and broad effort to convince and to persuade "the people" (of whom, more in a moment) of the necessity, the possibility, and the desirability of a struggle for socialism. We must expect that such a struggle in the U.S., even more than in Western Europe, would be prolonged rather than sudden, for *at least* two major reasons. First, a long and continuous socialist tradition and a degree of class-consciousness exists in Western Europe, which, muted and weak though it may be, is loud and strong in comparison to the U.S. Second, a socialist movement in the United States (as also in Europe) will have to include a *majority* of politically attentive people among its forces *prior* to any attempt to gain State power. In other words, *democracy* must be part of a socialist strategy and a socialist program, all along the way. What Tawney long ago said of the British, can today be applied to the Americans:

> The only version of socialism which . . . has the smallest chance of winning mass support, is one which . . . guarantees . . . personal liberty, freedom of speech and meeting, tolerance, the exclusion of violence from politics, [and representative] government. Its exponents must realize that the class which is the victim of economic exploitation, instead of merely reading about it, is precisely the class which attaches most importance to these elementary decencies. They [the exponents of socialism] must face the fact that, if the public, and particularly the working-class public, is confronted with the choice between capitalist democracy, with all its nauseous insincerities, and undemocratic socialism, it will choose the former every time. They must make it clear beyond the possibility of doubt that the socialist commonwealth which they preach will be built on democratic foundations.[11]

Whatever else this means, it implies a *long*-term strategy, as well as one for the "mid-term" and the immediate future; and it implies the development of *tactics* that will enhance the success of that strategy, rather than tactics which, as often seems true recently, assume sudden and explosive social change and which, if anything, probably vitiate the possibilities of a socialist movement.

Thus, an American socialist strategy must be complex both in its plans and in its expectations; it must be open to the frequent need for

---

[11] R. H. Tawney, *Equality** (New York: Capricorn Books, 1961), p. 227. First published in 1931. Until his death in 1962, Tawney was one of the most influential of British socialists.

significant alterations, in keeping with unpredictable but likely changes in the whole range of economic/political/social/national/international circumstances that occur over sustained (and even brief) time periods: it must be a dynamic and flexible strategy. Whatever the many reasons for such complexity, two at least are compelling: the powerful "ideological hegemony" of the capitalist class in the U.S. and the extraordinary diversity of the U.S. population—not just in the obvious (if also complicated) categories of class, race, and sex, but also the geographical, cultural, ethnic, and religious influences. All societies are complex, of course, but no capitalist society approaches the U.S. in terms of its social and geographic "spaces." No political strategy can neglect that diversity, nor do those of the capitalist parties; for a socialist strategy to do so is deservedly to die a-borning, as has repeatedly happened in the American past.

This moves us toward a closely related point: a socialist strategy must, as Tawney puts it, "wear a local garb." Indeed, it was Gramsci's attempt to adapt Leninism to Italy that led him to devise his quite different system of political theory. His theory centers on the notion of hegemony and the political party (the socialist's "Modern Prince"), but also treats systematically of the role of intellectuals, and distinctions between them; of the nature and distinctions between "civil" and "political" society and between "spontaneity" and "leadership" in the socialist effort; of the nature and meaning of "historical blocs"; of the necessity for anticipating and planning for intermittent defeats and leadership loss or displacement in what is necessarily a long struggle. Thus, a careful reading of Gramsci's works is required (most conveniently in his *Prison Notebooks*, cited above). It is striking that Mao Tse-tung quite independently moved along remarkably similar lines (in many, though not all respects) in the decades-long struggle within which the Chinese socialist movement developed and finally won out. Thus,

> A Communist is a Marxist internationalist, but Marxism must take on a national form before it can be applied. There is no such thing as abstract Marxism, but only concrete Marxism... that has taken on a national form. If a Chinese Communist who is a part of the great Chinese people, bound to his people by his very flesh and blood, talks of Marxism apart from Chinese peculiarities, this Marxism is merely an empty abstraction.... We must put an end to writing eight-legged essays on foreign models; there must be less repeating of empty and abstract refrains; we must discard our dogmatism and replace it by a new and vital Chinese style and manner, *pleasing to the eye and to the ear of the Chinese Common people.*[12]

[12] Quoted by Boggs, *Socialist Revolution*, Number 12, pp. 53–4. My emphasis. Speaking to the same point, Tawney says, ". . . a socialism which is to exercise a wide appeal must be adapted to the psychology, not of men in general, nor of workers

In working out his major ideas, Gramsci was led to use language "pleasing to the eye" of "common people" in part because he wrote his major works while in a fascist prison—and he was thus forced to disguise (and in doing so to clarify) the usual Marxian terminology in favor of more readily understandable words and concepts. What Gramsci *had* to do, those who seek to *develop* a socialist movement should choose to do.

The "how" and the "who" and the "when and where" all clearly overlap, the strategy concerning each very much interdependent with that concerning the others. So when the question of language is raised, it can only be raised as it relates to "who?" Traditionally, a socialist movement is seen as being developed by and for the industrial working class, the prime victims of capitalism. As Marx saw it, the working class is "the universal class," in the sense that its needs and possibilities, when realized, would comprehend those of all or almost all of the population, and there would be no need for a repressive State, or class rule—except, "for a while," the "dictatorship of the proletariat." This remains a firm principle among many on the Left, in the U.S. and elsewhere; I am convinced it is both strategically unsound and, in its programmatic implications, undesirably limiting, especially if by the "industrial working class" is meant—as usually is so—"blue-collar workers." It is one thing to say that no socialist revolution is either possible *or* desirable without the main participation of the industrial working class (defined narrowly or broadly) because of their condition, their numbers, and their possibilities. It is quite another thing to engage in or promote one or more of the following: the idealization of workers, whose obverse face is the feeling of shame by (or contempt for) those who are not "workers" (while raising the question of how to view Marx, Engels, Lenin, Mao Tse-tung, Che Guevara, Fidel Castro, Ho Chi Minh, and other nonindustrial workers in the socialist Hall of Fame); the neglect of the genuine exploitation and oppression of the overwhelming majority of the population that works for a living, but does not do so in mine, mill, factory, or field—including not only clerical and sales workers, but technical and professional wage and salary earners (such as teachers, nurses, computer programmers, et al.); the lumping together of racism and sexism with exploitation, thus muting the distinctions between exploitation and oppression, and between class, race, and sex—to say nothing of the programmatic implications of making versus not making such distinctions. In recent years much fruitful discussion of these and connected questions emerged, under the heading

---

in general, but of the workers of a particular country at a particular period . . . [and] be related, not only to the practical needs, but to the mental and moral traditions of plain men and women, as history has fixed them. It must emphasize primarily what it has in common with their outlook, not the points at which it differs from them. It must not dogmatize or brow-beat, but argue and persuade." *Equality*, p. 226.

of "new working class," "extended working class," "socialist feminism" (and vice versa) and the like. There must be more.

As such discussion and organizing proceeds, we should keep in mind the vast differences between nineteenth century and contemporary capitalism, whether in Western Europe, Japan, or North America. When Marx thought and wrote, not only the class structure but everyday life was simple by comparison with today: work from dawn to dusk for most people, almost all of whom were illiterate, subsisting on minimal diets, clothing, and shelter at best; with no political rights (until 1867, when *men* in Britain got the franchise). To bring about a socialist movement and a socialist world, the consciousness of people must be transformed. Marx saw that consciousness as being transformed principally by and because of the worker's life "at the point of production." He envisaged the intermittent crises of capitalism as coming together with the rising consciousness of an ever more organized working class to bring down capitalism and produce socialism. But the era of monopoly capitalism, which began to grow just after Marx died, produced a different world. As Perry Anderson puts it:

> Technological and economic evolution has not operated a dramatic simplification of the social structure, reducing it to a single, unbridgeable confrontation between exploiters and exploited. On the contrary, it has diversified and articulated the social structure into an ever more complex . . . ensemble. Exploitation and oppression are as real as ever, but they are masked and mediated in a thousand ways.[13]

It is that society and that social structure toward which our socialist strategy must be directed. We have touched only a few of the matters that are vital to such a strategy, and have done so in ways that are bound to be—and should be—controversial. There remains at least one major additional question of the "how?" to be taken up before we discuss a program.

The foregoing has centered on the appropriate *tone* and *assumptions* of a socialist strategy. But what about its *politics*, the day-to-day and long-term activities by those who seek to develop a socialist movement? What about electoral politics? Should there be a new socialist party? Should socialists participate in reform efforts, and if so, how? What about "popular front" efforts? Or coalitions on specific issues?

[13] In Perry Anderson and Robin Blackburn, eds., *Towards Socialism* (Ithaca: Cornell University Press, 1966), in his own essay, "Problems of Socialist Strategy," p. 240. Originally published in England by New Left Books. Anderson's massive historical studies, cited earlier, are aimed largely at understanding "superstructural" processes and relationships, in order to strengthen socialist strategy. His is only one of many important essays (including another one of his own) in this valuable book which, though mostly British in empirical focus, is of relevance to the U.S.

These are but a few of the fundamental and recurring questions those on the Left face. The debate over each question cannot be settled in this or any other book. But we can offer some general directions.

First, it is useful to remember that everyone wears several of many potential political "hats," each one representing an area of political struggle: we all live in a neighborhood, a town or city, a county, a state, and in a nation, concerning all of which there are constant political fights; we all have a function or occupation, as an industrial or white collar worker, or student, or teacher, or doctor, and there are always struggles going on in the area of that function; we are all men or women, white or black or brown or red or yellow, and there are always struggles in those arenas; and so on. In all the areas of life and conflict, there is much to be done to deepen and broaden the possibilities of democracy; the work of politics will never end, and for a long while to come, it will be "reformist politics."

Whatever it may be called, it is in the reformist arena in which the ongoing political activity of socialists has mostly taken place. It will continue to do so until the "moment of socialist transformation" is produced—whether the struggle is for a trade union, or for a *better* trade union, for day-care centers, for community control of schools or police, for improved housing, against militarism or any particular foreign policy, or any one of dozens of what are in fact reformist issues. Socialists neither can nor should abstain from participation in such struggles; but they should participate honestly, where honesty means *as* socialists as well as making every effort to achieve such reforms. To be a socialist in such a process is to believe and to argue that reforms are necessary but not enough, both because they leave so much untouched and because they often have been and often will be turned to the advantage of those with power ("co-opted") and to the disadvantage (and the disillusionment) of those for whom the reforms are presumably designed. Socialists must earn the respect of those not yet socialists; that can only be done in the political arena that is at least temporarily important to the nonsocialists. Socialists must come out of the closet, educating and learning to communicate with, and learning from nonsocialists. Socialism must cease to be a dirty word, through honest effort. So, what are we *for?*

Elements of a Socialist Vision for the United States

Most Americans, whether they approve or disapprove of it, view socialism as the system now existing in the Soviet Union, or in Yugoslavia, or in China, or in Cuba, or (among other places) in Tanzania. And, some believe and argue, socialism in the United States could, should, or would be similar to one or more of those—thus either great or awful. But socialism in the U.S. could not imitate *any* of those, because the movement could not originate by using any other system as a model. Nor could the realities of those other societies be replicated in any substantial way in the U.S.—presumably one of the kinds of things Marx had in mind when he noted that we make our own history, but not under circumstances chosen by ourselves. We Americans have the United States to work with in this part of the twentieth century: there is no place like it—like it or not.

If we are to have a successful socialist movement, we must and we can have a program that speaks to both the negative and the positive needs, as well as to the beckoning possibilities of this particular society. And if our movement is worthy of the name *socialist*, it will also move in solidarity with the global socialist movement. But let us first consider our present situation.

The differences between the United States and the other societies that have moved toward socialism are several, posing both greater and lesser difficulties for us. For example, the *economic* problems of a socialist United States would be quite minimal, because we already have a very strong economy. But the sociopsychological and political problems even of eliminating our widespread poverty would be (as they have been) imposing, given the depth and spread of racism and the bitterness of its victims in the United States. Given the hegemonic strength of capitalism in this country, the noneconomic problems of moving *toward* socialism are substantial indeed. Also, the great size and diversity of this society both require and enable a socialist program and society of heterogeneity—as has been true of China, say, but much less so of Cuba. In short, an American socialist program must be shaped to what Americans can be expected to prize and what this society makes necessary and feasible, making life harder *and* easier at the same time for those seeking to build such a society. Let me now attempt the bare outlines of such a program, under the headings of *principles, structures,* and *ways and means*—all connected in practice, but treated somewhat separately below.

Principles

Our principles are what we wish to live up to; they are our aims and goals, what we take to be of highest and enduring importance. A socialist United States could and should be one of continuous evolution toward (and the maximum practice at any time of) economic and political *democracy*, social *equality*, personal *freedom*, and *peace*. All very familiar, to be sure, and rightly so, but mostly as empty rhetoric. If such principles are to be realized in practice, we must take explicit account of what has to be offset and undone: economic autocracy and political oligarchy, institutionalized racism and sexism in all quarters of life, numerous de facto and legal constraints on the freedom of individuals to live as they choose even when such freedom would be harmless to others, the leukemia of militarism and violence in our system, and a broad range of encrusted and supportive attitudes toward all these matters. The "unlearning and undoing" process has already begun, as noted earlier, and it is part of the breakdown of capitalist hegemony; a socialist movement can and must carry that process considerably further, not just by attacking what exists, but by offering an alternative vision that would become part of a *socialist hegemony.* This entails spelling out details and procedures that would enable the abstract principles just noted to become real. It entails moving to a lower level of abstraction.

Contributing to the realization of democracy, equality, and freedom would be the maximum *decentralization* of power in the economy and in government. In addition there would be a connected maximum *debureaucratization* of all functions, not just in the obvious areas of economy and government, but also in education, in health care, and in the informative, entertainment, and cultural functions of the media.

Our analysis thus far has a vague quality, of course; but it is plausible to believe that in a democratic socialist society lofty principles would more likely than not be embodied in practice because they *could* be, because a healthy socialist system would thrive on their operation (whereas capitalism feeds on inequality, political oligarchy, and the like), and has everything to lose by their absence in practice. And it should be clear that this could occur not least because the dispersed power of a democratic socialist society would, if anything could, enhance the sense of individual and social responsibility, whereas the concentration and centralization of economic and State power of this society breeds alienation and apathy and encourages irresponsibility. Most Americans have come to see such behavioral shortcomings as part of a fixed "human nature." Instead, the needs and functions of the capitalist system, which profits from bringing out the worst in us, have encouraged such beliefs. It is a commonplace today that most citizens in our society believe it makes little difference what they do or don't do, that we "can't get no satisfaction." So why bother? To change that "system" means in part to alter patterns of social organization, to which we now turn.

Structures

The structures of *production* and *employment,* of *consumption* and *income,* and of *wealth* and *power* are all in continuous and dynamic interaction. Each must be changed substantially and qualitatively, but none can be without concomitant changes in all the others. Furthermore, although the foregoing refer to structures of the economy, they also intermingle with and act to shape political, social, and cultural relationships and processes.

Clearly, the pattern of production relates closely to the pattern of employment, especially when we implicitly include the technologies utilized. What is produced, and by whom, and how, is also the principal set of determinants of what and how much can be consumed, and by whom; and in turn, that is all directly and indirectly set by those with the wealth and the connected power to make decisions.

What of the structure of production itself? We produce too much of certain *commodities*—such as automobiles and guns—and too little of certain others—mass transit facilities and housing, for example. We have too many of certain *services*—those in advertising (on which we spend $30 billion annually), finance, and the military, for instance—and too few of certain others—such as those in health care and education.

In addition to those who labor at producing commodities and services we (as distinct from the capitalist system) don't need or want, there are many millions of able-bodied people who either don't work at all, don't work full-time, or who work at socially useless or trivial occupations. Almost all of such people could and would give their energy to full-time and meaningful work, which would greatly expand the "national income" in terms of needed and desired goods and services, work whose production would more than "pay for itself." And this points to a fundamental material argument for U.S. socialism, which runs quite contrary to the usual notion that socialism means a lowered level of life: an altered structure of production would eliminate the enormous *social waste* that keeps the present system going, with the result that the same amount of work and use of resources would provide a higher level of material well-being.

All this—suggesting a greatly altered pattern of production, employment, and consumption—is impossible so long as the decision-making processes remain in the hands of those who control and benefit from the existing patterns of production, consumption, income, and wealth: the hidden bottom of the iceberg that sinks liberal reforms. To change the patterns of production (and all the rest) requires a change in the structures of wealth and power: it requires the abolition of private ownership and control over the production process, and the democratic dispersion of both economic and political power.

That brings us to a basic principle of democratic socialism: not private, but *social ownership and control* of the means of production; not production for profit, but *production for use*. Does that mean that "everything must be nationalized"? And who has the decision-making powers?

An economy of social ownership and control in which production is for use must be a *planned* economy; if ownership is social, economic decision-making must be social. What does social ownership imply? Who would do the planning? How would the planners know what to decide? These questions have varying answers; what follows is what I take to be generally appropriate for U.S. conditions.

First, ownership and control: enterprises should be publicly-owned and *directly* controlled through the political process and structures *only* to the degree that their operations have the power to affect lives and other economic units significantly for better or for worse. This is easy to understand at the extremes: steel as compared with hairpins. The uncertain middle areas—beer, for example—would be a focus for political discussion and experimentation over time.

There could be no doubt about any industry using a large-scale technology, with all that implies about resource and employment demands and relationships with suppliers and users: they must be publicly-owned, and their key production decisions arrived at within the central planning mechanism (although decisions within the "enterprise" concerning work patterns, and the like, could often be dealt with on the spot by those involved). This would refer, for instance, to steel, petroleum, automobiles, machinery, public transport, and communications, and so on—in effect, to almost all the industrial corporations comprising the "Fortune 500" and "50" leading utilities, banks, etc.

At the other end of the spectrum, there would be ample room for individually-controlled small farms, retail outlets (whether stores, bars, or whatever), and small-scale production units where matters of design and taste are vital—such as, for furniture, or for bakery goods. Should production in such small enterprises be for *profit?* Should they be privately-*owned,* in the current sense? The answer depends upon the process by which socialism would come to the U.S., how long the process would take, and how deeply its principles would take hold in the first stages. An important distinction between the meanings of "ownership" and "control" in the process of production is badly blurred in capitalist society. It may be asserted that all individuals have a deep need to have control over their production, whether as a worker in a large plant, or as a craftsperson; and the ways in which that can be maximized must be explored. But ownership and property income are "needs" associated only with the particular characteristics of capitalist society. So long as productive people can be assured of comfort, security, and recognition for having done useful and good work, wages and salaries are likely to be sufficient—as they are already for a broad range of constructive and creative people (in the arts and professions, for instance). Experimentation in this connection, as in many others, would be appropriate; the possible results cannot be estimated by us, living now, when the "experiment" would be taken only later, after a process of socialist struggle and development.

Second, who would control the planners, and how would they know what to plan, what kinds and quantities of things to have produced? We will enunciate only two obvious points here: (1) The *goals* of the economy for short and longer periods of time would have to be, and *could* be decided upon through the political process. In general this would mean that political decisions would have to be made about real investment versus consumption allocations, and allocations within and between the various industries in the two sectors; and decisions would also have to be made about changing proportions of time to be spent on work or leisure, or education. Such political decisions would require political discussions and debates at all levels from the neighborhood and the factory to the nation—much as in China today (a process we often hear mocked in the U. S., because we know so little of serious political discussion in this country). (2) How could planners, or people in general, know what the people want now, or might want in the future? People can be asked.

To pause for a partial summation, there seems to be every reason for combining central planning with decentralized operations in a U.S. socialist economy, employing a broad variety of institutions. So long as we are determinedly bent on expanding the sphere of democratic control, which is easier to do in an economy as strong as ours than elsewhere, that is not likely to be as difficult in practice as it may appear in prospect. Errors would be only minimally damaging, and subject to mitigation over time. Once a socialist society has been popularly accepted and developed, "small is beautiful" becomes a practicable principle *along with* democratic central planning of large production units.[14]

Thirdly, and before proceeding to a fuller discussion of "ways and means," there is at least one other function that is vital to any socialist program: the distribution of income and wealth. Just about a century ago, Marx made a distinction that became a classic: between "socialism" and "communism." "Socialism" would be the social process replacing capitalism in which at least some capitalist attitudes survived *and* the problem of economic scarcity had not yet been eliminated; therefore, "from each according to ability, to each according to *work*." A "communist" society would be one in which the economic problem had been eliminated (through the growth and alteration of productive capacity), *and* the population had been living as socialists in practice and consciousness. Therefore, the principle of income distribution could become "from each according to ability, to each according to *need*." A classless society would have been achieved, in which the State had "withered away," in which government, as Lenin later put it, would "administer over things, not over people." How would these distinctions apply to the U. S.?

So far as *economic* considerations are concerned, the U. S. could move immediately to income distribution determined by the "communist"

---

[14] E. F. Schumacher, *Small is Beautiful** (New York: Perennial Press, 1974) is valuable both analytically and programmatically, except that, in not recognizing the need for transforming the structure of power through a socialist process, his arguments remain utopian.

standard: all *needs* could be satisfied, given our productive capacities; everyone could live comfortably, with much left over. That does not mean, however, that absolute income *equality* (as distinct from a sharp narrowing of differentials) would be politically and sociopsychologically appropriate for a socialist program. What might well be feasible immediately is a program arguing (1) for a high floor for incomes and a much lowered ceiling—say (at current prices), a minimum of about $15,000 and a maximum of about $30,000 for a family of four (with a much altered "budget," in which health care would be provided socially, paying for housing would be transformed, etc.), and (2) that all income should derive from either work or need, not from property ownership. In turn that means "wealth" would consist entirely of nonincome producing goods—that is, of consumer goods.

Setting other vital questions aside, let me now seek to suggest the ways in which important aspects of our everyday existence could and should be treated in a socialist program.

Ways and Means

We do not live by bread alone, we also live—that is, we thrive or languish—dependent upon how we "make our bread," by our conditions of work. There is much more to life than consumption and work, of course; there are our personal and social and political and cultural relations, our aesthetic and recreational lives, our schooling, and much else. Here I shall examine only work and education, leaving the rest to be seen as moving along comparable paths. First, work.

From at least Adam Smith's era to the present, conventional social scientists have treated work as something to be shirked. Under capitalist conditions that is, of course, appropriate, for it is a means only of *staying* alive, not of *being* alive, as we "work" for someone else. The common result is that workers hate their jobs and their bosses, and employers despise "their" workers. What we do, mostly, is what must be deemed "unnatural"—we have no say over what we produce, or how, or when, or why we produce it; we labor only to get an income we hope will keep us going. We are alienated, as Marx put it, from our work, from our fellow workers (whom we frequently must see as competing for our jobs), and, perhaps most importantly, from our human possibilities. We perform. We are like dancing bears or trained seals. (And we may assume that the latter are also "alienated.")

But has this not changed for the better in the industrial era? Or if it has worsened, is it not industrialism, rather than capitalism, which is at fault? The studies by Margolin and Braverman (cited much earlier) are meticulous and damning indictments of how the work process has been distorted and shaped by capitalist impulses and power; they should be read carefully. Braverman sums up the contemporary situation aptly:

> Thus, after a million years of labor, during which humans created not only a complex social culture but in a very real sense created themselves as well, the very cultural-biological trait upon which this entire evolution is founded has been brought, within the last two hundred years, to a crisis..., which Marcuse aptly calls the threat of "a catastrophe of the human essence." [15]

Industrialism has, of course, had some positive consequences, and some negative ones. Even under the best of socialist conditions, industrial production—because of its scope and its minute division of labor—poses a challenge; under capitalist conditions, the challenge is of a different sort: not, how can the complexity of work under industrial conditions be treated so as to allow human beings to realize their potentialities (on the job and elsewhere) but, how can that complexity be used so as to reduce the decisions and increase the output of the worker? "Scientific management" is the management of people for profit. A socialist program can and must be different from that. As Harry Braverman points out, it must also be more than "workers' control."

> The conception of a democracy in the workplace based simply upon the imposition of a formal structure of parliamentarism—election of directors, the making of production and other decisions by ballot, etc.—upon the existing organization of production is delusory. Without the return of requisite technical knowledge to the mass of workers and the reshaping of the organization of labor—without, in a word, a new and truly collective mode of production—balloting within factories and offices does not alter the fact that the workers remain as dependent as before upon "experts," and can only choose among them or vote for alternatives presented by them. Thus genuine workers' control has as its prerequisite the demystifying of technology and the reorganization of production. [16]

Some work is humanly rewarding, and much that is not could be made so; other work is not and cannot be rewarding. In a socialist society, all work than *can* be made rewarding should be retained and expanded, even at the cost of reduced efficiency. Much of the rest should and could

---

[15] Braverman, *Labor and Monopoly Capital*, p. 171.

[16] Ibid., p. 445, footnote. André Gorz has written much and well in this and connected areas. See his essay "Work and Consumption," in *Towards Socialism*, and his two books, *Strategy for Labor** (Boston: Beacon Press, 1964) and *Socialism and Revolution** (New York: Anchor, 1973). Ken Coates, "Democracy and Workers' Control," in *Towards Socialism*, is also illuminating.

be automated. What cannot be automated and what cannot be made rewarding—menial and/or "dirty work" (garbage collection)—should be shared and/or highly rewarded (whether in money income or other ways). Under present conditions, the worst work is the worst paid; the best work is the best paid. Those who, like research scientists, love their work, receive very high incomes; others, who hate everything about their jobs, receive the lowest incomes. The latter are among the "surplus" population, whose "marginal revenue productivity" is, as mainstream economists see it, low. It is merely the impersonal workings of supply and demand: you get what you deserve.

All that, of course, ignores the basic social processes within which people are "brought to market"—not least in importance being class, "racial," and sexual determinants of how much and what kind of education people get and how that connects with their working lives. We close our examination of elements of a socialist program in this crucial area.

Both the structures and the processes of education in the U.S., at all levels, are, like the economy and the State they serve, run by the wrong people, in the wrong ways, and for the wrong reasons, from the standpoint of human needs and possibilities. For the functioning and maintenance of the capitalist system, however, it's about right. Education now works to train and socialize; in a socialist society it could and should be the main means by which human beings would realize their constructive and creative possibilities.

Our education should be how and where we learn to understand and to appreciate our society, nature, and our culture, where we learn who we are and what we can and wish to be. At its best, today, it is where we pick up certain skills; at its worst—and its worst side grows faster than its best—it is where young people learn to hate learning, where using the mind and feelings is subject to coercion and distortion. The educational system always both reflects and shapes the society in which it exists; it has done that up to now, and it would continue to do so in a socialist society.

The development of skills would of course be part of education in a socialist educational system, but that would be the smallest part of it. A democratic socialist society would encourage, because it would need and want, self-reliance, independence, and creativity, and its "schools" would assist in achieving those goals; its students and teachers would exchange roles, alternatively; they would relate to each other cooperatively and voluntarily, not competitively and coercively; growth, not grades, would be stressed; the hierarchical structure of administrator, teacher, and student would be eliminated; education would be seen as a lifelong activity, with intermittent work leaves for all. Knowing the horror education has become, it would be developed for what it can be: a process for the enrichment of life.

The Seeds Sprout

Democracy, equality, freedom, peace, education as enrichment, and all the rest. . . . Pipe dreams, in a society that demonstrably moves to the Right? No, for as the U. S. moves to the Right, many of its people have been living lives that increasingly and consciously *incorporate* the ideals enunciated above (among others), whatever they may be called. In the past decade, steadily and increasingly, small groups of people have begun to live their lives differently, in ways and to degrees unmatched in our history. If, as has been argued above, any movement for socialism in the U. S. must be a long-term movement, the signs are there and growing that such a movement has begun its long march. The signs and sounds are subdued, not blatant, and as yet they do not have the traditional appearance of a *movement*, socialist or otherwise. Just as the raucous activities of the 1960's were part of an important liberating and learning process for the New Left and others, so the quiet searching and serious activities of today are: the seeds that were warmed in the 1960's have begun to sprout.

This may be said in contrast with the talk of recent years that "The Movement" has died. What has died is the sense of dynamism and of excited hopes, the reality of being part of a vast (if ephemeral) organized social *movement*. The reasons for the change are not entirely negative, however, for the activities of radicals in the U. S. now receive much less media coverage, and they are much more concerned with substantive and lasting day-to-day work, mostly at the local level– in the realms of health and day-care centers, publications, "food conspiracies," "people's garages," housing and rent control, liberation struggles, and, among many other radical activities, the now pervasive "radical caucuses," in virtually every profession (URPE's in economics) and in many trade unions. One writer, who has observed both the radicals and the main holders of power with great care has concluded:

> There are tens of thousands and perhaps millions of people who have come out of the Sixties with new ideas, new ways of looking at America, new perceptions of themselves, their families, and their communities, shorn of old loyalties and assumptions, no longer taking for granted the values and authority of things-as-they-are. These are the people, mostly but not exclusively young, who were truly "radicalized" in the last decade and haven't forgotten it in this one. . . . [T]he obituaries are, at the least, premature.[17]

[17] Kirkpatrick Sale, "The New Left: What is Left?" in the magazine *WIN* (June 28, 1973). Also see his *SDS* (New York: Random House, 1973), and *Power Shift: The Rise of the Southern Rim* . . . (New York: Random House, 1975).

An American revolutionary socialist movement must comprehend both analytically and programmatically the diverse and common problems, needs, and aspirations of the many groups that have been raised to consciousness and anger and effort in recent years and serve to encourage many others; it must understand both the strengths and the weaknesses of the existing system; it must have an analysis of power that tells it where and how and when to move or to hold back (for "action" can be counterproductive, as recent years have shown); it must move toward the liberation, the well-being, and the power of wage-earners, of women, of the nonwhite, of the young—but also of those who in their different yet serious ways are unfree and crippled: the middle-aged, middle-class whites, men and women alike. The revolution we need is one that at least removes the fangs of America in the world and that seeks to make the United States liveable for its own people and a force for cooperative constructive change in the world.

All that is asking a lot. But it is no more, as a perspective, than is necessary if there is to be hope for an effective socialist movement in this society, or if such a movement is to deserve the effort and the sacrifices it will entail. A socialist movement will have to learn, and act upon its knowledge, of the inherent possibilities of all human beings; see itself as comprising not morally or intellectually superior creatures, but men and women privileged to understand the plight of society and to have the energy to spread that privilege until the plight is replaced by what society can make possible for people.

Those who are angry can build such a movement; those who hate cannot. Committed men and women are essential; zealots are a hindrance. Thought, analysis, and reflection are indispensable; dogmatism is poison.

"America," the midwestern poet Carl Sandburg wrote long ago, "was promises." Decency, sanity, and safety require that those promises be redeemed; with effort, patience and impatience, and love, they can be.

Index of Subjects

(Note: The intent of this index is not to locate all subjects mentioned in the text or, for example, to identify all those pages where "capitalism," "imperialism," or other such central concerns of the book are discussed. Instead, the index seeks first of all to locate passages where critical relationships and processes are discussed; second, it identifies pages where matters deemed likely to be either especially interesting (e.g., alienation) or puzzling (e.g., enclosures) are discussed).

Conservationists, 166–67, 294
Consumerism: beginnings of in U.S., 96;
and post-World War II expansion,
114–15, 119
Conventional economics. *See* Economics,
neoclassical
Corn Laws, 13
Corporate liberalism, 289, 292, 294, 297–
98, 307–11
Council on Foreign Relations, 234
Creditor nation status. *See* Debtor/credi-
tor nation status
Cycles, business, 86–88. *See also* Fluctu-
ations, economic; Expansion, economic

Debt, 117–18
Debtor/creditor nation status: transformation of the U.S., 227–30
Dependency. *See* Underdeveloped countries
Depression: characteristics and consequences of, 1930's, 103–109; in U.S.
and Germany in 1930's, 22; of the
1890's, 94; of the 1930's and World
War II, 82; and economics, 21–25, 86;
and Malthus, 11–13; and mergers in
1890's, 70–71; and the New Deal, 107–
11; and stagnation theory, 111–13
Diminishing returns, principle of, 13
Dual economy, 78; in agriculture, 177;
internationally, 230; and Depression
of 1930's, 99–103; and poverty, 155;
and the State, 313; and underdeveloped countries, 259–63
Duplex Printing v. Deering, 147
Dust Bowl, 177

Earth Day, 196, 202
Ecological imbalance: nature and development of, 193–202; and agriculture,
179; and economic growth, 36*n*
Economics: as scientism, 27; *classical,*
4–5; nature and emergence of, 15–17;
neoclassical, inadequacies for present
needs, 3; and classicists, 4–5; and consumer sovereignty, compared to pluralism, 271; and the Depression, 22, 86–
87; and economic development, 11–
15; and hedonism, 18; and modern
economies, 20–21; and scarcity, 16;
and stagnation, 112–13; and urban and
environmental problems, 165–67
Education, 159–60, 347–50
Effective demand, 12–13, 24–25

Enclosure movement: and creation of
working class, 43–44, and distribution
of income and wealth, 47
Energy crisis/shortage, 178, 199–202. *See
also* Oil
Executive compensation, 141
Expansion, *economic:* after World War
II, 112–15; as essential for capitalism,
3, 86; role and nature of in capitalist
development, and relation to exploitation, 35–49; and Adam Smith, 10; and
the business cycle, 89–90; and debt,
117–18; and farmers, 168–72; and
growth of State, 313; and "growthmania," 180; and income distribution,
138; and inequality, 128; and investment, 24
Expansion, *geographic:* 53–55, 61–65,
208; changing conditions of and current crisis, 326–28; into underdeveloped countries, 260; "objectless," 214;
pre- and post-capitalist compared, 215;
viewed as solution of domestic problems, 254–55; and ecology, 212–14;
and militarization, 317
Exploitation: as intrinsic to capitalism, 3;
changing conditions of and current
crisis, 326–28; of human and natural
resources, 64; of nature and of labor,
181; of people in underdeveloped
countries, 262; and Adam Smith, 10;
and capitalist expansion, 35–39, 128;
and enclosures, 47; and geographic
expansion, 215; and income distribution, 138; and militarization, 317; and
monopoly capitalism, 340; and powerlessness, 44; and propertylessness, 19,
41–45; and taxation, 37
Export-Import Bank, 233
Exports. *See* Foreign economic relationships
EXXON, 76–77, 197, 201, 246, 256

Farmers. *See* Agriculture
Fascism, possibilities of in U.S., 328–30,
334–35
Federal Reserve System, 24, 93, 109,
277–78, 283, 294
Fluctuations, economic: analyzed, 91–92;
contrasted with growth and development, 85–86; record of in U.S., 92
Food shortage, 178, 205
Foreign economic relationships of U.S.:
compared with Great Britain's, 230–32,

241–42; nature and dependence of U.S. upon after Civil War, 227–29; overseas investment, 245–50, 255, 261–62; recent trade and payments changes, 240–43; and farmers, 157–58; and multinational corporations, 243–50; and underdeveloped countries, 250. *See also* Debtor/creditor nation status

Fortune 500. *See* Business, big

Free trade, and Ricardo, 13

General Motors, 59, 76–77, 100–101, 187, 245, 246, 247, 256

Gross national product (GNP), compared with sales of giant corporations, 255–56; components since 1929, 105–106; defined, 102n; fall in, 1929–33, 103–105, stability of since World War II, 114; and big business, 76; and the economic surplus, 307; and foreign trade, 207, 229; and government spending, 310–13; and military spending, 302; and State expenditures, 102

Growth, economic. *See* Expansion, *economic*

Hanseatic League, 210

Hegemony, ideological, 280, 332–34, 335–39, 343

Homestead Act of 1862, 172

Immigration, 51, 63–64, 146–47, 152

Imports. *See* Foreign economic relationships

Indochina War, 54, 83n, 118, 134, 143, 213, 236, 237, 239, 240, 243, 265, 281, 300, 303, 305, 318, 319, 320, 321, 335

Industrial Workers of the World (IWW, Wobblies), 145, 153

Inflation, since World War II, 115–19; causes, consequences, and beneficiaries, 121–23, 140; and Indochina War, 320; and military expenditures, 120–21, 201; and warfare-welfare State, 313

Investment: as percent of GNP, 102, 107; and expansion, 24; and expansion after World War II, 114

Irish workers, 144

Japanese-American Treaty, 236

Jim Crow laws, 153, 287

Keynesian economics. *See* Economics, *neoclassical*

Knights of Labor, 145

Labor: control over, and scientific management, 34–35, 45n; 347; and socialist possibilities, 348–49. *See also* Trade unions; Workers

Labor movement, contrasted with trade union movement, 150–52

Laissez-faire, 7–8, 11, 17, 25, 40, 49, 52, 69, 93, 269, 285, 294–96

Land policy and speculation, 169–70

Landrum-Griffin Act, 149

Legitimation, 279–82, 308–13

Lockheed, 109

Lorenz Curve, 135

Marshall Plan, 173, 235, 240

Mass communications: and deception, 282n; and legitimation, 280–82; and monopoly capitalism, 114

Mercantilism: "American," 52; compared with imperialism, 209–12; general nature of, 40, 51; and Colbert, 221; and power, 273; and the State and classical political economy, 5–8; private, 8, 67; and underdeveloped countries, 250, 262

Mergers: horizontal, vertical, and conglomerate, 73, 75; record of, 72, 74; waves of, 70–71, 73; and concentration and centralization of power, 75

Middle East Treaty Organization, 236

Military in the U.S.: expenditures since 1941, 89; purchases and sales, 303; and crisis of the cities, 190; and employment, 121, 319; and industrial complex, 68, 82; and post-World War II expansion, 112–15; and power, 278; and re-appraisal of U.S. realities, 321; and stagflation, 118–20; and warfare State, 300–306

Millionaires, 315n

Monopoly: as outcome of competition, 66–67; and neoclassical economics, 20–21; and technology, 69–71

Monopoly capitalism: as decaying, 117–19; as a social system, 123; main postwar characteristics, 114–15; and socialist analysis, 340

Multinational corporations (MNC): evolution and general nature of, 80–81; role, spread, and importance of, 243–50; and current uncertainties, 213; and underdeveloped countries, 250

110; and trade unions, 145; and World War I, 296

South, 61–63, 146, 168–69, 226, 285–86, 287–88

Southeast Asia Treaty Organization (SEATO), 236

Speculation. *See* Land speculation

Stagflation, 92, 98, 112, 115–19

Stagnation, economic: analysis of, in U.S., 111–22; in Great Britain, 21; signs of before World War I, 95–96; and conventional economics, 112–13; and inflation, 122; and monopoly capitalism, 119–20

Stationary state, 14

Subversive Activities Control Board, 236

Surplus, economic, 306–307

Surplus labor, 41–42, 307–309

Taft-Hartley Act, 111, 149

Taxation: and exploitation, 37; and income and wealth distribution, 135; and Progressive period, 294; and "tax expenditures," 161n; and "welfare-warfare state," 313–17

Technology: as seen by Schumpeter, 87; and competition, 46–49, 87; and economic growth, 15–16; and expansion, 38; and mergers, 69–71, 87; and monopoly, 39–40

Trade unions: compared with labor movement, 150–52; development of in U.S., 144–49; and foreign policy, 237; and

MNC's 248–49; and racism and sexism, 152–54; and the Wagner Act, 110–11. *See also* Workers

Truman (Greece-Turkey) Doctrine, 236

Underdeveloped countries: analyzed, 251–54, 259–63; and income, 135; and MNC's, 250; and military purchases, 303n; and population growth, 12; and power, 277n; and U.S. expansion after World War II, 213

Unemployment: in nineteenth century, 93–94; 1908–1915, 95; 1920–29, 98; in the 1930's, 103–105; relationship to military production, 120–21; and inflation, 122–23; and stagflation, 116; and understatement today, 98

Union for Radical Political Economics (URPE), 16n, 29, 350

United Farm Workers, 125

Urban problems. *See* Cities

Urban renewal, 191–93

Wagner (National Labor Relations) Act, 110–11, 148–49, 294

Waste, 119, 344

Watergate, 83n, 282n, 318, 320, 321, 330

Webb-Pomerene Act, 295

Wobblies. *See* Industrial Workers of the World

Workers: as alienated, 18–19, 45; and competition, 39; and exploitation, 41–44. *See also* Labor; Trade unions

Index of Names

Hacker, Andrew, 84
Hacker, Louis M., 31
Halberstam, David , 83n, 239n, 281n, 318
Hamilton, Alexander, 225, 232
Hamilton, Edward K., 311
Hammond, Bray, 284n
Hamrin, Robert D., 310n, 316
Handlin, Oscar, 146n
Hanna, Mark, 287
Hansen, Alvin, 111, 112, 304n
Harding, Warren G., 148, 296
Harriman, Averill, 234
Harrington, Michael, 156, 157
Hartman, Chester, 192n
Haveman, Robert D., 310n, 316
Hayes, Edward C., 205
Hays, Samuel P., 166n
Hayter, Theresa, 261n
Heckscher, Eli, 210n, 222n
Heilbroner, Robert L., 29, 79n, 205
Henderson, W. O., 47n, 269
Herman, E. S., 313n, 322
Hersey, John, 318
Herter, Christian, 234
Higbee, Edward, 178n
Hilgerdt, Folke, 230n
Hill, Christopher, 7, 56, 274n
Hoare, Quintin, 332n
Hobsbawm, E. J., 56
Hobson, J. A., 251, 262, 263
Ho Chi Minh, 339
Hodges, Donald, 264
Hoffman, Abbie, 142
Hoffman, R. J. S., 225n
Hollander, Samuel, 10
Hoover, Herbert, 108, 109, 148, 177, 296, 297, 298
Horowitz, David, 234n, 264
Horowitz, Irving Louis, 164, 322
Huberman, Leo, 31
Hunt, E. K., 30
Hutchins, Maynard, 160
Hymer, Stephen, 80, 244, 246

Imlah, Albert, 225n
Ingles, Jerry, 322

Jackson, Andrew, 52, 170, 283, 284, 285
Jacobs, Jane, 183n, 204n
Jacobs, Paul, 61n, 291n
Jalee, Pierre, 265
Jeffers, Robinson, 33, 207
Johnson, Dale L., 253n

Johnson, Lyndon Baines, 75n, 82, 113, 123, 157, 176, 193, 195, 201n, 254n, 258, 262n, 282n, 305, 318, 319, 332
Josephson, Eric and Mary, 32
Josephson, Matthew, 71n
Judis, John, 331n

Kahn, Alfred E., 225n
Kahn, R. F., 23
Kalecki, Michael, 23
Karp, Walter, 321
Katznelson, Ira, 322
Kemmerer, Donald, 58
Kemp, Tom, 217, 252n
Kennedy, John F., 23, 113, 123, 149, 193, 201n, 240, 258, 305, 318, 332
Kennedy, Robert, 318
Kesselman, Mark, 322
Keynes, John Maynard, 4, 5, 12, 16, 21–25, 31, 66n, 86, 90, 94, 102, 110
Kirkland, Edward C., 58, 63n
Klare, Michael, 242n, 303n, 317, 322
Kohlmeier, Louis M., 75n
Kolko, Gabriel, 52, 93n, 113, 132, 143, 144n, 264, 288n, 289n, 290, 292, 317, 322
Kolko, Joyce, 241, 243n, 245, 246n, 262n, 264
Kornbluh, Joyce L., 162
Kozol, Jonathan, 204
Kuhn, Thomas, 30

La Feber, Walter, 208n
Lampman, Robert J., 137n
Landau, Saul, 61n
Lane, Frederic C., 224n, 241
Lary, Hal, 231n
Laski, Harold, 45n, 270n
Lazonick, William, 44n
Lebergott, Stanley, 141n
Lefebvre, Henri, 123
Lekachman, Robert, 125, 265
Lenin, V. I., 57, 251, 252n, 322, 333, 338, 339, 346
Lens, Sidney, 162
Leuchtenberg, William E., 108n
Levinson, Andrew, 145n
Levy, Walter, 236n
Lewis, Sinclair, 100, 124, 175n
Lewis, W. Arthur, 101n, 104
Liebling, A. J., 282n
Ligh, Donald, 139n, 157n
Lincoln, Abraham, 204, 226
Lipset, S. M., 299n

Thernstrom, Stephen, 184n
Thompson, E. P., 57
Truman, Harry S., 83n, 113, 176, 235, 305
Tussing, Dale, 116, 155, 161n, 163, 323
Twain, Mark, 52

Upton, Letitia, 130n, 132, 135n, 137

Van Alstyne, Richard W., 54n
Vatter, Harold, 63n, 163
Veblen, Thorstein, 4, 17–20, 24, 25, 28, 31, 47n, 56, 57, 62, 65, 66, 67, 82, 83n, 86, 87, 88, 89, 90, 97, 100, 142, 143, 164, 169, 170, 175n, 176, 202, 209, 216, 263, 276, 279, 299, 313, 325, 326
Voltaire, 142n
Von Horn, General, 47

Wachtel, Howard, 159
Wallace, George, 176, 313
Wallerstein, Immanuel, 34, 54–55, 214n, 272n
Walzer, Michael, 274n
Ward, Benjamin, 30
Wasserman, Miriam, 159n, 205
Watkins, Myron W., 84
Watson, Tom, 171n
Weaver, James, 30, 159n

Webster, Daniel, 226
Wecter, Dixon, 124
Weidenbaum, Murray L., 312
Weinstein, James, 93n, 110n, 144n, 288n, 289n, 294n, 296n, 336n
Weisberg, Barry, 100n, 196–97, 198n
Weiss, Leonard, 83
Weisskopf, Thomas, 56, 218n, 251n, 255n
West, Nathaniel, 187n
Wiebe, Robert H., 288n
Wilcox, Clair, 156, 157
Will, Robert E., 163
Williams, Gwynn, 332n
Williams, William Appleman, 31, 54n, 171n, 172n, 173, 174, 175n, 208n, 234n, 264, 297, 298n, 317
Wilson, Charles (business), 59
Wilson, Charles (historian), 225n
Wilson, Thomas, 57
Wilson, Woodrow, 52, 291, 296n
Wolfe, Alan, 329n
Wolff, Robert Paul, 322
Woodward, C. Vann, 171n, 286–87n
Wright, Erik Olin, 268n

Young, Marilyn Blatt, 174n

Zaretsky, Eli, 163, 164
Zeitlin, Maurice, 321

Index of Periodicals